D0915430

INSIDE THE BLUE BERETS

Other Books by the Author

Soviet Tanks & Combat Vehicles of World War Two
(with James Grandsen)

The Polish Campaign, 1939
(with Victor Madej)

Soviet Bloc Elite Forces
(with James W. Loop)

Soviet Tanks & Combat Vehicles 1946 to the Present
(with James W. Loop)

Inside the Soviet Army Today

Soviet Air Defense Missiles: Design, Development, and Tactics

Red Thrust: Attack on the Central Front—
Soviet Tactics and Capabilities in the 1990s

Tank Attack: A Primer on Modern Tank Warfare
(with Michael Green)

Target America:
The Soviet Union and the Strategic Arms Race, 1945–1964

INSIDE THE BLUE BERETS

BERETS

A Combat History of Soviet
and Russian Airborne Forces,
1930–1995

STEVEN J. ZALOGA

PRESIDIO

Published by Presidio Press
505 B San Marin Dr., Suite 300
Novato, CA 94945-1340

Library of Congress Cataloging-in-Publication Data

Zaloga, Steven J.
    Inside the Blue Berets : A combat history of soviet and russian airborne forces, 1930–1995 / Steven J. Zaloga
        p.   cm.
    Includes index.
    ISBN 0-89141-399-5
    1. Special forces (Military science)—Soviet Union—History. 2. Soviet Union. Sukhoputnye voiska. Vozdushno-desantnye voiska—History. 3. Soviet Union—History. Military. I. Title.
UA776.S64Z35 1995
356'.16'0947—dc20   94-40927
                                                                CIP

Photographs are from the author's personal collection unless otherwise noted.
Typography by ProImage

Printed in the United States of America

*To
Bob Carey*

Contents

Illustrations

Tables

Introduction

Over the past decade, there has been a surge of interest in elite forces and special operations units. Much ink has been spilled over the exploits of the U.S. airborne divisions, the SEALs, the SAS, the Fallschirmjaeger, Delta Force, and a shadowy host of secret warriors. Of all the world's special operations units, the least appreciated are the Soviet, now Russian, airborne forces. Soviet airborne operations have been cloaked in secrecy for many years, and only recently have many of their missions been publicly disclosed. The aim of this book is to fill the gap in the history of elite forces. Although certain aspects of the history of the Russian VDV Airborne Force have been well covered in English, until now there has never been an overall account of its evolution and combat record. Besides the VDV Airborne Force, this book also surveys the evolution of other Russian special forces to help place the airborne forces in their proper context.

To military historians in the West, the tradition of airborne operations is most closely associated with three countries: Germany, Britain, and the United States. It was the paratroop units of these three countries that fought in the legendary World War II battles of Eben Emael, Crete, Normandy, and "the Bridge Too Far" at Arnhem. It is often forgotten that the Russians, with their daring experiments in the 1930s, were the inspiration of many of these paratrooper forces. Russian paratrooper operations in World War II are unknown among most Western military historians, except for a small circle of Eastern Front specialists. This is not altogether surprising. Most of the

1

large airborne jumps on the Eastern Front in World War II ended in
disaster and never entered the ranks of the great battles such as
Stalingrad, Kursk, Operation Bagration, or the drive on Berlin.

If the West ignored Russian airborne operations, the Soviet Army
certainly did not. In the Cold War years, the Soviet Army's airborne
forces became the largest in the world, equal in size to the entire
British army. Well trained and well equipped, they were the shock
troops for an invasion of capitalist Western Europe, an invasion that
never came. Instead, the VDV Airborne Force became the imperial
storm troopers of the Kremlin, dispatched to the dirty little imperial
skirmishes of the Cold War: Hungary in 1956, Czechoslovakia in
1968, and Afghanistan in 1979. For ten long years, the Blue Berets
of the Soviet airborne forces bore the brunt of the hard fighting in
the brutal mountains of the Hindu Kush in Afghanistan.

The Afghan experiences of the Blue Berets had particular rel-
evance in the post–Cold War world. With the sudden collapse of the
"Soviet Threat" and the premature announcement of a "New World
Order," Russia's Blue Berets have seen little peace. For all of its
bloody faults, the former Soviet Union kept most of Eurasia's warring ethnic groups from each other's throats. No sooner did the Communist regime fall but old grudges began to reappear: Azeri against
Armenian, Georgian against Ossetian, Ukrainian against Moldovan;
the list goes on and on. The guns from Afghanistan had hardly
cooled when the Blue Berets were asked to don their flak jackets yet
again to venture into exotic lands on Russia's frontier to help deal
with the New World Disorder. Nor was the VDV's fight limited to
exotic locales in the remote hinterland. The VDV played a prominent
role in the 1991 and 1993 coup attempts and has evolved into the
Praetorian Guard of the Kremlin.

This book looks at the Russian experience with airmobile forces
from their beginnings in the 1920s and 1930s to today's Russian
Mobile Force. The Russian Army may no longer be "The Threat,"
but the Blue Berets are likely to figure prominently in the headlines
over the next decade. In the New World Disorder, rapidly deployable
special forces are becoming the central focus of modern armies. The
Blue Berets are Russia's power projection muscle in these conflicts.
This book aims to establish Russia's legitimate claim as one of the
pioneers of airmobile forces and to explain how this tradition is
changing the face of today's Russian Army.

Chapter 1
We Are First!

Voronezh is one of southern Russia's most ancient cities. Its medieval fortress overlooked the Voronezh River and formed part of the Belgorod defensive line, guarding Russia's fertile black-earth regions from the bloody incursions of the dreaded Tatar raiders. But the Tatars were eventually conquered, and the wild steppes southeast of Voronezh became tame. Deep inside the Russian heartland, the city escaped the Napoleonic Wars of the nineteenth century and shed its military battlements. In recent times, it became a sleepy provincial capital, distinguished only by its synthetic rubber plant.

In the warm summer months of 1930, Voronezh's peace was often disturbed by the incessant buzzing of aircraft from the nearby Red Air Force base. A frequent visitor to the skies over the city was a huge Farman-Goliath biplane bomber, newly purchased from France. The Goliath was very advanced for its day, even though it looked almost comical by modern standards. On 2 August 1930, peasants on the outskirts of Voronezh were treated to a particularly odd sight. The Goliath began a slow circle over an outlying farm building. For no apparent reason, six airmen jumped out of the bomber in quick succession, from a height of only 1,500 feet. To the relief of the startled onlookers, parachutes soon blossomed over the six airmen, and they gently floated down into the fields. Parachutes were quite a novelty in 1930, especially out in the provinces. The Goliath was quickly followed by a procession of three smaller Polikarpov R-1

3

light bombers. Had any Western intelligence agents been in the audience, they would have recognized the parachutes as being of American manufacture, and the Polikarpov R-1 aircraft as being Russian copies of the British De Havilland DH.4 bomber of World War I fame.

It wasn't the novelty of the technology that was so impressive, it was the novelty of the tactics. The R-1 bombers buzzed over the field where the airmen had landed, and dropped six large bags by parachutes. As the bundles landed, the six airmen on the ground rushed to open them, unloading rifles and machine guns. About twenty minutes later, the big Goliath bomber returned, dropping another six airmen—this time from the daring altitude of only 300 yards. Fortunately, the farm field provided a soft landing area, and none of the men was injured. The second group rallied around the cargo bags and quickly armed themselves. The commander of the group, L. G. Minov, called the group to attention. After a brief inspection, he declared the exercise a success and ordered the airmen back to base. According to Russian accounts, it was the world's first combat parachute drop.*

MILITARY FUTURISM

Russia's pioneering role in the genesis of airborne forces goes against the grain of Western stereotypes. The prewar Red Army is usually seen through the distorting prism of Germany's experience fighting the Red Army in World War II. The image of the Red Army that has emerged from the German accounts is one of a massive, brutish opponent, ill prepared for modern warfare, led by terror, and depending on mass instead of skill. Because British and American accounts of the wartime Red Army have been so dependent on German sources, this image has dominated English accounts as well. In fact, the Red Army in the early 1930s was one of the most innovative military forces in the world; it was tragic political events in the late 1930s that would reverse these early advances.

The mood in Russia in the early 1930s was buoyant and optimistic. The Bolshevik Revolution of 1917 heralded the beginning of a

---

*In fact, Italy had conducted an experimental mass drop on 6 November 1927 from Caproni Ca. 73 biplane bombers.

new Russia, a Russia that would lead the world in industry, science, and political organization. The backward and lethargic attitudes of prewar Czarist society would be discarded for these new millenarian fantasies. No subject so ably captured the Soviet imagination as aviation. Russia had legitimate claims to a pioneering role in this field, particularly the creation of the world's first large multiengine bombers, the legendary Sikorsky Flying Ships. Stalin's regime had fastened onto aviation as a symbol of its progressive vision of technology. It sponsored the infant Soviet aviation industry to an extent not seen elsewhere in Europe at the time. It fostered a public awareness of aviation through spectacles such as the annual aviation days held every August in the Moscow area. Soviet organizations were set up to cultivate public enthusiasm in aviation through glider clubs.

The modernist aspirations of Soviet Russia were central to the dream of the Red airborne forces. Unlike the more tradition-bound armies of Western Europe, France and Britain in particular, the Russians were enthusiasts of nearly any novel technology or tactic. The Soviets viewed themselves as the vanguard of the future, and airborne forces had the futuristic appeal of an H. G. Wells novel. The idea of using paratroop forces sprang up from two distinctly different sources: air force and army officers who were experimenting with parachutes, and Soviet military thinkers who were attempting to create a new style of warfare for the Red Army in keeping with the modernist spirit.

In 1927, the Soviet government purchased a few hundred Irvin parachutes in the United States for six hundred dollars each. This was a fantastic sum of money at the time, especially for a country as strapped for hard currency as the Soviet Union. But the Russians were fascinated by American experiments with parachutes, and they sent a steady stream of unofficial visitors to the United States to study the exciting new technology. In 1929, L. G. Minov, the pilot who would later lead the first parachute drop at Voronezh, was sent to America to study the use of parachutes in air rescue missions.

Experimentation in Russia itself was hampered by the small number of parachutes available. The American parachutes were thinly spread among units of the burgeoning Red Air Force for use in their traditional role as airborne lifesavers. The Soviet Union couldn't afford to buy more American parachutes, so in 1929 the Air Force Scientific Research Institute began a program to manufacture American-style parachutes in Russia. A small workshop was established under the direction of M. L. Savitskiy, and in 1930 Savitskiy was sent to the United States to learn more about the American industry. In April 1930, the first small batches of parachutes began to enter production—the PL-1 for pilots and the PN-1 for navigators, both patterned on the American Irvin system. The workshop was later turned over to the aviation industry, and a special design bureau for military parachute technology was set up under P. I. Grokhovskiy. By the end of 1931, the first mass-produced parachute for paratrooper forces, the PD-1, was developed; of the first 5,000 parachutes manufactured in the Soviet Union, about 70 were of this type.

The availability of parachutes was an important step in the birth of the Russian airborne forces. Many other European countries had parachutes and parachute enthusiasts, but they did not develop a paratrooper force. The key difference in the Soviet Union was a group a visionary military theorists dreaming about the nature of future warfare. Mikhail Tukhachevskiy, the commander of the Leningrad Military District in 1929, proposed the idea of an aviation motorized division that could be airlanded behind enemy lines as part of his conception of "deep battle." In the early 1920s, small teams of Soviet soldiers had been landed by aircraft during the fighting with Muslim guerrillas in Central Asia, a tactic that the Red Air Force chief of staff, A. N. Lapchinskiy, promoted as a forerunner of modern airmobile forces.

The idea of airborne assault struck a responsive chord in the minds of Soviet military theorists, who realized that it was a futuristic echo of traditional Russian military concepts. The most forward looking of Russia's tsars, Peter the Great, had conceived of a *corps volant*, a "flying corps," in the seventeenth century. Peter described it as "a force so constituted that it can act without encumbrance in every direction, and send back reliable information of the enemy's doings . . . it would be detached at the disposal of the general, whether to cut off the enemy, deprive him of a pass, attack his rear, or fall on his territory and make a diversion." Of course, the unit that Peter was describing was a mobile cavalry force. But the tactical concept behind Peter's *corps volant* was almost identical to the type of force envisioned by Tukhachevskiy and Lapchinskiy more than two centuries later. Peter's concept remained an important one in Russian military thinking. Russia's borders were long and not easily defended. Russia's tsars favored the development of a highly mobile force, responsive to central government control, that could be dispatched to the frontiers to deal with unexpected threats. These ideas were forerunners of what today is called a strategic rapid-reaction force.

The vast expanses of the Russian steppe favored daring mobile operations. In the Napoleonic period, these became known by the Russian term *letuchie otriady*, "flying detachments." This tradition became embedded in Soviet military thinking as a result of the Russian Civil War in 1917–21. The civil war was fought over enormous distances by using mobile tactics completely dissimilar to the trench warfare tactics that had dominated World War I. Tukhachevskiy had been one of the most prominent Red commanders of the civil war, and an able practitioner of mobile warfare. The parachute added a thin veneer of modernity to a very old idea, and made Peter's *corps volant* literally possible.

EARLY AIRBORNE UNITS

The first practical test of these airborne assault tactics was conducted at Voronezh on 2 August 1930, as described earlier. This first experiment was a local initiative by parachuting enthusiasts such as L. G. Minov. News of the stunt quickly spread, and in September 1930 it was repeated at the same location. But the second drop had a more serious military flavor. The airborne raid was given a military mission: seizing documents from an "enemy" headquarters during district war games. An ANT-9 aircraft, a Soviet counterpart of the Ford Tri-Motor, dropped a raiding party of eleven paratroopers under the watchful eye of the military district commander, A. J. Kork. Impressed by the display, Kork dutifully reported his findings to the General Staff in Moscow. In view of Mikhail Tukhachevskiy's enthusiasm for such futuristic schemes, the General Staff decided to set up the first airborne unit in the Leningrad Military District.

The experimental airborne force was called the Parachute Assault Unit, or PDO in short for Parashutno-Desantniy Otryad. The PDO was commanded by Ye. D. Lukin and was based at the Komendantskiy airfield in the Leningrad area. It numbered 164 troops and was fully motorized, using light trucks and motorcycles, supported by its own armored platoon with two T-27 tankettes and three armored cars. Among its artillery were two DRP guns, the world's first recoilless rifles.

The tactics of the PDO were far more elaborate than those demonstrated at Voronezh in 1930. Tukhachevskiy was skeptical that a light infantry force landed by parachute could survive on the modern battlefield. Instead, the parachute element of the PDO would be dropped on an enemy airfield, or on a suitable area of open ground, and seize control of the area. Once this was accomplished, the main force would arrive and land on the captured strip with the PDO's vehicles and other heavy equipment. The PDO had an attached squadron of twelve Tupolev TB-1 heavy bombers and a detachment of ten R-5 light bombers specifically for this airlanding role. The paratrooper echelon of forty-six soldiers was attached to the 1st Aviation Brigade for training and was commanded by the head of the first Voronezh airdrop, L. G. Minov. The first demonstration of this combined parachute/airlanding raid was demonstrated to a curious group of Red Army generals during the autumn 1931 war games in the Leningrad Military District. Minov's detachment was also dropped near Mogilevka during the Ukrainian Military District's 1931 war games.

The Soviet approach to airborne operations was very different from the approach that would later be taken in Western Europe. The Soviets envisioned a combined-arms force with its own trucks, motor vehicles, and artillery support. In Germany, Britain, and the United States, airborne forces were light infantry forces with very little fire support and little or no motor transport.

The Red Army was far more enthusiastic than the air force about the results of these early paratroop demonstrations. I. P. Belov, who succeeded Mikhail Tukhachevskiy as commander of the Leningrad Military District, urged the formation of the first regular airborne divisions. Under Belov's plan, the divisions would have a parachute detachment to seize the landing area, a main force of a motor assault brigade, and an aviation brigade to provide the needed airlift. The Red Air Force was not so optimistic. All of the landings had been carried out under ideal conditions against no real opposition; in spite of this, the forces often landed widely dispersed. The air force thought that more attention needed to be paid to airlanding technology, including more advanced parachutes and more suitable equipment to carry and unload vehicles and equipment from aircraft.

Given the limitations of the Red Army budget in the early 1930s, Belov's proposal was wildly impractical. Instead, the General Staff agreed to the formation of four aviation motorized detachments in the Leningrad, Moscow, Ukrainian, and Byelorussian Military Districts. Not surprisingly, the Leningrad unit was the first in the field. Designated the 3rd Motorized Airborne Assault Detachment, it had three machine-gun companies with a total of 144 soldiers, plus three aviation squadrons for airlift. Two of the machine-gun companies were prepared as a paratrooper landing force; the third company would be airlanded, accompanied by the unit's fire support, including six 76mm howitzers and eighteen squad machine guns. The airlift component of the detachment included three Tupolev TB-1 heavy bombers, six Tupolev ANT-9 transport aircraft, six Polikarpov R-5 biplane light bombers, and three Polikarpov U-2 biplane utility aircraft. The Leningrad detachment was the only unit fully formed under the 1932 plan. A parachute platoon was formed in the Ukrainian Military District, but no other units materialized, owing to a lack of equipment and skepticism over the idea in the other districts.

In spite of the Red Air Force's wariness, Grokhovskiy's special design bureau was given considerable support in its schemes to develop airborne equipment. Grokhovskiy's most important innovation was the development of a static line for automatically opening parachutes. Previously, each paratrooper had to open his own chute with a ripcord. This was not an entirely dependable method when jumping at low altitudes; many novice paratroopers were gripped by a mind-numbing terror after leaping from the aircraft and forgot to pull the ripcord. The static line ensured that all the parachutes would open, no matter what the paratroopers' state of mind.

Grokhovskiy took his static-line idea one step too far. He designed a simple cradle, somewhat similar in shape to an ambulance stretcher, that could be mounted under the wings of TB-1 bombers. Each cradle would support a single paratrooper lying on his back, and each bomber could carry several of these cradles. On reaching the drop zone, the pilot would trigger the cradles much like bomb racks, and the paratroopers would be spilled out in quick succession. These paratrooper cradles were demonstrated in 1931 but were not popularly received. The paratroopers were buffeted about by the aircraft's slipstream, vibrated by the TB-1 bomber's noisy engines, and then unceremoniously dumped out without warning. The designers quickly appreciated that it was the camaraderie of the paratroopers before the jump that made the terrifying leap endurable. The cradle, although technically feasible, overlooked the critical human element in airborne operations.

Grokhovskiy did have success in the area of heavy-equipment technology. His bureau devised a number of cradles that could be attached underneath heavy bombers to carry tankettes, howitzers, and other unwieldy loads. Although technically successful, early experiments with airlanding raised concerns in the Red Air Force about the feasibility of the whole notion of airlanding heavy equipment. In the event of soggy ground, the aircraft became bogged down and could not return to base. In 1932, the total Red Air Force heavy-bomber force was only 152 TB-1 heavy bombers, and they could not afford to be lost in risky airlanding operations. As a result, Grokhovskiy was instructed to look at alternatives. These included heavy-load parachutes, and cargo pallets to protect vehicles and artillery when parachute-dropped.

COMBAT GLIDERS

The air force also sponsored another critical innovation, the assault glider. At the time, the Red Air Force was beginning to make extensive use of gliders for basic training of new aircrews. Gliders offered the hope of solving the airlanding problem. Instead of the risk of landing a priceless heavy bomber or transport in enemy territory, an inexpensive glider could land in its place. If made of inexpensive wood and fabric, it could be left behind if need be, or recovered after the operation. Gliders could be cheaper than expensive silk parachutes for landing large numbers of troops. And gliders saved on the expense of training specialized paratroopers; ordinary infantry could be airlifted without specialized training. Gliders also increased the carrying capacity of the aircraft tug. A TB-1 heavy bomber could carry only fifteen paratroopers, but it could tow a glider with up to fifty troops. Every added pound of parachute greatly detracted from the range or carrying capacity of the transport, but gliders assisted the transport tug since their wings provided much of the lift needed to carry their load.

Two airlanding gliders were ordered in 1932: the light G-63, towed by a Polikarpov R-5 biplane bomber, which could carry seventeen fully armed soldiers plus one thousand pounds of arms and equipment, and the heavy G-64, towed by a TB-1 heavy bomber, which could carry fifty troops. The G-63 was first test-flown in October 1932, but its performance was poor. As a result, no production was undertaken, and the larger G-64 never even reached prototype stage. Grokhovskiy turned his attention to a less conventional design, the G-31. Instead of carrying the cargo or troops in the fuselage, the G-31 had massive ninety-two-foot wings that contained sixteen compartments for either cargo or troops. This design was no more successful. Other attempts, such as Gribovskiy's G-11, also ended in failure. Grokhovskiy's appetite for novelty was not matched by his technical competence in aircraft design.

Other of his experiments were even more bizarre and earned him a special place in the annals of weird aviation schemes. While working on his gliders, Grokhovskiy became convinced that it would be possible to drop cargoes onto the landing field without parachutes if the cargoes were sufficiently cushioned by spring suspensions. He called these devices air buses. An air bus consisted of an aerodynamic container, resembling a cross-sectional portion of a heavy-bomber wing. At the front of the container was a pair of automobile tires with heavy-duty spring shock absorbers. At the rear was a reinforced tail skid. The capacity varied with size; Grokhovskiy envisioned several air-bus designs, carrying from three to twelve fully armed troops, tailored to the size of the transport aircraft. The airborne troopers would ride in the container in a prone position, stacked like cordwood on canvas shelves with their heads forward. Grokhovskiy also planned a special amphibious type, called a hydro-air bus, built with a boat hull, which could be dropped on water near a shoreline.

The air bus and hydro-air bus were to be carried under the belly of the transport aircraft. On nearing the drop zone, the pilot would lower his speed, bring the aircraft as near to the ground as possible, then release the air bus. This would then skid along the ground, with the tail skid gradually slowing it down. The first tests of the hydro-air bus from a TB-1 were not encouraging. When dropped onto a calm stretch of water, the container split open and sank. Grokhovskiy and his deputy, I. V. Titov, were the guinea pigs for the first test of the normal air bus, which was dropped without killing the designer or his hapless aide. The Red Air Force actually ordered a small number of these devices for further trials in 1932, but, mercifully, their fate has disappeared from the pages of history.

PRACTICE MAKES PERFECT

While Grokhovskiy was busily tinkering with the new airborne technology, the Red Army was still debating the future role of airborne forces. The first official description of the aviation motorized landing detachments released in February 1932 envisioned them as tactical raiding forces, able to attack vital enemy targets such as supply dumps and bridges, block enemy reinforcements, or disrupt enemy command and communication. Tukhachevskiy and his supporters viewed their role as even more significant—operating deep in the enemy rear and "arresting the action of [enemy] forces throughout the operational depth of the defense." Leningrad's 3rd Motorized Airborne Assault Detachment put on another able display of its skills in a September 1932 exercise at its training grounds near Krasnogvardeisk. At the drop was Stalin's confidant and the head of the Red Army, Klimenti Voroshilov, who was impressed by the display.

Another attempt was made to expand the airborne force in January 1933. The 3rd Detachment in Leningrad was enlarged to become the 3rd Special Purpose Airborne Brigade (3rd ABON), under the command of M. V. Boytsov. The paratroop element was raised to a battalion in size, and the airlanding element was designated as a moto-mechanized battalion. The brigade's airlift was substantially increased by substituting two squadrons of the new TB-3 heavy bomber for the earlier TB-1 and ANT-9 aircraft, and retaining a squadron of R-5 biplanes. The new brigade was first tested during a September 1933 airborne jump near Luga.

The 1933 plan also included the organization of twenty-nine special purpose airborne battalions attached to existing rifle corps throughout the Soviet Union, totaling some eight thousand troops. Although substantial in size, these units were intended for airlanding by aircraft or gliders, since there were neither sufficient parachutes nor sufficient training resources to prepare so many new troops for the difficult skill of parachute jumping. An attempt was made to rejuvenate the three airborne motorized detachments that had moldered away since the original 1932 plan, and a fourth was added in the Volga Military District. Several small platoon- and company-sized paratroop detachments were formed to increase the number of jump-qualified troops. One of the most important sources of jump-qualified personnel was the government-organized parachuting clubs organized by the Osoaviakhim Society to stimulate interest in technical military careers among teenagers.

In 1934, the four airborne motorized detachments were again expanded, this time being configured along the lines of the Leningrad 3rd ABON. The Byelorussian ABON was deployed in the 1934 summer district war games near Minsk. On 7 September, a force of 129 paratroopers was dropped in the "enemy" rear to prevent an enemy withdrawal. Two days later, in the largest airborne drop ever attempted, 603 troops were landed behind enemy lines to disrupt the advance of enemy forces. Both exercises were judged successful.

With the exception of a few small demonstration airdrops and airlandings, the early Soviet airborne maneuvers were kept secret. In 1935, however, it was decided to disclose the full extent of Soviet airborne experiments. Foreign military attachés in Moscow were invited to witness the 1935 Kiev Military District maneuvers. The district commander, I. E. Yakir, had planned an especially dramatic airborne operation. For months before the war games, the district's 13th ABON was enlarged in strength to a regiment, and the experienced paratroopers assisted in training two regular rifle regiments in airlanding tactics.

THE BIRTH OF THE MODERN AIRBORNE

The Kiev exercise of 1935 marked the birth of modern airborne forces. By 1935, the Soviet force had a distinct tactical doctrine on airlanding and a clear place in Soviet war-fighting doctrine. In both these respects, it predated any other paratrooper force in the world. Equally important, the Kiev exercise excited many other paratrooper enthusiasts around the world in the viability of the concept. Other armies had tested with paratroopers on a very small scale; Kiev proved that mass airdrops were possible.

The Kiev exercise began with an impressive show of force as wave after wave of TB-1 and TB-3 bombers flew in formation over the airfield near Brovary, protected by swarms of Red Air Force fighter planes. Two jumps were made, one regiment over the Brovary airfield, the other to the east of Darnitsa to form a blocking force to shield the landing field from an approaching "enemy" force. In all, some 1,188 paratroopers were dropped from about fifty TB-3 heavy bombers. The initial waves of paratroopers were lightly armed with rifles, submachine guns, and DP squad machine guns. Once Brovary airfield was secured, another wave of lumbering TB-3 bombers swept into the airfield 1,765 troops, a single T-37 light tank, ten artillery pieces, and six light trucks. Unlike the paratroopers in their blue coveralls and corn blue jump helmets, the airlanding troops were mostly regular Red Army riflemen in the usual dull khaki battle dress. In one hour and fifty minutes, 2,500 troops had either parachuted or airlanded, and soon afterward they repulsed an advancing enemy force in a mock battle.

Many of the foreign observers were stunned by the scale of the exercise. The deputy chief of the French general staff, General Loiseau, remarked, "I am impressed by the success of the airborne force. Western Europe is lagging behind!" The Italian army had already begun to experiment with airborne forces, and General Monti gushed, "I am literally amazed by the employment of such airborne landing forces." The French opened their first parachute training school in October 1935 and formed their first regular paratrooper companies in 1937. Italy followed suit in 1938.

Germany had been following the Soviet progress with some interest. Among the German observers of the grand displays in 1935 was Col. Kurt Student, a World War I pilot who would go on to establish Germany's vaunted Fallschirmjaeger airborne force. Student, probably more than any other observer, appreciated how far the Soviets had progressed in the airborne assault idea. The Germans recognized the potential value of airborne forces and began to gradually build up a paratroop and glider force that would reach divisional strength by the beginning of World War II. It would be the largest airborne force in the world next to the Red Army's.

The sole dissent came from Britain. The head of the British delegation, Maj. Gen. A. P. Wavell, would win fame a few years later in the Western Desert campaign. Wavell was far more skeptical in his evaluation of the Kiev exercise. "This parachute descent, though its tactical value may be doubtful, was a most spectacular performance. We were told that there were no casualties and we certainly saw none; in fact the parachutists we saw in action after the landings were in remarkably good trim, mostly moving on the double. They are, of course, a specially picked force and had had some months training. It apparently took some time after the first descent began landing, about one and a half hours after the first descent began, a part of the force was still being collected." The British army, beggared by a peacetime defense budget consumed by air force and naval priorities, paid no attention to such futuristic ideas. Britain would be a latecomer to airborne forces, not establishing its first significant airborne force until 1940.

The Kiev war games cemented the role of the airborne force into Red Army doctrine. The official assessment of the exercise concluded that "the great success of the real mass airborne landings completely proved the capability for employing this new combat arm for serious tactical and operational missions in future warfare." The Red airborne force came to form an integral part of the new Soviet doctrine of deep battle. The Red Army envisioned the use of mechanized violence to shatter enemy armies through their entire depth, not simply frontal engagements such as the trench war of World War I. Mobile forces using tanks, motorized infantry, artillery, and air support would crash through weak points in enemy lines. In the meantime, airborne forces would be landed a dozen miles behind the enemy lines to attack their second line of defense, destroy their logistical links, and paralyze the command structure by disrupting communications. Airborne units would also be dropped even farther behind the front line, in the operational depth of the enemy lines, to seize key bridges and facilities. These views were codified in the 1936 Field Regulations, the culmination of the Red Army's dynamic military thinking in the prewar years.

Further large-scale experiments with airborne forces continued after the Kiev debut. Parallel to the Kiev maneuvers, the Red Air Force airlifted an entire rifle division from the Moscow Military

District across the Eurasian continent to Vladivostok on the Pacific Ocean in 1935, involving more than 5,000 troops. It was one of the most remarkable peacetime exercises of the interwar years but is still little known due to the secrecy attached to the operation. This exercise was undertaken to show how the Red Army could rapidly deploy forces into the Far East to counter Japanese expansion in China. In the autumn of 1936, two major exercises were conducted in the Byelorussian and Moscow Military Districts. By this time, two more of the district battalions had been brought up to brigade strength on the Leningrad model, bringing the total to three. Other airborne units included three airborne regiments in the tense Far East districts facing Japan, and three battalions in the Moscow, Volga, and Transbaikal Military Districts. The Byelorussian District's 47th Special Purpose Airborne Brigade was used in the 1936 district war games, followed by an airlanding with tanks, artillery, and other heavy equipment. For the fall 1936 Moscow Military District war games, its paratroop battalion was expanded into an improvised regiment and supported by four new independent paratroop battalions. The most important innovation in this exercise was the largest airlanding yet attempted—the transport of more than 5,000 troops of the 84th Rifle Division aboard transport aircraft into the airfield seized by the paratroopers during the airdrop.

THE HIDDEN AIRLIFT PROBLEM

The gargantuan scale of these exercises concealed the most significant flaw in prewar Soviet airborne development: the lack of airlift. These military district war games pushed the limits of the Red Air Force's heavy-lift capacity. The 1935 Kiev maneuver required one special aviation brigade and two heavy TB-3 bomber brigades— about half the total Soviet heavy-bomber force of the time. This was conceivable in peacetime conditions, but in wartime the air force would have many pressing commitments for its heavy-bomber force other than acting as an airborne taxi service for the paratroopers.

Nor was the TB-3 an ideal choice for paratrooper operations. It was selected because it was the only Soviet military aircraft that could carry a reasonable load of paratroopers and their equipment. The normal capacity of the TB-3 was thirty-five to forty paratroopers, but up to fifty could be carried in exchange for less fuel. The main technical problem was that the TB-3 had not been designed for paratrooper missions. Exit from the aircraft was limited to a small access door on the right fuselage side, and a pair of machine-gun combings above and behind this door. These spaces were too small for easy exit by a fully equipped paratrooper, so they could not be used for the quick exit of a string of paratroopers. Instead, the Soviet technique was to move the paratroopers out onto the enormous wing and have them slide off in quick succession to minimize dispersion on the ground. Several minutes before reaching the drop zone, the paratroopers would clamber out onto the wing, where they would hang on for dear life. Climbing out of the machine-gun combings and the small side door while encumbered by more than seventy pounds of main parachute, reserve chute, and gear was no mean feat. On a faster aircraft, this technique would have been impossible, but the TB-3 was a slow aircraft, usually flying at eighty-five to one hundred miles per hour when approaching the drop zone. Films from the Kiev war games show the TB-3 lumbering into the drop zone with antlike swarms of paratroopers moving onto the wings.

The Soviet airborne's reliance on the TB-3 bomber was mainly due to the immaturity of Soviet civil aviation. The state airline, or GVF, was small by European standards. Air travel in Russia was a luxury that few could afford. In contrast, the German civil air fleet would later prove a vital ingredient in developing airlift for the German paratrooper force, the Fallschirmjaeger. Hitler's enthusiasm for air travel and the clandestine needs of the German Luftwaffe led to extensive government subsidies for Lufthansa. Most importantly, they led to the requirement for cargo and passenger aircraft, such as the legendary Junkers Ju-52. These aircraft were far more suitable for the needs of the paratrooper force than improvised bombers. The Junkers Ju-52 would prove to be the workhorse of the Fallschirmjaeger, just as the American Douglas DC-3, in its militarized C-47 form, would prove to be the principal means of airlift for the U.S. Army's airborne divisions.

Stalin did not share Hitler's enthusiasm for flying; his surly and paranoid nature made him wary of the risks involved. As a result, the Soviet state airline, Aeroflot, had a hard time obtaining government support for airliner development. The PS-35 airliner of 1937 was not

entirely satisfactory, and only eleven were built for Aeroflot. Swal-
lowing their pride, the Russians decided to license-produce the Douglas DC-3, powered by Soviet engines. The resulting aircraft, called
the PS-84, or later the Lisunov Li-2, entered Aeroflot service in 1941
on the eve of the war. Russia was not alone in neglecting airlift; Britain never developed an adequate military transport before World War
II and relied on Lend-Lease C-47s or modified bombers.

The second area of neglect was in the development of gliders. The
early plans for the Soviet airborne force had called for the construction of troop and equipment gliders. As mentioned earlier, the Grokhovskiy attempts in 1933 were unsuccessful, and subsequent attempts by other inexperienced designers were no better. The fact that
the main design bureaus such as Tupolev and Polikarpov weren't
given the assignment is testimony to the low priority assigned this
project by the air force. Gliders would have been a workable alternative to airliners or dedicated military transports since they could be
towed by a wide variety of aircraft, including medium bombers, that
would have been otherwise unsuitable for the airlift role.

The leaders of the Soviet airborne force were not oblivious to the
airlift problem. When the success of the 1936 war games led to widespread acceptance of the airborne concept, and it was officially en-
shrined in the 1936 field regulations, there was hope that the airlift
requirements could be satisfied in cooperation with the air force in
the next few years. But these dreams would be cruelly shattered in
1937 when the Red Army's airborne force was subjected to its first
test of fire.

Chapter 2
The Test of Fire

I f Joseph Stalin truly hated any Soviet commander, it was Mikhail Tukhachevskiy. And Stalin was not the type of person to forget a grudge. The enmity between Stalin and Tukhachevskiy, which stemmed from a long-simmering feud during the 1920 Russo-Polish War, would have tragic consequences for the Red Army.

The Russo-Polish War began in the early summer of 1920 when the Polish army, supported by an allied Ukrainian army, marched into Ukraine. The Red Army responded with a two-pronged blow: an attack by Tukhachevskiy's Western Front on Warsaw by way of the northern route over the Pripyat marshes, and an attack by the Southwestern Front toward the key city of Lvov, south of the Pripyat marshlands. Stalin was the Communist Party representative of the Southwestern Front attacking Lvov. At a critical phase of the battle for Warsaw, Tukhachevskiy insisted that the mobile cavalry army under Semyon Budenny from the Southwestern Front support his attack on Warsaw. Stalin, in connivance with the staff of the Southwestern Front, managed to evade Moscow's orders. Tukhachevskiy's drive on Warsaw was blunted by a masterful counterstroke by Marshal Pilsudski's forces, and the Red Army was sent scurrying back to Russia in an utter rout. Tukhachevskiy put part of the blame for this humiliating defeat on Stalin and the Southwestern Front commanders for obstructing the transfer of critical cavalry forces.

Stalin and Tukhachevskiy were polar opposites. Tukhachevskiy was the radical son of the Russian aristocracy. In World War I, he was a dashing young cavalry commander, radicalized by his fellow Russian aristocrats' inept handling of the bloody war. Handsome and charismatic, he quickly rose through the ranks of the infant Red Army in the civil war that followed the October Revolution of 1917. Stalin, the son of a Georgian cobbler, had an unsavory reputation as a provinical bank robber and political malcontent. Ill mannered and ill spoken, he made little impression on the inner circle of Lenin's Bolshevik Party but tenaciously advanced in the byzantine world of Communist politics. He was a treacherous schemer in a radical political movement that came to power by treachery and scheming. After Lenin's death, he outmaneuvered his political rivals and by the mid-1930s was the unquestioned dictator of the Soviet Union.

Tukhachevskiy's brilliance made him the most visible advocate of the modernist wing of the Red Army and the sponsor of many new technologies and tactics. Stalin, preoccupied with establishing his position within the Communist Party during the first decade of his rule, paid little attention to his old nemesis. No one doubted Tukhachevskiy's loyalty to the Soviet Union, and he made little effort to extend his influence outside the military. Once Stalin had consolidated his power, however, his attitude toward Tukhachevskiy began to change. Ever distrusting of the success of others, Stalin suspected that Tukhachevskiy's popularity in the military might be a stepping-stone to Bonapartist ambitions. Stalin projected his own devious manner in his judgment of potential rivals. And he was not about to tolerate any rivals.

In 1936, Stalin began eliminating the old Bolsheviks by staging show trials on trumped-up charges of treason and conspiracy. It was the beginning of a campaign of terror that would cost millions of lives. In 1937, the purge spread into the ranks of the military with the arrest of Mikhail Tukhachevskiy and all of his close associates. Tukhachevskiy was shot, allegedly for involvement in a preposterous plot against Stalin. In 1937 and 1938, the NKVD special police murdered nearly the entire upper leadership of the Red Army, including most divisional and brigade commanders. This senseless slaughter took place at a time when a new European war seemed ever more likely.

The Great Purge had both immediate and long-term effects on the

Soviet VDV Airborne Force.* The VDV was closely associated with Tukhachevskiy and so was harrowed mercilessly, as were Tukhachevskiy's pet mechanized forces. Many of the VDV's brigade and regimental commanders were killed or imprisoned, leaving the airborne force leaderless in the years before the beginning of World War II. Young commanders were pushed forward, but many were inexperienced and unprepared to cope in such dangerous times.

In the broader sense, the purge of Tukhachevskiy brought into doubt his concept of deep battle and so, too, the VDV Airborne Force. Leadership of the Red Army passed to Stalin's cronies from the days of the 1920 Russo-Polish War, especially those who had served in Budenny's cavalry army. The Soviet cavalry, like most cavalry branches in the 1930s, would never be accused of intellectual vitality or progressive attitudes.

VDV REORGANIZATION

The purges slowed—but did not stop—the planned enlargement of the airborne forces. The VDV underwent another reorganization in 1938. Three airborne regiments, including two in the Far East, were enlarged to brigade size, numbering three thousand troops each. This brought the combined VDV strike force to a strength of six airborne brigades. Three airlanding regiments were also added in the Moscow Military District. The diminished fortunes of the VDV were evident in other developments, or lack of development. The hallmark mass airborne drops so characteristic of the Red Army's summer and autumn war games in the mid-1930s were halted. The purges also distracted the VDV from attempting to ameliorate its continuing airlift problem. Glider design was ignored, and the lack of summer war games disguised the airlift problem.

Technical progress in other areas continued, but at a slower pace. Grokhovskiy's bureau was shut by the purges, but work on parachutes by other teams went on. Early Soviet parachutes were flat, circular canopies; these were acceptable for use with slow aircraft such as the TB-3 bomber, but they had high opening shock and were

*In the late 1930s, the Soviet airborne force became known as the VDV, the Russian acronym for Vozdushno-Desantniy Voisk.

not very stable. The Soviet airborne introduced a novel solution: using two canopies instead of one. The first backpack chute was opened by a static line in the aircraft; the front reserve chute was opened by a ripcord. The use of two chutes reduced oscillation and slowed the landing speed. During high-altitude jumps, the practice was to refrain from opening the second chute until the jumper was near the ground. In 1941, the Soviets began adopting a new square canopy design from Col. N. Lobanov, the PD-41.* This parachute opened slowly to reduce shock, had greater stability than circular chutes, was easy to collapse on the ground, and had some degree of steerability since it had a fin opening on one side. The PD-41 was also cheap to manufacture. This new chute was not without faults, however: it suffered from erratic opening, its slow-opening feature required higher altitude jumps, and its canopy fin tended to cause the parachute to glide laterally at a rate of about five to six and a half feet per second, which could cause dispersion problems during mass drops.

Even if the VDV Airborne Force had lost its favored position, it was still a formidable force by world standards. Germany was only beginning to form a divisional-sized airborne force in 1938, and most armies had only small, experimental units.

FIRST BLOOD

The first combat employment of the VDV brigades took place in 1939 in Mongolia during the border fighting with the Japanese. At the time, there were two VDV units in the area: Col. I. I. Zatevakhin's 212th Airborne Brigade and Maj. I. I. Gudarevich's 204th Airborne Brigade. A third unit, Col. I. S. Bezugly's 201st Airborne Brigade, was transferred to the Far East from the Leningrad Military District. Their use in the air assault role proved impossible due to the shortage of airlift. The 1st Heavy Bomber Regiment, equipped with TB-3 bombers, and the 150th Bomber Regiment, with the new DB-3F bombers, were the only significant bomber forces available in the

---

*This was the final prewar evolution of a series of parachute designs that can be traced back to Savitskiy's original PD-1, including the PD-2, PD-6, PD-6PR, PD-7, PD-8, PD-10, and PD-10U.

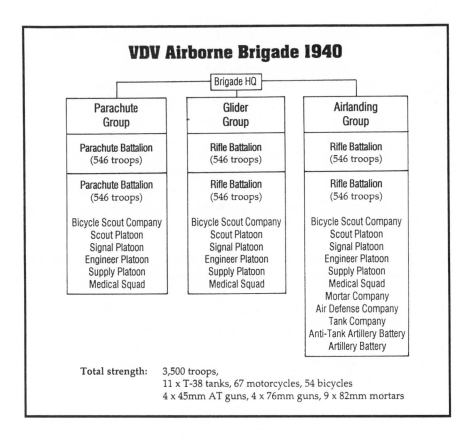

area. It was out of the question to employ these precious aircraft on airlift missions when they were so badly needed for their principal role of bombing Japanese troop concentrations.

As a result, the 204th and 212th Airborne Brigades were simply committed as light infantry forces. The theater commander, Gen. Georgiy Zhukov, kept the 212th Airborne Brigade in his reserve at the opening stages of the fighting around Khalkin Gol and finally committed the brigade's troops as light infantry in the assaults on the Fui Heights. They performed well in the battle, driving out the tenacious Japanese infantry in bloody hand-to-hand combat with bayonets and grenades. But their role was not particularly significant compared to the pivotal role of the Soviet mechanized brigades. The 201st Airborne Brigade served with the 15th Army during the fighting, and the 204th Airborne was kept in the 15th Army reserve until the final days of the campaign.

The glory of the Khalkin Gol victory over the Japanese was followed by the ignominy and embarrassments of the Russo-Finnish War of 1939–40. Stalin demanded territorial concessions from Finland to push back the border from the city of Leningrad. The Finns refused, fearing it would be the first step in a return to the Russian empire. As a result, the Red Army invaded southern Finland in 1939 in what would prove to be one of the most inept and humiliating wars of the era. The 201st Airborne Brigade returned to the Leningrad Military District too late to take part in the opening phases of the war, but it was later committed to the fighting in the light infantry role along with airborne regiments from the Byelorussian and Kiev Military Districts. Soviet histories of the VDV Airborne Force pass over these battles in silence, which suggests that the airborne's performance was not particularly distinguished. In contrast to the Soviet units in the Far East, which had been spared the worst excesses of the purge, the units of the Leningrad Military District taking part in the Finnish campaign displayed a shocking degree of unpreparedness. The near defeat of the Red Army in the Russo-Finnish War of 1939–40 showed how corrosive the effects of purge had been. The Red Army made small-scale use of paratrooper raiding parties during the war, including some groups disguised in Finnish uniforms. However, there were no drops larger than platoon size.

The VDV airborne brigades were committed to action a third time in June 1940 in what would be their debut in the paratrooper role. The battleground was Romania. As part of the German-Russian treaty of August 1939, which had preceded the German invasion of Poland, the erstwhile allies agreed to a series of territorial concessions. Stalin demanded the Romanian province of Bessarabia, which had been part of the Tsarist Russian empire, as well as the province of Bukovina, which had not been under Russian control. Confronted by both Hitler and Stalin, the Romanians had little choice but to accede to the demands. Stalin decided to seize the new territories quickly before Hitler had second thoughts about the matter. Stalin selected eastern Romania to be the showcase for a revived Red Army.

To counteract the impression created by the bungled campaign in Finland, Stalin insisted on a textbook demonstration of Tukhachevskiy's deep battle concept with mechanized thrusts supported by airborne assaults, much like the German blitzkrieg. The blitzkrieg in Poland, the Low Countries, France, and Norway had been a convincing demonstration of German prowess, and few operations were as stunning as the German airborne operation against the Eban Emael fortresses in Belgium in May 1940. Stalin no doubt wanted his own counterpart to Eban Emael. Since the bombers would not be needed for air attacks, they could be husbanded for airlift. Four regiments of TB-3 bombers—about 170 aircraft—were tasked with delivering the airborne units.

The Soviet occupation of eastern Romania began on the morning of 28 June 1940. The first wave consisted of mechanized and cavalry units, which raced forward to occupy the area as quickly as possible. The 204th Airborne Brigade, newly returned from Mongolia, spearheaded the attack by a mass airdrop north of Bolgrad. After forming up, the brigade marched seven miles into the city and occupied it. The 201st Airborne Brigade was sent from the Leningrad Military District to redeem its reputation after the Finnish debacle. The plan was to airland the brigade on the airfield near Izmail on the third day of the operation, 30 June. A reconnaissance of the air base made it clear that it was far too small to accommodate the big TB-3 bombers, so the force parachuted into Izmail instead. The city was occupied without opposition. The 214th Airborne Brigade remained as a reserve force under air force command during the Romanian operation and did not see any action.

The Romanian airborne operations were not a serious test of combat, as the Soviets were not opposed, but this success did help revive the fortunes of the airborne force. The German use of airlanding and airborne forces at Eban Emael meant that such forces had become a prerequisite for the new style of blitzkrieg warfare. Stalin dismissed the reservations of his horse cavalry cronies and embraced the deep battle doctrine of his murdered rival, Tukhachevskiy.

The new 1940 PU-40 field service regulations of the Red Army further defined the airborne's role. The regulations stated that the "VDV are an instrument of the high command, used to accomplish those missions in the enemy rear that cannot be accomplished by the other combat arms at a given time, but which if carried out might have a significant impact on the battle or the entire operation."

Although the VDV remained nominally under air force jurisdiction, in reality it was now regarded as the special operations force of Stalin and the Soviet STAVKA high command for use only in high-value missions, much as Peter the Great's *corps volant* had been the shock force of the tsar. The VDV was not intended to be wasted as light infantry, as had occurred in Mongolia and Finland.

In November 1940, the six airborne brigades were reorganized yet again, this time into three groups: paratroop, glider, and airlanding. The paratrooper and glider groups each consisted of two battalions of 546 men each with small arms and light machine guns. The airlanding group was organized in a similar fashion but would bring along the brigades' heavy weapons, including a company of eleven T-37 or T-40 light tanks, an artillery battalion with four 45mm antitank guns and four 76mm regimental howitzers, a mortar company with nine 82mm mortars, and an air defense company with twelve 12.7mm heavy machine guns. The organization showed several important changes from earlier brigades. The idea of motorized airborne formations that had been present since Tukhachevskiy's original concepts in 1930 was abandoned as unrealistic. There simply wasn't enough airlift to bring in any significant number of vehicles. The only mobile forces in the brigade were the scout companies in each battalion, equipped with eleven motorcycles and nine bicycles each. The organization still insisted on retaining an armored complement of eleven T-40 light tanks, to be delivered under the belly of the TB-3 bombers. The 1940 brigades revived the idea of using gliders to land a third of the force. A program was started to develop new gliders, including the seventeen-man BDP-1 glider by N. N. Polikarpov's design team. None of these was ready for production before the outbreak of the war in 1941.

The new brigade organization had not gone very far when in April 1941 the Red Army High Command announced the decision to reorganize five of the brigades into airborne corps, somewhat larger in size than Germany's 7th Airborne Division. Each of these corps would consist of three airborne brigades. To further add to the confusion, the new brigades were organized in a completely different fashion from the 1940 brigades. The 1941 brigades were based around four paratrooper battalions. The idea of having a mixed paratroop/glider/airlanding force was dropped in favor of paratroopers alone. The brigade's firepower was increased, and more attention was paid to specialized combat engineer equipment such as flame-throwers and explosives, based on the German tactics at the Eban Emael fortress. The tank companies were taken out of the brigades and consolidated into a separate tank battalion under the corps head-quarters. As a final change, the VDV was allowed to form its own headquarters directly under the Ministry of Defense, freeing it from air force control. On paper at least, it was a formidable force with more than 100,000 troops. The reality was very different.

VDV Airborne Force: Order of Battle, April 1941

Corps	Military District	Brigades*	Commander
1st Airborne	Kiev Special	1, 204, 211 VDB	M. A. Usenko
2nd Airborne	Kharkov	2, 3, 4 VDB	F. M. Kharitonov
3rd Airborne	Odessa	5, 6, 212 VDB	V. A. Glazunov
4th Airborne	Western Special	7, 8, 214 VDB	A. S. Zhadov
5th Airborne	Baltic Special	9, 10, 201 VDB	I. S. Bezugly
	Far Eastern	202 VDB	

*VDB = Vozdushno-Desantnaya Brigada, or airborne brigade.

OPERATION BARBAROSSA

The German invasion of the Soviet Union on 22 June 1941 caught the Red Army ill prepared for modern warfare. The more perceptive Soviet generals were expecting the Germans to attack, but Stalin blindly insisted that Hitler would not betray the 1939 Molotov-Ribbentrop alliance so soon. The Red Army's reorganization was not scheduled for completion until late 1942. Stalin did not permit Red Army units along the frontier to go to alert status in June 1941, in spite of German provocations such as reconnaissance overflights. Stalin did not want to give Hitler a pretext to launch the invasion. Hitler needed no pretext.

The VDV force was in complete disarray when the war broke out. The spring 1941 draft brought in a flood of fresh, young recruits, but

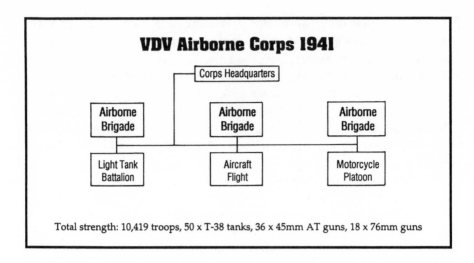

VDV Airborne Corps 1941

Corps Headquarters

Airborne Brigade — Airborne Brigade — Airborne Brigade

Light Tank Battalion — Aircraft Flight — Motorcycle Platoon

Total strength: 10,419 troops, 50 x T-38 tanks, 36 x 45mm AT guns, 18 x 76mm guns

none had any military training, and only a small fraction were jump-qualified from peacetime practice with Osoaviakhim parachute sporting clubs. Nearly 150,000 Soviet citizens had completed parachute training with the civilian clubs, but only a small portion of these were draft-eligible. The most severe shortages were in officers and NCOs. The VDV had expanded much too rapidly, and young company commanders were suddenly thrust forward to command battalions of equally inexperienced young paratroopers. Materiel for the new airborne corps also was in short supply, especially radios, tanks, and specialized equipment.

The German invasion on 22 June 1941 had a crippling impact on the VDV. The German tank attacks were preceded by devastating air raids on the forward Soviet airfields. The enormous TB-3 bombers that had been the mainstay of VDV airlift were easy targets for Luftwaffe attacks. Of the 800 bombers available on 22 June 1941, most of those in European Russia were either destroyed on the ground or shot down. Fewer than 200 survived by the end of 1941, mainly in regiments in the Far East. German air superiority, and the heavy losses suffered in the early stages of the Barbarossa offensive, made it impossible to contemplate using the new airborne corps in their intended fashion. Furthermore, the airborne corps were intended as offensive strike forces. They were too lightly equipped to

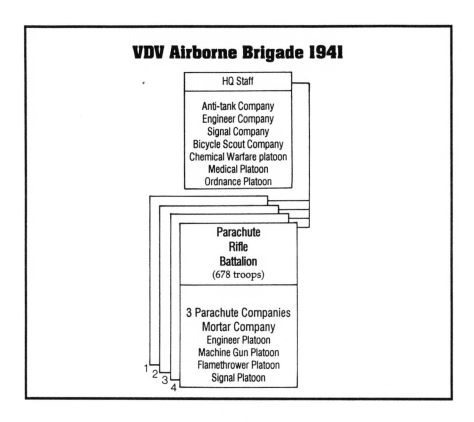

survive more than a few days of intense combat before being relieved by advancing Red Army columns. Under the conditions of
1941, no air assault operation could expect to receive relief.

In spite of the unfavorable conditions, the 204th Airborne Brigade
staged several small-scale airborne raids in July 1941 in Ukraine.
Small groups of paratroopers were dropped behind German lines to
disrupt communications, attack convoys, and destroy supplies. They
had little impact on the Wehrmacht attack but were a notable precursor to the Soviet partisan effort in later years.

The first VDV unit in combat was Gen. I. S. Bezugly's 5th Airborne Corps in the Baltic area. It was thrown into action as an infantry force, first in support of the badly understrength 21st Mechanized
Corps, and on 28 June 1941 with the 27th Army in the attempts to
push back the German 4th Panzer Group bridgehead over the Dvina

River at Daugapvils in Latvia. The German armored assault was aimed at Leningrad and was heavily supported by Stuka attacks. The paratroopers staged several local counterattacks against the German infantry positions at Daugapvils but could not resist the German tank attacks. The 5th Airborne Corps had no armor and only six artillery pieces. The survivors of the Daugapvils fighting managed to escape German encirclement, and the corps was finally withdrawn back toward Moscow in August to be rebuilt.

The 4th Airborne Corps took part in the fighting east of Minsk in Byelorussia. The fighting in Byelorussia had begun with some of the most devastating German attacks of the campaign. Panzer Gruppe 2 had crushed or bypassed the Soviet forces on the border and had smashed into the Byelorussian capital of Minsk in only a week. In desperation, a reserve force was cobbled together in an attempt to stop the German tanks along the Berezina River east of Minsk. The 4th Airborne Corps was based at Maryna Gorka and entered the field as infantry on 28 June. The 7th and 8th Airborne Brigades were assigned to cover the Berezina River on the approaches to Mogilev, while the 214th Airborne Brigade was positioned farther south on the western approaches to Bobruisk. Although the 214th Airborne Brigade was scheduled to be air-dropped behind German lines to attack the logistics of the advancing German tank columns, German air superiority and a shortage of aircraft prevented this mission. There were several small-scale airdrops by troops from the 214th Airborne Brigade, and they managed to cause damage far beyond their modest size.

Fast-moving columns from the 3rd Panzer Division drove a wedge between the two northernmost brigades on 30 June, cutting off the 214th Airborne Brigade on the west bank of the Berezina. The 7th and 8th Airborne Brigades were not able to hold their positions much longer when confronted by a renewed German offensive on 5–6 July, part of a major breakthrough toward Smolensk. These two brigades withdrew to the southeast with neighboring rifle divisions, eventually establishing a defensive line on the Sozh River toward the end of the month as part of the 13th Army. With the planned airdrop of the 214th Airborne Brigade now impossible, the brigade was ordered to remain in the German rear area and harass the German advance. After nearly three months of rear-area guerrilla fighting, the brigade's survivors made it back to Soviet lines in the autumn of 1941. The 7th and 8th Airborne Brigades had already been withdrawn back toward Moscow in August as the first step in rebuilding this decimated unit.

The heaviest commitment of airborne units took place in Ukraine. Three of the airborne corps—the 1st, 2nd, and 3rd—were in the second strategic echelon of the Red Army. The border battles against the Wehrmacht in June 1941 were a disaster. Attempts to stem the German advance were in vain, and in the second week of July the German tank units breached Soviet defensive positions near Novograd-Volynskiy and reached Zhitomir, on the approaches to the Ukrainian capital of Kiev. The three corps were shifted to the Kiev region as part of a desperate effort to defend the city. By the end of July, the Red Army's defensive positions in southern Russia and northern Ukraine were threatened by substantial German inroads both to the north and south. The Red Army's Southwestern Front around Kiev included four armies totaling some forty-four divisions. The Kiev bulge presented the Germans with the tantalizing opportunity to bag massive numbers of Soviet prisoners in another great strategic encirclement operation. At a STAVKA high command meeting on 29 July, the chief of the General Staff, Gen. Georgiy Zhukov, urged Stalin to abandon Kiev in favor of a more defensible line behind the Dnepr River. The suggestion led to Zhukov's dismissal for "defeatism." The Soviet generals were not the only ones earning their leader's disfavor. Hitler was inclined to shift some of the panzer forces southward, away from the drive on Moscow, to envelop the Red Army in the Kiev pocket, an option that was resisted by some officers, including Gen. Heinz Guderian. The battles around Kiev would continue to rage as the German generals argued over the fate of the city.

The new and inexperienced 3rd Airborne Corps, based at Odessa on the Black Sea, was loaded onto trains on 10 July for the journey to Kiev. Much of the unit was made up of raw recruits, so the corps disembarked at the Borispol station outside the city for further training. Two weeks later, at the beginning of August, the 3rd Airborne Corps was deployed as the main defensive force holding the southwestern suburbs of Kiev from lead German armored columns pressing forward along the Zhitomir highway. Hitler had issued a directive that Kiev be taken by 8 August, and plans were already under way for a victory march down Kiev's main avenue, the Kreshchatik. The tempo of the battle shifted as the Wehrmacht pulled back its panzer units and pushed the infantry forward. City fighting demanded infantry, not tanks. The lead elements of the 71st Infantry Division of the German 29th Army Corps began engaging the Soviet paratroopers on the afternoon of 6 August 1941. The initial fighting centered around the trolley-car depot at Golosieyevo and the nearby forest. The Germans managed to overcome the paratroopers' positions by 12 August after being reinforced by tanks. The airborne corps commander, Maj. Gen. V. A. Glazunov, was ordered to launch a counterattack on the German infantry the following morning after a short artillery barrage. The paratroopers managed to fight their way back into the Golosieyevo area.

The Germans attempted to envelop Kiev to the northwest by breaching a hastily erected Soviet defensive line running to the west of the capital toward Korosten. In early August, the 1st Airborne Corps had been committed to help reinforce the Soviet 5th Army there. The 1st Airborne Corps was only partly formed when called up, with only a single airborne brigade—the 1st Airborne. The corps was reinforced with elements of the 215th Mechanized Division and 124th Rifle Division. In an attempt to push the German 51st Army Corps away from the capital, brigades of the 1st Airborne Corps took part in a counteroffensive beginning on 5 August 1941 toward the Malin railroad station. The attack was partially successful but very costly. By the end of a week of fighting, the corps' strength was only about 3,000 troops.

In a bold move, Guderian's Panzer Gruppe 2 began to move south from the Smolensk area during the second week of August. Zhukov's forebodings had proven correct, and now the main concentration of Red Army forces in Ukraine was threatened. On 19 August 1941, Stalin and the STAVKA began to consider a staged withdrawal of the 5th Army behind the Dnepr River. The withdrawal began on 22 August, and by 25 August the 1st Airborne Corps was holding positions on the right bank of the Dnepr south of the town of Navozy.

The three airborne corps in the Kiev area—the 3rd on the outskirts of Kiev, the 1st to the north of Kiev, and the 2nd in the front reserve—saw little fighting during the following month. Their fate was decided elsewhere. Guderian's panzers pushed south past Konotop while Panzer Gruppe 1 smashed northward from the Kremenchug region, beginning a strategic envelopment of the entire Southwestern Front. The 3rd Airborne Corps was pulled out of Kiev, reorganized as the 87th Rifle Division, and sent north to Konotop as part of reinforcements aimed at stemming Guderian's attacks. It was the only one of the three airborne corps to survive the Kiev encirclement, retreating eastward after Guderian's capture of Konotop. The other two corps were trapped in the Kiev pocket, part of the nearly quarter of a million troops lost in the debacle.

By the autumn of 1941, the VDV Airborne Forces had almost ceased to exist. The 4th and 5th Airborne Corps had been pulled back toward Moscow in August for rebuilding but were mere skeletons. Two corps had been lost totally near Kiev, and the third had been pulled from the VDV as a rifle division. Major General V. A. Glazunov's superior performance as commander of the 3rd Airborne Corps led to his appointment as the new head of the VDV following the Kiev battles.

BACK INTO THE FRAY

The 5th Airborne Corps had little time to rebuild before being recommitted to the fighting. After the Kiev encirclement, German attention shifted back to the drive on Moscow. Guderian's Panzer Gruppe 2 was shifted back to its former location opposite the Red Army's Bryansk Front as part of the renewed assault on the Soviet capital on 30 September 1941. The German attack, spearheaded by the 24th Panzer Corps, began moving up the Orel-Tula highway to the southwest of Moscow. The STAVKA began shifting its reserves into position to blunt the German attack, but it progressed so quickly that desperate measures were needed. Colonel S. S. Guryev, the commander of the 5th Airborne Corps, was told to prepare his men for rapid deployment along the threatened highway.

At the time, only two brigades had been partly re-formed, the 10th and 201st Airborne Brigades, numbering about 6,000 troops. The plan was to airland the paratroopers at airfields along the Orel-Tula highway to form an improvised blocking force until the planned rifle and tank reinforcements arrived. The lack of aircraft and parachutes precluded an airdrop. Only eighty transport aircraft could be spared, a mixture of TB-3 heavy bombers and PS-84 airliners impressed from the Civil Air Fleet (GVF). The first wave consisted of a battalion from the 201st Airborne Brigade, landed at Orel airport on 3 October. The scene at the airport was demoralizing. As the eighty aircraft approached, the sky was full of sooty black clouds from the burning fuel dumps at the airport. The airfield was under German artillery attack, and the runway itself was under fire. The airborne troops disembarked as quickly as possible, but several of the transport aircraft were hit by artillery bursts and had to be abandoned after catching fire. The airborne battalion hurried to the northwestern outskirts of the city where the fighting was most intense.

The surviving transport aircraft returned to air bases near Moscow to pick up other units. The 3/201st Airborne Brigade was the next to land, being deposited at Optukha airport about five miles northeast of Orel. The remaining battalions were landed around Mtsensk during the next eighteen hours, after a total of about 300 sorties. The lack of airlift meant that the units had been landed with minimal equipment and ammunition. There were no antitank guns and only small numbers of antitank rifles. The lead elements of the Soviet 4th Tank Brigade, with new T-34 tanks, arrived on 4 October to stiffen the Red Army positions. But the tanks were too few in number. Without any tank support of their own, the troops of the 201st Airborne Brigade crouched in trenches as German tanks attacked their positions. Their only antitank equipment was bundles of hand grenades, a dubious expedient with little chance of stopping a tank. One of the platoon commanders, Lt. N. V. Bondarev, managed to knock the tread off one tank with a grenade bundle, and as a second tank approached his trench, he threw himself underneath it with a bundle of grenades. Bondarev's sacrificial heroism could not stop the German tanks, however, and on 5 and 6 October 1941, the 201st Airborne Brigade and 4th Tank Brigade were forced to continually fall back toward Mtsensk along the Moscow highway. But the T-34 tanks took their toll. Guderian in his memoirs recalled that "this was the first occasion on which the vast superiority of the Russian T-34 tank became plainly apparent. The [4th Panzer] Division suffered grievous casualties." On the night of 6–7 October, the first snow of the season fell, but it melted the next morning, turning the roads to mud.

The Soviet defensive positions finally coalesced on 7 October with the arrival of the 1st Guards Rifle Corps and another T-34 unit, the 11th Tank Brigade. The remaining battalions of the 5th Airborne Corps were moved forward, reinforced with 45mm antitank guns from neighboring rifle divisions. The German units finally broke through the defenses at Mtsensk on 10 October, and the airborne forces formed a rear guard to hold the last remaining bridge over the Zusha River. The Soviet forces counterattacked the next day with T-34 tanks, again inflicting serious losses on the 4th Panzer Division. The early snow had turned to rain, and the Germans found it difficult to reinforce their positions along the muddy roads. With the front stabilizing, the 5th Airborne Corps was pulled out of the line and shipped by train to the trenches near Podolsk, where another German drive was threatening. The 5th Airborne Corps would remain in the Podolsk trenches for nearly two months until the Moscow counteroffensive.

The Orel battle of 1941 was the only significant use of the VDV forces in their intended role as a rapid-reaction force. Although they served heroically in these skirmishes, the VDV was ill suited to this type of fighting. It was poorly prepared to handle German mechanized units due to the general lack of defensive antitank equipment.

The more typical use of the VDV before and after the Orel-Mtsensk battles was as light infantry. There were several reasons for this. The disastrous harrowing of the Red Air Force in June 1941 left the VDV without airlift; it would not be until 1942 that enough transport aircraft could be scraped together from scattered locations and from the Far East to consider an airborne operation. Furthermore, an airborne operation in 1941 would have been extremely risky due to German air superiority over most of the Eastern Front. Soviet airborne doctrine was also a problem; the airborne forces were designed to be used as the spearhead of Red Army offensive operations. In the summer and fall of 1941, the Red Army was fighting for its life, and offensive operations were out of the question. The VDV troops no longer had their special mission. Given the extreme shortage of trained troops, it was inevitable that the airborne corps would be committed as ordinary infantry. These two factors—the lack of airlift and the desperate need for troops—were problems that would continue to afflict the VDV through most of the war and severely limit its intended use in the paratrooper role.

Chapter 3
The Moscow Airborne Operations

The battles on the approaches to Moscow in the cold autumn of 1941 were the beginning of a bitter struggle for the Soviet capital. But the German Wehrmacht had run to the end of its tether and by December was forced onto the defensive after penetrating as far as the Moscow suburb of Khimki. The stalemate at the gates of Moscow could not help but remind the combatants of the parallel to Napoleon's invasion more than a century before. In a burst of optimism, Stalin became convinced that the Germans could be decisively defeated and sent hurtling back to the Berezina River in headlong retreat. The Red Army was able to bring forward reserve forces from the Urals and Siberia to help launch a series of offensive operations with an aim toward precipitating a catastrophic German rout. As would soon become apparent, the Germans were neither weak enough, nor the Russians strong enough, for these plans to be carried out.

The first phase of these battles began on 5 December 1941 with a Soviet counteroffensive. The greatest threat to Moscow came from Panzer Gruppe 3 to the northwest of the capital. General Georgiy Zhukov's Western Front began a counteroffensive with the hopes of trapping and destroying as much of this force as possible. By Christmas, Panzer Gruppe 3 had been forced to retreat westward.

These offensives were difficult to conduct due to a lack of tank and other mobile units. The Red Army had lost more than 20,000 tanks in 1941, and only about 2,200 tanks were available all along the vast front line. There were about twenty-four tank brigades on hand for the Moscow counteroffensive, but they were terribly weakened by the previous fighting and possessed only 667 tanks. The other traditional mobile force, the Soviet cavalry, was also at a low ebb due to the bloody summer battles. A total of twenty-four cavalry divisions were available, but, in reality, most of these units were at less than half strength. Out of sheer desperation, the STAVKA planned to use any other mobile force, including ski battalions and the airborne force.

The VDV Airborne Force in December 1941 was poorly prepared to handle these new assignments. In September 1941, at the height of the Kiev battles, the VDV had been reorganized on paper yet again. But training facilities, parachutes, and transport aircraft were lacking. Many of the new VDV divisions were raised in the Volga region where there were no jump towers or any other means to train the troops in paratroop techniques. And by this time, most of the Soviet Union's meager transport fleet was involved in a desperate airlift effort in the Leningrad area. The VDV reorganization was accompanied by a revision in its intended role, scaling back its missions to more reasonable objectives. New missions included cooperative engagements with Red Army ground forces to encircle enemy formations; disruption of enemy command, control, and logistics by rear-area raiding; special missions to secure high-value objectives such as key bridges and rail crossings; the destruction of enemy airfields; and the seizure of beach landing areas in advance of naval infantry assaults. The latter was a good example of the type of tactical mission now considered suitable for the VDV. For example, on 22 September, a small airdrop of twenty-three paratroopers was conducted near Odessa on the Black Sea in support of a naval landing at Grigorevka. Again on 31 December, a battalion from the 2nd Airborne Corps was dropped on the Kerch peninsula in the Black Sea area to support an amphibious landing there. The value of these forces led the Black Sea Fleet to raise its own airborne company from the ranks of attached naval aviation units in May 1942; the company was used in several operations through the war.

The STAVKA planned a substantial airborne force in spite of the heavy losses of the 1941 summer debacle. The five original airborne corps were rebuilt beginning in August, and five new corps were gradually added through December. Once again, these grandiose plans overlooked the critical issue of airlift.

The fighting in 1941 had led to the destruction of 70 percent of the Soviet bomber force, which had been the primary source of VDV airlift in the prewar years. A total of 7,200 of the 8,400 bombers available to the Red Air Force at the beginning of the war had been destroyed. In particular, the TB-3 heavy-bomber force had suffered grievous losses. Although precise figures are lacking, less than 200 TB-3s survived, mostly in regiments in the Far East. The new Soviet heavy bomber, the Pe-8, was available in miniscule numbers and reserved for special long-range bombing missions such as raids on Berlin. Medium bombers, such as the Ilyushin DB-3/IL-4, were ill suited to airborne operations due to their internal configuration. One of the few bright spots in this otherwise dismal situation was the new PS-84 airliner, of which seventy-two had been manufactured up to June 1941. This license-built copy of the American DC-3 airliner had proven very suitable for airlift operations, as had been demonstrated during the airlift of the 201st Airborne Brigade at Orel in October 1941. But the VDV Airborne Force was not the only force requiring their services. From October through December 1941, most of the GVF Civil Air Fleet was committed to the evacuation of key government and industry personnel from encircled Leningrad, flying out 50,000 persons and 6,000 tons of key war materiel. Furthermore, the German assault on Moscow nearly captured the PS-84 plant in Khimki, in the Moscow suburbs. The main production effort was shifted to Tashkent, meaning that there was a temporary shortfall of vital transport aircraft production in the winter of 1941–42.

In September 1941, the core of a new airlift force had been created, based around five transport squadrons and five independent transport flights. But this small force was hardly adequate to lift a single airborne battalion. In anticipation of the planned airborne operations in the Moscow sector, the Red Air Force began forming a new transport force called the Moscow Special Operations Aviation Group (MAON). This was based around Aeroflot and other GVF airliners, mainly the precious PS-84 airliners returning from the Leningrad evacuation.

THE AIRBORNE RAID ON TERYAYEVO SLOBODA

Ironically, the first major Soviet paratrooper mission of the war did not even involve a regular VDV unit. On 5 December 1941, the Soviet Kalinin Front began its part in the Moscow counteroffensive by attacking German units north of Moscow, near the city of Klin. The Germans began withdrawing in an attempt to form a new defensive line along the Lama and Ruza Rivers. The STAVKA decided to drop an airborne force behind the German lines in an attempt to disrupt the retreat and destroy as many German units as possible. The unit selected for the mission was an improvised airborne detachment commanded by Capt. I. G. Starchak.

In August 1941, Starchak had formed a special operations detachment of the Western Front air force based on volunteers. It was reinforced with about fifty paratroopers from the 214th Airborne Brigade to provide some parachute training. Like most airborne units, it was committed as infantry in the 1941 battles, being used mainly for rear-area raiding.

The objective of the drop was to cut off as many German troops as possible by severing key roads and bridges. Starchak's battalion, numbering 415 paratroopers, parachuted into the fields near Teryayevo Sloboda on the night of 14–15 December 1941 in subzero temperatures. The detachment was too small and too scattered to attack the town of Teryayevo Sloboda itself, so it began to attack German columns on the Klin–Novo Petrovskoye and Klin-Volokolamsk roads. Over the next ten days, it harassed German convoys, attacked German railroad traffic, and blew up bridges in the area. It was finally ordered to rejoin advancing Soviet forces on 25 December. The detachment claimed to have killed four hundred German troops, destroyed about fifty vehicles, and blown up twenty-nine bridges during the sixteen-day raid.

Starchak's raid had no significant impact on the fighting in the area. The raid was too little too late. Hitler had approved the withdrawal from Klin on 13 December, and the majority of forces had pulled back by Thursday, 14 December. By the time Starchak's unit landed that night, all that was left were stragglers and rear-guard units. In any case, Starchak's unit had too few men and was too poorly equipped to attack any significant German force, such as the rear guard from 1st Panzer Division. The raid was not focused on

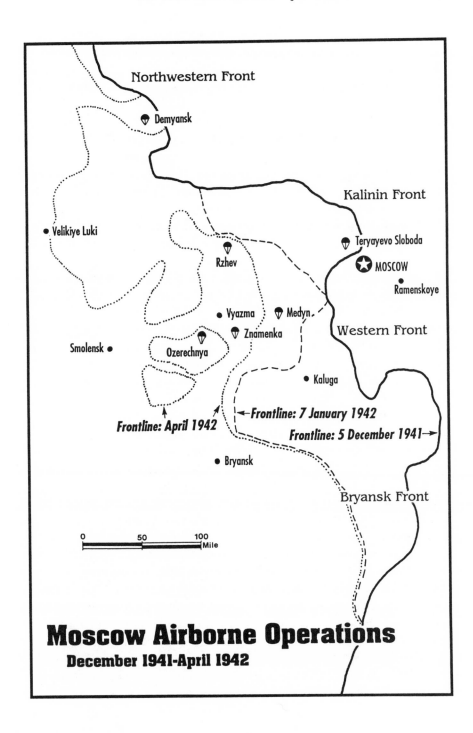

Northwestern Front

● Demyansk

Kalinin Front

● Velikiye Luki

Teryayevo Sloboda

★ MOSCOW

Rzhev

● Ramenskoye

● Vyazma   Medyn

Znamenka

Western Front

Smolensk ●

Ozerechnya

● Kaluga

←Frontline: 7 January 1942

Frontline: April 1942

Frontline: 5 December 1941→

● Bryansk

Bryansk Front

0   50   100
Mile

Moscow Airborne Operations
December 1941-April 1942

any particular objective such as a key bridge or command post, which further diluted its impact. Nevertheless, after months of disastrous failure, even the modest accomplishments of Starchak's raid impressed the Red Army leadership.

THE RZHEV-VYAZMA OFFENSIVE

The success of the Teryayevo Sloboda raid encouraged the STAVKA to consider the use of larger airborne formations in the next stage of its counteroffensive southwest of Moscow. The plan was a coordinated assault by the Kalinin Front north of Moscow and the Western Front, which covered the city itself and the areas south of the capital. The counteroffensive was conceived as a gigantic envelopment of the German Army Group Center. The Kalinin Front's 29th and 33rd Armies, spearheaded by the 11th Cavalry Corps, would drive westward in an attempt to catch the Germans in a huge pocket. From the south, the Western Front's 50th Army, spearheaded by the 1st Guards Cavalry Corps, would link up with the Kalinin Front near Rzhev, trapping the German forces nearest Moscow. It was an ambitious scheme, especially considering the harsh weather, the lack of strong mechanized forces, and the general exhaustion of many of the troops from the previous several weeks of fighting. The Western Front commander, Gen. Georgiy Zhukov, enthusiastically supported continued offensive actions but warned that "for successful offensive operations it is essential to reinforce our forces . . . above all with tank units, without which we can have no basis for anticipating particular success." Zhukov would not get the tanks he sought and would have to make due with light mobile forces such as the inexperienced VDV airborne brigades.

The offensive was planned to begin on 5 January 1942. In late December, the Western Front staff began planning for an airborne raid a few days before the main offensive began, to cut the roads behind the front line. The specific objective was the road net around the key town of Medyn, interdicting the retreat of German units from positions to the southeast and leading to their capture or destruction by the advancing Western Front during the ensuing offensive. In view of Starchak's success, a larger airborne raiding group was formed, led by the commander of the 250th Rifle Regiment, Maj. N. L. Soldatov.

The airborne group, numbering about 1,300 troops in all, consisted of Soldatov's regiment, Captain Starchak's battalion, and a battalion of the 201st Airborne Brigade under Capt. I. A. Surzhik.

The size of the airborne group created a problem. There was not enough airlift to drop the entire force into the area at one time. So the plan was to drop Surzhik's VDV battalion first, to begin carrying out raiding operations against the German rear areas and roads near Gusevo. The next night, Starchak's battalion would parachute near the Bolshoye Fatyanovo airfield outside the town of Myatlevo. After Starchak's force captured the airfield, Soldatov's regiment would be airlanded, and the airborne group would attack German logistics and command centers in the Medyn area.

Surzhik's battalion of 348 men jumped on the night of 2–3 January. The drop was reasonably compact, and the battalion formed up quickly. It then overran several small German garrisons from the 267th Infantry Division near Gribovo and Maslovo. Surzhik had been assigned to capture and hold a bridge over the Shanya River, but under the circumstances he decided to blow it up instead. This was the only portion of the operation that went smoothly.

The next night, Starchak's battalion prepared to jump on the Bolshoye Fatyanovo airfield. The main airdrop was preceded by a weather reconnaissance flight, since severe snowstorms were common in the area at this time of year. There was also supposed to be a special pathfinder flight that would drop flares along the flight path to assist the inexperienced transport pilots. Apparently this never took place. The airlift force consisted of twenty-one TB-3 bombers and ten PS-84 airliners, barely enough to lift Starchak's battalion. The drop by Surzhik's battalion the night before had alerted the Germans to the possibility of further Soviet night missions, so on the night of 3–4 January, the German antiaircraft gunners were waiting for Starchak's battalion. The transport pilots, mostly civilian airliner pilots with no combat experience, were shaken up by the flak and tracer fire over the drop zone. The careful plans for a concentrated drop were soon forgotten as the pilots began evasive maneuvers. The hapless paratroopers were scattered all over the dark countryside below. About six of the aircraft simply returned to base with their paratroopers aboard. Instead of attacking the airfield, the detachment was forced to waste precious time regrouping.

The second wave consisted of the control group that would set up radios and beacons for the airlanding of Major Soldatov's regiment. The control group had to be airlanded since it was carrying the medium-range radios needed to communicate with the next wave of aircraft, as well as communicating with neighboring Soviet units during the later phases of the mission. The Soviet radio sets of the period were large and heavy, and too delicate to be parachuted. The control group also included demolition teams to destroy any obstructions that the Germans may have erected on the runway. Their aircraft flew over the airstrip at 03:00 on 4 January but found that the runway was still covered with snow and was partly in German hands. The fighting for the runway continued into the late afternoon of 4 January, by which time Starchak's battalion had established a firm defensive perimeter. But Starchak had no way to communicate this fact: none of his short-range radios had survived the drop, and the control group had not been able to parachute in with their long-range radio equipment. Lacking any communication with Starchak, the Western Front headquarters sent a U-2 biplane escorted by two MiG-3 fighters to try to establish contact. The U-2 landed at Bolshoye Fatyanovo, but the jumpy pilot mistook Starchak's men for Germans and promptly flew off. The front commander mistakenly believed that Starchak's drop had been a failure, so he canceled the main airlanding of the 250th Rifle Regiment.

Starchak made the best of a bad situation and sent his men out on raids to disrupt German supply columns in the area. The main offensive broke out on 5 January 1942, and Starchak's men could hear the sound of the preparatory artillery bombardment in the distance. The small airborne detachment destroyed several bridges, and on the night of 7–8 January seized the Myatlevo train station, blowing up two locomotives and a load of twenty-eight tanks and armored vehicles. Starchak's unit fought in the German rear until 20 January, when it joined up with advancing Red Army units near Nikolskoya. By this stage, there were only eighty-seven men left in the unit, and Starchak himself was wounded. Surzhik's battalion had been luckier, linking up with advancing 43rd Army units on 11 January near Kremenskoye. The Medyn raid failed to accomplish its main missions, since the majority of the raiding force, the 250th Rifle Regiment, never landed. The Medyn raid made it glaringly clear that the

VDV and the Red Air Force had not perfected the techniques needed to conduct a successful airborne mission. Serious training was needed by the transport crews, but there was neither the time nor the resources to do this before the next mission.

THE ZNAMENKA RAID

A second airborne raid was in preparation in mid-January before Starchak's unit broke out. The raid was a repeat of the Medyn raid, except it was set deeper behind German lines. The January offensive in this sector had ruptured the weakly held German defensive perimeter, and Gen. P. A. Belov's 1st Guards Cavalry Corps was advancing rapidly toward the key city of Vyazma. The objective of the next VDV mission was to place a large landing force near Znamenka airfield, about twenty miles behind German lines, to trap German forces, cut off supplies to the front, and harass the German forces in the area in support of Belov's cavalry. The shortage of air transport continued to plague the airborne force. For the next raid, only twenty-one PS-84 airliners were available from the MAON, along with a small number of TB-3 bombers, needed to carry 45mm antitank guns.

The plan was to drop the 1st and 2nd Battalions, 201st Airborne Brigade, on Znamenka airfield to seize the runway. With this accomplished, a control group would be landed to prepare the runway for the main airlanding party. Finally, the troops of Soldatov's 250th Rifle Regiment, scheduled to be used in the previous Medyn raid, would be airlanded at Znamenka.

The first phase of the operation began in the early-morning hours of 18 January. Sixteen PS-84 airliners left Vnukovo air base near Moscow with 425 paratroopers aboard. The aircraft reached the drop zone before dawn but were dispersed by the weather and the pilots' lack of night flying and airdrop experience. The paratroopers were scattered between the Znamenka airfield and the village of Zhelanye. The main body of the paratroopers was from Captain Surzhik's 1st Battalion, veterans of the Medyn raid. The battalion began forming up about 09:00 near the village of Zhelanye. The snow was about twenty inches deep, which hampered the paratroopers, since many of the PDMM *(parashutno-desantniy-materialniy-magazin)* containers with skis and snowshoes could not be found. Surzhik's battalion launched an attack on the German garrison at Znamenka. The German defenses at the airfield were sufficient to resist the paratroopers, and Surzhik withdrew toward Zhelanye to await the next drop. The control group arrived in four PS-84 airliners after dusk on 18 January. Russian partisan units in the area had been informed by radio to set up a landing strip for the aircraft, less than a mile from the German air base at Znamenka. With the runway lit up with bonfires, the aircraft landed safely, but only one of the PS-84s was fitted with skis. The deep snow prevented the three other aircraft from departing, so they had to be abandoned. The 65 men of the control group left to join up with Surzhik's group. Later that night, the next wave of paratroopers arrived on ten PS-84 aircraft, but a severe snowstorm intervened and only about 200 paratroopers jumped. By the morning of 19 January, the VDV forces in the area numbered 642 men, bolstered slightly by local partisan forces. The Germans discovered the three PS-84 aircraft and burned them.

Rather than risk heavy casualties with another attack on the Znamenka air base, Surzhik decided to create an improvised airstrip near the hamlet of Plesnovo. With the help of local partisan forces and civilians, a large area of farm fields was cleared, and the control group set up their radios. On 20 January, Surzhik radioed the Vnukovo air base that the improvised airstrip was ready. Between 20 and 22 January, 1,100 troops from the 250th (Airborne) Rifle Regiment were airlanded, mainly at night, with the runway illuminated by bonfires. The Germans finally caught wind of the operation and shot down three transports, killing twenty-seven paratroopers and wounding nine others. Major Soldatov, commander of the 250th Airborne Rifle Regiment, took charge of the operation shortly after landing. By this time, a portion of the force had been provided with skis. But many of the paratroopers had never used skis or snowshoes, and the skills to navigate on them are not easily acquired.

With the improvised runway secured by 20 January, the paratroopers began fanning out in the area to disrupt German supply convoys. The Germans heard the nighttime activity and became concerned that the paratroopers might attempt to seize the key bridge south of Vyazma over the Ugra River. Four infantry companies from Kampfgruppe Haase were sent to defend the bridge. The paratroopers, however, were unaware of the significance of the bridge due to poor intelligence, so they ignored it.

The front commander, Gen. Georgiy Zhukov, ordered Soldatov to occupy the Znamenka area, link up with Belov's cavalry forces near Temkino by 22 January, transfer two battalions to Belov, and "at all costs" halt enemy movement on the Yukhnov-Vyazma highway. Zhukov's instructions were hopelessly optimistic. Operations in the area were hampered by the deep snow, which severely limited the mobility of the units. The two battalions of paratroopers from the 201st Airborne Brigade overcame several small German garrisons in the area and finally linked up with Belov on the Moscow-Warsaw highway on 28 January 1942, nearly a week late. In the meantime, the bulk of the 250th Airborne Rifle Regiment attacked the Znamenka air base again, without success. The air base was defended only by an improvised Luftwaffe group, but its 20mm antiaircraft guns made fearsome antipersonnel weapons, and the thick snow favored the defenders. Only one of Soldatov's battalions was used to attack the Yukhnov-Vyazma highway. Soldatov's forces managed to capture many of the smaller garrisons in the area, but Znamenka and the neighboring airfield resisted all attacks, including another major night attack on 29–30 January. Soldatov's forces finally linked up with Belov's cavalry on 31 January. Their destination was to the northwest, where an even larger airborne operation was taking place.

THE VYAZMA AIRDROP

By the end of January, the Red Army's January counteroffensive was running out of steam. The German forces were retreating in an orderly fashion, even though badly weakened from nearly two months of fighting in brutal winter conditions without adequate clothing or equipment. Stalin insisted on another major blow along the key Moscow-Minsk highway by the Kalinin Front, coordinated with another blow along the Moscow-Warsaw highway by the Western Front to encircle and destroy the German Army Group Center. To assist in the Red Army ground actions, Stalin ordered a major VDV airdrop to the west of Vyazma, the key rail and road junction on the way to Smolensk. The immediate objective of the airdrop would be to link up with neighboring Red Army units to pinch off German forces in

Vyazma and Yukhnov, the German troop concentration nearest and most threatening to Moscow itself.

The 4th Airborne Corps, held in reserve since the summer debacles, was selected as the main shock force in the Vyazma operation. It would form the key link between the Kalinin Front's 33rd Army to the north and the Western Front's 1st Guards Cavalry Corps to the south. Two of the 4th Airborne Corps brigades, the 8th and 9th, had escaped the worst of the summer 1941 fighting. The third brigade, the 214th Airborne Brigade, had been brought back up to strength after its decimation in the Byelorussian fighting in August 1941. Due to the size of the planned operation and the usual shortage of transport aircraft, it was decided to base the transports as close to the drop zone as possible, rather than close to the air bases near Moscow. It was hoped that by using air bases at Kaluga, several sorties could be flown each night. This plan would prove to be a fatal mistake.

The troops of the 4th Airborne Corps moved forward from their home base at Ramenskoye southeast of Moscow to the Kaluga air bases for the new mission. Kaluga had been recaptured from the Germans only a few weeks before, so the area around the city was devastated. The trip by rail was constantly delayed by blown bridges and torn-up track, so by the time the paratroopers arrived, they had little time to prepare. The same applied to the air transport crews. None of the air bases near Kaluga was large enough to accommodate the force, so it had to be scattered among three small fields at Grabtsevo, Zhashkovo, and Rzhavets, further slowing preparations and complicating logistics.

The amount of airlift available for the operation was pathetic: forty PS-84 airliners and twenty-five TB-3 bombers, of which one PS-84 and three TB-3s proved nonfunctional. The plans called for round-the-clock airdrops to make up for the shortage of airlift. But airdrops in the daylight were dangerous due to the presence of German fighters. The plan called for the use of one fighter regiment of seventy-two fighters to cover the drop zone, and one squadron of thirty fighters to protect the forward airfields. In the end, only nineteen fighters could be scraped together. The plan overestimated Soviet resources and underestimated the German Luftwaffe.

The Red Army's intelligence on German forces in the area was poor and misleading. There was little or no aerial reconnaissance due to a lack of resources. The Vyazma area was swarming with Soviet partisans, but at this stage of the war the partisan movement was disorganized and amateurish, particularly in regard to the collection of tactical intelligence. The STAVKA was under the mistaken impression that the area west of Vyazma was free of any serious German troop concentrations, and that the majority of German forces were in a disorganized rout to the west.

German forces in the drop zone, although weakened by the constant fighting, were still formidable. Most of the small villages were occupied by German infantry companies or battalions, huddling in the peasants' log huts to escape the subzero weather. The main Moscow-Minsk highway passing through Vyazma was patrolled by the 11th Panzer Division, with the 3rd Motorized Division patrolling east and south. As the Red Army offensive surged forward, Vyazma became the collection point for many German units withdrawing westward, including the 309th Infantry Regiment and parts of the 5th Panzer Division. These forces were far more than Zhukov had bargained for in his plans.

The 4th Airborne Corps commander, Maj. Gen. A. F. Levashev, received simple and blunt orders from General Zhukov:

Mission:
26–27 January—land corps and occupy positions in accordance with the map.
Objective:
Cut off the withdrawal of enemy units to the west. Zhukov.

General Levashev received the final start order at 04:00 on 27 January and selected his 8th Airborne Brigade to lead off the assault. The first wave of the 2/8th Airborne Brigade, under Capt. M. Karnaukhov, left Zhashkovo airfield at 14:30 that afternoon in twenty-nine aircraft, intending to parachute near the town of Ozerechnya. In the dim light of dusk, over a featureless landscape swathed in snow, the pilots became disoriented. The paratroopers were dropped from high altitude, 5,000 feet instead of the usual 1,500 feet, to avoid antiaircraft fire. As Karnaukhov watched with alarm, the cold winter wind dispersed his men across the wild terrain below. The first wave was scattered over a fifteen-mile area near the village of Tabory, a dozen miles south of the intended drop zone. The second flight of seventeen aircraft did little better. Of 678 men dropped in the two waves, only 476 had linked up by morning.

The headquarters of the German 4th Panzer Army in the area was aware of the airdrops almost immediately. The 11th Panzer Division reported that 20 transport aircraft had dropped about 400 paratroopers at dusk near the Mitino rail station, and within a few hours, reports began to come in of attacks against the 309th Infantry Regiment and patrols on the Moscow-Minsk highway by small groups of paratroopers. Although the paratroopers' aggressiveness was laudable, this was not their intended mission. They were supposed to be arranging a drop zone for the succeeding flights.

Karnaukhov's problems were just beginning. Not only was his battalion badly scattered, but his troops had been able to find only about 30 percent of the PDMM supply containers that carried all the battalion's heavy weapons, radio equipment, skis, food, and ammunition. In spite of the problems, Karnaukhov set up a small landing zone near Tabory, guarded by a small force, in case the rest of the 8th Airborne Brigade made the same mistake. He then led his remaining troops to the intended drop zone at Ozerechnya. On arriving there, his scouts discovered that the village was occupied by a German rear-service unit of a few hundred men. It took three night attacks to overwhelm the Germans, by which time there were few German survivors. The battles around Moscow were savagely fought, with no quarter given and little effort to capture prisoners.

The 8th Airborne Brigade headquarters received only a brief message from Karnaukhov that his battalion had landed, then his damaged radio died. The 4th Airborne Corps in Kaluga had not even received that message due to the weak signal. Levashev took Karnaukhov's short message to be sufficient and ordered the 3/8th Airborne Brigade, under Maj. A. G. Kobets, to land that evening, 27–28 January. The airdrop was as confused as the night before, with about half of the battalion landing near Ozerechnya and the other half near Tabory. Kobets attempted to contact the 4th Airborne Corps headquarters by radio, with no luck. Finally, General Levashev ordered his assistant chief of reconnaissance to fly in a U-2 biplane to the drop zone and locate Karnaukhov's forces. The aircraft never made it that far, but Kobets did finally manage to reach the headquarters at Kaluga by radio late on 28 January.

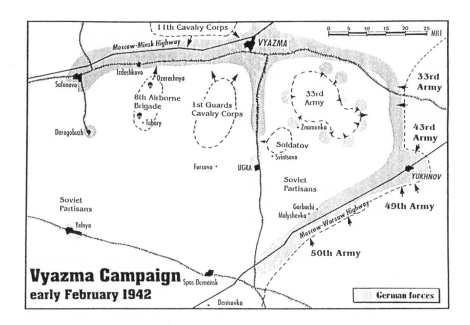

Vyazma Campaign
early February 1942

THE BATTLE FOR THE AIRFIELDS

The Germans did not stand idly by. The Luftwaffe was familiar with airfields around Kaluga, having occupied them only a few weeks before. On the afternoon of 28 January 1942, they sent out a Focke Wulf FW-189 reconnaissance aircraft to pinpoint the Soviet bases. On the night of 28–29 January, the Luftwaffe began raiding the forward transport bases, starting at Zhashkovo, where the 2/8th Airborne Brigade had departed two nights before. Bf-110 fighters strafed the runways, followed by bombers. The German raid came while the 4th Airborne Corps was attempting to resupply the drop zones, and TB-3 bombers and PS-84s lined the runways, loaded with fuel and supplies. After hammering Zhashkovo, the Luftwaffe night intruders turned their attention to the alternate bases at Grabtsevo and Rzhavets. By night's end, the Germans had destroyed seven of the irreplaceable TB-3 heavy bombers and one fighter, as well as damaging many more aircraft and setting several tons of aviation fuel ablaze. Of the sixty-five transport aircraft originally assigned to the Vyazma mission, only ten PS-84 airliners and two TB-3 bombers were operational by morning. After frantic repair work, a few surviving transports were able to drop 500 sets of skis and ammunition to the airborne battalions at Ozerechnya that evening to replace the PDMM containers lost the first night of the drop.

The heavy aircraft losses forced the STAVKA to order additional transport aircraft from MAON reserves near Moscow. This enabled the 4th Airborne Corps to drop another 540 troops on the evening of 29 January. The Germans retaliated by raiding the main air base at Kaluga, destroying more transports. The next night, a snowstorm and minus forty degree Fahrenheit temperatures limited Soviet airdrops to only 120 men. But the Germans were back out in force, bombing the transport bases at Zhashkovo and Rzhavets yet again, with little resistance from Soviet fighters. Under great strain from the relentless German air attacks, the 4th Airborne Corps was able to drop only 215 paratroopers on the night of 31 January. This drop included the 8th Airborne Brigade commander, Lt. Col. A. A. Onufriev, and part of his staff. Onufriev linked up with Karnaukhov's 2/8th Airborne Brigade. Kobets and part of his 3/8th Airborne Brigade, numbering 131 men, were still out of touch near Androsovo. The area was swarming with German patrols, so Kobets decided to carry out his raiding mission rather than waste further time trying to effect a link-up. Kobets's men overran several isolated German detachments in the villages nearby and raided supply convoys at every opportunity.

By 1 February, another 389 paratroopers had been dropped, bringing the total to 2,081 men and nearly thirty-eight tons of weapons, food, skis, and medicine. The weapons dropped with the 8th Airborne Brigade included 120 PPSh submachine guns, 72 antitank rifles, 20 mortars (82mm), and 30 mortars (50mm). The intensity of the German air operations, however, made it impossible to continue the missions from so near the front. General Levashev called a halt to the operation from Kaluga. His air bases were a shambles, and the losses of precious transport aircraft were unbearable. The transport aircraft were withdrawn to the safety of the Moscow area, where the fields were amply protected by antiaircraft guns and by patrols of MiG-3 interceptors. The headquarters of the 4th Airborne Corps returned to its main base at Ramenskoye to await new orders. (The performance of the air force in this operation and other failures would prompt Stalin to order the execution of the Moscow Military District aviation commander, Lt. Gen. Petr Pumpur, on 23 March 1942.)

Zhukov soon had another mission planned for Onufriev's two brigades, which had already landed west of Moscow. Belov's 1st Guards Cavalry Corps and Soldatov's 250th Airborne Rifle Regiment (from the earlier Znamenka airdrop) were ordered to march to the northwest and link up with Onufriev's forces. Onufriev had managed to collect about 1,320 men of the 2,081 who had jumped since the beginning of the operation.

The linkup would not be easy to accomplish. The Germans had managed to cut off Belov's cavalry force, so that his force was behind German lines and could not relieve Onufriev. Any semblance of a front line had disappeared, and the combat soon came to resemble guerrilla warfare. The Germans clung to the main Moscow-Minsk and Moscow-Warsaw highways and had garrisons scattered in the major towns south and west of Vyazma. Much of the wild, forested countryside between the two highways was under the control of paratroopers, Belov's roving cavalry units, or local partisans. The paratroopers continued to harass the German supply lines and overrun isolated detachments in the villages west of Vyazma. In the meantime, the Soviet 11th Cavalry Corps from the Kalinin Front was attempting to sever the Vyazma-Smolensk portion of the Moscow-Minsk highway from the north and to link up with the paratroopers and 1st Guards Cavalry Corps west of Vyazma near Izdeshkovo. The head of the German High Command, Gen. Fritz Halder, noted in his diary for 2 February: "The enemy elements that infiltrated behind our front are now being attacked by the 5th Panzer Division. The scenes in this battle behind the front are absolutely grotesque and testify to the degree to which this war has degenerated into a sort of slugging match that resembles no form of warfare we have ever known."

The German forces in the area made repeated attempts to crush the Soviet units, but the heaviest Soviet casualties came in the several disjointed attempts by Belov's corps and by Onufriev's men to attack prepared German defenses. Belov's cavalry tried to take Vyazma from the south on 5–6 February, without success. Operations by the separate cavalry and paratroop units had proven futile, and STAVKA again ordered Belov and Onufriev to link up in the hopes of forming a more potent and concentrated battle group. After finally linking up in the second week of February, Onufriev's paratroopers

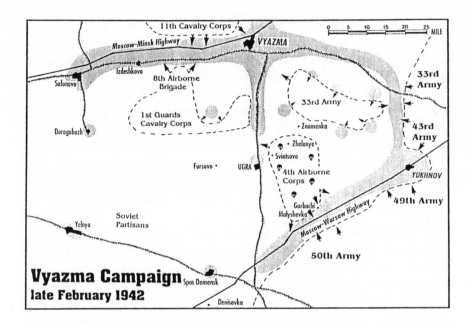

Vyazma Campaign Spas Demensk
late February 1942

were put under Belov's command. At the same time, the 11th Cavalry Corps, to the north, was ordered to attack southward again to link up with Belov and the paratroopers. But it was already too late. By now, Belov's 1st Guards Cavalry Corps and the 11th Cavalry Corps had been severely weakened by the weeks of costly fighting without reinforcements, rest, or adequate supplies. The paratroopers, although fresher than the cavalry troops, were considerably less mobile due to the shortage of skis and adequate winter training.

The linkup of the cavalry and paratroopers attracted German attention, and on 11 February 1942, the 106th Infantry Division and 11th Panzer Division smashed into the 8th Airborne Brigade and separated it again from Belov's cavalry force. Zhukov continued to insist that Belov and the paratroopers link up with the 11th Cavalry Corps to the north in anticipation of attacking Vyazma from the west yet again. Neither side was strong enough to deliver a death blow to its opponent. The Soviet forces, cut off from sources of supply and attacked repeatedly by German armored units, were gradually being reduced. Soldatov's group, which had been dropped near Znamenka at the end of January, didn't link up with Belov until 14 March with only 75 men from his original group of 1,100.

RELIEF AT RZHEV

While Onufriev's paratroopers were fighting in the pocket west of Moscow, the Red Army staged another, much smaller, airborne mission to the north near Rzhev. In late January, the Red Army's Kalinin Front to the northwest of Moscow launched a renewed offensive with the 29th and 39th Armies. After penetrating as far west as Rzhev, the Red Army forces changed direction southward toward Vyazma to close the huge pocket stretching north from Vyazma. By mid-February, the German 9th Army opposing the Kalinin Front managed to cut off the 29th and 39th Armies from the main elements of the Kalinin Front to the east. The German forces were far too weak to destroy the 39th Army, but they managed to constrict the 29th Army into a small pocket, only about five miles across, west of Rzhev. The 29th Army was ordered to break out of the encirclement and join back up with the 39th Army to the southwest, but it was opposed in this direction by the 1st Panzer Division and 86th Infantry Division. The front commander decided to send in reinforcements by parachute.

On the evening of 16–17 February, the 4th Battalion of the 204th Airborne Brigade loaded on TB-3 bombers of the 23rd Bomber Division at Lyubertsy airport east of Moscow. There were insufficient aircraft available to drop the 500 troops in one sortie, so two sorties were planned. The drop zone was supposed to be identified by fires arrranged in geometric patterns. The big, ungainly bombers approached the drop zone at night, at an altitude of 3,500 feet. About five miles from the drop zone, they cut back their engines to avoid alerting German troops on the ground. As the bombers descended in a shallow glide toward the center of the pocket, it was impossible to find the individual drop zones, since the whole area was ablaze with fires from the intense fighting. Nor could the aircraft maneuver with their engines idling. The pilots began to give the paratroopers the signal to jump from an altitude of about a thousand feet, and most of the paratroopers landed in the hotly contested southwest corner of the pocket instead of in the center as had been planned. Several of the bombers could not find the drop zone at all, and so returned to base with their paratroopers.

In total, 312 paratroopers jumped. About 75 were lost during the jump after landing outside the Soviet pocket in German-occupied

territory; a further 38 landed completely off course near the town of
Staritsa, to the northeast of Rzhev. The 1st Company under Lieutenant Kovalevskiy and part of 2nd Company landed inside the town of
Yeverzovo and almost immediately were engaged in house-to-house
fighting with German infantry. The rest of 2nd Company landed near
the town of Monchalovo and was soon under fire from German infantry. The 3rd Company, commanded by Lieutenant Borismanskiy,
landed near Okorokovo on the southwest edge of the pocket, and was
brought under fire even as they were landing. By the evening of 17
February, the battalion commander, Sr. Lt. P. L. Belotserkovskiy, finally managed to gather together 166 paratroopers out of the original
500-man battalion. After finally alerting the commander of the 29th
Army that his unit had arrived, Belotserkovskiy was instructed to
lead his men to the southwest sector of the pocket to assist in the
breakout attempts. Although the airdrop helped bolster the morale of
the encircled Soviet soldiers, so few men actually reached the intended destination that the mission had little impact. The linkup with
the 39th Army finally occurred on 22 February after bitter fighting,
and the decimated remnants of the battalion were used as part of the
hard-pressed rear guard.

REINFORCEMENTS

By late February, the front west of Moscow was largely stalemated,
and the trapped Soviet forces were being slowly mauled by the better-equipped German forces near Vyazma. Stalin and the STAVKA
decided to try another limited offensive to relieve the cut-off forces
while at the same time trapping the German 4th Armies in the
Yukhnov salient. The two principal elements of the attack would be
a ground attack by the 49th and 50th Armies into the southern shoulder of the Yukhnov salient, supported by another major airdrop by
the two remaining brigades of the 4th Airborne Corps into the
Zhelanye area to threaten the rear of the German 4th Army.

The airdrop suffered from the usual lack of airlift. The drop was
supposed to be completed in three nights even though the size of the
paratrooper force was larger than on the previous missions. But with
only forty-one PS-84 airliners from MAON and twenty-three TB-3
bombers from the 23rd Bomber Division, only one battalion could be

dropped at a time. The first unit in was the remaining battalion of the 8th Airborne Brigade, which parachuted into the Zhelanye area on the night of 17–18 February. Plans to pre-position teams with radio beacons never materialized, and the transport pilots had to rely on bonfires and other improvised ground signals—the same methods that had worked so poorly during the Rzhev drop the night before. Over the course of the next five nights, the transports made nightly flights out of Lyubertsy and Vnukovo airfields near Moscow, dropping 1,350 men of the 9th Airborne Brigade and 2,239 of the 214th Airborne Brigade into the area around Bolshaya Elenka near Zhelanye. The transport airfields were deep enough behind Soviet lines to prevent German night intruders from raiding them, as had been the case in the January missions. The weather continued to be a problem, with fog frequently obscuring the drop zones.

After the first airdrop on the night of 17–18 February, the Germans began to try to disrupt the flights. Luftwaffe actions were not very effective, but German soldiers set up bonfires, which disoriented the Soviet transport pilots and caused many airdrops to take place miles off course. Instead of taking three nights, the airdrops took seven. The Germans scored one of their few victories on the last night of the airdrops, 22–23 February, when a German fighter intercepted the transport carrying the 4th Airborne Corps commander, General Levashev. Levashev was killed and several of his staff were wounded.

In total, some 7,373 paratroopers were dropped in seven nights. It was a remarkable accomplishment for such a small transport force under such appalling conditions. But the rugged, forested terrain in the drop zone, abysmal weather, and pilot errors led to wide dispersion of the paratroopers. Some paratroopers fell directly into German garrisons and were killed. Others landed so far off course that it took them months to find Soviet lines. In total, about 5,000 paratroopers finally were assembled under the command of the corps' chief of staff, Col. A. F. Kazankin. The dispersion problem also affected the collection of the PDMM supply containers. These held all the heavy weapons (DP machine guns, 50mm and 82mm mortars, antitank rifles, and associated ammunition), skis, medicine, medical equipment, and additional rations. Each paratrooper had carried in only a three-days' supply of dry rations, one unit of fire of small-arms ammunition, two hand grenades, a TNT block, and a shovel or an ax. The drop zone was heavily forested and covered with snow, so locating the PDMMs proved difficult. After three days of searching, only 33 to 55 percent of the materiel had been found, and because the paratroopers who had packed the containers were inexperienced, a portion of the recovered equipment was damaged beyond repair. As a result, additional emergency air supply missions had to be flown into the area. The long delays in carrying out the airborne landing robbed the operation of its element of surprise, and the days wasted on assembling the force allowed the Germans to begin preparing their defenses.

The first stage of the associated Soviet offensive had not proceeded as quickly as planned. The attack by the 50th Army into the southern shoulder of the Yukhnov salient had stalled, and twenty miles of rough, wooded terrain separated the 4th Airborne Corps from the 50th Army. Kazankin ordered his two brigades southward to the Moscow-Warsaw highway to link up with the 50th Army. In four days of marching, the paratroopers overwhelmed several German garrisons and reached the German strongpoint of Malyshevka, a little more than a mile from the Warsaw highway. Reconnaissance in front of the main body was weak. Colonel Kazankin did not have a good appreciation of the layout of the German garrisons in front of him, so it was hard to determine where the main thrust should be directed. The paratroopers stumbled into prepared German defenses.

By now, the Germans were well aware of the 4th Airborne Corps' objective and had moved artillery and armor into the area. The towns initially attacked by the paratroopers contained about two regiments of troops. The 9th Airborne Brigade attack on 27 February finally took the town of Kliuchi, killing some 600 German troops of the 12th Infantry Division. But other attacks toward the highway were bloodily repulsed. Both sides pulled back to lick their wounds. The paratroopers found shelter in the neighboring villages and forests, whereas the Germans continued to control the towns and roadways in the area.

Time was on the side of the German infantry. The Soviet paratroopers had managed to stretch out three days of rations for eight days, but in the intense cold the lack of food was beginning to show its effect. The paratroopers were exhausted from a week of fighting and exposure to the harsh, subzero winter weather. The Germans had the advantage of strong defensive positions in the villages, with warm accommodations and a steady supply of food and ammunition. Coordination between the paratroopers and the 50th Army to the south was nonexistent due to radio problems. The brigades had a number of Sever transceivers, but they were either provided with the wrong preset channels, or damaged. Contact was not established until 1 March. Another attack toward the highway was launched that evening, but it ran into a counterattack by the German 131st Infantry Division supported by Stukas and two ski battalions. Paratrooper losses by now had been heavy, totaling 1,200 men, or about a quarter of the force. The effective strength of the Soviet airborne force in early March totaled less than 2,500 men, the remainder of the men being sick or wounded.

On 4 March 1942, the German Army Group Center decided to withdraw from the Yukhnov salient to more defensible positions on the west bank of the Ugra River. The withdrawal was not particularly deep, and the German defensive line on the Moscow-Warsaw highway remained in place. The withdrawing German units reinforced the garrisons standing between the 4th Airborne Corps and the 50th Army. Two German infantry companies tried to drive a wedge between the 4th Airborne Corps' two main concentrations on 5 March, but without success. On 6 March, the Soviet forces launched another coordinated attack on Malyshevka in hope of linking up. One paratrooper battalion was stopped in its tracks by German fire before reaching the start line, and the other two battalions from the 9th Airborne Brigade were halted when the Germans surprised them with a flank attack by ski troops. The German infantry in the area had a distinct edge in mobility because of the more skillful use of ski troops. The Germans responded with a counterattack of their own, but it too was beaten back with heavy casualties.

By early March, the air bases near Moscow were finally able to organize regular supply missions, averaging about fifteen tons per day, to the 4th Airborne Corps. The area to the north of the airborne force was held by a Russian partisan unit, called the Zhabo detachment, which helped recover the supplies. Depending on the weather, Red Air Force units near the front also began flying small U-2 biplanes into the rear areas to evacuate wounded paratroopers one or two at a time.

On 11 March, the German 131st Infantry Division launched a major attack with two companies supported by artillery and mortars and, for the first time, tanks. The Germans had limited success against an exposed company from the 214th Airborne Brigade, but the main Soviet defensive perimeter held. On 13 March, two German infantry battalions assaulted the main paratrooper stronghold in the village of Gorbachi after heavy artillery preparation. Although the Germans made some inroads into the Soviet defense, the intervention by a paratrooper company on skis turned the tide in favor of the Soviets. But the fighting in the first two weeks of March had cost the Russians another 500 lives.

In the middle of March, the Germans reinforced the battered 131st Infantry Division with the 449th Infantry Regiment and a fresh unit, the 107th Infantry Regiment of the 34th Infantry Division. On 18 March, the Germans hit the village of Pushkino, which was abandoned by the thirty survivors of 4/214th Airborne Brigade. The day after this battering, the paratroopers moved back into the forests to establish a more defensible line. This withdrawal coincided with the start of a major German antipartisan operation, Operation Munich, around the Yelnya area on the western edge of the pocket occupied by Belov's cavalry and supporting partisans who were harassing German supply convoys along the Moscow-Warsaw highway. The campaign involved some nine German infantry and security divisions.

At the end of March, the Soviet forces trapped in the Vyazma region were in three main groups. The Kalinin Front's 29th and 39th Armies were in a pocket northwest of Vyazma, with its 11th Cavalry Corps trying to break through to Belov's 1st Guards Cavalry Corps to the west of Vyazma. Remnants of several divisions of the 33rd Army were isolated in a pocket to the southeast of Vyazma. Belov's 1st Guards Cavalry Corps and the 4th Airborne Corps controlled a huge but thinly held area between the Moscow-Minsk and Moscow-Warsaw highways. Control of all Soviet forces in this pocket was entrusted to Belov, who commanded not only the regular cavalry and paratrooper forces but a significant partisan force as well.

At the beginning of April, elements of the 4th Airborne Corps and 2nd Guards Cavalry Division formed the southern flank of Belov's pocket, aimed at the Moscow-Warsaw highway. This narrow salient was about ten miles wide, with the rear areas held by the Zhabo partisan detachment. The 9th Airborne Brigade held the left (southeast-

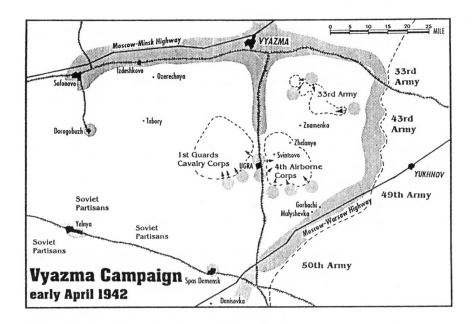

ern) shoulder of the pocket, the 214th Airborne Brigade the center, and the 2nd Guards Cavalry Division the right (southwestern) flank. The corps' 8th Airborne Brigade was still serving with Belov's 1st Guards Cavalry Corps farther north along the Vyazma highway.

A major German attack on 31 March marked the beginning of a German effort in the sector. The Germans had planned to launch a major attack with two panzer divisions and a security division, but when the panzer forces were pulled away for other operations, the attack had to be substantially scaled back. Instead of a thrust to cut the Soviet pocket in half along the rail line running south of Vyazma through Ugra, only a southern thrust was made, directed against the area held by the 4th Airborne Corps. Three German infantry battalions with tank support succeeded in recapturing several small villages along the center of the salient. The new attack was aimed to punch through the Soviet positions to reach the Ugra rail station, about eight miles behind the Soviet lines, where an 800-man German garrison had remained isolated and partly surrounded for nearly a month. The attack was directed up the north-south rail line, which roughly divided the 2nd Guards Cavalry Division to the west and the

214th Airborne Brigade to the east. The Germans pressed their attacks, finally breaking through the Soviet defensive trenches on 2–3 April. On 5 April 1942, Hitler demanded that Field Marshal H. von Kluge, the commander of the German Army Group Center, consolidate the German forces in front of Moscow by eliminating Belov's forces. In spite of the directive, von Kluge's forces were still too weak to stage anything more than local assaults in narrow sectors. Besides the attack toward the Ugra station, von Kluge was also trying to eliminate the trapped 33rd Army east of Belov's encircled forces.

The German attacks toward Ugra finally forced Belov to dispatch reinforcements from less threatened sectors of the pocket. After months of fighting along the Vyazma highway, the survivors of the 8th Airborne Brigade were transferred back to the main body of the 4th Airborne Corps. Although now reduced to battalion strength, the 8th Airborne Brigade was committed to the area of most intense fighting, along the rail line to Ugra. In spite of these last-minute reinforcements, the Germans finally divided the Soviet pocket and captured the Verterkhovo railroad station on 9 April. This allowed the main German forces to finally link up with the isolated garrison at Ugra, and it separated the Soviet 2nd Guards Cavalry Division from the airborne forces. Soviet casualties by this time were very high. The 4th Airborne Corps' effective strength was down to 1,500 paratroopers, and 2,000 sick and wounded, from the more than 7,300 troops who had jumped in late February. They were supported by about 1,700 partisans. The cold winter weather had given way to the first signs of spring, and the battlefield began turning to mud with the onset of the first spring rains.

The Germans appreciated the precariousness of their position at Ugra, a narrow salient twenty miles from the main German lines along the Moscow-Warsaw highway and only about five miles wide, with Soviet forces on either side. Von Kluge did not have sufficient forces to hold Ugra or push northward to link up with forces along the northern stretch of the rail line, since the German Army Group Center at the same time was trying to crush the 33rd Army pocket east of Belov's forces. Beginning on 12 April, with the Ugra garrison rescued, the Germans began withdrawing southward again, with the Soviet forces harassing them the entire time. The German withdrawal prompted Belov to order the 2nd Guards Cavalry Division to launch yet another attack on the night of 13–14 April toward the Warsaw highway in hopes of linking up with the 50th Army. After initial success, the attacks bogged down when German rear-guard units were encountered about ten miles north of the highway.

By mid-April, Belov's cavalry and the 4th Airborne Corps paratroopers had little chance of overcoming any serious German positions in the Vyazma pocket. Yet Stalin and the STAVKA were intent on keeping them in the field to force the German Army Group Center off balance and to prevent the Germans from planning any further actions toward Moscow itself. To keep the effort going, on 19 April 645 paratroopers of the 4/23rd Airborne Brigade parachuted into a drop zone near Svintsovo to reinforce the 4th Airborne Corps, bringing the effective strength of the Soviet paratroopers back up to about 2,000 men. This was of little consolation, as on 25 April, the trapped divisions of the Soviet 33rd Army were finally overcome by von Kluge's assault, further isolating the Vyazma pocket from any potential relief effort directly from the Moscow area to the east.

The fighting calmed down at the end of the month as the rainy spring weather turned roads to thick, gooey mud. Neither the Germans nor the Soviets could easily move under these conditions. The 4th Airborne Corps held much the same area as before the April German counterattacks. Belov's forces saved their strength for an anticipated summer counteroffensive by Soviet forces.

During May, the Germans reinforced their garrisons all around the 4th Airborne Corps, including newly gained positions to the north and east. Ironically, the only area free of large German concentrations was to the west, a no-man's-land of swamp and forest coveted by neither side. The Germans decided to wait until the spring rains had ended before staging a final attempt to crush the paratroopers. The unsatisfactory results of the early spring fighting convinced Field Marshal von Kluge that small-scale operations were inadequate. What was needed was a major offensive to clear the entire pocket occupied by Belov and the paratroopers.

OPERATION HANNOVER

The campaign to crush Belov and the paratroopers was code-named Operation Hannover. German preparations began in early May. Rather than relying entirely on force, the Germans decided to try persuasion and subterfuge as well. The Luftwaffe began dropping leaflets urging Soviet soldiers and partisans to defect; political commissars, formerly shot on capture, were promised that their lives would be spared. A special unit of about 350 Russian defectors, dressed in Red Army uniforms, was formed for special operations during the campaign. Called the Graukopf Battalion, this unit was assigned the mission of penetrating Soviet lines, disrupting Soviet defenses, and seizing General Belov and his headquarters.

The principal forces for Operation Hannover came from General–oberst Gotthard Heinrici's 4th Army. The main blows would be directed from positions on the eastern end of the pocket, toward the west, to minimize the chances for Belov's forces to escape. In the northeastern corner, the 46th Panzer Corps at Vyazma would launch assaults by the 23rd and 197th Infantry Divisions toward the town of Dorogobuzh, supported by the 5th Panzer Division to their south. In the southeastern sector, the 43rd Corps would launch parallel attacks toward the west by the 19th Panzer Division and 34th Infantry Division, while at the same time preventing Belov from escaping across the Moscow-Warsaw highway by reinforcing the cordon with the 221st and 442nd Security Divisions. The 12th Corps was assigned a holding action on the eastern end of the salient, to prevent the Soviet forces from breaking out at the point closest to Moscow.

In total, Operation Hannover could muster three corps and seven divisions, plus a substantial number of assorted security units. However, these forces had not been rebuilt since the costly winter fighting and were only a shadow of their usual strength. For example, the 19th Panzer Division had less than a tenth of its tanks, only eighteen in total; 5th Panzer was not appreciably stronger. The total German force committed to Operation Hannover was about 18,000 troops, or roughly the same size as Belov's encircled forces. Nevertheless, the Germans had substantial advantages in artillery and air support. Moreover, their troops were in better physical condition than the haggard and emaciated paratroopers and cavalrymen of Belov's command.

Operation Hannover was planned for mid-May but was repeatedly delayed due to weather. Field Marshal von Kluge insisted on clear skies to ensure Luftwaffe support. In addition, he wanted a few days of clear weather to help dry the muddy roads. There were growing fears that Belov's troops would escape out of the trap, as there was clear evidence that the Soviets had discovered the preparations for the assault. The attack was ordered to begin on the night of 23 May. The weather was worse than expected, with spring cloudbursts in the eastern sector of the pocket. The Ugra River was three times its usual width, and streams in the already swampy area overflowed their banks. The German infantry pressed forward in spite of the mud, supported by a substantial artillery barrage.

Facing the German 43rd Corps, the Zhabo partisan detachment numbered about 1,400 troops, burdened with many women and children. The rain delayed the first operations, but the poorly trained and equipped partisans could do little to resist the German advance. The turncoat Graukopf Battalion had surreptitiously entered Soviet lines on their mission to capture Belov. The defectors never managed to do so, but they caused considerable consternation to Belov after at least one officer was captured and revealed the mission. Belov was forced to assign about 1,000 troops to tracking them down, a substantial drain on his resources at a critical moment.

The 19th Panzer Division attempted to seize a bridgehead over the Ugra River on the first day of fighting, only to have the paratroopers blow up the bridge at Vskody in front of their noses. At the time, the Soviet 4th Airborne Corps mustered 1,565 effectives and a further 470 sick and wounded. But the 4th Airborne Corps defenses were much too thin, and by nightfall on 24 May, the 19th Panzer Division secured a small bridgehead over the river, reinforced the following day by a pontoon bridge. The main attack by the 19th Panzer Division and 34th Infantry Division against the 4th Airborne Corps sector came on the second day of the offensive, 25 May, and was directed mainly at the 2nd Guards Cavalry Division and the Zhabo partisan detachment. In one day of fighting, the Germans destroyed about 60 percent of the Zhabo partisan group and killed 3,000 partisans and Soviet soldiers. Although the Red Army troops and partisans resisted fiercely at first, they were soon overwhelmed by superior firepower, mobility, and numbers. Much to the surprise of the Germans, the Red Air Force intervened and attempted to bomb the 19th Panzer Division's bridge over the Ugra River—without success.

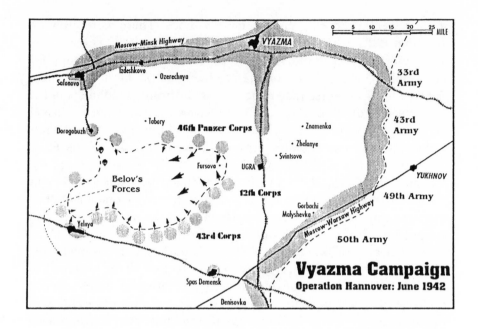

By 27 May, all contact between the paratroopers and the partisans had been lost, and Belov ordered the 4th Airborne Corps to withdraw westward to avoid encirclement. It was in the nick of time. Later on 27 May, elements of the two German corps met up at Fursovo, about ten miles west of the Ugra rail station, trapping any remaining Soviet forces in the eastern part of the pocket. The paratroopers finally managed to join up with Belov's cavalrymen on 30 May. In the first week of fighting, the Germans took 5,361 prisoners and killed about 4,000 partisans and Soviet soldiers; German casualties were about 500 dead and 1,500 wounded. The Germans did not race after Belov and the paratroopers; von Kluge insisted that the eastern portion of the pocket be thoroughly tidied up. It was impossible to distinguish partisans from civilians, so all Russian males between the ages of fourteen and sixty were dumped into the German's hellish prisoner of war (POW) camps. The Wehrmacht estimated that about a third of Belov's forces had been destroyed in the first phase of Operation Hannover.

In late May, the STAVKA decided to airdrop additional reinforcements. The role of the reinforcements was not so much to help the paratroopers escape as to ensure that Belov's forces held out as long as possible. There was some fear that the Germans might make another attempt to capture Moscow in the summer of 1942, and the longer Belov held out, the less likely became any German operation against Moscow. Some thought was also being given to another Soviet offensive in the Moscow area, and Belov's resistance helped in this eventuality as well. Beginning on the night of 29 May 1942, paratroopers from the 23rd Airborne Brigade (10th Airborne Corps) and 211th Airborne Brigade (1st Airborne Corps) were dropped in the Dorogobuzh area in the western end of the pocket. There is some mystery about this operation, and Soviet accounts are almost completely lacking. In six nights from 29 May through 3 June, more than 4,000 paratroopers were landed. But details of the airborne drops remain very sketchy.

Unbeknownst to Belov and the paratroopers, the promised Soviet summer offensive in the Moscow area never materialized, owing to the defeat of the Red Army in Ukraine near Kharkov. Under intense German pressure from Operation Hannover, Belov and Kazankin were forced to concede that their positions had become untenable. They were finally authorized to break out and return to Soviet lines in early June. Field Marshal von Kluge ordered Operation Hannover to resume on 3 June, in spite of another spate of rainy weather. After nearly two days of painfully slow advances through the mud, the German forces ran into the new airborne forces about fifteen miles east of Dorogobuzh. The weather did not allow Luftwaffe support, and the muddy roads made it impossible for tanks to provide aid. In a grim infantry battle, the Wehrmacht managed to outflank the Soviet airborne positions. Dorogobuzh itself did not fall until 7 July, when it was encircled by the 23rd Infantry Division and the 5th Panzer Division. By the time the city was captured, it was being held by a skeleton partisan force. Belov and the surviving paratroopers were already farther south, trying to escape the trap.

Von Kluge correctly assumed that Belov's forces would try to break out to the southwest, near Yelnya, as Soviet partisans still held a wooded area there. The 221st Security Division, a third-rate police unit, was ordered to reinforce its positions there. General Heinrici ordered the 19th Panzer Division to the area as well. A motorcycle battalion from the 19th Panzer Division reached Yelnya on the afternoon of 8 June, followed by an understrength infantry battalion and about five tanks. A single tank was sent out along the Yelnya-Smolensk road to begin patrolling the area, but it was stopped by a mine.

Belov's forces had traversed nearly eighty miles in the first week of fighting before reaching the southwestern perimeter of the pocket. Local partisans had already reconnoitered the area and had spotted a gap between the villages of Berniki and Petrovo. Aside from one artillery battery about five miles west of Yelnya, and a motorcycle battalion five miles farther east, there were only scattered forces from the security division. Around 20:00 hours on 8 June, while it was still light, Belov's forces made a mad dash through the gap. The motorcycle battalion was alerted and rushed to the area. The battalion commander was killed in the ensuing firefight, and the battalion disintegrated under the overwhelming pressure of thousands of fleeing Soviet troops. The debacle was not reported to Heinrici's command until the afternoon of 9 June, and by the time the Luftwaffe arrived overhead, Belov's cavalrymen and paratroopers were safely ensconced in the swamps of the Desna River. About 6,000 troops managed to flee.

Belov's group gathered their strength and moved southward, looking for another gap in German lines. After the embarrassment of 9 June, von Kluge ordered a more serious effort to finally seal off Belov's forces. The Germans at the time thought that only about 2,000 troops had escaped, and they had a great deal of trouble finding their elusive enemy. After another twenty-five-mile march, the remnants of Belov's two corps reached the Warsaw highway near Denisovka. Soviet scouts reported that the sector was held by a dug-in German infantry regiment with a company of tanks in support. The emaciated Soviet troops were in no position to overcome such defenses, so they decided on a mad dash across the Warsaw highway on the night of 16–17 June. The Soviet forces numbered about 5,000 troops at the beginning of the escape attempt and included the families of partisan fighters. The units moved toward the highway without artillery preparation in hope of overwhelming the Germans by sheer mass.

The escape was chaotic and bloody. The Germans began firing on the retreating Soviet columns with mortars and heavy machine guns. Soon, tanks of the 19th Panzer Division got into the act, moving up and down the Warsaw highway with guns firing. Unit after unit screamed *"Urra"* and ran forward over the road. The Soviet troops had to run a gauntlet of fire, the road eerily lit up by descending flares, the night sky ablaze with machine-gun tracers. Only about half of the 4th Airborne Corps made it across the road. Some units arrived near the road too late and retreated back into the forest rather than risk certain death. The next day, many of those who had escaped over the road were hunted down by the Germans and killed. In desperation, the survivors who had not made it across the highway attempted it again the following night. The Germans were ready, and the Soviet troops faced a wall of fire. Few survived.

The paratroopers and cavalrymen who had crossed the highway on the night of 16–17 June reached Soviet lines on 21 June after one last skirmish near Zhilino. A small group of soldiers from the 8th Airborne Brigade, the first of the paratrooper units to have jumped in January, crossed into Soviet territory on the night of 27–28 June. In total, the Germans counted 11,061 Soviet prisoners and 5,034 dead in the month of fighting. German casualties were about 750 dead, and several hundred more dead from typhoid. A postwar U.S. Army study of the operation concluded that "by any standard, Operation Hannover was one of the toughest battles the German Army fought in the East."

ASSESSING THE VYAZMA OPERATION

As an airborne operation, the Vyazma airdrops were a costly failure. Of the 14,000 troops parachuted or airlanded in the Vyazma area, less than 2,000 survived, and most of these were prisoners or were left behind in the Vyazma pocket to fend for themselves. The reasons for the failure are many. From a strategic perspective, the initial operation had little chance of success after the Red Army's January counteroffensive bogged down east of Vyazma. Postwar Soviet assessments of the operation have focused on the failures of the STAVKA in planning and executing the operation. Soviet capabilities were overestimated and German tenacity was not adequately credited. There was insufficient coordination between the airborne forces and the main Soviet attack. Once the January offensive lost its momentum, it took the STAVKA too long to realistically assess the prospects of the 4th Airborne

Corps mission and reorient its actions and those of other trapped units such as Belov's 1st Guards Cavalry Corps.

From a tactical perspective, the airborne operation suffered from a severe shortage of resources, which adversely affected the conduct of the mission. The lack of airlift inevitably meant that the airdrops were conducted over long periods of time, in which the operation had lost its natural advantage of surprise. The combination of atrocious weather, rough terrain, and poor communications equipment caused the airborne forces to take days, if not weeks, to mass for an attack. Once surprise was lost, the airborne forces posed a limited threat to the main German defensive positions. Their combat utility was sapped by their lack of mobility in the snow-covered countryside, due to the dearth of skis and ski training. They were further weakened by the debilitating effects of prolonged exposure to cold weather and frequent lack of food. They fought without artillery fire support and often with too little ammunition. The airborne units could overcome isolated villages but were never able to overcome a regimental defensive position supported by artillery or armor. By their very nature, the airborne forces were light, possessing little firepower. Heroism was a thin shield against such odds.

Once it became clear that the January counteroffensive could not succeed, the strategic objective of the Belov forces changed. STAVKA was still fearful of German intentions toward Moscow, so it was inconceivable to withdraw Belov and the paratroopers in spite of their haggard state. The new mission became the prolonged harassment of German forces west of Moscow to hamper any further German attempts against the capital. Although the initial airborne mission had failed at its objective, the later objective was successfully met, but at a horrible cost. The chief of staff of the German 4th Army, General of the Infantry Guenther Blumentritt, derisively commented about the operation: "The red louse in one's hide was unpleasant . . . although the whole matter was very annoying, it had no strategic consequence." This was not entirely true. The determined Soviet resistance in the western approaches to Moscow made it difficult to prepare for any operations against the city in the summer of 1942. Hitler abandoned his dream of 1941 and instead aimed the Wehrmacht southward toward the Caucasus oil fields and Stalingrad.

THE LOST CORPS

In spite of the bloody ending of the Vyazma operation, the heroic battles of the 4th Airborne Corps in the Vyazma pocket have long been given an honored place in the history of the VDV Airborne Force. The same cannot be said for the disastrous Demyansk operation by the 1st Airborne Corps in March 1942. Standard Soviet histories of the VDV omit the operation entirely. It has been only through the research of noted American military historian Col. David Glantz that the story of the lost airborne corps has finally emerged after years of secrecy, culled from German rather than Soviet archives. The Demyansk operation was a grim conclusion to Soviet airborne operations in the bloody year of 1942.

In January and February 1942 while the Vyazma battles were raging, the Red Army's Kalinin and Northwestern Fronts launched a coordinated offensive as part of the effort to drive the Germans back from the Moscow area. This was an immediate counterpart of the Vyazma operations but located to the northwest of Moscow. The counteroffensive was extremely successful, trapping a major portion of the German 16th Army totaling six divisions, or about 70,000 troops, in a pocket around the town of Demyansk. Colonel General P. A. Kurochkin, commander of the Northwestern Front, decided to employ the 1st Airborne Corps in a unique fashion. The considerable difficulties in airlanding the 4th Airborne Corps during their operations to the south near Vyazma, combined with a continuing lack of airlift, forced Kurochkin to devise another approach to landing the 1st Airborne Corps in the German rear. He decided to use infiltration tactics. The 1st Airborne Corps would clandestinely penetrate German lines on skis and move deep into the enemy rear. Their mission was to capture the commander of the German forces, General Brockdorff-Ahlefeld, and seize the vital airfield at Demyansk, where the encircled German troops were being resupplied from the air. Supplies to the raiding party would be provided by airdrop, and the corps would cripple the German defenders from within while other Red Army units gradually constricted the Demyansk encirclement from without.

The 1st Airborne Corps was a new and inexperienced unit, replacing the corps that had been lost in September 1941 in the Kiev pocket.

The new corps was formed at Saratov, received practically no paratroop training, and was moved to the Moscow area as a reserve force during the critical battles in the winter of 1941. In March 1942, its component brigades—the 1st, 3rd, and 204th Airborne Brigades—were moved to Bologoye air base, fifty-five miles northwest of Moscow, for the Demyansk operation.

The preparatory act of the operation was a parachute jump by Maj. A. V. Grinev's 4/204th Airborne Brigade on the night of 15 February 1942 near Demyansk and Iasski. It was the only airborne jump of the operation. Grinev's paratroopers were to conduct reconnaissance for the corps and apparently were assigned the mission of capturing the German commander. The airdrop was conducted with about 100 aircraft, which alerted the German SS Totenkopf Division to the presence of Soviet paratroopers.

The three airborne brigades followed on skis over a ten-day period from 6 to 16 March so as to avoid German attention. The 1st Airborne Brigade entered the German pocket near Vereteika on the night of 6–7 March, crossing through German lines with few casualties. But German garrisons in neighboring Pustynia and Pochinok gradually became aware of the nighttime activity. By 12 March, when the 204th Airborne Brigade began to cross into German territory, it came under intense small-arms fire, punctuated by artillery. The German actions inflicted heavier and heavier casualties as the missions continued over the next few nights. The Germans also noted the flight of Soviet transport aircraft into areas behind their own lines, evidently dropping supplies to the advanced airborne groups. Some troops without parachutes were also dropped during the course of the operation. Slow-flying U-2 biplanes would skim close to the ground, and the paratroopers would leap off into deep snowdrifts. The first major attack occurred on 15 March when the garrison at Maloye Opuevo was overrun by about twelve hundred paratroopers from the 1st and 204th Airborne Brigades.

The nighttime airdrop missions of the transport aircraft proved unable to keep the airborne units adequately supplied. Paratroopers went for days without food, in bitterly cold winter conditions. By 17 March, the front was being forced to sneak supplies into the Demyansk pocket by dogsled. The lack of food, and the brutal weather conditions, delayed the beginning of the 1st Airborne Corps' planned attacks on the Demyansk airfields. These airfields were absolutely essential to the German 2nd Army. During the campaign, German transport aircraft flew more than 32,000 sorties into Demyansk airfields, bringing in more than 64,000 tons of supplies and 30,500 troops. The airfields were not objectives that the Germans would surrender easily.

By 19 March, nearly two brigades from the 1st Airborne Corps were in the middle of the German pocket on the northern outskirts of Demyansk itself. The 2nd Airborne Brigade did not follow the other two brigades into the center of the German pocket but veered to the east in order to attack the rear area of the German 30th Infantry Division. An attack on German positions east of Lychkovo on the night of 18 March by the 2nd Airborne Brigade was repulsed, with about 200 Russian dead.

On the night of 19 March, two attacks were launched by the 1st and 204th Airborne Brigades in the outskirts of Demyansk, one at the airfield near Globovshchina and the other against the town of Dobrosli. The Germans repulsed both attacks with heavy losses, amounting to at least 650 Russian dead. The Germans were well entrenched and supported by the deadly 20mm antiaircraft automatic cannon and machine guns, whereas the Soviet paratroopers were weakened by lack of food and the bitterly cold weather. The detachment commander realized that his main mission was hopeless in the face of such odds and decided to abandon any further attempts. Both airborne brigades continued their way south past Demyansk, striking German garrisons at Igoshevo and Staroe Tarasovo on 24 March with little success. The retreating Soviet forces were pounded by artillery, and their plans were compromised by poor radio security.

The weather began to change, with temperatures rising above the freezing point. Movement was made difficult as roads and paths turned to mud, and the paratroopers began to throw away their skis. By now, the German forces were well aware of the presence of the paratroopers, and German signal intelligence units were listening in on radio conversations and pinpointing their origin. The Soviet units were subjected to repeated attacks by German artillery. The airborne forces were becoming increasingly desperate for food and ammunition. They were too deep in German territory for dogsled supplies, and the nightly airdrops had dried up. A small airfield was prepared in the Gladkoe swamps, and the Red Air Force flew in light Po-2 biplanes to bring in supplies and evacuate the wounded. But these small, two-man aircraft could not bring in the volume of supplies needed.

German reconnaissance pinpointed the Soviet position and correctly assessed the likelihood of a Soviet attempt to break through the southern edge of the German lines on 28 March. The 1st Airborne Brigade ran into elements of the SS Totenkopf Division and 123rd Infantry Division. The skirmishes cost the Soviets at least 130 dead and forced the brigade to break up into several smaller groups. Rebuffed in their first breakout attempt, the 1st Airborne Brigade was forced to withdraw into swamps to avoid the German forces. Another attempt to break out in the early-morning hours of 29 March was also bloodily repulsed by the German infantry. Elements of the SS Totenkopf Division were dispatched to deal with the Soviet paratroopers, and the main Soviet base camp was overrun after a two-hour battle. By this time, any organized effort by the survivors of the 1st and 204th Airborne Brigades had collapsed. Isolated groups of paratroopers tried to sneak out of the pocket on their own. On the night of 6–7 April, 600 paratroopers tried to break out, and the 1st Airborne Brigade commander, Lt. Col. N. E. Tarasov, was captured. The starving paratroopers stubbornly continued the desperate attempt, and later in the day the new 1st Airborne Brigade commander, Lieutenant Colonel Ustinov, was killed along with 80 of his men. A German report indicated that from 21 to 29 March, at least 1,500 paratroopers had been killed and 70 taken prisoner. Of the 5,000 paratroopers in the 1st and 204th Airborne Brigades, probably no more than 400 escaped. The 2nd Airborne Brigade, which had remained in the northeastern portion of the Demyansk pocket, was able to extricate about 500 troops, or about a quarter of the brigade's initial strength.

Soviet silence over the fate of the 1st Airborne Corps is not altogether surprising, considering its utter lack of success and its tragic ending. The whole notion of infiltrating a large force behind an encircled German garrison was doomed from the start, given the inability of the Red Air Force to conduct an adequate number of supply missions to the isolated force.

NAVAL RAIDERS

The successful use of small teams of paratroopers during the raid near Odessa in September 1941, and in the amphibious operation on the Kerch peninsula on 31 December 1941, prompted the Soviet Navy to raise several special operations parachute units during the war. In May 1942, the Black Sea Fleet's aviation branch formed an air assault company of 160 men under the command of Capt. M. A. Orlov. Although intended for the support of amphibious operations, this company had as its first mission an adventurous raid. During the fighting in the Caucasus in the autumn of 1942, the Luftwaffe conducted many of its missions from an air base near Maikop. On the evening of 23 October 1942, Maikop was attacked by a mixed group of aircraft of the 63rd Bomber Aviation Brigade, including SB bombers, DB-3 bombers, and a pair of old I-15 biplane fighters. Trailing the strike force was a single PS-84 airliner with eighteen paratroopers, and a TB-3 bomber with twenty-two troops from the naval paratrooper company, commanded by Capt. A. P. Desyatnikov. The plan was to distract the Germans with the air raid, then parachute and land the raiding force to destroy any surviving German aircraft. The PS-84 made its pass first but was caught by several German antiaircraft searchlights; only fifteen paratroopers jumped before the pilot was forced to maneuver to avoid antiaircraft fire. The TB-3 bomber followed by gliding into the base with its engines shut off in the hope of attracting less attention from the German antiaircraft gunners. On touching down at the center of the air base, the bomber was hit by a German antiaircraft gun and burst into flames. The landing party managed to escape the burning bomber in good order and quickly scattered over the runway to plant demolition charges on any German aircraft in sight. Of the sixty-two German aircraft on the runway, the Soviet landing teams managed to destroy twenty-two before being driven off by German counterattacks.

The Black Sea Fleet formed a second paratrooper unit in January 1943 to support a combined operation against the port city of Novorossisk on the northeastern corner of the Black Sea. The Soviet 47th Army planned to attack from the land side of the city in conjunction with an amphibious assault to the south of the city. About eighty sailors and naval aircrew and naval infantry volunteers were formed into a special operations battalion under Col. V. D. Gordeyev. On the night of 4 February 1943, they were loaded aboard four Li-2 transports and dropped over Iyuzh Ozereika, on the southern flank of the amphibious landing area. Their mission was to conduct sabotage and to attack the headquarters of the German 10th Infantry Division, which was defending this sector. The group was unable to carry out its raid on the German divisional HQ but managed to destroy a German artillery battery and ambush several companies of German infantry. Of the fifty-seven paratroopers who jumped, twenty-eight were rescued by navy small craft several nights later.

The failure of the Demyansk mission, and the limited success of the Vyazma airdrops, forced the STAVKA to seriously reconsider its attitude toward airborne operations. Aside from the small-scale use of paratroopers by the navy after the Demyansk fiasco, there would be no major airdrops for more than a year, until the autumn of 1943. In the summer of 1942, after suffering enormous losses in Ukraine, the entire VDV force was converted to infantry. STAVKA would turn to other forces to carry out special operations in early 1943.

Chapter 4
Airborne Alternatives

The failure of the Vyazma airborne operations put an end to Soviet airborne operations for more than a year. The long interlude between the Vyazma operation and the Dnepr bridgehead airdrop in the autumn of 1943 was due to a complex interplay of factors, including continued shortages of air transport aircraft, an inability of the VDV to maintain a reserve force of trained airborne divisions because of the manpower demands of the Red Army, and the increasing importance of an alternative to airborne operations—the growing partisan movement.

The STAVKA studied the lessons of the Vyazma operation and concluded that reform was needed before another airborne operation could be staged. But any hopes of using the VDV divisions evaporated in the summer of 1942. The costly failure of the Red Army's offensive plans at Kharkov led to a massive loss of troops and equipment. It was followed by a German offensive into southern Russia, reaching Stalingrad and the Caucasus by the autumn. Under these circumstances, the ten airborne divisions and five separate airborne brigades were converted into Guards rifle divisions to help make up for the heavy summer losses. The fact that not a single division, or even brigade, was kept in reserve for continued airborne training and development was an indication of the desperation of the Red Army for manpower, as well as the skepticism attending the airborne concept among the Red Army leaders.

The value of these units was too precious to waste. The former VDV divisions had won a hard-earned reputation for tenacity and bravery. During the Stalingrad battle in the autumn of 1942, the 37th Guards Rifle Division suffered 90 percent casualties while defending the Barrikady and Stalingrad tractor factories in the center of the city; the neighboring Red October Plant was stalwartly defended by the 39th Guards Rifle Division. The 13th Guards Rifle Division also figured heavily in the critical fighting in Stalingrad.

Reorganization of the VDV Corps, Summer 1943

1st Guards Airborne Corps	37th Guards Rifle Division
2nd Guards Airborne Corps	32nd Guards Rifle Division
3rd Guards Airborne Corps	33rd Guards Rifle Division
4th Guards Airborne Corps	38th Guards Rifle Division
5th Guards Airborne Corps	39th Guards Rifle Division
6th Guards Airborne Corps	40th Guards Rifle Division
7th Guards Airborne Corps	34th Guards Rifle Division
8th Guards Airborne Corps	35th Guards Rifle Division
9th Guards Airborne Corps	36th Guards Rifle Division
10th Guards Airborne Corps	41st Guards Rifle Division
1st Airborne Brigade	5th Rifle Brigade
2nd Airborne Brigade	6th Rifle Brigade
3rd Airborne Brigade	7th Rifle Brigade
4th Airborne Brigade	8th Rifle Brigade
5th Airborne Brigade	9th Rifle Brigade
4th Reserve Airborne Brigade	10th Rifle Brigade

THE PARTISAN ALTERNATIVE

The Vyazma operation had highlighted a new phenomenon in Red Army tactics in World War II—the extensive use of partisan forces alongside regular army formations. Partisan forces were not new to the Soviet way of war; indeed they had been a characteristic of the early Red Army during the years of civil war in 1917–21. Under Stalin, however, the partisan tradition withered. Stalin was uneasy about the partisan concept, with its heavy emphasis on spontaneous uprisings and decentralized control. Partisan movements contained the seed of possible insurrections against Soviet control, and this would not be tolerated.

The 1941 debacle in the western Soviet Union had left tens of thousands of Red Army soldiers behind German lines. Rather than surrender to the Germans, these young men simply blended into the local population. These ex-soldiers represented a potential pool of recruits for partisan forces. Early attempts in the summer and fall of 1941 to form partisan bands relied primarily on Communist Party stalwarts and government officials, due to Stalin's concerns about the loyalty of local warlords. These groups were not militarily successful. As German occupation policy became more brutal, the incentive for spontaneously forming partisan groups increased. Many partisan units were spearheaded by former Red Army officers and enlisted men without any contacts with Moscow. Red Army policy began to change, viewing partisan units as useful adjuncts to the regular Red Army.

From the outset, Red Army leaders were well aware of the shortcomings of partisan forces. The units lacked the usual level of military discipline, and they could not be expected to carry out orders with the immediacy of regular formations. As was typical of irregular forces, their training and tactics were not up to the standards of the regular military. This had been evident in the Vyazma operation. The 6,000-man partisan detachments north of the 4th Airborne Corps were destroyed in only a single day of fighting when the Germans launched Operation Hannover, and nearly 2,000 partisans were slaughtered in the initial skirmishes. In contrast, the better-trained and better-led paratroopers, although poorly equipped and weakened by constant fighting, remained a cohesive fighting force and managed to withdraw in order.

Yet the partisan forces had significant strengths. Their use was not a costly option for the Red Army. This was of no small concern in 1942, when resources were still stretched thin. The partisans could partly arm themselves from caches of weapons hidden after the 1941 disasters. They could live off the land, and they would require only modest levels of supplies, including such specialized items as radios, explosives, and ammunition. Even if not as effective as regular troops, the partisans could use ambushes and sabotage to wreak havoc in German rear areas and tie down significant numbers of German troops on security duties. The Germans would have to waste precious manpower guarding every major rail junction, supply depot, headquarters, and army facility and would have to form special antipartisan groups to combat this menace. With improved leadership and training, partisan formations might accomplish many of the same missions as airborne forces. Prior to a major Red Army offensive, they could seize important lines of communication, harass the German defenders, and destroy key installations.

Stalin gradually changed his opinion about the value of partisan forces for political as well as military reasons. Large segments of the Soviet population, especially the non-Russians, had welcomed the Germans as liberators from Communist oppression. Stalin began to realize that the partisan movement would help reassert Soviet control over occupied areas. Even if the partisans could not totally control occupied areas, their very presence would be a warning to any potential collaborators that revenge was near. The partisans served as a reminder that Soviet power would return.

The partisan movement had its dark side. Some other resistance organizations in Eastern Europe, notably Poland, had a strategic doctrine opposed to armed resistance while German control was still firm. Armed action against the Germans invariably led to savage reprisals against the local civilian population. The Polish Home Army's controversial doctrine was to wait until the German army was on the verge of collapse before initiating armed struggle, concluding that their modest military power would have far greater impact under such circumstances. The Soviet policy was exactly the opposite. Partisan activity was encouraged in spite of German reprisals. Indeed, the German reprisals served a broader Soviet objective of turning the population against the Germans. Such a policy exacted a horrible cost. Soviet civilian casualties in World War II were on the order of sixteen million dead, a significant part of which can be directly traced to the bloody partisan war in the Soviet hinterland.

The Soviet partisan movement had direct impact on the VDV Airborne Force for two reasons. The partisans could carry out some missions that otherwise would have been assigned to the airborne force, therefore weakening the Red Army's resolve to maintain specialized airborne formations. In addition, the partisan movement competed with the VDV Airborne Force for resources, at a time when resources were scarce. The Soviet partisan force in 1941 and early 1942 was an improvisation, little more than an armed rabble. What the Red Army had in mind by the summer of 1942 after Vyazma was a better-organized, better-led, better-trained, and better-equipped partisan force. This would require the dispatch of men and materiel to the occupied territories—in many cases the same type of resources that could have been used to maintain the VDV Airborne Force.

On 30 May 1942, the STAVKA formed the Central Staff for the Partisan Movement (TsShPD, or Tsentralniy Shtab Partizanskogo Dvizheniya), nominally commanded by Stalin's crony, Marshal Klimenti Voroshilov. In reality, the movement was heavily controlled by the Communist Party apparatus. Partisan activity was strongest in Byelorussia, so the chief of staff position was assigned to P. Ponomarenko, the Communist Party head of Byelorussia. Control of the partisan groups was shared by territorial staffs, under the control of the Central Staff, and local front commanders, who had special partisan warfare officers assigned to their staffs to coordinate actions. Within the partisan groups themselves, there were multiple links as well. Trained military officers began to be dispatched on a regular basis in April 1942, often accompanied by watchdogs from the NKVD special police. Some idea of the scale of the operation can be seen from the fact that 2,600 officers and specialists were sent into Byelorussia alone from April to October 1942.

For a variety of reasons, the partisan movement concentrated its efforts on the wooded areas west of Moscow and in Byelorussia. To begin with, this area was strategically important since it was the rear area of the Wehrmacht's Army Group Center, which still threatened Moscow itself. The partisan movement helped to tie down and weaken German forces in the area. Second, this region was far more receptive to the partisan movement than other areas, notably Ukraine and the Baltic states. The Baltic states had been under Soviet occupation for less than two years before the German invasion, and the brutality of the Soviet occupation had deeply embittered the residents. The same was true of western Ukraine and western Byelorussia, which had been seized from Poland in 1939. The Soviets never managed to create a local partisan force in western Ukraine, due to local antipathy to Soviet rule and the presence of a competing nationalist Ukrainian partisan movement, the UPA. In central Ukraine, memory of Stalin's anti-Ukrainian policies, especially the famine of the early 1930s, had created lingering resentment toward Moscow. Although the sentiment did not lead to a vigorous nationalist movement as in western Ukraine, it meant that there was little popular support for a Moscow-led partisan movement. Without active local support, Soviet attempts to form partisan groups in Ukraine withered until the victories of 1943, when it became expedient to assist the partisans.

Byelorussia was also suitable for the partisan movement for geographic reasons. The area was still heavily forested in the northern and central districts, and filled with inaccessible marshlands along the border with Ukraine to the south. The forests and swamps provided natural refuges for the partisans, whether or not the meager local populations supported them. In the exposed and open countryside of Ukraine, on the other hand, popular support was far more important to shield the partisans from the German occupation forces.

The partisan movement also flourished because of the policies of the German occupation forces. In contrast to the situation in German rear areas in Russia during World War I, where the local peasants were indifferent to the German presence, German racial policy in World War II guaranteed resentment. The Germans began by exterminating the local Jewish population, Communist Party officials, and most local community leadership in 1941–42. The Germans hoped these policies would terrorize the local population into submission. The Reich Commissariats established in the occupied territories then began to exploit the region economically, by confiscatory seizure of grain and livestock. Coming on the heels of a Soviet policy of scorched earth during the 1941 retreat, this policy left the local rural population on the verge of starvation. The Germans were the target of most of the blame, and the alienation of the local peasants from the Germans ensured support for the partisans.

Nor could the Germans afford to keep the territories under control by force of arms. The Wehrmacht was simply spread too thin by the vastness of the Soviet Union. For example, in central Byelorussia at the end of 1941, the German 707th Infantry Division guarded an area of 31,000 square miles, much of it heavily forested. The Germans introduced restrictions on movement by the local population and nighttime curfews in an attempt to gain some measure of control, which only served to further embitter the peasants. The Germans had lost "the hearts and minds" of the population in the northern Soviet Union by the spring of 1942, making the area ripe for partisan expansion. The Germans attempted to counteract the weakness of their security forces by escalating the harshness of their occupation policy. A directive issued before the outbreak of the war made it clear that "troops [will] take ruthless action themselves against any threat from the enemy population." The war between the German occupation forces and Soviet partisans was punctuated by frequent atrocities on both sides, with the civilian population bearing the brunt of the casualties due to the harsh German reprisal policies.

Military support of the partisan movement in the immediate vicinity of the front lines was fairly simple. Most of the men and much of the equipment could be slipped through gaps in the German lines on foot. Alternately, men and light equipment could be flown short distances using the ubiquitous U-2 biplane. The U-2, and similar aircraft such as the larger Polikarpov R-5 biplane, became a hallmark of the partisan effort. The U-2 (later called the Po-2 after its designer, Nikolai Polikarpov) was the standard means of supporting partisan movements located within a hundred miles of the front line. More than 12,000 U-2s had been built since 1929, and more than 14,000 of these inexpensive little aircraft were produced during the war years. The U-2 was a twin-seat design, with the pilot and passenger sitting in open cabins; on short hops, additional passengers and supplies could be crammed in. The airplane was affectionately called the *kukuruzhnik* (little cornhusker) by the partisans. During the war years, several ingenious improvisations were developed. Special containers were designed to enable the U-2 to carry stretcher cases. This became the main way of transporting wounded from the partisan areas. During 1942–43, there was an average of 150 flights every night into Byelorussia alone, increasing to as many as 900 nightly in 1944 prior to the Soviet offensive there. Up to the end of 1942, the GVF and other air force units flew 58,000 sorties in support of the partisan movement, including 4,645 involving landings behind German lines, mainly by the little U-2 biplanes. These flights delivered 6,400 tons of arms, ammunition, and supplies.

Many of the young officers and soldiers who would have formed the core of the VDV Airborne Force in 1942 were dispatched instead to lead the partisan movement. The new OMSBON (separate special

operations motor rifle brigade), not the VDV, became the new magnet for adventurous young volunteers. The OMSBON was used to
prepare Red Army troops for service in the partisan movement. After
special training, troops from this cadre were airlifted into occupied
territory and eventually used to form the core of about 200 partisan
units. These troops were parachuted into some areas, or airlanded in
regions where the partisans were able to hack improvised airstrips
out of the forest. There was a constant stream of personnel from the
"Great Land," as Soviet territory was dubbed, into the occupied
provinces via U-2s and larger transports. Besides officers and NCOs
sent to lead the partisans, many specialists were also used, especially
training officers and radio operators.

In addition to supporting the partisan movement, the flights also
served to carry tactical and strategic reconnaissance teams. These
razvedchiki, or scouts, were the forerunners of the modern Spetsnaz
troops. U-2s delivered the *razvedchiki* on tactical assignments, whereas
Li-2 transports were used for more distant flights. These flights not
only dropped the *razvedchiki* into Soviet territory but into neighboring countries as well. Soviet scout teams were dropped into Poland
in 1942 and 1943 to report on German train movements and collect
other forms of intelligence. On occasion these groups were airdropped
to carry out specific raiding missions, such as the demolition of
key bridges.

The PS-84 transports were also needed for supporting partisan
movements in Byelorussian districts too far to be reached by the
small U-2 biplanes. The extensive diversion of the transport fleet to
support the partisans was another factor undermining the training
and employment of airborne forces in 1942 and 1943. Take, for example, the 10th Guards Transport Division, formed on the basis of
the Moscow Special Aviation Group, which had carried the VDV
into battle at Vyazma in 1942. This single unit delivered 340,000
troops to the partisans during the course of the war, along with
52,000 tons of equipment, and evacuated 44,000 wounded partisans.

THE DEVELOPMENT OF AIRLIFT IN 1942

Air transport was still given a relatively low priority by the Soviet
Union in 1942. The dislocation of the aviation factories around Moscow in the autumn of 1941 had led to a temporary shortage of com-

bat aircraft in the spring of 1942. As a result, production priorities focused on the essential needs of the Red Air Force, namely fighters, ground attack aircraft, and bombers. Transport aircraft, such as the PS-84 airliner, were assigned to marginal aviation plants such as the one in Tashkent and given low priority for crucial subcomponents such as engines. Some measure of the low priority of the PS-84 transport (called Li-2 after September 1942) is evident from the fact that only 2,362 of these were built from 1940 to 1945. In contrast, the United States manufactured 10,349 C-47s as well as many other transport aircraft, and Germany manufactured more than 4,850 Ju-52s.

Through the early part of 1942, transport aviation was in the hands of the Civil Air Fleet (GVF). There were no transport regiments in the Red Air Force, although on occasion some bomber regiments were committed to this mission in an improvised fashion. The GVF was organized into regional or functional operational groups and was subordinated to the military in 1941. The most important of these groups was the Moscow Special Operations Aviation Group (MAON), formed in late 1941 around several regiments of the PS-84 airliner, the best transport aircraft in Soviet service. It was MAON that provided most of the airlift for the 4th Airborne Corps in the 1942 Vyazma operation. Other major formations included the Special Liaison Aviation Group (responsible for the transport of high government officials), Northern Aviation Group, Kiev Aviation Group, and North Caucasian Aviation Group. In 1942, the possibility of conducting airborne operations hinged on the availability of these groups. From October 1941 through December 1942, airborne operations were not really practical, since most of the resources of the GVF were committed to the Leningrad area, where the transports were used to evacuate key government personnel and equipment. The difficulties in conducting airborne operations in the Moscow area in January 1942 were largely due to the delays in transferring aircraft from the Leningrad operation back to the capital. Even if the entire PS-84 force had been committed to the VDV airborne operations, this probably would have amounted to no more than a hundred PS-84 aircraft, which could carry only twenty paratroopers per aircraft at maximum loading.

With the shift in Soviet policy toward the partisan movement in May 1942, the resources of the GVF were shifted accordingly. The resources of the aviation groups were reorganized, and two GVF divisions were formed specifically to support the partisan movement. These were subordinated to the STAVKA but directed by the Central Partisan Staff. During the war years, these units flew 40,000 missions behind the lines in support of the partisan movement, not including the many missions flown by air force U-2 biplanes. As previously stated, the heavy diversion of resources to support the partisans was a major factor in limiting the role of the VDV Airborne Force in 1942–43. The few transport aircraft available, the PS-84s and Li-2s, were tied down with partisan supply missions, making airborne training difficult. Preparation of the VDV Airborne Force ceased for all intents and purposes. In addition, other missions intervened, which further strained the limited air transport resources. For example, during the Stalingrad battles in the autumn of 1942, a large portion of the GVF transport fleet had to be transferred to this theater for support missions. From August 1942 to February 1943, the GVF flew 46,000 transport sorties carrying 30,000 troops and 2,587 tons of vital cargo into the Stalingrad area. Following the Stalingrad airlift, many of the aircraft reverted back to the partisan support missions. In 1943, some 12,000 sorties were flown by transport aircraft of the GVF and Soviet ADD (Aviatsiya Dalnogo Deistviya) strategic bomber force to supply the partisan movement.

By Soviet standards, the Stalingrad airlift was an operation of heroic proportions, pushing men and machines to the limits of endurance. But the scale of the Stalingrad air transport operation also highlights the continued weakness of Soviet aviation as late as 1943. At the same time and with equally heroic effort, the Luftwaffe was able to airlift 6,591 tons of supplies into the encircled 6th Army at Stalingrad and evacuate 24,910 wounded. This was about double the scale of the Soviet operation, made possible by the larger Luftwaffe transport fleet, based around the old but reliable Junkers Ju-52. The German transport force numbered about 750 Ju-52s at the time, whereas the Soviet transport fleet could count on less than 300 Li-2s plus an assortment of impressed bombers.

Soviet airlift was modestly aided by Lend-Lease aircraft. In January 1943, the United States began providing the first of 708 C-47 transport aircraft allotted through Lend-Lease during the war. In view of the shortcomings that the inexperienced GVF civil pilots had displayed during the Vyazma operation, the Red Air Force decided to absorb these new aircraft directly into its own units. The C-47s, as well as new Soviet-produced Li-2s, were used to replace the worn-out TB-3 bombers in the 5th, 6th, and 7th Long Range Aviation Corps of the ADD strategic bomber force. As more transport aircraft became available, they were eventually provided to other special operations units, including the 1st Long Range Bomber Division.

The Red Air Force decision to subordinate the new transport units to the ADD strategic bomber force had mixed results. On one hand, it ensured a steady stream of combat-experienced aircrews for the growing transport fleet. On the other hand, the ADD was preoccupied with the bomber mission. C-47s and Li-2s began sprouting bomb shackles under their wings, and the precious transports were frequently diverted from their intended airlift role to supplement the Red Air Force's already substantial bomber force. Moreover, there was little effort made to develop specialized air-dropping skills such as formation flying, glider tugging, or precision airdrop navigation. In 1944, the growing transport fleet allowed the ADD to form several special long-range units to support the airdrop of *razvedchik* detachments behind German lines in occupied Poland, Czechoslovakia, and even in Germany itself. These included the 8th, 44th, 62nd, and 87th Transport Aviation Regiments and the 5th Special Operations Squadron. By the end of the war, the ADD air transport regiments deployed about 800 Li-2 and 600 Lend-Lease C-47 transports.

THE GLIDER ALTERNATIVE

The commitment of the small Soviet transport force to missions other than the VDV airborne role put real limits on the possibilities of airborne operations through the summer of 1943. Nevertheless, the potential of the airborne force was not helped by the failure of the VDV staff to press for other alternatives, namely assault gliders. This is all the more ironic considering that the VDV had been the world's first airborne force to extensively experiment with gliders in the 1930s and the first to consider gliders to be an essential element in its doctrine.

During World War II, assault gliders were a central element in the airborne forces of all the major combatants except the Soviet VDV. The German airborne attack on the key Eban Emael fortifications in

Belgium in 1940 was conducted by gliders, not paratroopers. The German invasion of Crete involved the use of 74 gliders and about 450 glider troops in the initial waves, supporting the main paratrooper and airlanding forces. Anglo-American airborne units were the most avid practitioners of glider attack, some 144 gliders being used at Sicily in 1943, 490 during the airborne landings preceding the Normandy invasion in 1944, and nearly 2,600 gliders during Operation Market Garden in the Netherlands later in 1944—the largest airborne operation of the war.

Gliders were a viable alternative for the VDV in place of transport aircraft for several reasons. Gliders did not require transport aircraft as tugs. They could be towed aloft by bombers, which were available in far greater numbers than transport aircraft. At the beginning of 1942, the Soviet bomber force stood at 3,700 aircraft (about ten times the size of the transport fleet) and at the beginning of 1943 had risen to 5,300 due to the spectacular recovery of the Soviet aviation industry. These aircraft were mainly Pe-2 light bombers, IL-4 medium bombers, and small numbers of Lend-Lease aircraft. An IL-4 medium bomber could not carry a significant number of paratroopers due to its specialized internal layout, but it could easily tow a KTs-20 glider that contained twenty troops, the same payload as a Li-2 transport. Gliders were also an economically viable alternative since they were not very demanding from an industrial standpoint. Constructed of wood and fabric, they could be built in wood-working plants or airliner repair facilities and so did not detract substantially from the rest of the aviation industry.

The story of the Soviet glider force is largely one of missed opportunities. As mentioned earlier, experiments had been conducted with gliders in the early 1930s, though there was never any series production. Soviet glider design tended toward the fanciful and futuristic, such as Grokhovskiy's G-31 and Rafaelyantsa's "Flying Tank." There were also some practical designs, such as Groshev's GN⁰.4 from 1934, but these were unfairly ignored. The purges put an end to assault glider experimentation, and Grokhovskiy's institute, which had been at the center of airborne equipment design, was closed.

The revival of assault gliders came as a fluke. In 1939, the editor of the Osoaviakhim aviation journal proposed a design contest for a five-place glider. Osoaviakhim was a government organization aimed

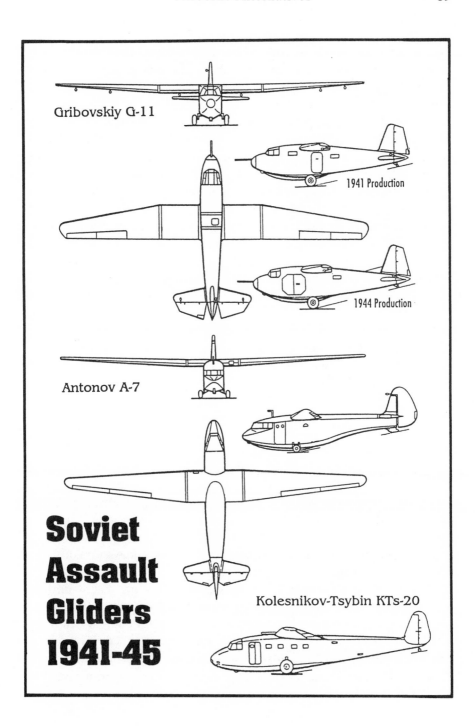

Gribovskiy G-11

1941 Production

1944 Production

Antonov A-7

Soviet Assault Gliders 1941-45

Kolesnikov-Tsybin KTs-20

at encouraging sports—sailplaning, parachuting, and car racing—
among Soviet teenagers to build up skills that would be useful to the
military when these young people were drafted. Most paratroopers of
the early Soviet airborne units were recruited via their membership
in Osoaviakhim-sponsored skydiving clubs. Likewise, Osoaviakhim
had an active sailplaning program to provide rudimentary flying
training for future Red Air Force candidates. Two talented young
designers, Oleg Antonov and V. K. Gribovskiy, who had designed
many sailplanes for the Osoaviakhim clubs, were among the entrants
in the competition. In 1940, shortly after the Germans had used
DFS.230 gliders during their stunning airborne raid on Eban Emael,
the design contest came to the attention of the head of the Red Air
Force, Ya. V. Smushkevich. Smushkevich expressed interest in an air
force examination of the winning contenders and spoke to Osoaviakhim leaders about changing the requirement to eleven seats. This
was based on the German DFS.230 glider, which had ten seats. One
of the clear favorites among the entrants was Antonov's RF-8, an
elegant wood and fabric design with good handling qualities. Nothing much came of the competition, however, due to the outbreak of
the war in June 1941.

In the months prior to the war, the VDV was substantially reorganized, as described earlier. This revived interest in assault gliders,
although little could be accomplished in the few months before the
German invasion. One glider prototype was ready when war broke
out—a seventeen-man assault glider created by a Polikarpov design
team. (The well-known aviation designer Nikolai Polikarpov had
designed most of the Soviet Union's fighters in the 1930s, but he had
fallen out of favor during the purges.) The design employed sophisticated aerodynamic refinements typical of fighter construction, which
would have made the glider expensive to produce. As a result, the
program was eventually shelved.

The VDV was looking for a rudimentary design that would be
cheap and easy to produce by factories not familiar with conventional aviation construction. On 7 July 1941, the People's Commis-
sariat for Aircraft Production (NKAP) ordered V. K. Gribovskiy at
the OKB-28 design bureau to devise a simple eleven-seat assault
glider, based on Smushkevich's recommendations from a year before. Gribovskiy was told that the design was needed as quickly as

possible. The drawings for the Gr-29 glider were hurriedly finished in three days, and a prototype was ready on 25 August 1941. It was sent to the Red Air Force test field at Ramenskoye, near Moscow, where it was test-flown along with Oleg Antonov's RF-8, one of the contenders in the 1940 Osoaviakhim contest. Both designs were judged acceptable with certain modifications. Antonov's glider was too small, and he was ordered to increase the seating from five to seven; Gribovskiy was told to incorporate several refinements in his design. On 18 September, Gribovskiy's glider, now called the G-11, was ordered into production at two former wood-processing plants in Shumerle and Kozlovka (Chuvash ASSR); the first ten G-11 gliders were turned over on 7 December 1941. These were the first mass-produced assault gliders in Soviet service.

Series production of the Antonov glider was delayed by the turmoil in the Soviet aviation industry brought about by the unexpectedly rapid German advance on Moscow. Production was scheduled to begin at a small Tushino plant and at the GVF airliner repair facility at Bykovo, both in the Moscow suburbs; at the end of 1941, these facilities were evacuated to Tyumen before any manufacture could start. Production of the Antonov glider, named the A-7 in Red Air Force service, later took place in a factory in Alopayevskiy (Sverdlovsk oblast) as well.

A third, medium glider design was added to the VDV wish list after the trials of the A-7 and G-11. The VDV wanted a larger glider, with twenty seats, which would more efficiently use the power of larger tugs such as the IL-4 medium bomber. A prototype of this glider, called the KTs after its designers, D. N. Kolesnikov and P. V. Tsybin, was built at the Bykovo factory, where series A-7 production was being undertaken. The first prototype was completed in October 1941 but crashed during trials. After improvements, there were plans to start production at a furniture factory in Ryazan, but these were upset by the Moscow evacuations. After long delays, production began at an evacuated factory at Lopatino, near Kazan, in the summer of 1943. The service designation for this type was KTs-20; it would prove to be the most troubled of the three designs produced during the war.

The delivery of the first Soviet assault gliders prompted the VDV to form the Saratov Military Aviation Glider School (SVAPSh) near the training area where many of the new airborne corps were being organized. The first fifteen glider pilots began training in May 1942. As glider pilots became available, two VDV glider regiments were formed, the 1st and 2nd Glider Regiments; a third was added later in 1943.

The glider effort might have revived the fortunes of the VDV by providing another, more accessible means of airborne landing, not subject to the usual bottleneck of Soviet transport aviation. Instead, the program became sidelined by the aviation production ministry, which assigned the manufacturing to wood-processing plants, furniture shops, and abandoned factories with no aviation production experience. As a result, the production rate was glacially slow. Many of the early gliders suffered from excessive weight problems and inadequate workmanship, which led to several crashes. It is not clear why the VDV did not put more pressure on the aviation production ministry to speed up glider manufacture, whether through a lack of attention by the VDV command, or sheer incompetence. But during the entire war, only about 50 KTs-20, 400 A-7, and 500 G-11 gliders were built—enough for only one large airborne operation.

To add insult to injury, the VDV glider regiments were gradually bled of their equipment and trained pilots to support the partisan movement or other adventures. The first glider operation was one of the most unusual. In November 1942, at the height of the Stalingrad battle, several Soviet tank brigades were sidelined due to a lack of antifreeze solution for their radiators. After forward deploying from Saratov to Voronezh, the VDV glider force was assigned to carry antifreeze to the tank units from 12 to 16 November. This permitted these tank units to take part in the major Soviet counteroffensive that trapped the German 6th Army in Stalingrad.

The majority of the gliders were expended in support of the partisan movement. The first mission took place in the summer of 1942 when a small group of gliders was landed in the forests outside Bryansk to assist a partisan group under Col. A. F. Kazankin.* There were insufficient trained glider pilots, so the mission was headed by

*Kazankin had led the 4th Airborne Corps during the Vyazma airborne operation earlier in the year.

S. N. Anokhin, the famous Russian test pilot. The glider pilots often remained behind and became part of the partisan group, though key individuals such as Anokhin were usually flown out by aircraft to lead later missions. Anokhin flew several of these partisan support missions, becoming a legend among the glider pilots for his actions, and eventually being decorated with the highest Soviet distinction, the Hero of the Soviet Union award. The Bryansk mission was one of the few glider operations conducted on Russian soil; most would take place in Byelorussia.

In the spring of 1943, a new organization, headed by P. V. Tsybin, one of the designers of the KTs-20 assault glider, was set up to coordinate air supply to the partisans. A forward staging base was established at Andreapol air base, northwest of Moscow, where supplies and aircraft were concentrated. The first large-scale glider operation took place in March 1943 when thirty-five A-7 and thirty G-11 gliders were landed behind German lines in support of Capt. I. Titkov's Zhelezniak (ironman) partisan brigade near Staraya Tropa in Byelorussia. They brought in 150 demolition specialists, 109 command staff, and 60 tons of supplies including 10 radios and 2 million rubles. By May 1943, a total of 100 gliders were flown in to support this brigade. Most other missions were not so large in scale, usually involving only a few gliders.

The next mass glider operation was conducted in the area of Selavshchyna in Byelorussia in April 1943, totaling some 138 glider flights. This operation brought in 215 tons of supplies as well as 472 troops and partisan leaders. On 4–5 May 1943, a total of 39 A-7 and G-11 gliders of the 2nd Glider Regiment were flown into the Begoml area of Byelorussia. The first wave of 18 gliders contained 119 troops and 2.4 tons of supplies. Smaller groups made even more distant journeys, including a flight by more than 20 G-11 gliders to aid a Soviet partisan group in Latvia. Usually, the flights were conducted at night to avoid German fighters. Nevertheless, the Germans did manage to shoot down at least one SB bomber tug and its A-7 glider during operations near Vitebsk in March 1943. The missions continued through the winter of 1943–44, mainly from the 1st Glider Regiment base at Teykovo and the 2nd Glider Regiment base at Kirshach, and directed toward Byelorussia via the Andreapol staging base.

THE VDV REBORN?

The STAVKA could not resist the idea of airborne operations, especially in late 1942 when it appeared that it would be going over to the offensive after the Stalingrad battles. Eight new airborne corps were formed, only to be reorganized yet again into ten airborne divisions in December 1942. In contrast to the earlier 1942 airborne corps, these new units were actually given some training. Russian accounts suggest that most of the new airborne troops conducted six to ten training jumps, though it is not clear if this was from a tower or actual jumps from aircraft.

These divisions suffered the fate so typical of the VDV during the war. In February 1943, all ten divisions were transported by rail to the Northwestern Front, where they were committed to action in the battles at Staraya Russa and Demyansk. In the spring, after these battles, they were transferred southward. Seven divisions were assigned to the Central Front in the Kursk bulge, and three were assigned to the Kharkov area. Two of the divisions—the 4th and 9th Guards—especially distinguished themselves in the massive tank battles at Kursk in July 1943. The 4th Guards Airborne Division held the town of Ponyri against German tank attack, the high-water mark of the German assault on the northeastern shoulder of the bulge. The 9th Guards Airborne Division was dug in along the approaches to the town of Prokhorovka and faced the final attacks of the German 4th Panzer Army, the high-water mark for the Germans on the south side of the Kursk salient. Yet in all these battles, the paratroopers fought as ordinary infantry. None of the ten VDV airborne divisions would be used in a major airborne mission for the duration of the war.

In the spring of 1943, as the existing airborne divisions were being shipped to Kursk, STAVKA made yet another attempt to create a VDV reserve force. Starting in April and May 1943, twenty new airborne brigades were formed and began to train for paratroop operations that were expected to follow the summer campaign around Kursk. Three brigades from this new levy would serve in the last major Soviet airborne operation of World War II and the last recorded Soviet combat parachute jump in history.

Chapter 5
A Bridge Too Few

On the chilly, damp evening of 24 September 1943, German Sd.Kfz.251 armored half-tracks sloshed forward on a wet and muddy Ukrainian road leading to the town of Dubari. *Panzergrenadiers* huddled inside the hard steel shells trying to catch some fitful sleep before arriving at their next combat assignment. The weary troops were the advance guard of the 73rd Panzergrenadier Regiment, 19th Panzer Division, and they had been on the move since midnight of the previous day. Their division was one of the lucky ones. They had crossed the Dnepr River near the Ukrainian capital of Kiev the day before, with Russian tanks fast on their heels. Other German divisions had not been so lucky and had been encircled or smashed by the rampaging Red Army offensive. The 19th Panzer Division was given no time to regroup or refit before being sent on another emergency assignment. Their objective was to relieve the division's reconnaissance battalion, stationed along the Dnepr River, which had been trying to hold back small Soviet bridgeheads there for nearly two days. The entire division was being sent to the area to make certain that the small bridgeheads didn't grow into major encroachments of the new German defensive line.

The half-track battalion arrived in Dubari at dusk, followed by the rest of the regiment in trucks. Strung out along the road from Kiev to the north was the remainder of the division, with the Panther and Pz.Kpfw.IV tanks of the 19th Panzer Regiment close behind the *Panzergrenadiers*. The infantry barely had time to light up the fires on their field kitchens for a late supper when, around 19:30, they heard the sound of aircraft engines coming from the east. The division's mobile flak unit, equipped with quadruple 20mm Flak 38 autocannons mounted on brawny Sd.Kfz.7 half-tracks, rushed to get its weapons ready. The evening sky was gloomy and overcast, with the sodden cloud cover drooping down to 2,500 feet. Instead of the expected bombers, the aircraft were lumbering transport planes. The lead aircraft was a Soviet twin-engine Lisunov Li-2 transport, flying at about 2,000 feet. The Germans were astonished to see a string of paratroopers leaping out of the aircraft, their white parachutes catching the fading light of the setting sun.

The parachute jump was unusually high due to the inexperience of the Soviet pilots. It gave the Germans ample time to prepare a hot arrival for the hapless paratroopers. The 20mm autocannons opened fire first, aiming at the transport aircraft, and then at the paratroopers once the plane had escaped. The roar of the 20mm flak guns drowned out the sounds of the many smaller weapons that had joined the bloody fray—7.62mm MG-42 machine guns from the half-tracks and tanks, and the rifles and submachine guns of the German infantrymen. The tracers from the 20mm autocannon and signal flares helped illuminate the paratroopers in the darkening sky. Several half-tracks raced forward into the neighboring fields to attack the helpless paratroopers as they landed. Within moments, a second Li-2 transport appeared and spilled out its cargo, dropping the paratroopers to their certain deaths. Not until the fourteenth or fifteenth transport aircraft did the pilots finally realize what was happening below and begin to veer away from the bloody drop zones.

So began the last major Soviet airborne operation of World War II, which even by the standards of the botched 1942 Vyazma operation was a tragic fiasco. Unlike the Vyazma operation, undertaken in the most desperate of circumstances, the Dnepr bridgehead mission had been thoroughly planned as part of an audacious river crossing. But the execution was hopelessly flawed.

THE DNEPR BRIDGEHEADS

By the early autumn of 1943, the Wehrmacht was on retreat along most of the Eastern Front. The German summer offensive, Operation

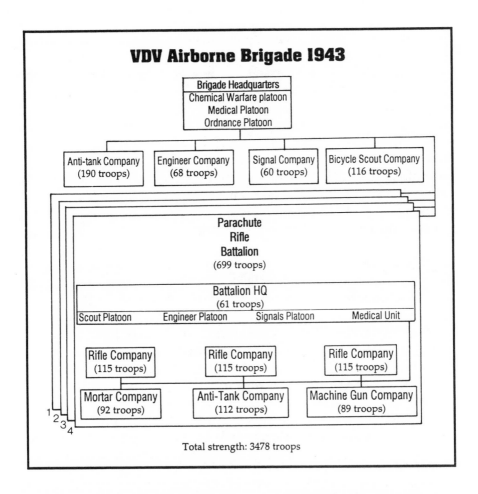

VDV Airborne Brigade 1943

Brigade Headquarters
Chemical Warfare platoon
Medical Platoon
Ordnance Platoon

| Anti-tank Company (190 troops) | Engineer Company (68 troops) | Signal Company (60 troops) | Bicycle Scout Company (116 troops) |

Parachute
Rifle
Battalion
(699 troops)

Battalion HQ
(61 troops)

Scout Platoon   Engineer Platoon   Signals Platoon   Medical Unit

| Rifle Company (115 troops) | Rifle Company (115 troops) | Rifle Company (115 troops) |
| Mortar Company (92 troops) | Anti-Tank Company (112 troops) | Machine Gun Company (89 troops) |

1 2 3 4

Total strength: 3478 troops

Citadel, in the Kursk-Orel salient, had been decisively routed in a titanic series of tank battles often called "the death ride of the panzer force." The Red Army responded with a massive counteroffensive in Ukraine, spearheaded by its tank forces. Kharkov had already fallen, and the Red Army was racing toward the Dnepr River. Hitler forbade the Wehrmacht to prepare fixed field fortifications for fear of encouraging retreat, so the German High Command held out hope that the Dnepr could serve as a natural defensive line to stem the Red Army's advance. It was a natural choice. In the area north of Kiev, the river widens to form a broad lake, called the Kiev reservoir. South of

Kiev, the river is wide and not fordable, and eventually widens again southeast of Kanev into another lake, called the Kremenchug reservoir. The area between Kiev and Kanev was the most likely location for a Soviet attempt to leap this formidable natural barrier since it was the only stretch narrow enough to bridge.

By the end of the summer, the German situation on the eastern side of the Dnepr had become desperate, and on 15 September, the German High Command ordered all units to withdraw to the western side of the river. The Soviet Voronezh Front, commanded by General of the Army N. F. Vatutin, was racing for the river at a rate of nearly sixty miles a day. Substantial German forces were still on the east bank of the Dnepr, notably the 24th Panzer Corps, strung out along the eastern shore of Kremenchug Lake in the area opposite Kanev to Cherkassy. On the morning of 22 September, a company of Soviet infantry from the 51st Tank Brigade made its way across the Dnepr, largely unopposed, and established a small bridgehead in the Bukrin River bend.

The Bukrin River bend area, known as the Velikiy Bukrin bend in Russian, was a natural point for a Soviet bridgehead. The Dnepr River makes a sudden turn to the east during its course southward, forming an eastward-pointed bulge of land. Not only was it the nearest possible river-crossing point, but the area was weakly held, forming a junction between the German 8th Army to the north of Bukrin on the west bank of the Dnepr, and the 24th Panzer Corps to the south of Bukrin, still on the east side of the Dnepr. To further complicate matters for the Germans, the Red Army was pressing tank attacks against the main river bridge at Kanev, trying to isolate the 24th Panzer Corps on the east bank of the Dnepr by cutting their main escape route over the river. The first attempt by the Soviet 6th Guards Tank Corps was halted when it ran into a 75mm PaK 40 antitank gun supporting the 253rd Grenadier Regiment, 34th Infantry Division, and two self-propelled antitank guns of Panzerjaeger Battalion 34 near Reshetki.

Vatutin's plan was bold and ambitious. Without halting to bring up reinforcements or heavy pontoon bridging equipment, the Voronezh Front would attempt to secure bridgeheads over the Dnepr from the march before the Germans could consolidate their defenses. Vatutin was gambling that small groups of infantry could get across by improvised means. If they could gain footholds on the opposite bank, they might be able to secure bridgeheads deep enough to eventually bring up the heavy bridging equipment needed to move across tanks and mechanized equipment. The bridgehead had to be deep enough to protect the bridges from the German artillery. To obtain this needed depth, the Soviets planned an airborne drop.

PLANNING THE DNEPR AIRDROP

The conditions in the bridgehead area appeared to be ripe for an airborne operation—precisely the type of conditions that the VDV airborne doctrine had dreamed about. The enemy was in disarray, and a modest airborne force could provide crucial leverage with its unique vertical envelopment capabilities to influence the outcome of a major operation. The STAVKA had been planning since the late summer to use the VDV Airborne Force in the Dnepr river-crossing operation. The painful lessons of the Vyazma operation were not forgotten, but the STAVKA refused to give up on the airborne concept. Other new means of warfare, although difficult to implement, had proven ultimately successful. The Red Army's use of large tank formations in 1941 and 1942 had been a bloody failure; by 1943, the better-trained and more experienced armored force formed the fast-moving vanguard of the Soviet offensive. So, too, the STAVKA hoped that the VDV had applied the lessons of Vyazma and were ready for a demonstration of their new concept of warfare.

Nominally at least, in the autumn of 1943, the Red Army possessed a significant airborne force in the form of several airborne divisions. In reality, these divisions had received little or no actual airborne training and, as mentioned earlier, had been used mainly as elite infantry divisions. In August, STAVKA ordered the commander of the VDV, Maj. Gen. A. G. Kapitkokin, to begin preparing a new corps actually trained for paratrooper missions. Kapitkokin took no chances and delegated the deputy commander of the VDV, Maj. Gen. I. I. Zatevakhin, to command the new corps. As a preliminary step, Col. P. A. Goncharov's 3rd Guards Airborne Brigade (3rd GVDB) began conducting airborne training exercises in the Moscow area, including badly needed jump training. That August, the 3rd Guards Airborne Brigade along with Col. P. I. Krasovskiy's 1st Guards Airborne

Brigade and Lt. Col. P. M. Sidorchuk's 5th Guards Airborne Brigade conducted a major field exercise along the Moscow River near Ramenskoye, simulating the airborne support of a bridgehead operation. By September, about half the men had some parachute training, on average about six to ten jumps, but the late arrivals had no jumps at all beyond minimal tower training. It would have to do.

On 15 September, the German High Command ordered that remaining units on the east bank of the Dnepr withdraw to the west bank and reestablish defensive positions there. The STAVKA became aware of this instruction from signals intercept or other intelligence means, and on 16 September, the STAVKA and VDV staff put the finishing touches on operational plans for the Dnepr bridgehead operation, aimed at securing the Bukrin River bend to establish the Voronezh Front's main bridgehead over the river. The plan called for the use of Zatevakhin's airborne corps, supported by two glider regiments. The 3rd Guards Airborne Brigade would land north of Potaptsy to form the right flank of the airborne landing; 1st Guards Airborne Brigade would be in the center, to the south of Potaptsy; and, finally, 5th Guards Airborne Brigade would jump south of this to form the left flank. The drops would take place on a line about ten miles west of the Dnepr River, with the nearest landing zone—that of the 3rd Guards Airborne Brigade—about twelve miles from the planned Soviet bridgeheads in the Bukrin River bend area. The main jumps would be preceded by small pathfinder teams, which would mark the landing zones in conjunction with local partisan groups.

The Vyazma failure had shown that far more attention was needed in planning and executing the airlift phase of the airborne operation. By the autumn of 1943, the GVF Civil Air Fleet had been completely absorbed into the Red Air Force's ADD strategic bomber force, making coordination simpler. A special operational group of the ADD long-range aviation force was formed at Lebedin airfield, the main air base in support of the Voronezh Front. Lebedin was nearly 200 miles from the bridgehead area, sufficiently far away to remove the threat of German air attacks on the airfields. The planners remembered that German attacks had crippled the forward airfields during the initial stages of the Vyazma airdrop, and they were determined to avoid a repeat performance.

The basis for the special operational group was the 1st Separate Transport Aviation Division, a militarized title given to the transport branch of the GVF Civil Air Fleet after a reorganization in late 1942. The operational group was assigned 180 transport aircraft, nearly all modern PS-84s, Li-2s, and C-47s, not the lumbering and inefficient old TB-3 bombers. Ten glider tugs were also provided, mostly Ilyushin IL-4 or Lend-Lease B-25 bombers, with thirty-five A-7 and G-11 gliders. Although generous by the standards of the 1942 Vyazma missions, the airlift was still not adequate to lift all three brigades in one drop. Instead, the 1st Guards Airborne Brigade and 5th Guards Airborne Brigade would be dropped the first night in three waves, and the 3rd Guards Airborne Brigade would be dropped the second night.

The landing zone was near enough to Soviet lines that artillery support could be provided from the east bank of the Dnepr. To assist in this, Zatevakhin's airborne corps was assigned artillery spotters, and a squadron of Po-2 biplane artillery spotting aircraft was to coordinate fire support. A force of thirty-five Li-2 transports was permanently assigned to the corps for the duration of the mission to carry in needed supplies and to evacuate the wounded.

On 19 September, the main STAVKA representative, Gen. Georgiy Zhukov, reviewed the plan and approved it. But he warned the Voronezh Front commander, General Vatutin, that the plan should be updated to reflect unfolding events in the bridgehead area. The drop was then scheduled for the night of 23–24 September 1943.

THE FRICTION OF WAR

In a grim repeat of the initial stages of the Vyazma operation, transport bottlenecks began to interfere with the airdrop plans from the beginning. The three airborne brigades were transferred to the 2nd Air Army's forward air bases at Smorodino and Bogodukhov, near Lebedin, by rail rather than by aircraft due to the lack of sufficient transport aircraft. On reaching Ukraine, the trains were slowed to a snail's pace, in part because of damage inflicted on the rail lines by the retreating Germans and general congestion stemming from the Soviet offensive. It hardly mattered, as the weather also conspired against the plans. Cold rain descended on the area south of Kiev, making it impossible to move all the necessary transport aircraft to the staging bases. Only eight aircraft had arrived by the afternoon of 23 September.

General Zatevakhin, the airborne corps commander, and General Vatutin, the Voronezh Front commander, met at 40th Army headquarters to alter their plans. The airdrop had to be delayed a day due to the obvious shortfall of troops and airlift. It appeared that the 3rd Guards Airborne Brigade would arrive sooner than 1st Guards Airborne Brigade, so the plans were amended to drop 3rd Guards Airborne Brigade and 5th Guards Airborne Brigade the first night, and 1st Guards Airborne Brigade the second night. Colonel Sidorchuk's 5th Guards Airborne would land, as originally planned and briefed, in the southernmost drop zone. Colonel Goncharov's 3rd Guards Airborne would drop south of Potaptsy, in the landing zone originally planned for 1st Guards Airborne. Colonel Krasovskiy's 1st Guards Airborne would drop in a new landing zone, immediately to the east of the two other drop zones and nearer to the base of the Bukrin bend and the Dnepr River.

Vatutin and Zatevakhin planned the changes, however, without adequate intelligence on German dispositions in the drop zone. Early partisan reports that the area was unoccupied had changed dramatically as the Germans began to consolidate their defenses. The Red Army leadership was unaware of the extent of these changes due to the sudden change in the weather. The planned photographic reconnaissance flights by the 2nd Air Army never took place; the reconnaissance aircraft were grounded by the weather, or found that the cloud cover was too low for photographic passes.

Instead of landing in relatively unoccupied areas, the Soviet airborne force would be dropping into a hornets' nest. The small landing by Soviet forces in the Bukrin bend the day before had alerted the Germans to the threat and led to the dispatch of the reconnaissance battalion of the 19th Panzer Division. The small Soviet foothold had been followed by two other small bridgeheads by the evening of 23 September. The Red Army was unable to exploit their initial bridgeheads due to a lack of heavy pontoon bridges or other engineer equipment to move tanks across, but the Germans were aware that the substantial weight of the Soviet 3rd Guards Tank

Army sat on the east bank of the Dnepr, ready to race across once bridging was brought forward. To smash this bridgehead before the engineering equipment arrived, the full weight of the 19th Panzer Division would be brought to bear. The division began moving south from the Kiev area late in the evening of 23 September and was scheduled to arrive near the northern drop zone by the evening of 24 September, unbeknownst to the Soviet planners, just as the first waves of Soviet paratroopers were scheduled to land.

As if that were not enough, the 24th Panzer Corps continued to move the bulk of its forces out of the pocket on the east bank of the Dnepr and across the Kanev bridge. This exodus was moving directly into the landing zone area of the 5th Guards Airborne Brigade, five miles west of Kanev. These forces included the 10th Panzergrenadier Division and three infantry divisions. The exodus out of the east-bank pocket was completed at 05:00 on the morning of 24 September, and the Germans destroyed the Kanev bridge behind them to prevent their pursuit by Soviet tanks.

Besides these forces in the immediate landing-zone area, the SS Viking Division was moved into positions south of the 5th Guards Airborne Brigade drop zone, and the SS Das Reich Panzer Division was moving into the area south of Rzhishchev behind the 19th Panzer Division. The Germans were absolutely determined that the Red Army bridgehead at Bukrin would be smothered before it could become a serious threat.

The Soviet commanders failed to anticipate these moves. The airborne operation continued as though the Bukrin bend was lightly held. Having received Vatutin's change of plans, Zatevakhin and the VDV airborne staff at 40th Army headquarters began preparing revised assignments for the brigades on the afternoon of 23 September. The revised orders were not received by the brigade commanders until 24 September. Colonel Goncharev's brigade was the most severely affected, since the new plans meant that it would land in a new drop zone, with very different objectives. The chaos at the forward air bases at Smorodino and Bogodukhov due to the late arrival of the troop trains and aircraft meant that the battalion commanders didn't get their instructions until ninety minutes before takeoff, and company commanders received theirs fifteen minutes before takeoff, while loading the aircraft.

The airlift situation was confused. By late afternoon, only forty-eight of the planned sixty-five Li-2 transport aircraft had arrived at the 5th Guards Airborne Brigade airfield at Bogodukhov; 3rd Guards Airborne Brigade was more fortunate and had a nearly complete force at Smorodino. The Li-2 was rated at a maximum of twenty air-drop units, meaning a mixture of twenty paratroopers or light PDMM airdrop containers. Due to the weather conditions over the drop zones, the transport regiment commanders refused to load the transports to the maximum, permitting only fifteen to eighteen units per aircraft. The drop plans had been based on the presumption that each aircraft would carry twenty units, so there was a mad scramble to reassign men and equipment. This most severely impacted the distribution of radios. Due to the hasty reassignments and bad planning, many battalion commanders took off without radio teams, whereas in the 3rd Guards Airborne Brigade, the entire command group and its assigned radios were crammed onto a single aircraft along with the brigade commander, Colonel Goncharov.

For reasons that remain unclear, no pathfinder teams were dispatched in advance of the main group. Russian accounts suggest that weather interfered, but it seems more likely that it was confusion at the air bases. This was unfortunate for two reasons. Had the pathfinder teams been dropped ahead of the main waves, as originally planned, they would have discovered the critical change in German forces in the drop-zone area. Second, a pathfinder group was essential, especially in bad weather, to establish radio communication with the main air-drop wave and to mark the landing zone with flares or fires. The lack of an initial pathfinder flight was a tragic mistake and a sad reflection of the VDV's lack of experience in conducting airborne drops. It was to have tragic consequences in the hours to come.

INTO THE FIRESTORM

The 3rd Guards Airborne Brigade began taking off from Smorodino airfield at 18:30 on the evening of 24 September. The 5th Guards Airborne Brigade was scheduled to depart from the neighboring runways at Bogodukhov two hours later. The Lebedin area was nearly 200 miles from the drop zone, so the flight took nearly an hour. The

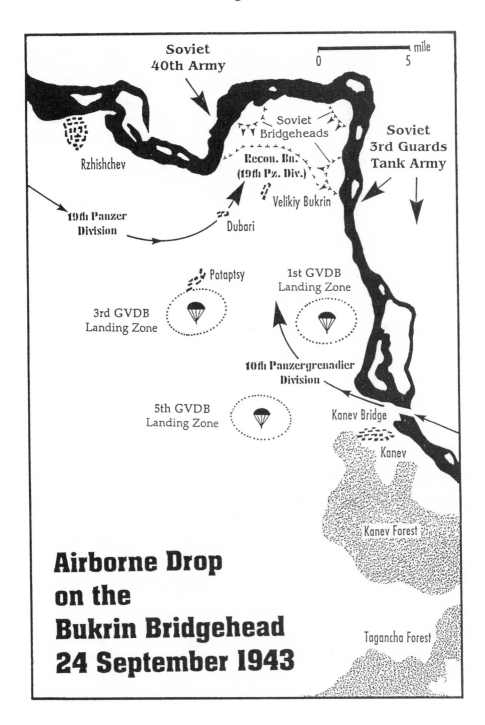

**Airborne Drop
on the
Bukrin Bridgehead
24 September 1943**

first wave of aircraft appeared over the Bukrin River bend at around 19:30. Unfortunately, the landing zone southwest of Potaptsy took the transport aircraft right over the lead elements of the 19th Panzer Division, as described earlier. The intense antiaircraft fire decimated the lead elements of the first wave and caused following aircraft to begin wild evasive maneuvers. The airdrop quickly degenerated into complete chaos.

The chief of operations of the 19th Panzer Division recalled:

> The Soviet formation was very open. The big machines arrived singly, or two at a time at most, at intervals of half a minute, and then dropped their paratroopers. This made our defense even more effective. Some of their aircraft evidently realized the disaster and wheeled back to the north. Our devastating defensive fire and the brilliant white flares that were zooming everywhere clearly unnerved the Soviets. Now they dropped their men haphazardly, all over the place. Split up into smaller and smaller groups, they were doomed. They tried to take cover in narrow ravines, but were soon winkled out; they were killed or taken prisoner.

Paratroopers were dropped all over the area north and south of Dubari in no particular pattern. Some pilots ascended to 6,000 feet to avoid the worst fire, which only meant that the paratroopers had an even longer descent, under fire all the while from German forces on the ground. The skies over Dubari and Potaptsy became a grotesque shooting gallery, with many Soviet paratroopers killed before landing. Nightfall might have shielded the paratroopers' descent, but the Germans used signal flare pistols to illuminate the area, and the white parachutes made easy targets. Nor did the paratroopers find refuge on the ground. The German infantry began moving into drop areas and attacking surviving paratroopers before they could regroup and pose a serious threat.

Units that descended away from the main drop zone did not fare any better. Several aircraft dropped paratroopers near the town of Balyka, more than ten miles north of the intended drop zone. They came down in the midst of the 10th Panzergrenadier Division, also moving into the Bukrin bridgehead. The scene at Dubari was repeated as the paratroopers were blasted by antiaircraft and machine-gun fire. The Germans were surprised to find women in the group. The Germans captured some of the brigade's medical detachment, consisting of several women doctors and medics. One of the Germans' most important finds—on a dead officer—was a set of map instructions that explained the drop pattern and missions of the operations.

The fighting was not entirely one sided. One paratrooper from the 3rd Guards Airborne Brigade landed on the onion dome of the village church in Grushevo, catching his parachute on the spire. Unable to cut himself free, he killed six German infantrymen before being killed. Private Drozdov descended toward a German field kitchen and killed several German soldiers by dropping a hand grenade. He then landed directly on top of the field kitchen, overturning it, and made his escape after snatching the Schmeisser submachine gun of a startled cook. The commander of the 3rd Guards Airborne Brigade, Col. P. A. Goncharov, managed to gather about 150 paratroopers near the village of Grushevo and establish a defensive position in nearby woods. A company from the 73rd Panzergrenadier Regiment took serious losses trying to overcome them. Soviet snipers claimed many casualties before the woods were finally overrun. Most of the paratroopers were killed in the skirmish, and Colonel Goncharov was captured.

The 3rd Guards Airborne Brigade drop in the Potaptsy area lasted about ninety minutes, at which time the transports returned to Smorodino to pick up the second wave. It is remarkable that a second wave was dropped at all after the carnage of the first wave. The pilots did not fully comprehend the severity of the situation on the ground, and the landing paratroopers were not able to establish radio links with either the aircraft or the 40th Army communications units to warn them. The later waves of aircraft were hopelessly scattered, doing little to help the chaotic situation on the ground.

The 5th Guards Airborne Brigade mission from Bogodukhov was far more disorganized than the 3rd Guards Airborne Brigade mission from Smorodino. There was a shortage of fuel trucks, and few of the aircraft were ready on schedule. Instead of taking off en masse, the aircraft began leaving the airfield in driblets starting at about 20:30. As a result, the aircraft arrived singly, in the dark, often astray due to poor night navigation training. One aircraft dropped its passengers into the middle of the Dnepr River, where they all drowned. Several dropped their load of paratroopers on the wrong side of the river, whether due to poor navigation or a sense of mercy. The 5th Guards Airborne did not run into the intense opposition encountered by the 3rd Guards Airborne, but the confusion and inexperience of the pilots and the lack of clearly marked drop zones led to the brigade being wildly scattered over the southern area of the drop zone. For example, the 5th Guards Airborne Brigade commander, Colonel Sidorchuk, landed near the edge of the Kanev forest, and first linked up with a private from the 3rd Guards Airborne who was supposed to have been dropped nearly ten miles away. Sidorchuk was not able to link up with the survivors from his brigade staff, who had been on the same aircraft, until nine days later.

The airlift of the 5th Guards Airborne Brigade out of Bogodukhov had to be halted about five hours after the initial takeoffs due to a lack of fuel. As a result, only 1,525 troops of the 5th Guards Airborne were actually dropped, compared to 3,050 from the 3rd Guards Airborne. A total of 2,017 men, mainly from the 5th Guards Airborne, were left behind at the airfields due to the cancellation of further missions in the early-morning hours of 25 September.

Aside from the massive casualties suffered in landing, the greatest problem was the radio situation. In total, twenty-nine radio teams had been dropped, including four high-power radios with the operations group of the corps headquarters. Only five low-power 12-RP radios were found after the drop. Some of the others were hidden by their operators on landing, but the locations were lost when their operators were captured or killed. Most of the other radios were not accompanied by a communications officer, who possessed the operating frequencies and codes necessary to communicate with the neighboring 40th Army or 3rd Guards Tank Army. As a result, by the morning of 25 September, no communications had been received from the drop zone. In fact, none would be received until 6 October 1943, some twelve days after the initial drop. Light Po-2 biplanes were sent to the drop zone but failed to reach the area due to German flak, or found no evidence of Soviet paratroopers when they arrived. The lack of information led General Zatevakhin to cancel any further drops into the Bukrin bridgehead.

During the Dnepr airborne operation, a total of 4,575 paratroopers and 660 supply containers were dropped in 298 sorties, instead of the planned 6,600 paratroopers in 500 sorties. At least 230 paratroopers were dropped on the wrong side of the river and joined up with Red Army forces. The Germans estimated that they killed about 700 paratroopers and captured more than 200 on the night of 24–25 September, and more during the cleanup operation that followed. The Soviet paratroopers had not been trained to bury or hide their chutes. As a result, on the morning of 25 September, German light reconnaissance aircraft quickly detected the locations of the main Soviet drops and helped to coordinate the German counterattacks against surviving groups. There were scattered Soviet attempts to ambush German convoys and carry out small-scale diversionary raids, but for all intents and purposes, the airdrop had failed completely.

Over the next few days, the scattered paratrooper units managed to form about thirty-five groups of various sizes, totaling 2,300 men—meaning that about half the force, 2,200 men, were dead or missing. About twenty groups operated in the northern area, numbering about 1,100 paratroopers, with the remainder in the south near Kanev. The largest of these groups, about 600 paratroopers from the 5th Guards Airborne Brigade, eventually formed up in the Kanev woods at the southernmost edge of the intended drop zones. The largest group, from the harrowed 3rd Guards Airborne Brigade, formed up in the woods near Chernyshi, east of Potaptsy, and eventually numbered about 200 men. The other groups were significantly smaller, seldom more than 100 men.

The immediate problem of most of the groups was to retrieve the ammunition containers. The paratroopers had dropped with only about a day's supply of ammunition and two days' supply of dry rations. Since it was expected they would link up with Soviet troops from the bridgehead the next day, equipment was kept to a minimum. They were not even issued ponchos, in spite of near-freezing nighttime temperatures, and they were not issued normal entrenching spades. Retrieval of the containers was hazardous, as some German infantry units used them as bait to attract the paratroopers into ambushes.

Lacking communications to the corps headquarters, the isolated groups began operations on their own initiative. The scattered paratroopers in the northern sector near Potaptsy were the most hard pressed. Their positions were immediately behind the main German defensive positions in the Bukrin bend, and the Germans vigorously attempted to rout them out and destroy them. After a few days of disjointed raiding efforts, most of these groups attempted to join up with the 40th Army across the Dnepr or with the 3rd Guards Tank Army in the bridgehead.

Not only did the airdrop go sour, but in the days that followed, the Soviet bridgehead operations were halted by the heavy influx of German tanks and infantry. The Red Army did manage to consolidate its three small bridgeheads into a larger, continuous bridgehead, but by the time this was accomplished, the Germans had stuffed the narrow Bukrin bend with tanks, guns, and troops. The bridging areas were within range of German artillery and were mercilessly pounded. The tanks of the 3rd Guards Tank Army were gradually brought across and, in a month of intense fighting, suffered heavy losses. Indeed, the German forces held the area so securely that when the Red Army did finally move past the Dnepr in 1944, the Bukrin bend was the last area of the river line still in German hands.

The paratrooper groups farther south near Kanev had more freedom of movement due to the lower concentration of German forces in the area. By the beginning of October, a group of about 600 coalesced around the 5th Guards Airborne Brigade commander, Colonel Sidorchuk. They were organized into a regular formation with three rifle battalions, as well as engineer, antitank rifle, reconnaissance, and communication platoons. On 6 October, they finally established voice radio contact with Soviet forces on the eastern bank of the Dnepr. But by then, their codes were useless, since new codes had been introduced. The Russian radio operators would not believe that the Soviet forces on the eastern bank were really the lost paratroopers until an officer who knew Sidorchuk had a conversation with him over the radio. Beginning on 8 October, General Zatevakhin arranged airdrops into the Kanev forest to supply Sidorchuk's forces with equipment and food.

The airdrops attracted German attention, and on 11 October, a German security unit attempted to wipe out the paratroopers. The attempt failed, but the intense pressure forced Sidorchuk's group to withdraw to the more defensible Tagancha forest farther south. The Germans made a second effort to stamp out Sidorchuk's group on 23

October, but the paratroopers managed to withstand the attack and withdraw in good order into the Cherkassy forest even farther south. Sidorchuk's force had steadily gathered scattered paratroopers during the course of its movements, finally adding a detachment of 300 men under Senior Lieutenant Tkachev on 25 October, bringing the brigade's strength up to 1,200 troops. The brigade continued to receive significant air support, and so built up its strength. Finally, in the early-morning hours of 13 November 1943, it was ordered to attack German positions from the rear while the 254th Rifle Division of the 52nd Army attempted to cross the Dnepr near Lozovko. After several days of intense fighting, the 52nd Army finally clawed a position into the western bank of the Dnepr with the invaluable assistance of Sidorchuk and his men. The survivors of the 5th Guards Airborne Brigade subsequently joined up with the 254th and 294th Rifle Divisions in expanding the bridgeheads near Cherkassy, and were finally pulled out of the line on 28 November 1943.

DNEPR POSTMORTEM

The Dnepr airborne operation had practically no beneficial consequences for the Red Army. The Wehrmacht decimated the airborne force as it was landing, and the 3rd Guards Airborne Brigade was lucky to pull even small numbers of its men out of the drop zone alive. The 5th Guards Airborne Brigade was luckier and landed in less defended areas. The stalwart actions of the brigade in a guerrilla warfare role attested to the training and determination of the paratroopers, but their conduct had little consequence during the fighting for the Dnepr bridgeheads in November.

The causes of the disaster were many. The lack of intelligence was a crucial factor in this tragedy. The failure to insist on reconnaissance flights over the drop zones was unfortunate. The weather undoubtedly was bad, but this didn't prevent the transport pilots from flying and shouldn't have prevented reconnaissance flights. Napoleon's adage that "a general never knows anything with certainty, never sees his enemy clearly, never knows positively where he is" certainly applied in this operation. But Napoleon's observation was not a stoic rationalization for failures based on intelligence shortfalls. It was a warning that, in the absence of sound intelligence, officers should have the foresight and intuition to anticipate their opponent's moves. The Soviet planners first failed in not demanding reconnaissance, then failed again to anticipate likely German reactions to the earlier Soviet footholds on the Bukrin bridgehead. To expect that the Germans would leave the Bukrin bend empty of forces for several days was naive folly. After the delays in staging the mission, the planners allowed their concerns over staging the airdrop to absorb all their attention, without pausing to reflect on whether the mission might be too late or misdirected.

Even if the Bukrin airdrop had occurred before the German tank units arrived, the combat potential of such a force must be questioned. To limit weight due to shortages of aircraft, the paratroopers were dropped without entrenching tools into terrain consisting of open fields with few villages or woods. Without proper equipment for creating defensive positions, the Soviet paratroopers were very vulnerable to German artillery, to say nothing of tank attack. In addition, the paratroopers almost entirely lacked any realistic antitank weapons. Some of the usual PTRD antitank rifles were dropped into the bridgeheads, but these became a grotesque joke when facing the thickly armored German tanks of late 1943. Even if the paratroopers had landed unopposed, they might still have been quickly wiped out due to their vulnerabilities.

The airdrop displayed cookbook tactics—a preoccupation with the prescribed doctrinal role of the airborne as a blocking force during the establishment of a bridgehead. The commander of the 24th Panzer Corps, Gen. W. K. Nehring, later observed that the airborne drop could have had far more dramatic and valuable impact if a smaller attack had been launched one or two days before against the Kanev bridge, even as late as the morning of 23 September. By seizing or destroying the bridge, the bulk of the 24th Panzer Corps would have been trapped on the eastern bank of the Dnepr, where they could have been destroyed. Nehring concluded that such an operation against the key Kanev bridge

> would have meant a really critical situation for our Corps; and not only for the Corps itself, but the whole Army . . . at that moment, a combined operation by their ground and airborne forces could have achieved their strategic objective of unhing-

ing our front on the Dnepr. Indeed, even in the early afternoon of 23 September, the sudden seizure of the bridge by a coup from the air might have been decisive.

From a technical standpoint, the airborne drop was a hopeless mess, relying on boldness and good luck instead of careful execution. The failure to dispatch a pathfinder group into the drop zone ahead of the main body was an inexcusable mistake and attested to the VDV's inexperience. The transport force, although larger than during the Vyazma airdrops, was still unprepared for such missions. Nighttime navigation skills were completely inadequate, no attention was paid to formation flying and other techniques to help ensure tight landing zones, and basic skills such as the rapid dispatch of a stick of paratroopers from the aircraft were not demonstrated. In view of the pilots' poor night navigation, the VDV planners could have considered a daylight drop, or an early-evening drop by the first wave, with the later waves dropping under the cover of darkness into drop zones already established and marked by the first wave. Preparations for the paratroopers to link up on the ground were based on the hopelessly optimistic assumption that the multiple waves of aircraft, shuttling battalions forward from Lebedin in the dark at two-hour intervals, would land the paratroopers close to one another. The provision of radios to help link up scattered groups was undermined by the lack of compact, durable radios and the unfortunate consequence imposed by excessive radio security, which kept the enlisted radio operators ignorant of necessary operating frequencies.

German commander Gen. W. K. Nehring's later assessment was to the point:

The Soviet command simply lacked the necessary sensitivity for the timing, the target area, and the possibilities for such an operation, and lacked a correct evaluation of the German forces. The whole action is marked by the stamp of dilettantism. Fundamentally, the reasoning was sound, but apparently they lacked an expert to implement the plans. Accordingly, the operation was a failure. The units were much too scattered to be rallied quickly for systematic, coordinated action. Of course, it was a lucky accident for us, and a disastrous one for the Soviets,

that three German divisions happened to be moving through the
drop zone. But even without the accident, the operation would
not have succeeded because the timing was wrong.

The STAVKA had planned a second corps-sized airborne operation later in October in the northern theater to assist the assault by
the 1st and 2nd Baltic Fronts and the Western Front in their offensive
drives toward eastern Byelorussia. Three of the independent airborne
brigades prepared in the summer were formed into an improvised
airborne corps. The mission never took place, as the offensive
bogged down with the onset of the autumn rains and the ensuing mud
and overflowing rivers.

The Bukrin debacle soured STAVKA confidence in airborne operations, much as the German airborne's Pyrrhic victory at Crete
marked the end of Hitler's tolerance for these risky ventures. STAVKA
could easily write off the Vyazma operations due to the paucity of
resources, the desperation of the moment, and the inexperience of
the new VDV leadership. These excuses were not valid for Bukrin.

Airborne operations required a commitment from both the Red
Army and Red Air Force that was lacking. The Red Air Force was
unable to dedicate an air transport division to the airborne role due
to the overwhelming demands on its small transport force, and using
ill-prepared cargo pilots for airborne missions was simply not good
enough. The Red Army's voracious appetite for troops to replace the
staggering battlefield infantry losses subverted all efforts by the
VDV to sequester and reserve a force of airborne-qualified commanders and troops for the airborne missions. The Red Army's failure with airborne forces contrasts sharply with its success in other
areas of new military technology and tactics: for example, tank operations, after the disastrous summers of 1941 and 1942, had by late
1943 become a hallmark of the Red Army. But success in conducting
joint operations, such as airborne operations, eluded Soviet commanders during World War II.

FINAL AIRBORNE MISSIONS

The last Soviet airborne operation of the war against Germany did
not involve troops of the VDV. In August 1944, the Red Army was
fast approaching the borders of Slovakia, a region of occupied

Czechoslovakia that had formed an independent state and was allied to Germany during the war. Now, however, elements of the Slovak army and Slovak political leaders decided to switch sides, forming the Slovak National Council. They informed both London and Moscow of their plans, fearing that Germany and Hungary would catch wind of the insurrection and try to occupy Slovakia. The insurrection was triggered by Slovak partisan units who captured a German military delegation and then shot them on 27 August. Besides the Slovak partisans, there was a strong Soviet partisan operation in the area, supported from the air by the advancing Red Army. The Germans responded to the deteriorating situation by dispatching the 357th Infantry Division with orders to suppress the Slovak insurgents. This forced the hand of the Slovak National Council, and by 29 August, heavy fighting had broken out between elements of the Slovak army and partisans against the Germans. The Slovak army was not entirely behind the insurgency, and the Germans had little problem disarming the Eastern Slovak Corps.

The Soviet Union decided to support the uprising, viewing it as a useful weakening of the German position in eastern Czechoslovakia. The plan was to attack into Slovakia via the key Dukla pass, using Gen. I. S. Koniev's 1st Ukrainian Front. The Red Army had already formed a 1st Czechoslovak Corps from volunteers and internees in the Soviet Union, including Colonel Prikyl's 2nd Czechoslovak Separate Airborne Brigade *(2.cs.samostatna paradesantni brigada v SSSR)*. As a first step in aiding the insurgents, the Red Air Force committed the Li-2 and C-47 transports of the 4th and 5th Aviation Corps of the ADD strategic bomber force to fly arms into the improvised Tri Duba airfield.

Koniev's attempt to breach the Dukla pass failed due to intense German resistance, and the 1st Guards Cavalry Corps (the same unit that had taken part in the 1942 Vyazma battles) found itself trapped once again after it had attempted to open a corridor through German defenses. The transport planes were diverted to supply the cavalry from the air. The STAVKA decided to try to also reinforce the Slovak insurgents from the air and, on 13 September, transferred the 1st Czechoslovak Fighter Regiment, flying Lavochkin La-5FN fighters, to Tri Duba to provide air support. On 15 September, the STAVKA gave permission to begin airlifting the 2nd Czechoslovak Airborne Brigade into Tri Duba using the 5th Aviation Corps of the ADD.

A control team of twelve Czechoslovak paratroopers with two radio sets was parachuted into Tri Duba on 17 September to prepare for the landings. The airlandings did not begin until 27 September, a company at a time; the bulk of the brigade—700 troops and 104 tons of supplies—did not arrive until the first week of October. The sight of the paratroopers was an enormous morale booster in Slovakia. By the third week of October, the 5th Aviation Corps had flown in 1,855 Czechoslovak paratroopers and 360 tons of supplies and flown out 784 wounded partisans and Slovak soldiers. Air operations late in the month were hampered by poor weather and the growing strength of the German Luftwaffe.

By late October, the German army managed to smash the uprising by a heavy infusion of brutal and experienced Waffen-SS anti-partisan units. Surviving paratroopers of the 2nd Czechoslovak Airborne Brigade were ordered to withdraw into the wilds of the nearby Carpathian Mountains, from which they continued to wage guerrilla warfare through the bitter winter ahead. This last Soviet airborne operation of the war in Europe was a typical amalgam of Soviet special operations in World War II: the combined use of airborne and partisan units linked by common air support.

As a curious side note, the Red Army conducted about twenty successful airlanding operations during the final phase of the brief war with Japan in August 1945. Following the Japanese announcement of a cease-fire on 14 August 1945, the STAVKA decided to continue to push the Red Army forward to seize key objectives in Manchuria and Korea. In many cases, infantry were loaded onto Li-2 transports and other aircraft and flown into Japanese air bases. Some of these landings were substantial in size, involving twenty aircraft and as many as five hundred troops. They did not represent true combat operations, as none was seriously opposed. But they were curious forerunners of Soviet airborne operations in the Cold War years, where unopposed airlandings by the VDV spearheaded the Soviet invasions of Hungary in 1956, Czechoslovakia in 1968, and Afghanistan in 1979.

Chapter 6
A Cheap Gamble

W hy didn't the Soviet Union abandon airborne forces after World War II? Certainly, the Soviet experience with its paratrooper forces during the war was extremely disheartening. Yet the same might be said of many other branches of the Soviet armed forces: Soviet strategic bombers, submarines, and warships had equally impoverished war records. The Soviet General Staff began to examine the lessons of the war—not only Soviet experiences but those of other combatants.

Several considerations helped preserve the airborne force in the Soviet order of battle. The combat performance of other countries' airborne forces suggested that the concept still had merit. The Anglo-American use of airborne forces during the Normandy invasion was a clear example of the potential role of airborne forces in supporting offensive operations. Operation Market Garden, the largest and most ambitious airborne operation of the war, carried mixed messages. Although the Anglo-American forces failed to take the key Arnhem bridge during the operation, the near success of the mission kept alive the dream of airborne enthusiasts.

If the successes of the Anglo-American airborne forces helped to convince the Soviet General Staff of the potential value of this form of warfare, their own experiences encouraged continued experimentation. Airborne forces were a cheap gamble. What little specialized equipment they required, such as transport aircraft, had many other practical applications, as the wartime experience clearly showed.

Even if the conditions for an airborne operation never occurred, the airborne divisions were not a waste. They could be fielded as elite light infantry, as the Red Army had done so often in the Great Patriotic War.

In June 1946, the VDV was put directly under the Ministry of Defense, and a new commander, Col. Gen. Vasily V. Glagolev, was appointed. Glagolev was a decorated veteran of the Great Patriotic War, earning its highest distinction, the Hero of the Soviet Union award, in 1943. He began the war commanding cavalry and rifle divisions, then rifle corps, and finally an army. His units fought in many of the key battles: the Crimea, the Caucasus, the Kursk bulge, and the Dnepr River offensive. But his leadership of the VDV would be short lived; he died in September 1947.

The selection of an experienced officer such as Glagolev suggested that Stalin did not expect the VDV to retreat into obscurity. The VDV was gradually rebuilt and within a decade would be the world's largest airborne force, with six divisions in its order of battle. Indeed, by the mid-1950s, the Soviet VDV outnumbered the rest of the world's airborne forces combined. Part of this was due to the sheer size of the Soviet military. In the 1950s, the Soviet Army numbered some 175 divisions, so the six VDV divisions were not disproportionate. By way of contrast, the U.S. Army, which seldom exceeded 20 divisions after World War II, had 2 airborne divisions during most of the Cold War period.

The new VDV was based around new guards airborne divisions. Most of these divisions evolved from wartime rifle divisions but could ultimately trace their lineage to the wartime airborne units. The 98th Guards Airborne Division evolved from the 44th Guards Rifle Division, itself based on several guards airborne brigades. The 13th Guards Airborne Division was a descendant of the 13th Airborne Division of 1943, the 104th from the wartime 11th Airborne, the 105th from the wartime 12th Airborne, the 106th from the wartime 16th Airborne. Several of the new divisions were recent arrivals in the airborne business, descending from traditional rifle divisions. The new divisions contained several innovations, including a revival of the glider assault regiments, badly neglected during the war.

There is little available in Russian literature to suggest any major innovations in the airborne divisions of the late 1940s and early

1950s. The configuration of the divisions was very similar to that of the wartime units. Nor was there much debate about airborne tactics during the late 1940s and early 1950s. This period was marked by stagnation in Soviet military doctrine due to Stalin's dominance of military policy. The main focus appears to have been reconstructing the airborne after the devastation of the war, and studying the lessons of the war, including the lessons of Anglo-American and German airborne forces. Innovation would wait nearly a decade, until the death of Joseph Stalin in 1953. In the meantime, the role of the VDV Airborne Force remained as a strategic power-projection force of the Soviet high command. The Soviet Air Force did not have long-range airlift to seriously consider employment of the VDV much beyond Soviet borders, so the principal area of operations would be against NATO in Western Europe.

In a secret 1952 assessment, the U.S. Army's Military Intelligence Division had the following to say about the postwar VDV: "The principal weaknesses of the Soviet airborne forces are the lack of experience in the coordination and control of large scale airborne operations, the lack of suitable aircraft for long-range flights and the lack of ability to drop heavy equipment by parachute." These three areas would be the central focus of the VDV until the mid-1950s.

AIRLIFT REVIVED

If there was any single technical lesson learned from the wartime experiences, it was that Soviet airlift needed serious attention. At the end of the war, the air transport regiments of the Red Air Force were still attached to the ADD strategic bomber force. These consisted of about 800 Li-2s and 600 Lend-Lease C-47s in the 4th, 5th, 6th, and 7th Aviation Corps of the ADD. In 1946, with the revival of the VDV, the airlift regiments were regrouped into a new air force formation called the Air Landing Aviation branch (in Russian: TDA, meaning *transportno-desantnaya aviatsiya*) headed by Col. Gen. Nikolai Skripko. Skripko's task was made somewhat easier by Stalin's commitment to modernize the Soviet Union's hopelessly backward civil aviation industry. The new Aeroflot's efforts to establish a civil passenger and freight transport service required new and more modern transport aircraft not dissimilar to those needed by

Skripko's new TDA. Efforts to modernize Aeroflot and the TDA were mutually beneficial.

Work on new transport aircraft had begun during the war but had low priority. The Ilyushin design bureau, which developed the legendary IL-2 *shturmovik* ground attack aircraft, began work on a transport in 1943 to surpass the Lisunov Li-2 in performance. The new aircraft, designated IL-12, was intended to carry up to twenty-nine passengers over distances of three thousand miles. The IL-12 flew for the first time in August 1945 and entered production in 1946 at Khodynka and later at Aviation Plant Number 82 in Tashkent. A total of about 1,500 were built by 1949, a significant new start for the TDA, since a large fraction of the production was of the IL-12D military transport version. A more refined derivative, the IL-14, followed and entered production in 1953. Some 2,200 of these were built through 1959, many going to the new TDA regiments. The production of the IL-12 and IL-14 allowed the Soviet Air Force to deploy a TDA air transport division alongside each of the VDV corps. This was an essential element in the revival of the VDV, since a readily available TDA division provided the necessary airlift for peacetime training. Generally, each VDV division would be located near an air base equipped with a regiment of 45 transport aircraft from its assigned division. By 1952, the Soviet Air Force deployed about 1,100 Li-2 and IL-12 transport aircraft, which could be strengthened by a further 1,000 Aeroflot airliners in the event of war. The TDA itself was allotted 450 Li-2s and IL-12s, though additional aircraft could be made available for some missions.

The size of the TDA in the early 1950s gave it the capability to lift about one airborne division at a time. Airborne divisions of the period numbered about 6,000 to 8,000 troops. Assuming a mission involving 7,000 troops in the first wave, this would have required 425 IL-12D transports: 370 for paratroops and 55 for the necessary 70 tons of heavy equipment, arms, and supplies. To sustain the division over the course of a mission, another 70 tons of supplies would be needed daily, amounting to 11.5 pounds per man per day, plus ammunition and other requirements. This was well within the capability of the expanded TDA airlift force. This force was large enough to be able to reinforce the first airborne division with another division during a five-day mission, assuming that the 450-aircraft transport force did not suffer too heavily from attrition. Any larger mission would have required the allotment of additional transport aircraft from air force or Aeroflot reserves, which was not out of the question.

Heavy Lift

Although the advent of the new IL-12 and IL-14 aircraft significantly boosted the airlift capacity of the Soviet Air Force, the configuration of the aircraft was shaped by the Aeroflot requirements more than military needs. The aircraft were well suited to either airliner passenger service or to paratrooper missions but were not well laid out for heavy, out-sized cargo such as vehicles or artillery. The Soviet aircraft industry had not recovered sufficiently from the wartime losses to afford the luxury of both a new civilian airliner and a dedicated military transport design. It would be several years before the air force would sponsor a dedicated military transport aircraft with heavy cargo airdrop capabilities. In the meantime, the VDV made do with improvised solutions. Relying on prewar practices, the Soviet Air Force assigned some heavy bombers to the TDA. These were mainly the new Tupolev Tu-4 heavy bomber, a copy of the American Boeing B-29 Superfortress. Although aerodynamically superior to the wartime TB-3 bomber, the Tu-4 was not ideal as a transport. Its main advantage was that its substantial lifting capacity could accommodate very heavy cargo loads, including light armored vehicles or artillery. It was used as an expedient solution until a dedicated military transport aircraft was developed in the late 1950s. Another solution was the cargo glider.

The wartime neglect of the glider force abated in the postwar years. The Soviets experimented with mixed paratrooper/glider regiments, but these were short lived. Interest in troop-carrying gliders waned in favor of their use for carrying heavy cargo, in spite of the success of Anglo-American glider tactics in 1944. This may have been due to the fact that both the British and Americans eliminated their own glider forces after the war, and the Soviet VDV decided to follow their example.

One of the lessons of the war was the need to land heavy weapons and vehicles to support the paratroopers. Gliders offered a practical alternative to airlanding heavy loads, as the British Hamilcar glider had demonstrated during World War II. The Hamilcar was large

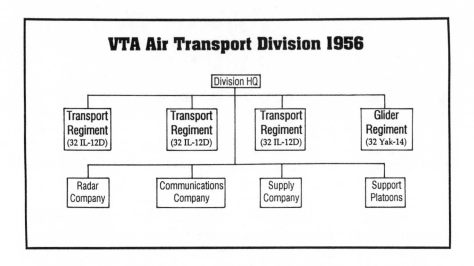

enough to carry a light tank, yet small enough to be towed by existing piston-engine aircraft. Germany even built the enormous twelve-ton Me-323 Gigant glider during the war, which could carry a tank, or a howitzer with its tractor. The Soviets studiously avoided re-creating such a monstrosity but were interested in gliders such as the Hamilcar.

With the British example in mind, work on a heavy cargo glider began in the Soviet Union. Toward the end of the war, the Tsybin design bureau had developed the first Soviet heavy cargo glider, the Ts-25, and a small number were manufactured in 1945–46. The Ts-25 could carry a jeep towing a light antitank gun, but something heavier would be needed to carry light armored vehicles. New designs for a six-ton glider were begun by the Gribovskiy design bureau in 1946 and by the Tsybin bureau in 1947. Neither of these materialized. The growing respectability of the VDV led the Ministry of Aircraft Pro-duction to take the glider requests more seriously than in the war years. The ministry assigned the requirement to the two premier Soviet design bureaus, Yakovlev and Ilyushin, in 1948.

Two design requirements were issued, a medium glider require-ment to Yakovlev and a heavy glider requirement to Ilyushin. Yak-ovlev's inexpensive wood Yak-14 was reminiscent of the Hamilcar, with its cockpit located above a cavernous, box-shaped wood fuselage, but it was designed to carry only a three-and-a-half-ton load, less than half that of the Hamilcar. Ilyushin's more modern aluminum IL-32 glider was equally boxy but substantially larger, with an empty weight of eight tons and an eight-ton cargo capacity. Like that of the wartime British Horsa glider, the nose could be swung out of the way to allow large cargo, such as vehicles, easy access to the interior. The Ilyushin IL-32 was not accepted for production, as it was judged too expensive and complicated for what was essentially an expendable aircraft. The smaller and cheaper Yak-14 was accepted for production in 1948, and a total of 413 Yak-14s were manufactured. They were the last mass-produced combat gliders manufactured in the world; after the war, most other air forces abandoned the glider concept altogether.

Although smaller than the IL-32, the Yak-14 was still a substantial aircraft, with an eighty-six-foot wingspan. It compared closely to the wartime German Gotha Go-242 in capacity and performance, though it resembled a shrunken Hamilcar in configuration. It was fairly efficient as gliders go, with an empty-to-loaded weight ratio of about 46 percent. This meant that its designers had been careful not to include any excess weight in the design that would detract from the amount of cargo that could be carried. The glider's construction was designed to be inexpensive, since the aircraft was to be expendable in wartime. The internal fuselage structure was made from steel tubing, but the remainder of the construction was wood and fabric. The cargo compartment was more than seven feet wide, to accommodate light vehicles. If used in a troop-carrying role, thirty-five fully equipped soldiers could be carried. However, it was intended mainly for lifting heavy cargo into the drop zone. In this role, its carrying capacity was three and a half tons. Typical loads could include a GAZ-67B jeep towing a 76.2mm ZiS-3 divisional gun or 57mm antitank gun with crew, or an ASU-57 self-propelled gun with crew. The nose of the aircraft was hinged to the side, and small ramps were provided so that the vehicles could drive out the front of the fuselage. The Yak-14 was designed with fixed landing gear so that it could be employed during peacetime for exercises. Little has been written about its service career, though some Yak-14s did take part in 1955 Warsaw Pact exercises. A handful were given to the small

Czechoslovak airborne force in 1955. The aircraft remained in service until the late 1950s, by which time heavy cargo parachutes and pallet systems had been developed.

Parachute Development

In the years after the war, efforts were also begun to improve the technical quality of Soviet parachutes and to develop specialized designs, especially heavy cargo parachutes. In 1946, the Parachute Research Engineering Institute was established in Moscow to develop new equipment for the airborne forces. The first major postwar design was the PD-47, a square parachute with a descent speed of sixteen feet per second. It largely replaced the wartime PD-6 and PD-41 types, which were relegated to training and sporting use. The PD-47 parachute was widely used for training in the Soviet Union and in the Warsaw Pact countries for many years, and was itself replaced by the new circular T-4 parachute in 1955. The Soviet practice of using two parachutes during a jump remained a common practice until 1954. By this date, the reliability of Soviet parachutes had improved, as had their design quality. It was still common to outfit a paratrooper with both a main parachute on the back and a reserve on the chest, but the reserve was not intended to be deployed except in emergencies.

The first postwar cargo parachute was the PG-125-47, a replacement for the wartime PG-8 used with PDMM or PDBB cargo containers. The PG-125-47 could carry cargo bundles up to 310 pounds. Experimental work was also undertaken on ribbon parachutes and multiple-canopy parachute systems for dropping considerably heavier loads. In the late 1940s, the first serious experiments were made in dropping heavy weapons such as artillery and light armored vehicles. In 1949, the TDA conducted an airdrop exercise with the 7th Guards Airborne Division in Latvia, dropping GAZ-67 jeeps on a special pallet with an unusual double canopy parachute. Although the jeeps survived, the concept needed refinement.

One of the main problems was that existing transport aircraft such as the IL-12 and IL-14 did not have cargo doors of sufficient size to drop such loads. As a result, the loads had to be carried under heavy bombers such as the Tupolev Tu-4. Carrying such cargo was awkward. Early attempts were made to fit vehicles within the open bomb-bay area, but the bomb-bay doors had to remain open during the flight in order to accommodate the load, causing serious drag. Other alternatives, such as carrying the loads under the wing, also induced drag, which degraded the aircraft's performance.

The solution to this problem was the P-90 parachute container. This was an aerodynamically streamlined aluminum shell, large enough to enclose a small artillery piece, light truck, or light armored vehicle. The aluminum container reduced the aerodynamic drag, which made it possible to carry two heavy loads under the wing. The main problem was weight. The loaded P-90 containers weighed five tons each, reducing the combat radius of the Tu-4 to 500 miles. The container and parachutes weighed about 60 percent as much as the cargo they were carrying. In fast descents, the containers sometimes became damaged, making it difficult to extract the cargo. A number of exercises used these unwieldy devices in the early 1950s, but the containers faded from view by the end of the decade as new transport aircraft and new parachute systems became available.

Airborne Firepower
One of the reasons for the 1947 glider program was the VDV decision to field air-portable armored vehicles. During the 1942 Vyazma battles, the paratroopers occasionally had been supported by T-60 light tanks from Belov's 1st Guards Cavalry Corps. In spite of their small size and puny armament, the little T-60 tanks were a godsend to the lightly equipped paratroopers. They supported attacks on heavily defended German positions that had proven impregnable to infantry attack alone. The lack of armored vehicles or antitank guns at other phases of the Vyazma battles was remembered with some bitterness. The VDV desperately wanted weapons such as these for any future operations.

Conventional tanks were of no use. Even light tanks weighed far more than the carrying capacity of the gliders. The last Soviet light tank design of World War II was the T-80 of 1943. Armed with a 45mm antitank gun, this tank weighed more than eleven tons. A vehicle of this weight would have required a heavy glider such as the aborted Ilyushin IL-32 and, even then, would have needed some weight cuts. Furthermore, the armament on the T-80, a 45mm gun such as that used on prewar tanks, was completely inadequate for modern tank fighting.

The Astrov design bureau, which had developed the T-80 and most other wartime Soviet light tanks, suggested a different approach. This took the form of airborne assault guns, called ASU in Russian *(aviadesantnaya samokhodnaya ustanovka)*. The Soviet Army had built only 120 T-80 tanks, preferring instead an assault gun based on the same chassis, the SU-76. Assault guns dispensed with the tank turret; instead their weapon was mounted in an open fighting compartment at the rear of the vehicle. The weight savings allowed the designers to fit a heavier gun. In the SU-76 assault gun, a 76mm ZiS-3 divisional gun replaced the T-80's 45mm "sparrow-shooter" gun.

Astrov proposed that this approach be taken one step further. The design of the SU-76 was lightened even more, and the vehicle was shrunk in size. This reduced the weight to only three tons. Armor protection on these tiny vehicles was minimal—only on the fronts and sides, and only enough to defend against rifle bullets. There was no armor protection on the roof or rear. The vehicles were armed with lightweight artillery such as the new 57mm airborne antitank gun, or lightweight 76mm guns. On so light a chassis, the recoil of the guns was ferocious.

Several of these designs were built in prototype form in the late 1940s, including an amphibious version and even a troop-carrying type. But in the end, only one was accepted for VDV service, the ASU-57. This was armed with a 57mm antitank gun and weighed only three tons. The long Ch-51M 57mm gun was selected over the medium-length 76mm gun since it offered better antitank performance. It could penetrate one hundred millimeters of armor at a thousand meters, whereas the 76.2mm ZiS-3 gun could penetrate only fifty-eight millimeters. On the other hand, the Ch-51 gun (57mm) fired a much smaller high-explosive round, but its role was antitank defense, not fire support.

The ASU-57 entered production in 1951. Its 57mm gun was not adequate to duel with a contemporary main battle tank except from ambush. But new armor-piercing ammunition made it capable of penetrating the frontal armor of older NATO tanks such as the M4 Sherman, which were still common in the 1950s. Newer designs such as the American M26 Pershing or the British Centurion could be pen-

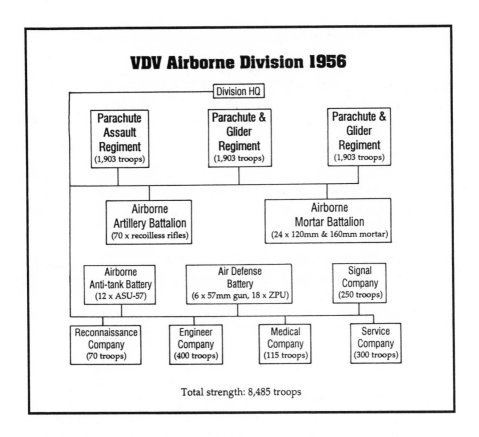

VDV Airborne Division 1956

Division HQ

Parachute Assault Regiment (1,903 troops)

Parachute & Glider Regiment (1,903 troops)

Parachute & Glider Regiment (1,903 troops)

Airborne Artillery Battalion (70 x recoilless rifles)

Airborne Mortar Battalion (24 x 120mm & 160mm mortar)

Airborne Anti-tank Battery (12 x ASU-57)

Air Defense Battery (6 x 57mm gun, 18 x ZPU)

Signal Company (250 troops)

Reconnaissance Company (70 troops)

Engineer Company (400 troops)

Medical Company (115 troops)

Service Company (300 troops)

Total strength: 8,485 troops

etrated from the sides or rear, but the little 57mm gun was inadequate to deal with the thicker frontal armor. In spite of these limitations, the ASU-57 was a substantial increase in paratrooper firepower and mobility.

There were several other important technical innovations in airborne firepower. During the war, the Soviet VDV units were conspicuously ill equipped in antitank weapons. The standard wartime man-portable Soviet antitank weapon was the PTRS or PTRD antitank rifle. These 14.5mm single-shot rifles were satisfactory in 1941 when they were first fielded. They could penetrate thirty-five millimeters of steel armor at three hundred meters, which was adequate to deal with common German tanks such as the PzKpfw.II and early models of the PzKpfw.III. But by 1943, tank armor had grown so thick that such weapons were useless. Other armies developed rocket-propelled weapons using new shaped-charge antitank warheads, for example, the German *Panzerfaust* and *Panzershreck,* or the American bazooka. These gave the infantryman some capability to defend against tanks, even though these weapons were dangerous to use and not always effective. The Soviets understood the shaped-charge principle, and used it in some tank ammunition and grenades, but they failed to connect shaped-charge warheads with rocket technology and thus missed one of the most important infantry innovations in World War II. Ironically, Soviet engineer Leonid V. Kurchevskiy had pioneered these types of weapons in the 1930s, but he was imprisoned by Stalin during the purges of 1937–38, before these weapons could be perfected.

After the war, the Soviet Army remedied this situation very quickly. Captured German engineers were dispatched to the new KB-3 (design bureau 3) in Sofrino to develop lightweight antitank weapons alongside Soviet scientists. After producing a copy of the wartime German *Panzerfaust* as the RPG-1, a new antitank grenade launcher was developed, called the RPG-2 (*raketniy protivotankoviy granat-2,* or antitank rocket grenade). This was closely patterned on the *Panzerfäuste,* but the launcher assembly was reusable. The RPG-2 was an effective weapon for its day, capable of penetrating 180 millimeters of tank armor. The main problem was that such weapons were not terribly accurate, and their range was short, only 150 meters, which meant that other antitank weapons such as the ASU-57 were still needed. But they did give the Soviet paratrooper a measure of protection sorely lacking during the war years.

To further enhance airborne firepower, the Soviet Army also began manufacturing recoilless rifles; a type of lightweight artillery system. Conventional artillery is inevitably heavy since the gun carriage must withstand considerable recoil energy when the gun is fired. Recoilless rifles avoid the weight burden by using a special type of projectile that delivers a blast of propellant gas backward when firing to compensate for the force in the other direction. These weapons can be considerably lighter than conventional artillery, although they do not usually have the range.

Once again, Soviet inventor Leonid Kurchevskiy had developed these weapons back in the 1930s. In fact, small numbers of Kurchevskiy 76mm recoilless rifles were actually used in the famous 1935 airborne exercises, the first time such weapons were deployed in any army. But the technology was immature at the time, and their evolution was halted by the purges. Few of these recoilless rifles were in service with VDV in 1941, though some were captured in Finland in 1940. The German airborne forces made widespread use of recoilless rifles during the war as a form of lightweight artillery. The U.S. Army also developed lightweight recoilless rifles in 1944–45, and these became a staple infantry weapon in the 1950s.

Two recoilless rifles were fielded by the VDV in the late 1940s, the B-10 and B-11. Developed by Boris Shavyrin's design bureau in Kolomna, both rifles were similar in features except for size. The B-10 was an 82mm recoilless rifle, weighing 160 pounds fully equipped. This fired a ten-pound high-explosive projectile to a range of almost three miles. The weapon was manned by a crew of four, and it was mounted on a small wheeled carriage so that it could be towed by its crew. This was an important feature for airborne units, since vehicles were seldom available. The B-11 was essentially a scaled-up 107mm version. It weighed more than 650 pounds fully loaded, making it too large to be man portable. However, it was small enough to be towed by GAZ-69 light trucks of the type used in airborne units. It fired an 18-pound high-explosive projectile to ranges up to four miles. The B-10 was generally used for antitank defense and fire support for airborne battalions; the larger B-11 served the same role at the regimental level. The rifles did not give the airborne the firepower of conventional infantry units but did provide a great deal more firepower than was available in World War II, when VDV units considered themselves lucky to have a few of the weak but overweight 45mm infantry guns.

Last but not least, the VDV benefited from important advances in communications technology in the early 1950s. Although Soviet radio development was not prompted by VDV requirements, the general trend toward lighter and more robust tactical radios was especially important to the VDV. So many wartime VDV missions ended in disaster when airlanded forces lost communications due to radio failures. The new radios were smaller, lighter and more durable, being based on wartime German and Lend-Lease U.S. Army designs.

Testing of the new weapons began during war games in the early

1950s. There were no mass jumps on the scale of the prewar maneuvers. In 1951, an airborne battalion was deployed to Altenburg in East Germany as part of the 8th Guards Army. In 1952, the 8th Guards Army war games included the jump of 300 paratroopers. This became a fairly regular practice in Germany, with further war game participation in 1955 in the maneuvers near Ohrdruf.

Airborne maneuvers in the Soviet Union itself were still fairly small scale, seldom over battalion size. Paratroop drops became a staple of the summer aviation festivities in the Moscow area, but the carnival atmosphere of the events meant that they were of little importance except as a demonstration of new parachutes and airdrop equipment.

OPERATION WHIRLWIND

The first airborne operation of the postwar Soviet VDV took place in 1956 in Hungary. Although the Soviet intervention in Hungary in 1956 is well known, the participation by Soviet airborne forces has been a state secret until recently, as have many details of this operation. The desire of the Warsaw Pact countries to escape Soviet domination threatened the propaganda image of Soviet–Warsaw Pact fraternity, and discussion of the Soviet invasion of Hungary in 1956 was officially off-limits for many years to avoid undermining this illusion. This is the first account of this operation in English and is based on recently declassified Soviet documents and accounts.

In 1956, Eastern Europe was in turmoil. Nikita Khrushchev delivered a speech to the 20th Party Congress in the spring, denouncing Stalin's crimes for the first time. It was the first step in the painful and tumultuous process of de-Stalinization, an attempt to remove hard-line Stalinists from high party positions in the Soviet Union and replace them with Communists aligned with Khrushchev. The de-Stalinization campaign had unintended consequences in the satellite countries of east-central Europe.

The contents of Khrushchev's speech soon leaked out, spread in part by the American Central Intelligence Agency (CIA). Khrushchev's revelations were no news to the inhabitants of Poland or Hungary, who were familiar first hand with Stalin's crimes against humanity. Many people in the Warsaw Pact countries interpreted the speech as the beginning of a policy of liberalization. Poland, Hungary, and Czechoslovakia were chafing under the oppressive Soviet rule imposed by the Red Army in the mid-1940s. The puppet governments were led by a particularly reprehensible group of servile mediocrities who helped the Soviets create police states. East Germany had seen mass demonstrations bloodily repressed by Soviet troops in 1953. Khrushchev's de-Stalinization program contained the hint that some changes might be tolerated.

In Poland, the de-Stalinization campaign triggered popular unrest and a power struggle within the Polish Communist Party. As Stalin had said, communism fit Poland like a saddle fits a cow. Communism had been brutally imposed on Poland after World War II, causing a bloody but little-known civil war. The populace tried to squirm out from under the grip of the Communists at every opportunity. In 1956, workers rioted in Poznan, and Communist control seemed ready to unravel. The government headed by Boleslaw Bierut was toppled by another Communist faction led by Wladyslaw Gomulka. Gomulka played the nationalist card and won popular support with promises of reform and liberalization. Even the mildest reforms scared the Kremlin, and the Soviet leadership rushed to Poland in hopes of averting catastrophe. Poland was the largest and most populous of the Warsaw Pact countries; if it slipped from the Soviet grip, others would surely follow. Khrushchev threatened that the Soviet Army stood ready to invade Poland to restore Communist power. Gomulka brazenly argued with Khrushchev, saying that his coup represented the type of de-Stalinization that Khrushchev himself had sought. Gomulka warned Khrushchev that a Soviet invasion would be met with force by the Polish army.

No one doubted that the Polish army could be quickly crushed by the massive Soviet Army. But Khrushchev was well aware of the wartime Polish resistance movement and the likelihood that an invasion would be followed by prolonged guerrilla resistance. A civil war in Poland could spread to neighboring Czechoslovakia and Germany. Worst of all, the North Atlantic Treaty Organization (NATO) might intervene. Khrushchev was astute enough to realize that the de-Stalinization he sought in the Soviet Union meant that Moscow would have to relax its control over its Warsaw Pact satellites. Even if Gomulka was a pigheaded Polish nationalist, at least he was a

Communist. So Khrushchev finally reached an accommodation with the defiant Poles.

Hungary would be a very different case. The root of the popular discontent in Hungary was the same as in Poland—the tyranny of the Communist system imposed by Moscow. There were critical differences, however. The leadership of the Polish Communist Party offered some alternatives to the Moscow-trained stooges so common in the Warsaw Pact countries of the early 1950s. Gomulka had spent the war years with the underground resistance in Poland. This experience earned him grudging popular support and gave him a more independent viewpoint than that of the Communists who had spent the war under Stalin's thumb in Moscow. In Hungary, the Communist opponents of the Rakosci government were just another clot of Moscow-trained mediocrities with no popular appeal. The second difference was that Hungary had been a wartime German ally. The Soviet government had little or no sympathy for the "fascist" Hungarians. The Poles had fought against Hitler, and their stubborn anti-Nazi resistance movement, even if pro-Western, had earned the grudging admiration of the Kremlin.

In the face of growing discontent in Hungary, the thoroughly hated leader of the Hungarian Communist Party, Matthias Rakosci, fled to Moscow on 21 July 1956. His place was taken by the equally despised Erno Gero. The turmoil in the Communist leadership and the Polish example emboldened Hungarian university students. Mass meetings were begun, ostensibly to support the Polish reform movement, but in fact to ignite similar reform in Hungary. The three Soviet divisions stationed in Hungary were put on alert on 18 October in response to the growing ferment. On 22 October, the Soviet Army erected pontoon bridges over the Prut River near the Romanian frontier at Zahony in case reinforcements were needed from the east. The Special Operations Corps (Osobiy Korpus Sovetskoi Armii) was formed in Hungary under the command of Gen. P. Lashchenko. This consisted of the three divisions already in Hungary, the 2nd Guards Mechanized Division near Kecskemet, Gen. G. I. Obaturov's 33rd Guards Mechanized Division, and Col. N. A. Gorbunov's 128th Guards Rifle Division. These would be supported, if necessary, by additional units from the 25th Guards Mechanized and 32nd and 34th Mechanized Divisions in neighboring Romania. The Special Operations Corps numbered 31,550 troops, 1,130 tanks and assault guns, 380 armored infantry vehicles, 3,930 trucks, and 615 howitzers and mortars.

The Hungarian revolt began spontaneously on 23 October 1956. Students in Budapest called for a rally to express solidarity with Poland; it was in fact a thinly disguised excuse to protest the new Gero administration. The march was officially banned by the police, which only served to encourage workers from the large factories in Budapest to join the students. The solidarity between the students and the workers frightened the government and alarmed Soviet officials. The size of the demonstrations grew as the day went on, giving the crowds new confidence. Soon they began shouting antigovernment slogans: "Get lost, Gero!" "Soviet Army out and take the Stalin statue with you!" By late afternoon, the thuggish AVH secret police opened fire on the crowds at several locations in the city. The Communist Party leadership was terrified and confused. Instructions to the police and army were being ignored, and the AVH secret police force was too small to counter the emboldened crowds. Statements and warnings from the government were treated with derision.

By late in the day, the street demonstrations escalated into violence. The hated AVH secret police continued to fire on the crowds and were themselves soon the victims of mob retribution. The Hungarian army, its ranks victimized in previous years by the AVH's sadistic purges, would not fire on ordinary Hungarians. Most units stayed neutral, but several units in key towns threw in their lot with the discontented citizenry. The crowds soon obtained arms from sympathetic army and police garrisons, and full-scale fighting with the AVH broke out all over the city.

The head of the Soviet delegation in Hungary was a senior KGB officer and future head of the USSR, Yuriy Andropov. On the evening of 23 October, he telephoned Khrushchev and recommended that Lashchenko's Special Operations Corps move on Budapest to restore order and stop a "fascist counter-revolution." General Lashchenko received a direct phone call from the minister of defense, Marshal Georgiy Zhukov, telling him that "not one soldier would show his face in Budapest" without direct instructions from Moscow. Khrushchev was still hoping that some sort of accommodation could be reached in Hungary—a preferable solution to a brutal restoration of order by the Soviet Army. But local conditions deteriorated more rapidly than Moscow expected, and the troops were ordered into the city.

Soviet armored units began moving on Budapest at midnight. At the discretion of local commanders, tanks and armored vehicles rolled toward the city as a show of force, hoping to intimidate the crowds without the need for any real fighting. The troops were expressly forbidden to fire on the crowds unless fired upon, for fear of worsening the situation. The first Soviet T-34 tanks of the 33rd Guards Mechanized Division began clanking into the outskirts of Budapest around 04:30 on 24 October 1956. There was a thick fog along the Pest River in the center of the city. By dawn some of the Soviet tanks had reached the parliament building.

The Hungarian reaction to the Soviet forces was mixed. Many young Hungarian students approached the tank crews and tried to convince the Soviets not to intervene on the government side. Most of the tank crews were naive, young draftees completely befuddled by the actions taking place. They had been told by their officers that they were guarding Budapest from fascist reactionaries, so they were bewildered to find that the "fascist beasts" were friendly teenagers like themselves who spoke good Russian. An alarming number of young Soviet soldiers defected to the Hungarian side or refused to follow orders. By later in the morning, attitudes began to harden. Fighting between the Hungarian insurgents and the AVH police became more intense, and in some areas the AVH was supported by Soviet troops. Hungarians began throwing Molotov cocktails at the Soviet armored vehicle convoys moving along the narrow, cobbled streets. By afternoon, the city was shaken by the constant sound of explosion, gunfire, and artillery. Instructions or not, the Soviet Army was heavily involved. Earlier gestures of Hungarian-Russian solidarity were quickly forgotten.

By 25 October, General Obaturov's 33rd Guards Mechanized Division had suffered heavy casualties. Out of the 400 tanks committed to the city fighting, about 200 had been knocked out or severely damaged. The troops of the Special Operations Corps were suffering from poor morale because of deceptive propaganda received from the political officers, their distaste for firing at civilians, and their poor preparation for the rigors of intense street fighting. The heavily mechanized forces were not adequately provided with infantry due to the failed plan to overcome the Hungarians by intimidation rather than brute force and thus minimize Soviet casualties. In the narrow city streets, tanks were largely ineffective and soon became isolated and vulnerable to the Hungarian insurgents. By evening, infantry units from the 128th Guards Rifle Division had taken up positions in the city.

To seal off any incursions from NATO, Marshal Zhukov ordered the 17th Guards Mechanized Division, stationed near Szombathely, Hungary, toward the Austrian border. More units from Romania moved into Hungary. Nine tank and infantry divisions from the Carpathian Military District in western Ukraine, consisting of Gen. Khadzhi Mamsurov's 38th Army and Gen. Amazasp Babadzhanyan's 8th Tank Army, were ordered to seal the Hungarian border and take up positions in western Hungary to prevent any possible action by NATO.

Soviet units in Budapest attempted to stay aloof from the street fighting, under direct orders from Moscow and the corps command. The main emphasis was to maintain government control over key buildings in the center of the city. Sporadic fighting continued for several days. The Hungarians concentrated on routing out the AVH and usually avoided direct confrontation with the well-armed Soviet units.

By 28 October, a Communist faction led by Imre Nagy had formed a new coalition government and deposed the Gero government. Realizing that the presence of Soviet troops only inflamed popular sentiment, Nagy asked Andropov and the Soviet embassy to withdraw the tanks from the city. Khrushchev agreed to do so, hoping that Hungary would follow the peaceful Polish example. The majority of the Special Operations Corps pulled out of Budapest, leaving small detachments to guard key government buildings. Local Soviet commanders were infuriated. Their troops had taken severe casualties during the four days in Budapest, with more than 500 dead and 1,100 wounded. The streets were littered with burned-out Soviet tanks and BTR-152 armored personnel carriers. The 33rd Mechanized Division alone had lost twelve T-34 tanks, one IS-3 Stalin heavy tank, one SU-100 assault gun, six BTR-152 and four BTR-40 armored transporters, thirty-six vehicles, and many weapons and small arms.

Behind the scenes, Khrushchev and the Soviet leaders were watching and contemplating their options. After a few days, it became clear that the new Communist government under Imre Nagy was unable to take control. Nagy was being forced into concessions by the insurgents, who were demanding that Hungary leave the Warsaw Pact and that the Soviets leave Hungary for good. The Soviet leadership was losing its patience with Nagy; they recruited another Hungarian Communist, Janos Kadar, to form yet another puppet government.

Khrushchev also ordered Marshal Zhukov to prepare a military option. Code-named Operation Whirlwind, the plan called for Lashchenko's Special Operation Corps to reenter the city and crush the Hungarian insurgents in Budapest. The task of subduing the towns and cities in the rest of Hungary was assigned to the two armies of the Carpathian Military District. Lashchenko desperately needed infantry to make up for previous casualties. Moreover, he needed experienced troops, not recent conscripts such as those in the rifle divisions, who showed no enthusiasm for the disagreeable tasks of imperial policing. Zhukov decided to test the mettle of the new VDV divisions by committing two of them to action in Hungary. It was not a relevant display of their specialized military capabilities, but it would demonstrate their political reliability in awkward situations.

The timing for Operation Whirlwind was determined by unfolding developments in the Mideast. Egypt's nationalistic leader, Gamal Nasser, had nationalized the Suez Canal from its British consortium in the summer of 1956. France and Britain considered the action a threat to their supply of oil from the Middle East. Israel was already on the verge of war with Egypt over a number of grievances. In a secret agreement, France, Britain, and Israel decided on a joint military action to resolve the crisis. The war between Israel and Egypt began on 30 October 1956. French and British amphibious forces began massing in the Mediterranean, threatening to intervene to protect the canal.

While the world's attention was focused on the Suez Canal, Khrushchev acted. To lend a semblance of legitimacy to its actions, Moscow recognized a new Hungarian government under Janos Kadar, and

Kadar obliged his hosts by requesting the assistance of the Soviet Army "to help break down the resistance of the rebels in Budapest and restore lawful power and public order in the country." On 2 November, the head of the Special Operations Corps, General Lashchenko, was summoned to the headquarters of Marshal I. S. Koniev at Szolnok, in the Budapest suburbs. Koniev had been assigned by Marshal Zhukov to direct Operation Whirlwind. Koniev explained the objectives of the operation and promised Lashchenko that VDV paratroopers would be sent into Budapest to make up for the shortages of infantry in the Special Operations Corps. At 05:00 on 4 November 1956, Koniev ordered the start of Operation Whirlwind.

Airborne Whirlwind
Participation of VDV airborne units in the Hungarian fighting had begun weeks before the start of Operation Whirlwind. The first unit activated was the 108th Guards Airborne Regiment (108 GVDP) of the 7th Guards Airborne Division. On 19–20 October 1956, the regiment had

deployed forward to the airports at Vilnius in Lithuania and Kaunus in Latvia along with ninety-nine IL-12D transport aircraft. This regiment was fairly typical of airborne regiments of the period. It counted 1,046 troops, a bit understrength from the official tables. Fire support consisted of twelve 82mm mortars, eighteen B-10 82mm recoilless rifles, and six ZPU-2 antiaircraft machine guns. Platoons were armed with the new RPG-2 rocket grenade launcher—eighty-one of them when the unit was called up. To provide some mobility on the ground, the regiment had fourteen GAZ-67 and GAZ-69 light trucks. The regiment had no specific assignment but was kept on alert.

On 28 October, Maj. Gen. P. M. Ryabov's 31st Guards Airborne Division was ordered from its base at Novograd-Volynskiy to deployment airfields at Lvov and Khemilnitskiy in Ukraine. Their mission was a combat jump against the Hungarian air base at Veszprem. The paratroopers began to prepare their parachutes and specialized equipment, including recoilless rifles, mortars, and light trucks.

Veszprem, at the eastern end of Lake Balaton, was headquarters to the Hungarian 30th Artillery Division and housed several regiments from the neighboring 32nd Infantry Division as well. From intelligence sources in Hungary, the VDV command learned that the Veszprem garrison had not sided with the insurgents. So, instead of parachuting into Veszprem, Ryabov was ordered to airland his two regiments (114th and 381st Guards Airborne Regiments) at Veszprem air base a few days before the start of Operation Whirlwind. The 114th Airborne was landed in the early afternoon of 30 October, and the 381st Airborne just before midnight.

The landing operation had unexpected results. The Hungarian garrison had planned to stay neutral in the Budapest disputes, but the sudden arrival of Soviet troops prompted several units to go over to the insurgent side. Hungarian unit commanders and political officers considered sympathetic to the Soviets were told to leave, and several who refused were arrested. Some of the soldiers began arming local hotheads. The Hungarian insurgents in Veszprem eventually numbered about 3,000, including several hundred armed civilians. The units of the 31st Guards Airborne Division set up defensive positions around the Veszprem airfield and began preparing their equipment for a probable attack on the town.

The order to seize Veszprem was given at dawn on 4 November

1956 as Operation Whirlwind began. The troops started a careful advance on a military garrison complex to the northeast of the town, reaching it around 10:00. The Hungarian garrison was largely abandoned, but a firefight eventually broke out between insurgents and the paratroopers. A recent Russian account of the skirmish melodramatically referred to the garrison as "a factory of death." In fact, the Hungarian forces were mostly local teenagers with a smattering of soldiers, and were overwhelmed by the better-trained Soviet paratroopers. After disarming the Hungarian force, the paratroopers marched into Veszprem and occupied the town hall and other key buildings. Total Soviet casualties in Veszprem were 10 dead and 25 wounded. Hungarian casualties were 217 killed. The paratroopers took 3,000 prisoners and captured ten SU-76 assault guns, sixteen 57mm antitank guns, twenty-five machine guns, and more than thirteen hundred small arms.

The two regiments of the 7th Guards Airborne Division were assigned missions in Budapest itself. The 80th Airborne Regiment was moved to Beregovo air base in Ukraine and flown into the air base at Tekel, in the suburbs of Budapest, late in the evening of 3 November, before Operation Whirlwind was scheduled to begin. It is not clear if they were airlanded or parachute-dropped, but their assignment was the capture or destruction of five Hungarian antiaircraft gun batteries that had been blocking the airport. They completed this mission by morning.

Due to a lack of air transport, the 80th Airborne Regiment of the 7th Guards Airborne Division was moved by truck from Mukachevo in Soviet Ukraine to Szolnok in Hungary. In the early-morning hours of 4 November, as the 80th Airborne Regiment moved toward Szolnok, the column was ambushed near Terekszentmiklosz. The paratroopers were pinned down for only a few minutes until the officers led a short counterattack that drove away the Hungarian insurgents. Soviet accounts of the ambush described it as "well organized," but that is belied by the fact that total Soviet casualties were only one dead and five wounded. The regiment arrived in Budapest later in the day and took part in street fighting there. The superior performance of the paratroopers during the street fighting led to the decision to deploy them as the bodyguard force for the commander of Operation Whirlwind, war hero Marshal I. S. Koniev.

The hardest fighting fell on the division's other unit, the 108th

Guards Airborne Regiment. Two detachments of about 150 troops each were sent from the air base at Tekel into Budapest on the morning of 4 November to help in the street fighting. The detachments were formed into special assault units, put under the command of KGB special operations officers K. E. Grebennik, P. I. Zyryanov, and A. M. Korotkov, and provided with BTR-152 armored transporters and supported by ten to twelve T-34-85 tanks each. These small units lost twenty-five men in the bitter street battles, and many more were wounded.

The Hungarian insurgents were not prepared for military action on the scale of Operation Whirlwind. The militias had few antitank weapons aside from Molotov cocktails. The Hungarian army had seventy-seven T-34-85 tanks in Budapest, but they were sandwiched into a parade ground at the Petoki barracks on Budaorsi Road. There was some suspicion that the tanks had been deliberately parked there by pro-Soviet officers to prevent the militias from using them, and none were disentangled before they were seized by Soviet forces. Few regular Hungarian army units sided with either the rebels or the Soviets.

The initial Soviet assaults were conducted mainly with tanks and heavy assault guns. The Soviet officers, enraged by the numerous casualties suffered in late October when their hands were tied by strict rules of engagement, were determined to minimize their own casualties this time, even if it meant heavy Hungarian civilian casualties from indiscriminate shelling. The toughest fighting took place at the university, in the Corvin district, at the royal fortress, and in Moscow Square. On the first day of fighting in Budapest, Lashchenko's Special Operations Corps captured 4,000 rebel troops. The Hungarian uprising was crushed in a few days of fighting with minimal casualties on the Soviet side. The paratrooper units lost thirty-eight soldiers on 4 November, four the next day, and twenty-five on 6–7 November as they helped to clean out several last strongholds of Hungarian rebels such as the Killian barracks. Hungarian casualties during the fighting for Budapest included at least 2,000 dead and 19,000 wounded, mainly civilians.

Total VDV paratrooper casualties during the Hungarian operation were 97 dead or missing and 265 wounded. This was a small fraction of the 720 killed and 1,540 wounded Soviet troops during the entire

Hungarian operation. However, the majority of Soviet casualties had been suffered in the first few days of the uprising in October; casualties in the mechanized units during Operation Whirlwind were light. The VDV bore the brunt of the heaviest street fighting in Budapest on 4–7 November 1956 and so suffered disproportionate casualties for such small units.

The performance of the VDV in the operation was highly regarded by the Soviet high command, which decorated 1,710 paratroopers for their role in the fighting. Four paratroopers, all officers, were awarded the Hero of the Soviet Union distinction, three of them posthumously. The VDV awards were disproportionate to the size of the units, garnering 18 percent of the decorations even though they were less than 6 percent of the total Soviet forces during Operation Whirlwind.

Hungary did not represent a real combat test for the VDV. The Hungarian insurgents were a disjointed group of poorly trained, poorly armed, and poorly led civilians. Nevertheless, the VDV performed significantly better than other Soviet units. Several mechanized units had young conscript soldiers defect or refuse to fight civilians; there were no such embarrassments among the paratroopers. The VDV also showed its ability to pack up and move from its bases quickly and in good order. The strategic mobility of the VDV, as well as its reliability in ticklish political conditions, helped change the perceptions of the Soviet General Staff toward the paratroopers. Operation Whirlwind suggested a new and important role for the VDV: imperial storm troopers.

Chapter 7
Imperial Storm Troopers

The Hungarian revolt revealed a new role for the VDV Airborne Force. The Kremlin was beginning to view it as a reliable enforcer of Soviet power in the face of unwanted reform and revolution on the peripheries of the Soviet empire. It was not a role the VDV had sought, but it would come to be its dominant mission through the last four decades of the Cold War.

The VDV's use as imperial storm troopers can be traced to several factors. The VDV was the last stronghold of light infantry in the Soviet Army. In the wake of military reforms in 1957–59, the Soviet rifle divisions were gradually converted to mechanized infantry formations, or, to use the Russian expression, motor rifle divisions. The light infantry talents of the VDV were more useful than mechanized infantry in certain environments, such as city fighting. In addition, the VDV was gradually transformed into a true elite force. The VDV was given preference in recruitment, whereas the Ground Forces* ended up with whatever draftees were left over after the Strategic Missile Force, air force, and navy had their pick. The parachute skills needed in the VDV demanded robust and fearless soldiers.

---

*The Ground Forces (Sukhoputnykh Voisk) were the Soviet equivalent of the U.S. Army; the term "Soviet Army" (Sovetskaya Armiya) refers to all elements of the Soviet armed forces except the navy.

Whereas the composition of Ground Forces motor rifle divisions was often 40 percent or more non-Slavic minorities, the VDV became heavily Slavic. The majority of troops were Russians, or kindred Byelorussian or Ukrainian draftees, with a smattering of draftees from the more distant provinces. Non-Slavic draftees were not specifically excluded from the VDV; indeed some of the VDV's best troops and officers came from non-Russian areas. But the non-Slavs accepted into the VDV tended to be heavily assimilated into Russian society. The ethnic composition of the airborne made the paratroop units more reliable in imperial policing missions. Furthermore, the homogeneity of the units reduced the level of ethnic tension among the enlisted men, a significant factor in helping to build unit morale. In contrast, many Ground Forces divisions suffered from serious ethnic tensions. The Soviet General Staff accepted the elite recruitment of the VDV personnel as an important element in the creation of a special reserve force tailored for assignment to particularly difficult missions. The VDV retained its traditional wartime missions but took on a new, and seldom acknowledged, role as imperial police force.

The individual most closely connected with the transformation of the VDV was Gen. Vasiliy F. Margelov, the head of the VDV in 1954–59 and 1961–79.* Margelov was a Byelorussian who had grown up in the Russian industrial towns of eastern Ukraine. He entered the Red Army in 1928 and as a young officer served in the invasion of Poland and Finland in 1939. During the siege of Leningrad in World War II, he commanded an elite naval infantry regiment and eventually served as the commander of the 49th Guards Rifle Division. He was decorated with the Hero of the Soviet Union award for his division's success in seizing and defending a bridgehead over the Dnepr River near Sadoviy in March 1944. Margelov was a charismatic leader who would leave a deep imprint on the organization and outlook of the VDV.

Margelov's leadership of the VDV coincided with dramatic changes

---

*Margelov's short hiatus was due to his relief from command after involvement in a party prank in which a paratrooper was injured while wrestling a pet bear.

in the Soviet Army. In the waning days of Joseph Stalin, army doctrine stagnated under the benighted concept of "the permanent factors of war." Stalin's stultifying influence ended with his death in 1953. The Soviet General Staff then began to examine the effect that tactical nuclear weapons would have on the conduct of conventional war in Europe. Stalin had previously forbidden detailed study of this issue for fear that it would expose the Soviet Union's inferiority in nuclear technology. By the late 1950s, this was no longer the case. Furthermore, the U.S. Army was clearly moving in the direction of tactical nuclear weapons to make up for its numerical inferiority in the event of a clash between the Warsaw Pact and NATO in Europe.

In 1954, the Soviet Army staged a tactical nuclear explosion near Totskoye to examine the psychological effects of such weapons on the troops. Other tests were conducted to examine the destructive effects of tactical nuclear weapons on various types of equipment, including tanks and artillery. More importantly, Soviet Army tacticians began to consider the consequences of such weapons on the battlefield of the future. The "revolution in military affairs" brought about by tactical nuclear weapons led to a dramatic reorganization of the Soviet Army. The cavalry force was finally disbanded in 1956, and all rifle divisions were gradually mechanized and transformed into motor rifle divisions. Soviet tacticians realized that neither cavalry nor unprotected infantry could easily survive on a nuclear battlefield. Conventional infantry divisions were extremely vulnerable to tactical nuclear weapons. A single nuclear artillery projectile could destroy an entire division. Infantry divisions lacked the mobility to disperse, and so were deprived of one of the most obvious means to diminish the destructive implications of tactical nuclear weapons. By mechanizing the infantry with armored transporters, the blast and radiation effects of nuclear weapons on individual soldiers could be reduced. A concentrated infantry division was a lucrative target for nuclear weapons. But a motor rifle divisions' vehicles allowed it to operate in a dispersed configuration, and so it was less vulnerable to a single, crippling nuclear strike. Also, the division's newfound mobility allowed it to concentrate again if necessary for missions.

The new tactical doctrine raised questions about the viability of the VDV on the modern battlefield. The problem was complicated. On the one hand, a VDV unit was unlikely to be a target of a NATO nuclear strike, since its most likely mission would be to land within NATO territory to carry out deep raiding missions. However, in the rear areas, which probably would have been struck by Soviet tactical nuclear weapons, the paratroopers would be vulnerable to any residual radiation. This reopened the debate regarding the future of the VDV.

The Hungarian experience helped the VDV cause since it was a clear reminder that the Soviet Army would be used in missions other than all-out war with NATO. This point was reinforced again in 1956 when the Anglo-French operation against Egypt, Operation Musketeer, employed airborne forces with considerable success. It was not unreasonable to retain 6 light airborne divisions for such missions when the Soviet force structure was more than 150 divisions. Though Hungary and the Suez crisis ensured the survival of the VDV in the Soviet order of battle, it left unanswered the question of the utility of the VDV in a war with NATO.

Margelov's long-term solution was to mechanize the VDV. At first glance, the proposal seemed absurd. Paratrooper forces were by their very nature light infantry units. It had been painfully difficult to provide even modest numbers of "toy tanks" such as the ASU-57 to the airborne, never mind mechanizing the entire force. Nevertheless, some in the VDV argued that new developments in airlift and airborne technology made such a concept viable even though expensive. Work on a mechanized vehicle for the VDV began in the early 1960s, but it had to await improvements in airlift before becoming a practical solution.

ENHANCING AIRLIFT

The most important single factor in realizing Margelov's dreams of modernizing the VDV was the new generation of transport aircraft. The Soviet Air Force had changed its attitude toward the air transport role since World War II, and reequipment of the TDA air transport branch was steady.

The first of the new transports developed strictly for military needs was the innovative Antonov An-8. It was designed by Oleg Antonov, the same man who had designed the A-7 assault glider of

World War II. After the war, Antonov had formed a small aircraft design bureau in Ukraine to develop transport aircraft. His first important design was a remarkable anachronism, the An-2 biplane transport. The An-2 was widely dismissed in the West when it first appeared. The very idea of a biplane in the jet age seemed ludicrous. Yet the An-2 was an exceptionally rugged and dependable aircraft, well suited to its task of air transport in the less developed regions of Russia. A testament to its durability is that thousands still remain in service today. They also became a critical ingredient in the rebirth of the VDV after World War II, since they provided an economical, dependable, and rugged means of airlift for training paratroopers.

Antonov's next major design, the An-8, was based on a 1952 requirement for a new military transport aircraft. The VDV specifically sought a transport aircraft that could handle large loads such as the ASU-57 airborne assault gun. The existing IL-12 and IL-14, although perfectly capable in the paratrooper role, were nearly worthless with any large cargo. The design requirement coincided with a significant breakthrough in aircraft propulsion, the turboprop engine. A German wartime invention, the turboprop used a small jet engine as the source of power, but instead of relying on the jet principle as its main source of thrust, it harnessed the jet's turbine to turn a conventional propellor. There were several advantages to turboprops over conventional reciprocating engines: they were far more reliable and durable, they were extremely powerful for their size, and they were very economical in terms of fuel consumption. Several German engineers were dragooned into Soviet service and served at the new Kuznetsov design bureau developing these new power plants.

Antonov employed a pair of the new engines on his An-8. The VDV requirement heavily shaped the design. Many contemporary American and European transport designs, such as Britain's Bristol Type 170, or the U.S. C-123 Globemaster, used opening doors at the nose of the aircraft to handle heavy loads. This was a practical solution to airland cargoes but was useless for parachuting the payload. The other conventional approach was a twin-boom design with central fuselage pod, epitomized by the American C-119 Flying Boxcar but also used on other types such as the French Nord 2501 Noratlas and the British Blackburn Beverly. Antonov conceived a more elegant design, placing the cargo doors in the tail. This solution was reached at about the same time in the United States for the C-123 Provider transport aircraft. This layout required an unusually high rudder and tail assembly. But the configuration proved successful and would be repeated in later transport aircraft designs.

The An-8 cargo configuration allowed heavy cargoes such as light armored vehicles to be parachuted out the rear end. This is easier said than done, and it took years of experimentation before satisfactory techniques were developed. Two innovations were needed: parachute pallets and roller-bearing aircraft floors. The pallets were needed to simplify handling the vehicle and rigging it with a multicanopy parachute. The pallets served the secondary function of providing some cushioning when the armored vehicles were dropped. The floor design was needed to permit such pallets to be easily moved into the aircraft and, more importantly, easily pulled out during the parachute phase. Tracked vehicles without pallets would have been impossible to extract, using drogue chutes or other techniques, due to the tremendous friction created by the tracks against an ordinary metal floor.

The Antonov An-8 did not prove entirely successful, even though it pointed the way. Its new turboprop engine was troublesome, and its high tail configuration led to unexpected aerodynamic problems. Nevertheless, about a hundred were built, and all were delivered to the Soviet Air Force. Some would occasionally appear with Aeroflot markings, but this was a thin disguise for what was obviously a military transport.

The Antonov An-8 was followed in short order by an enlarged transport, the four-engine Antonov An-12. The An-8 had been designed to accommodate relatively small armored vehicles such as the ASU-57. Its cargo bay was capable of lifting up to ten tons. The next generation An-12 could carry medium armored vehicles, specifically the airborne's new ASU-85 assault gun, as well as specialized equipment such as air defense vehicles. The cargo capability was doubled to more than twenty tons through the use of a four-engine layout. The first An-12 became operational in 1959, three years before its American counterpart, the Lockheed C-130E Hercules. Eventually, about 740 An-12s were built for the airlift role, with several hundred more for specialized tasks in the civilian Aeroflot branch.

The entry of the An-12 into Soviet service corresponded with organizational changes in the Soviet Air Force. The TDA Air Assault Landing branch was reorganized as the VTA (Voennoe-transportnaya Aviatsiya), or Military Transport Aviation, the Soviet equivalent of the U.S. Air Force's Military Airlift Command (MAC). The reorganization was necessary due to the changing role of aviation in the modern Soviet armed forces. In the late 1940s when the TDA was first organized, transport aircraft were used mainly in specialized roles such as airborne operations. By the late 1950s, aviation had matured into an important transportation service, used regularly for moving troops and cargo around the Soviet Union. The new VTA recognized this by organizing its air transport units into two major elements. The transports earmarked to support the VDV Airborne Force were designated VTA–Airborne (VTA–Desantniy). By the mid-1960s, as more An-12s became available, VTA–Airborne deployed six transport divisions (one per airborne division) and several independent regiments. It was eventually renamed VTA–Central (VTA-Tsentralniy) but retained its primary mission of delivering the VDV airborne divisions. The remainder of the VTA was devoted to supporting the Soviet Air Force and other branches of the Soviet armed forces with light transports, liaison aircraft, and other airlift. But under its new commander, Marshal Nikolai Skripko, the VTA's primary focus was delivering the airborne force.

ARMORED FIREPOWER

As the airlift capabilities of the VTA increased, the firepower of the VDV Airborne Force grew as well. The little ASU-57 was a weak attempt at an antitank weapon. In the late 1950s, a new assault gun, the ASU-85, was developed to take advantage of the airlift available in the Antonov An-12. The ASU-85, also called the SU-85, was armed with a long 85mm gun. The new vehicle was based on components from the PT-76 light tank and weighed fourteen tons fully loaded, more than four times the weight of the ASU-57. It was fully armored, including the roof, and the armor was sufficient to protect against small arms and heavy machine-gun fire. The 85mm D-70 gun could penetrate more than 140 millimeters of armor, enough to deal with most medium tanks of the period.

As was so often the case with VDV armored vehicles, the ASU-85 was too little too late. As the ASU-85 was entering service in 1961, the U.S. Army was introducing a new generation of main battle tank, the M60A1, with armor in the frontal quadrant that was too thick for the ASU-85's gun to penetrate. Likewise, the new British Chieftain was much too thickly armored for the ASU-85. The Russian vehicle could still penetrate the armor of older tanks such as the American M48 and British Centurion, but its own armor was so thin that the only practical tactic was ambush. In an open engagement, any contemporary NATO tank could destroy the ASU-85 long before it came within effective striking range.

In spite of its shortcomings, the ASU-85 was produced in modest numbers. Eventually, each airborne division received a tank destroyer battalion equipped with thirty-one of these vehicles. It was still useful as an assault vehicle, even if its antitank performance was barely adequate. The ASU-85 was first demonstrated in East Germany at a secret 1963 Warsaw Pact exercise dubbed October Storm.

The VDV was not overly concerned about the limitations of the ASU-85, since a new type of weapon was entering service. It was the guided antitank missile, which made tank destroyers such as the ASU-85 obsolete. The first of these, the 3M6 Shmel (bumblebee) was a large, awkward design that used a simple joystick control system. After the missile fired, the operator had to keep an eye on the missile and the target, and steer the missile to impact. These missiles could be mounted on the lightweight GAZ-69 truck or on the BRDM-1 armored vehicle. In both cases, the missile-armed tank destroyers were much lighter and more portable than the ASU-85. The new missiles packed a warhead big enough to penetrate any NATO tank. The early guidance systems were awkward to use and took extensive training, but the weapon pointed the way toward future lightweight antitank weapons.

By the late 1960s, each airborne regiment had received an antitank battery of four missile-armed tank destroyers. A typical example was the 9P113, a BRDM-2 wheeled armored vehicle armed with six 9M14M Malyutka antitank missile launchers. In addition, man-portable versions of the missile were also introduced to provide more depth to airborne antitank defenses. But it took almost a decade before these missiles became truly practical. By the early 1970s, an improved guidance method was introduced, technically called semiautomatic command to line of sight, or SACLOS. This meant that the missile gunner no longer had to actually steer the missile. Instead, he aimed the missile sight at the target, and a calculator in the missile guidance tracker automatically sent course corrections to the missile. This made the missile much more likely to hit its target, and reduced the amount of time needed to train the gunner.

The growing sophistication and weight of VDV firepower led to the development of one of the most remarkable Soviet aircraft of the 1960s, the Antonov An-22 Antei. The An-22 was based on a 1962 VDV requirement for a military transport aircraft capable of airlanding tanks or other heavy off-sized loads. When the An-22 entered service in 1967, it was one of the world's largest transport aircraft, second only to the U.S. Air Force's C-5A Galaxy. Production was very slow, and only seventeen An-22s were in VTA service by 1972, five years after series production began. Ultimately, the aircraft proved inadequate in the long-range airlift role, which was demonstrated during an attempted relief operation to Peru in 1970 and an arms resupply to Egypt and Syria in the wake of the October 1973 war. In total, only forty-five An-22s were finally completed for VTA service. The An-22 was replaced in the 1980s by the even larger Antonov An-124 Ruslan jet-powered heavy-lift transporter.

BLUE BERETS

Elite forces have traditionally distinguished themselves from the rest of the military by adopting distinctive uniforms or insignia. The Soviet VDV was no exception. Colonel General Margelov was an enthusiastic proponent of this effort, feeling that it bolstered unit morale. The first step was the adoption of the Soviet Navy's striped blue and white sailor's shirt, the *telnyashka,* under the normal khaki tunic, to distinguish the paratroopers from the rest of the Soviet Army. This was an odd choice for an army unit, and was due to Margelov's combat career in World War II. In the early years of the war, Margelov had served on the Leningrad Front. Many Soviet warships were bottled up in harbors in Leningrad, so the sailors of the Baltic Fleet were brought ashore and used as elite infantry. Although an army major, Margelov was assigned to command the 1st Naval Infantry Regiment, which was used for raiding behind German lines.

Margelov associated the striped sailor's shirt with this highly effective unit. He had kept his own naval shirt as a memento of past glories, and now he decided the sailor's shirt would serve as the basis for the new VDV paratrooper's uniform. In spite of its odd beginnings, the blue-and-white–striped shirt became the predominant symbol of Soviet and Russian elite forces, especially after Afghanistan. It is now used not only by the VDV, but by other elite formations, including the Spetsnaz and elite special police units.

Another of Margelov's innovations was more traditional—the beret. The use of crimson berets by paratroopers can be traced back to the British practice, later picked up by the United States. The initiative for a Soviet paratrooper's beret came from a Russian military artist, A. B. Zhuk, who did some paintings of a proposed paratrooper uniform heavily influenced by the Anglo-American tradition. Margelov thought the idea was a good one, since it would further distinguish his forces from the great dull mass of the Soviet Army. Margelov authorized two berets, a khaki beret with the service uniform and a crimson beret with the dress and parade uniform. The new berets were officially approved in June 1967, and crimson berets began to be issued later in the summer. They first appeared publicly on 7 November 1967 during the big fiftieth anniversary parade for the 1917 October Revolution.

The crimson berets were short lived and disappeared within a year. No official explanation has been put forward to explain the sudden change. It may have been that the crimson berets were seen as too heavily influenced by the NATO style. In any event, the crimson berets gave way to cornflower blue berets. These had a more satisfactory Soviet lineage, since the original Soviet paratrooper units of the 1930s used pale blue helmets during the great summer war games. The blue berets were issued in 1968 and became the most popular element of the Soviet paratrooper's uniform. Indeed, Soviet paratroopers have been colloquially known as Blue Berets ever since.

OPERATION DNEPR

The growing capabilities of the VDV Airborne Force and the associated VTA–Airborne transport force were first put to the test in the autumn of 1967. The Soviet General Staff planned another of its impressive fall exercises, always a combination of real training and lavish propaganda. The Dnepr exercise was the largest postwar Soviet war game, aimed at impressing NATO as much as training Soviet troops. Like most of these major exercises, the missions were tightly choreographed, and there was little doubt that the good guys would win.

One of the most intriguing features of Operation Dnepr was the decision to drop an entire VDV airborne division, the first time this would be done in the USSR since the 1930s. Indeed, this exercise was the largest single drop of airborne forces since the 1944 Arnhem operation. The division selected for the main drop was the 76th Guards Chernigov Airborne Division, based near Pskov in the Leningrad Military District. It was supported by elements from another VDV division. This exercise required a large fraction of the VTA–Airborne airlift force, since the plan called for delivering the entire division in a single lift, the first time this had ever been attempted in the USSR.

The Dnepr war game was a front-level exercise, with the Soviet Union represented, not surprisingly, by the "Eastern Front" and NATO by the "Western Front" opposing force. On 26 September, the Eastern Front conducted a river-crossing exercise over the Dnepr and Pripyat Rivers north of Kiev, using a helicopter force to seize the western bank. At this point, the Western Front began mechanized attacks to crush the bridgehead. In a textbook plan somewhat similar to the October 1943 Dnepr airborne operation, the airborne division would be landed behind the bridgehead to weaken the Western Front. The exercise was given a more modern flavor by its tactical missions. The airborne force was to capture the Western Front headquarters, seize a neighboring airfield, and capture the Western Front's tactical nuclear weapons.

The exercise was a clear demonstration that the technical lessons of the World War II Dnepr debacle were clearly appreciated. The first stage of the airborne drop began on the afternoon of 26 September with the insertion of reconnaissance platoons to secure the drop zones around the town of Ovruch. Once the areas were cleared, the main drops began before dusk. The first elements to land were the antitank companies with their little ASU-57 assault guns. These were important not only to defend the drop zones, but to provide the assault units with mobility. The heavy drop elements were followed by a massive drop of 8,000 paratroopers. The main drop took only twenty-two minutes. In another echo of wartime lessons learned, the first objective seized was a nearby airfield. Once secured, VTA aircraft flew in a battalion of ASU-85 tank destroyers. That battalion was used to stop a tank attack by the Western Front, attempting to overwhelm the drop zone.

The airborne drop helped to collapse the Western Front defense, and the following day a second airborne division was dropped farther to the southwest in the Western Front rear area, near Korosten, to seize key highway and rail bridges. The aim of the mission was to demonstrate the role of the airborne force in the operational depth of the enemy to prevent the opponent from moving up the reserves or, in other circumstances, to trap retreating enemy forces so that they could be eliminated by the oncoming friendly forces.

The Ultimate World War II Airdrop?

The Dnepr war games were remarkable for several reasons. For the VDV, they represented a return to the forefront of the Soviet armed forces. After nearly two decades in the shadows, the paratroopers were now being regarded as an important element in Soviet doctrine. Margelov's vigorous advocacy of the VDV with the leadership of the Soviet Army had finally paid off.

Also remarkable was the scale of the Dnepr war games, which would have delighted airborne enthusiasts of the 1930s and 1940s. Ironically, the Dnepr war games were probably the last example of the classic World War II airdrop. The skies west of Kiev hummed with the drone of hundreds of transports dropping paratroopers much as they had three decades before in the 1935 maneuvers. But was this a realistic depiction of the modern battlefield? Even ignoring the sensitive question of nuclear weapons, the war game was a World War II scenario two decades too late.

In the intervening twenty years, the threat to large aircraft had dramatically changed, brought about by significant improvements in air defense, especially air defense missiles. In World War II, divisional air defense was limited to small numbers of semimobile guns or mobile autocannons on half-tracks. As was evident from the 1943 Dnepr operation, these weapons could cause grievous losses if they were in the right place at the right time, but they actually could shoot down very few transports.

By the mid-1960s, this had begun to change. At the divisional level, NATO units were fielding the MIM-23 HAWK surface-to-air missile (SAM), a highly effective weapon against nimble strike fighters, and a murderously efficient system if used against lumbering propellor-driven transports. Although HAWK batteries were still few in number, their range made them a formidable defensive system. At the lower end of the scale, 1967 marked the year that the U.S. Army introduced the FIM-43 Redeye, a man-portable SAM with four to six gunners per maneuver battalion. These little systems could make short work of a transport aircraft, since the aircraft's turboprop engine was an enticing attraction to the infrared seeker in the nose of the missile. This became evident in 1972–73 when North Vietnamese troops used the Redeye's Soviet equivalent, the Strela-2 (SA-7 Grail) missile, against America and South Vietnamese transport aircraft with considerable success.

Air defense continued to thicken with the deployment of radar-directed gun systems such as the U.S. Army M163 Vulcan in 1968 and the German Gepard in 1973. Medium-range missile systems, such as the U.S. Army's M48 Chaparral in 1969 and the Franco-German Roland in 1977, added to the lethal mix. This pattern was followed in the Soviet Army itself.

It wasn't so much the increase in numbers of air defense systems as the increase in lethality and accuracy. Nonmaneuvering, low altitude, slow targets such as transport aircraft were sitting ducks for the new missiles and radar-directed guns. The vulnerability of large multi-engine aircraft was one of the lessons of the many air wars since World War II. In the 1940s, tactical bombers were often large, cumbersome aircraft. In the age of the SAM, tactical bombers had to be fast and maneuverable, and multiplace bombers eventually gave way to one- or two-seat strike aircraft not much different from fighters. Transports could not follow suit and so remained vulnerable. Although air defense systems could be suppressed by a vigorous campaign of air strikes and electronic warfare, in the 1960s and 1970s the Soviet Air Force was poorly equipped to carry out such missions.

Nor was air defense the only problem. As the Soviets learned in the 1942 Vyazma airdrops, enemy fighter aviation posed a considerable threat to airborne operations. The 1943 Dnepr operation had been conducted under conditions of Soviet air supremacy. But in a war with NATO, local air superiority by the Warsaw Pact was the best that could be hoped for, and there was the very real chance of the transports being confronted by hostile fighter aircraft.

Parachute operations since World War II have been few in number precisely because of these contemporary hazards. The successful airborne missions since the 1960s have been only in Third World environments where advanced air defenses were few: the Congo, Grenada, and Panama. There were no large-scale paratroop drops in the midintensity conflicts of recent years—the Mideast wars of 1967, 1973, and 1982; the Iran-Iraq war of 1980–88; and the Gulf War of 1991—although all of these armies had airborne forces and the airlift necessary to carry out such missions. The Dnepr exercise of 1967 was the last gasp of a fading idea.

OPERATION BOHEMIAN FOREST

The VDV's role as imperial storm troopers was well demonstrated by their next postwar mission: the 1968 invasion of Czechoslovakia. Unlike Hungary in 1956 where the VDV performed mainly as elite infantry, in Czechoslovakia their rapid airborne insertion tactics were put to the test.

A decade had passed since the ruthless suppression of the Hungarian revolt, but the promises of political and social liberalization never materialized. In Poland, Gomulka backed away from his pledges of reform and in 1968 was faced with growing student protests. In Czechoslovakia, there was the hope of liberalization when Aleksandr Dubcek took control of the government and promised "socialism with a human face." Unfortunately for the Czechs and Slovaks, the Kremlin's aging dinosaurs did not approve. The Soviet ambassador in Czechoslovakia, Stepan Chervonenko, was a smug and dull-witted party apparatchik who viewed the plans for modest economic reform as "bourgeois counter-revolution." His reports on the Prague spring reforms were recently declassified: Aleksandr Dubcek characterized the ambassador's words as "simply idiotic" and the work of a "miserable observer."

By the late spring of 1968, the Czechoslovak reforms, or at least Chervonenko's jaundiced reports on them, were causing considerable alarm in the Kremlin. The Poles were already grumbling about the need for "a Polish Dubcek," so there was fear that the liberalization might spread. In April, the Soviet General Staff began plans for military intervention into Czechoslovakia if necessary. A repeat of the bloody Hungarian revolt was feared, so invasion was to be preceded by pressure and intimidation; force would be the last resort. As a first step, the General Staff recommended pushing up the date of the Warsaw Pact war games in Czechoslovakia from September to June. This would allow the Soviet Army to insert 27,000 additional troops and associated equipment into Czechoslovakia under the guise of normal peacetime training. The Czechoslovak government realized that this move was the first step in a game of intimidation and blackmail, and Marshal Ivan I. Yakubovskiy's attempt to gain Dubcek's acquiescence was politely rebuffed. Instead, the Warsaw Pact staged a major staff exercise in Czechoslovakia in June, code-named Bohemian Forest, which served as a planning exercise for an eventual invasion.

Czechoslovakia in 1968 presented a much greater problem than did Hungary in 1956. The Hungarian army in 1956 was small and poorly developed; its officers were cowed by political purges and secret police infiltration. In contrast, the Czechoslovak army in 1968 was one of the most modern in the Warsaw Pact, well trained and well equipped. Its officers had been chosen for their loyalty to "the ideals of socialism," meaning that they were not blatantly anti-Soviet, but there was always the risk that Dubcek's alluring promises of reform would subvert their allegiance from the Warsaw Pact to Czechoslovak nationalism. If the Czechoslovak Peoples Army (CSLA) decided to fight, an invasion would quickly become far bloodier than the 1956 Hungarian uprising.

As a result, the Soviet General Staff insisted on a lightning invasion. One of the most important actions would be a quick decapitation of the government. This would be the primary mission of the VDV. The Czechoslovak leadership would be seized at the very onset of the operation. The Soviets presumed that without official orders the Czechoslovak army would stay in its barracks.

The Soviet GRU military intelligence did not have to rely on blockheads such as Ambassador Chervonenko; there were Soviet advisers in all major Czechoslovak units. Moreover, the Soviet General Staff had a skeptical view of the warrior spirit of the Czechoslovak army. The Czechs were not romantic hotheads as were the Poles or Hungarians. The Czechoslovak army did not fight in 1938 when the Germans occupied their country, and there was no substantial popular resistance movement against the Nazis as there had been in Poland. Czech military tradition was epitomized by "the Good Soldier Svejk," the antihero from Husak's satirical novel.

OPERATION DANUBE

On 8 April 1968, General of the Army V. F. Margelov received a secret directive from Soviet Minister of Defense Marshal A. A. Grechko, countersigned by the chief of the General Staff, Marshal M. V. Zakharov. The directive stated that, "The USSR and the other socialist countries, true to their internationalist duties described in the Warsaw Pact, must call upon their forces to offer help to the Czechoslovak Peoples Army in order to protect the Homeland from the current danger." The VDV and its command staff were put under the immediate command of the General Staff. Margelov was told to put two of his divisions on alert: the 7th Guards Airborne Division in the Baltics and the 103rd Guards Airborne Division in Ukraine. Their missions were spelled out in the April directive. The 7th Guards Airborne Division would be assigned to airland or parachute into Prague to carry out special missions against the Czechoslovak government. The 103rd Guards Airborne Division would arrive by parachute and airlanding at Pribram (the headquarters of the Czechoslovak 1st Army), Blatna (near the headquarters of the Czechoslovak 4th Army), and Tabory (headquarters of the Czechoslovak Western Military District). Five VTA divisions were assigned to support Margelov's Special Operations Group. Margelov was told to prepare his units and await the orders for the operation to begin, the code word being *BURYA* (blizzard).

   The overall invasion plan for crushing the Czechoslovak reform movement was code-named Operation Danube and was put under the command of General of the Army Ivan G. Pavlovskiy. There were several Soviet units already stationed in Czechoslovakia as part of

the Central Group of Forces. From the Soviet Union itself, the Carpathian Front, commanded by General Colonel Bisyarin, would invade eastern Slovakia with one tank and two combined-arms armies, supported by an air army, and would also control allied Polish troops from eastern Poland. The Central Front, under the command of General Colonel Aleksandr Mayorov, was formed from units in Germany and southwestern Poland and would include two armies from the Baltic Military District and the 20th Guards Army already stationed in Germany. Although the Soviet General Staff did not expect NATO to intervene, it was not prudent to commit too large a portion of the Group of Soviet Forces–Germany to the invasion. A Southern Front was formed in Hungary from Soviet units along with allied Hungarian and Bulgarian units, but only the Balaton Operational Group was used during the invasion. The Soviet General Staff made certain that German, Polish, Hungarian, and Bulgarian units would participate, even if in token numbers, to aid the pretext that the invasion was a joint Warsaw Pact operation to provide "fraternal assistance" in the forced suicide of Czechoslovak reform.

Interestingly enough, the plan included the use of units of the Polish 6th Pomeranian Airborne Division, the Warsaw Pact's only other airborne division. The 6th Pomeranian was assigned to take the air base at Pardubice. There are rumors that the division was reorganized after the 1968 invasion due to the Poles' lack of enthusiasm for this unwelcome excursion to Bohemia.

The Czechoslovak leadership seriously misunderstood the Kremlin's attitudes. Dubcek in his memoirs recalls that he thought

> the 1956 crushing of Hungary was way behind us; this was a different era. . . . The challenge was to maneuver around [the Kremlin] long enough to make them accept us on civilized terms . . . the Soviets had for years preached the principle of peaceful coexistence and noninterference in the internal affairs of other countries. Was it rational to expect that they would contradict all this by attacking us militarily? I did not think so, and I do not think I was a dreamer.

On Sunday, 18 August 1968, the leaders of the other Warsaw Pact states met secretly in Moscow and signed a declaration authorizing the Warsaw Pact to invade Czechoslovakia. Margelov's Special Operations Group was put on alert and began to move forward to air bases in western Ukraine and Poland to prepare for Operation Burya.

SUMMER BLIZZARD

Around 20:30 on the evening of Monday, 20 August 1968, an Antonov An-24 transport aircraft with Aeroflot markings landed at Ruzyne airport in the western outskirts of Prague. It taxied to the end of the runway and remained parked. It was in fact a Soviet Air Force air control aircraft placed there in case the main control tower had to be knocked out. A few hours later another special Aeroflot flight came from Lvov in Ukraine; the passengers in civilian garb were met by officials from the Czechoslovak state security service. The visitors were Soviet government officials and KGB agents. At midnight, the control tower at Ruzyne was contacted by unidentified government officials and told to close the airport to any outgoing or incoming civilian flights. A Soviet KGB special operations team in civilian clothes arrived soon afterward and took up positions around the airport.

At 03:37 in the early morning of Tuesday, 21 August 1968, two Antonov An-12 military transports, escorted by MiG-21 fighter aircraft, landed at Ruzyne airport. They carried the commanders of the

7th Guards Airborne Division (7 GVDD) and the 7th Guards Aviation Transport Division of the VTA, the divisional operations group, and the 2nd Paratrooper Assault Company of the 108th Guards Paratroop Regiment of the 7th Guards Airborne Division. Within fifteen minutes, the 2nd Company had deployed and sealed off the airport. The VTA division's operations group seized the control tower in conjunction with a KGB special operations team already at the airport. With the airport under control, the remainder of the 7th Aviation Transport Division began to arrive in a steady stream, thirty seconds apart. The big Antonov An-12 transports quickly maneuvered to the sides of the runway, and the troops and vehicles of the 7th Guards Airborne Division disembarked.

Special assault groups formed up around 04:30, made up of troops from the division's reconnaissance company and the 108th Guards Paratrooper Regiment. They had a few ASU-85 and ASU-57 assault guns, plus a small number of BRDM-2 antitank vehicles. Although paratroopers could ride on the outside of these vehicles, the reconnaissance team seized two seventy-passenger tourist buses and four cargo trucks. One column moved on the presidential palace on Hradcany Hill in the center of Prague, surrounding it and placing President Ludwig Svoboda under house arrest.

Another column from the reconnaissance company under Lieutenant Seregin proceeded to the Communist Party headquarters building, led there by a black Volga manned by KGB personnel from the Soviet embassy in Prague. The team quickly overpowered the bewildered Czech security guards. The team was expecting to find only the first secretary, Aleksandr Dubcek, who lived in room 79 of the party building. Instead, when the team broke down to door to room 79, they found themselves facing not only Dubcek, but most of the Czechoslovak government, including J. Smrkovsky, F. Kriegel, J. Spacek, and about two dozen other top government officials. Dubcek reached for the phone to call Leonid Brezhnev in the Kremlin, but the phone was ripped from his hands by a young paratrooper officer. By now, the assault team had been joined by Lieutenant Colonel Shishkin, deputy chief of the 7th Airborne's political section. Shishkin greeted the Czechoslovak officials, and Kriegel demanded to know why the Soviet Army had invaded. Being a well-indoctrinated political officer, Shishkin impudently replied, "The Soviet Army has come to protect socialism in Czechoslovakia!"

The government officials had heard about the invasion over the telephone, but they presumed it would take ten to eleven hours for the Soviet Army to drive into Prague from the Polish or German border. The paratroopers' sudden appearance completely surprised them. The paratroopers finally lined up the officials against a wall, frisked them, and told them to sit down. The orders were to drive the government officials back to Ruzyne airport. By the time the party headquarters building was secured, around 07:00, a large crowd of Czech civilians had gathered. Several of the young men attempted to force their way into the building, and two were shot by the paratroopers. After the shooting, the crowd kept its distance, but its growing size made it impossible to move the government delegation until 18:30 that evening.

By 06:15, while the reconnaissance company was seizing the Czechoslovak government, the remainder of the first wave of the 7th Guards Airborne Division had landed at Ruzyne airport. This included the entire 108th Guards Paratrooper Regiment, the antitank battalion, air defense battalion, engineer battalion, and divisional communications battalion. As each planeload arrived, the divisional operations group formed them into assault teams and sent them into Prague.

By early morning, the paratroopers had set up their ZU-23 antiaircraft guns in positions on Letza Hill on the west bank of the Vltava River. Other units sealed off the Old Town, the radio and postal buildings, and other key communications points, including several bridges. The main radio station on Vinhradska Street was one of the last points to be seized. In the meantime, Czech civilians had created a barricade using a city tram and two heavy trucks. The barricade halted the paratroopers, who were uncertain what to do. The Czechs began to reinforce the barricade, and the paratroopers retreated into their ASU-85 assault guns and BRDM armored vehicles. Some of the more adventurous Czech teenagers began sneaking up on the armored vehicles, attempting to set them on fire with oily rags. As the armored vehicle crews noticed what was happening, they began to fire on the crowds with machine guns to warn them off, and also began firing at cars on the street to prevent the Czechs from adding them to the growing barricade. In frustration, the ASU-85s finally began firing on the barricade, with little effect but to start a smoky fire. After two nearby trucks exploded from the blaze, the paratroopers finally decided to use their ASU-85s to bulldoze the barricade. Once past the obstruction, the paratroopers piled out and smashed their way into the radio building. It was the last major communications center still in Czech hands, and the radio broadcasts soon ceased as the paratroopers spread out into the building.

Later in the day, the remainder of the 7th Guards Airborne Division arrived in downtown Prague and took up positions. As the General Staff expected, there was no resistance from the Czechoslovak army. The 103rd Airborne Division had done its job in seizing Czechoslovak army headquarters outside of Prague, so instructions about resistance were never given by the Czech General Staff. The sudden appearance of the Soviet troops had prevented Czech civilians from seizing weapons from police stations or army barracks, as had occurred in Hungary in 1956. Later that day, motor rifle and tank regiments from the Central Front began arriving in Prague, and soon the city was securely in Soviet hands. Unlike Hungary in 1956, casualties were minimal—eleven dead and eighty-seven injured—mostly as the result of accidents rather than fighting. "Socialism with a human face" had been decisively crushed, and the Brezhnev doctrine had been demonstrated to the world. The Czechoslovak longing for freedom survived, but it would not emerge victorious for another two decades.

The coup de main of the VDV paratroopers in Prague was an important reason for the quick and relatively bloodless success of Operation Danube. The Czechoslovak invasion proved that Margelov had succeeded in transforming the VDV from an inept, second-rate bunch into the pride of the Soviet Army. The VDV basked in the glow of success. In contrast, afteraction reports castigated the tank and motor rifle forces for their poor levels of preparedness and their logistical failings. The VDV was becoming a true elite force, attracting the best conscripts and some of the top officers into its ranks.

A Soviet paratroop exercise in the 1930s. One of the interesting differences between Soviet parachute techniques and those elsewhere in Europe was the use of two small canopies simultaneously as seen here.

In the early 1930s, the Soviets experimented with many unusual techniques for airborne delivery of troops, including these curious containers under the wing of a Polikarpov R-5 biplane bomber. *Sovfoto.*

The Soviets were the pioneers of many airborne technologies and were the first to use lightweight recoilless rifles like the DRP gun seen in this rare view from a 1930s wargame.

The workhorse of the Soviet VDV Airborne Force was the Tupolev TB-3 heavy bomber. Obsolete as a bomber by 1941, it took part in all of the early Soviet airdrops in World War II, including the Moscow battles. *U.S. National Air & Space Museum.*

During the desperate battles to the east of Moscow in February 1942, it was the Lisunov Li-2 that carried most of the paratroopers into German-held territory. The Li-2 was a copy of the legendary Douglas DC-3 airliner.

The supply demands of the expanding partisan movement drained away much of the airlift that might have been used for paratrooper operations during the war. Here, a partisan airbase in the northern Caucasus in October 1942. On the ground are a pair of Polikarpov Po-2 biplanes, while an old Tupolev PS-9 airliner flies overhead. *Sovfoto*.

The Polikarpov Po-2 biplane, first known as the U-2, was the workhorse of the partisan airlift effort. This version has been modified with a rear compartment to accept stretcher cases. These aircraft flew thousands of missions behind German lines to support the partisan movement.

A pair of Lisunov Li-2 transports conduct practice airdrops in central Russia in the summer of 1943 prior to the last major airdrop operation near the Dnepr River. The heavy commitment of these transports to other missions gave them little time to practice airborne drops, often with tragic consequences for the paratroopers. *Sovfoto.*

Although little known outside Russia, the legendary *razvedchik* scouts were the World War II forebears of today's Spetsnaz special operations troops. Like the Spetsnaz, the Red Army deployed special deep penetration scout teams for special missions behind German lines.

One of the lessons of the World War II airborne missions was the need for heavier firepower in VDV airborne units. This 85mm antitank gun was one of a number of new weapons adopted in the 1950s as airlift capabilities grew.

For airborne soldiers the world over, the rudiments of paratrooper training will seem familiar. Here, recruits at the main VDV Airborne Forces school at Ryazan practice basic landing techniques during February 1973 training. *Sovfoto.*

To drop heavy loads, the Soviets first used multi-canopy parachutes like the ones here. The smaller chutes nearer the pallet are the drogue chutes, which initially drag the load out of the rear of the aircraft.

In the 1960s, the Soviets developed the PRSM pallets. These needed only a single parachute, since, when near the ground, a large retrorocket is fired to slow the pallet before impact. The Soviets occasionally dropped airborne troops inside armored vehicles using this technique, surely one of the most frightening means of air delivery. *Sovfoto.*

A BMD-1 airborne combat vehicle with its parachutes packed and ready for airdrop at the Khodynka airfield in 1993. The long aluminum poles at the side of the vehicle hinge downward and contain contact sensors at their base which trigger the retrorocket of the PRSM pallet.

Company commanders review their troops prior to a winter airborne exercise in central Russia. The aircraft in the background is an Ilyushin IL-76 Candid. *Sovfoto.*

The first of the airborne combat vehicles was the diminutive ASU-57 tank destroyer introduced into service in the early 1950s. It carried a two-man crew, but other paratroopers would often ride on the outside to help clear away parachute static lines in the drop zone. *Sovfoto.*

The ASU-85 was introduced in the 1960s to make up for the inadequate firepower of the tiny ASU-57. However, it was so large that it had to be airlanded, an awkward tactical limitation. Here a pair of ASU-85s drive out of Antonov An-12 Cub transports during an exercise. *Sovfoto.*

The VDV Airborne Force began to mechanize in the late 1960s using the BMD-1 airborne assault vehicle. Up to six paratroopers could be carried inside besides the two-man crew, but it was definitely a cramped ride!

The successor to the BMD-1 is the new BMD-3, introduced in 1993. It is nearly twice as heavy as the earlier BMD-1 family, having been based on the lessons of the Afghan war where it became clear that the BMD-1 was too delicate for prolonged operations.

The VDV Airborne Force is armed more heavily than most other paratrooper forces in the world. Here, an airborne D-30 122mm howitzer battery prepares to fire. *Sovfoto.*

The Spetsnaz are the special deep reconnaissance troops of the GRU military intelligence service. They were well trained compared to other conscripted Soviet troops, but their capabilities were widely exaggerated in the West.

The Navy's special operations force is the Naval Infantry, a Soviet equivalent of the U.S. Marines. One of the tactical differences between the U.S. Marines and the Soviet Naval Infantry is the Marine preference for helicopters for rapid insertion, compared to the Soviet technique of amphibious assault air-cushion vehicles like the Project 1232.1 Dzheyran seen here. *Sovfoto.*

The Soviet VDV was the single most capable element of the Soviet Army during the bitter fighting in Afghanistan in 1979–1988 The VDV Airborne Force spearheaded the invasion and were the last regular units to leave.

The war in Afghanistan changed VDV combat tactics. They gave up their fragile BMD-1 airborne vehicles for the more robust BMP-2 Hedgehogs seen here. The Afghanistan experience demonstrated the limitations of parachute operations in modern wars, and the value of helicopters instead.

The advent of reliable gas-turbine powered helicopters like the Mil Mi-8M
Hip seen here marked the beginning of a revolution in airmobile tactics.
Helicopters proved a more versatile tool for special forces than parachutes,
a lesson quickly learned by the Soviet VDV in Afghanistan. *Sovfoto.*

The Afghan mujahideen called the Mi-24 Hind attack helicopter the "devil's
chariot" due to its ferocious firepower. This is a Mi-24P armed with an
especially potent twin 30mm cannon besides its usual assortment of rockets
and guided missiles. *Michael Jerchel.*

The workhorse of the Afghanistan war was the Mi-8MTB Hip assault helicopter, seen taking off from a base near the Soviet frontier in 1988. The
appearance of man-portable missiles like the Stinger made helicopter operations more dangerous, but this machine sports devices to lure away the
missiles, including an Ispanka IR jammer on its spine, a pair of scab-mounted
IR flare dispensers, and a large gas mixer over the engine exhaust.

The VDV Airborne depended on the airlift provided by the VTA Military
Transport Aviation branch of the Soviet Air Force. In the 1960s and 1970s,
the Antonov An-12BP Cub was the backbone of the VTA's airlift force.

By the late 1970s, the turboprop Antonov An-12 began to give way to the more advanced Ilyushin IL-76 Candid jet transport. The IL-76 has double the lift and double the range of the An-12, making mechanization of the VDV with new armored vehicles practical for the first time.

Since the fall of the Soviet Union in 1991, the VDV Airborne Force has been particularly busy along the borders of the former USSR. Here, a patrol of Russian paratroopers during peacekeeping operations in Georgia in 1993. *Dodge Billingsly.*

The future of the VDV Airborne Force is more likely to be tied up with the helicopter than the parachute. The VDV is expected to form the core of the new Russian Mobile Force, part of a strategic restructuring of the army in the wake of the momentous changes in Russia since 1991. *Sovfoto.*

The VDV frequently have been paratroopers deployed as "Blue Helmets" with the UN in locations such as Bosnia-Hercegovina, as well as many trouble spots in the USSR. These paratroopers wear the new tri-color flash of Russia as well as the old Soviet VDV insignia on their shoulders. *Dodge Billingsly.*

Chapter 8
Armored Airborne

The ultimate dream of Russia's earliest airborne visionaries had been an airlanded combat force no different from conventional army units. This meant a motorized and mechanized airborne force. This dream had proven to be impractical for nearly four decades due to the limits of airlift. But by the late 1960s, with the expansion of the VTA airlift force and the development of new transport aircraft, the dream of armored airborne forces had come within reach.

The desire for mechanized airborne forces in the 1930s was based on the same tactical reasons as the desire for mechanization in the army in general. Armored vehicles provided far more mobility, protection, and firepower than conventional infantry. The Soviet Union's "revolution in military affairs"—the post-Stalin renaissance in military thinking in the late 1950s—had added another reason. As mentioned earlier, there was concern about the viability of the airborne force on the nuclear battlefield. Unprotected paratroopers would soon fall victim to the debilitating effects of residual radiation if landing in areas previously hit by tactical nuclear weapons. Armored vehicles offered a solution to this problem. The steel armor of the vehicle, combined with plasticized lead pellet liners, offered a significant means of protection against this type of radiation. In addition, the air within the armored vehicle could be filtered to minimize the risk of inhaling fallout particles. The infantry within the vehicles could disembark to carry out traditional infantry tasks (at some risk of contamination) and return to the relative safety of the vehicle.

The idea of armored airborne combat vehicles had been examined in the late 1950s but was not treated seriously. The VTA airlift force was only beginning to be capable of lifting conventional paratroop forces; armored forces would have resulted in the same airlift/airborne force mismatch that had plagued the VDV since its combat debut in 1941. Furthermore, the Antonov An-12 was not the most suitable transport for this role. Although the An-12 could carry armored vehicles, the weight did impose constraints on range and performance.

The innovation that made airborne armor possible was the Ilyushin IL-76 transport aircraft, the first Soviet jet military transport. Development of the Ilyushin jet began in the mid-1960s as a Soviet counterpart to the U.S. Air Force Lockheed C-141 Starlifter. The requirements for the new aircraft were simple: double the range and double the payload over the existing An-12. The new aircraft also had to be suitable for landing and taking off from unprepared fields in the event that no suitable runways were available. The first prototype of the new transport began flying in 1971, slightly behind schedule, and was introduced into service in 1974. It would become the backbone of the VTA and remains so to this day.

While work was progressing on the IL-76 transport, design of its heavy cargo was also under way. The new vehicle was designated the BMD *(boevaya mashina desantnaya),* or airborne combat vehicle. The BMD was designed as an airborne counterpart of the army's best armored infantry vehicle, the BMP. Both vehicles shared the same armament system: a single-man turret with a 73mm low-pressure gun and a launcher for the 9M14M Malyutka antitank missile. There the similarity ends. Because the BMD was designed for airborne drop, its size and weight had to be considerably trimmed. The BMP weighed more than thirteen tons combat loaded; the BMD requirement called for a vehicle of less than seven tons, about half the weight. However, the VDV could not afford to build twice as many BMDs, so the troop requirement was not cut in half. The BMP carried eleven troops (including the crew), and the requirement for the BMD insisted on at least eight.

The design of the BMD was entrusted to the Volgograd design bureau, headed by Ivan V. Gavalov. Gavalov's design team had been

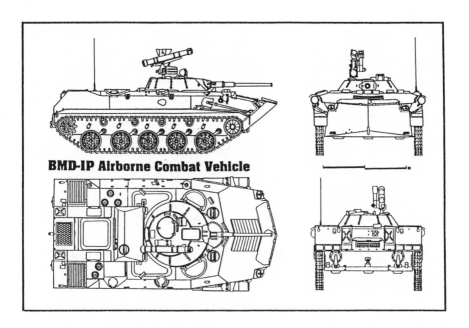

BMD-IP Airborne Combat Vehicle

an unsuccessful competitor in the Soviet Army's BMP design, losing to the Isakov design bureau from Chelybinsk. But the BMP competition had given Gavalov important experience in designing infantry vehicles. The BMD prototype, code-named Obiekt 915, was basically a shrunken version of Gavalov's Obiekt 914 BMP design. The one concession to the airlift requirement was to reduce the armor required on the BMD. The BMP was sufficiently armored to protect it against heavy machine guns such as the American .50-caliber Browning. The BMD requirement was protection against .30-caliber rifle fire. The lower armor requirement, combined with the reduced troop size, allowed Gavalov and his team to substantially reduce the size and weight of the BMD. Development of the BMD-1 was much delayed, first starting in 1961. The problems were more than technical and budgetary: some were still questioning whether it was prudent to mechanize the VDV. Both Margelov and his deputy, Gen. Dmitri S. Sukhorukhov, strongly supported the concept.

The first BMDs entered trials in the late 1960s. They were formidably armed for so small a vehicle. Indeed, when the BMD was first seen by Western intelligence, it was presumed to be a new light tank. Its compactness came at a cost: the vehicle was incredibly cramped inside. In the center of the forward portion of the hull was the driver; the squad leader and squad machine gunner were on either side. A single gunner sat in the turret. Behind him sat the remaining four squad members, shoehorned into an awkward cavity between the turret and the rear engine compartment. The space in the rear was so cramped that normally only three soldiers would ride in this compartment instead of the theoretical four. Riding in the BMD was not for the claustrophobic.

Production of the BMD began in 1968, and the new vehicle appeared in limited numbers for trials in 1969 with the 7th Guards Airborne Division in Lithuania. It was the only armored vehicle of its kind to enter service anywhere in the world. Although other armies had developed airborne tanks—the World War II U.S. M22 Locust and British Tetrarch, and the postwar U.S. M551 Sheridan—no other army ever fielded an airborne infantry vehicle. The U.S. Army was content to keep its one airborne division, the 82nd, a light infantry formation. The 82nd Airborne received one battalion of the new M551 Sheridan light tanks (officially dubbed armored reconnaissance/airborne assault vehicle), but armored infantry carriers were never seriously considered. This was due to major doctrinal differences between the U.S. and the Soviet Union. In the early 1970s, Soviet doctrine envisioned the use of the VDV as a significant element in a conventional high-intensity war in Europe. Since Soviet doctrine was essentially offensive in nature, the VDV was seen as a shock force suitable for landing deep in NATO's rear. The U.S. Army's orientation in Europe was more defensive, and it was difficult to see a paratroop role for the 82nd Airborne in most NATO scenarios. However, the 82nd Airborne did play a critical role in army plans for operations in low-intensity scenarios, especially in the developing world. In this context, armored vehicles seemed a heavy and burdensome luxury.

PROJECT CENTAUR

The BMD-1 first entered operational trials at the VDV's main training center at Ryazan in 1968. The original test drops used the new MKS-350-9 multicanopy parachute, with the BMD strapped to a standard cargo pallet. During the trials, one of the paratroop instructors, Maj. Leonid Zuyev, proposed to experiment with part of the crew actually riding inside the BMD during the drop. Before receiving official permission to do tests with a loaded BMD pallet, Zuyev began a series of tests to simulate the physical forces to paratroopers riding such devices. He had a paratrooper ride an unloaded pallet to examine the way it impacted on the ground.

When General Margelov heard about the experiment, he lost his temper. The Soviet system frowned on individual initiative, preferring all orders to come from the top. Margelov ordered the major into his office for a stern rebuke: "Do you think you can just throw people around and act on your own?" Zuyev apologized, and his sterling record protected him from more serious consequences.

Within a few days, Margelov's attitude had mellowed; he began to think that actually landing troops inside the BMD was not such a bad idea. There had always been problems when the crew jumped separately from a heavy load, even with the little ASU-57 assault guns: inevitably, the vehicle landed miles away from the crew and it took precious time to link up the crew and vehicle. By landing the crew with the vehicle, this problem would be avoided.

By this time, operational trials of the BMD were beginning with Col. Vladimir Krayev's 7th Guards Airborne Division in Kaunus, Lithuania. Margelov intended to test the concept during the trials. However, higher authorities intervened. During a meeting with Defense Minister Marshal Andrey Grechko, Margelov was told in no uncertain terms that the experiments were unacceptable. If the main parachutes failed, the paratroopers inside the vehicles would have no means of escape and would plummet to their certain deaths in a horrifying fashion. It was impractical for the BMD crews to wear their own parachutes. They could not get in and out of the small vehicle hatches if wearing parachutes, and, in any event, the hatches were blocked by the vehicle's parachute harnesses. Furthermore, film footage of the unmanned drops of the BMD showed that they tumbled violently after release from the aircraft before the main chutes deployed. Even if the parachutes opened properly, there was a good chance the crew would be seriously injured during the drop itself.

Although Grechko forbade the actual tests, research into the concept was permitted under a classified project called Kentavr (Centaur).

Project Centaur was headed by Leonid Zuyev, now elevated in rank to lieutenant colonel after Margelov's change of heart. Centaur consisted of ground experiments to examine the forces exerted on the crew during the drop and landing. The project developed a cushioned seat for the crew, patterned after the *kazbekov* seats used in Soviet spacecraft. The ground trials suggested that such manned drops were feasible.

After enduring much badgering, Defense Minister Grechko finally agreed to permit actual trials. Margelov had shown such enthusiasm for the project that his youngest son, a VDV lieutenant, volunteered for the first drop. (Of Margelov's five sons, four were parachute-qualified; the fifth, a naval officer, was not.) Leonid Zuyev sat in the driver's position and Lt. Aleksandr Zuyev sat in the troop compartment, strapped into the special seats. The first test drop was conducted on 5 January 1973 from an Antonov An-12 transport.

The concept worked, but the landing forces involved were severe. The most serious complication was the frightening ride immediately after the BMD left the aircraft: the seven-ton BMD and pallet fell several hundred feet before the parachutes finally opened with a jarring jolt. The impact on the ground came as an unexpected shock since the paratroopers could not see out of the vehicle except through a small periscope, which had very little downward view. Nevertheless, the Centaur experiments continued on Margelov's insistence. Several hundred other VDV paratroopers were put through the experience, though it was by no means a standard operation. The procedure was to drop two men in the vehicle: the driver and the squad leader or vehicle gunner. It was pointless to risk the whole squad, so the five-man dismount squad parachuted separately.

The operational trials of the BMD raised questions about the use of a multicanopy parachute. It was not very economical since this expensive item was sometimes lost during an exercise. In addition, the multicanopy parachute was heavy, adding about a ton of weight to the aircraft's cargo, and the parachute imposed speed limitations on the aircraft. This became a significant problem with the arrival of the new IL-76 jet transport. Furthermore, the parachute posed a serious hazard to the BMD itself. When the BMD was driven away from the pallet, some of the parachute lines inevitably became caught in the running gear of the vehicle. This could actually stop the vehicle, since the suspension of the BMD was relatively delicate compared to that of other armored vehicles. A solution was to develop a technique to slow the vehicle during the impact so that only a single-canopy parachute would be needed.

The Parachute Research Engineering Institute in Moscow began exploring new ideas for the delivery of BMDs. The French firm Aerazur had developed a cargo parachute system using air bags or other cushioning devices under parachute pallets. This was examined but eventually rejected. The parachute institute eventually developed a retrorocket system, called the PRSM-915, an acronym for rocket parachute system for 915-type vehicles.

The PRSM-915 system was based around a conventional pallet. Before the mission, the BMD was driven onto the pallet and strapped in place. The BMD had a hydropneumatic system that collapsed and locked the suspension into place for the drop, also lowering the height of the vehicle to make it easier to load into the aircraft. Once the BMD was firmly on the pallet, the PRSM-915 system was attached, along with a large, single-canopy parachute. The vehicle was now ready for airdrop.

When the aircraft was over the drop zone, the drogue chute from the parachute system was deployed. This small chute streamed out of the aircraft and eventually exerted enough force to pull the entire BMD, pallet, and parachute pack out of the aircraft. The BMD exited the IL-76 transport aircraft in a terrifying screech of metal on metal. Even though the IL-76 had a roller-bearing floor, the BMD's violent extraction was accompanied by mind-numbing noise. Once free of the aircraft, the BMD was buffeted by the strong airflow and vortices of the transport aircraft. The vehicle was in free fall for several seconds as the drogue chute and then the main chute deployed. The deployment of the main chute gave the vehicle a hard jolt, followed by a sickening pendulum motion as the vehicle dangled beneath the canopy. During actual combat jumps, the BMD would be released from as low an altitude as possible, about 1,500 feet. As a result, the time between exiting the aircraft and hitting the ground would be short—less than a minute. The final stage of the descent was the most dramatic . . . from the outside at least! After the main chute deployment, lanyards holding a set of four rods under the pallet pulled free. This caused the four rods to hinge downward, hanging several feet below the pallet. These rods contained contact sensors on their tips. Because of their location under the pallet, they struck the ground before the rest of the load. When the first one touched the ground, it triggered an electrical signal to the PRSM. The PRSM rocket pack was suspended under the main parachute, and above the BMD and pallet. When the rod struck the ground, the PRSM retrorocket fired, abruptly slowing the descent of the BMD. The PRSM fired from a position about fifteen feet above the BMD, spraying the roof of the vehicle with a fiery rocket blast and suddenly braking the rapid descent speed.

This system proved a practical alternative to multicanopy parachutes for heavy loads, and it entered service in 1975. The system allowed IL-76 jet transports to drop their loads at speeds about 25 percent higher than the older multicanopy parachutes. However, the BMD descended at a much higher rate of speed with the single canopy until the retrorockets fired.

General Margelov insisted that another study be conducted to see if the crew could be dropped inside a BMD when using the PRSM-915 system. The new program was code-named Reaktavr, or Project Rocketeer. The first test was again conducted by Margelov's son; now a major, he was one of the most experienced of the "airborne tankers." The Rocketeer tests showed that the PRSM-915 retrorocket system was not significantly different from the normal parachute methods, though it too required a fair amount of courage on the part of the crew.

Russian accounts of the VDV insist that the Rocketeer airdrop method, with one or two crewmen dropping with the vehicle, is still in use in Russia. However, this probably remains more a theoretical capability than a regularly employed tactic. It isn't known how many BMDs have had failed airdrops over the years, but such heavy-cargo airdrops are inherently risky for many reasons. And if the risk of an accidental landing is not bad enough, the drop itself is frightening. The crew is locked into the armored vehicle about an hour before the drop. The interior of the BMD is very cramped, and pitch black. When loaded for an airdrop, the entire roof of the BMD is laden with the parachute, harness, PRSM rocket, and loading paraphernalia, sealing the hatches. In a real combat jump, the vehicle also would be fully loaded with fuel and ammunition. It is of little consolation to the Rocketeer crew, but if the BMD did crash into the ground without its parachutes, death would be instantaneous—there would probably be a spectacular explosion from the detonation of the 73mm ammunition, 9M14 missiles, and other stored munitions. To add to the discomfort, there is no intercom between the BMD crew and the aircrew, though presumably there are improvised means to communicate, such as keeping the rear vehicle cargo hatch open a crack. The Rocketeer tactic is not for the faint of heart!

Some of the more sober leaders in the VDV must have questioned the Rocketeer idea, as BMDs are now fitted with remote landing aids. One of the main problems of airdrops has always been that the wind scatters paratroopers and cargo. This is a particular risk in combat operations when only a fraction of the paratroopers are trained in driving and operating complex combat vehicles such as the BMD. The alternative solution to dropping the crew inside the vehicle was to develop some method for the crew to locate the vehicle quickly. This was provided in the form of a small radio directional receiver preset to a particular frequency. When the BMD lands, it gives off a beeping radio signal that can be picked up by the receiver. Each crew has set its receiver to a different frequency to avoid confusion among the different squads.

IMPROVING THE BREED

The BMD-1 became the standard armored vehicle of the VDV Airborne Force in the 1970s, but it was not the only new airborne vehicle. The basic turreted BMD-1 is too cramped inside to be used for specialized roles such as command vehicles. So in 1974 a modified version, the BTR-D (armored transporter–airborne), was first issued to the troops. This version lacks the normal BMD-1 turret, which frees up a considerable amount of space in the center of the vehicle. In addition, the vehicle hull was lengthened to provide additional internal volume. Whereas the BMD-1 can carry eight troops in cramped conditions, the BTR-D can carry up to thirteen.

The basic BTR-D is used in BMD units to transport heavy-weapons squads, including AGS-17 automatic grenade launcher teams. The usual crew complement in this case is twelve men plus the driver; enough space is still available for the grenade launchers when stowed inside, as well as their ammunition. In addition to the basic BTR-D, several specialized versions have been developed.

The BTR-ZD air defense vehicle is used to tow regimental ZU-23 twin-barrel 23mm antiaircraft guns. The BTR-D can tow the gun behind, but the vehicle is also fitted with ramp attachments to allow the gun to be carried portee style atop the vehicle roof. The BTR-ZD also carries additional air defense weapons, including man-portable missiles such as the Strela-2M (SA-7 Grail). The BTR-RD is used in a similar fashion to carry antitank missile teams armed with the Fagot/Konkurs (AT-4 Spigot/AT-5 Spandrel) antitank missiles.

The BMD-1KShM is a specialized command version of the BTR-D used by battalion and regimental commanders. The larger internal volume of the BTR-D chassis allows the vehicle to carry the necessary R-123 radio, data links, and other command and control electronics typical of the modern battlefield. One of the most unusual BMD variants is the ODB, a BTR-D fitted with the R-440 satellite communications system. On this vehicle, the whole roof is taken up by a large circular communications dish that is used by the R-440 system. This vehicle allows the VDV divisional headquarters to communicate with Moscow via satellites or other data transfer systems.

The BREM-D (armored repair and towing vehicle–airborne) is a specialized armored recovery version of the BTR-D used to support BMD regiments. It has a small crane fitted to the roof to carry out basic repairs.

In the early 1970s, there was the desire to replace the outdated ASU-85 assault guns still in VDV service. By this time, these weapons were ineffective against contemporary NATO main battle tanks. With the advent of the BMD, their role had gradually shifted from antitank defense to direct fire support. One potential replacement for the ASU-85 was a new light tank being developed by the Soviet Ground Forces to replace the old PT-76 amphibious tank. Two prototypes of this light tank were constructed by two old rivals, Gavalov's BMD design bureau and Isakov's BMP design bureau. The requirements called for amphibious light tanks armed with a new 100mm smoothbore antitank gun. Both light tanks were designed to be airdropped. In the end, the Soviet Army decided against adopting these vehicles. Instead, the VDV turned to another BMD derivative.

Dedicated tank destroyers were less necessary for VDV units in the 1970s since each BMD-1 had considerable antitank firepower, both with its low-pressure gun and its antitank guided missile launcher. VDV interest shifted toward a self-propelled artillery vehicle. Conventional howitzers have substantial recoil, which requires a sturdy and heavy chassis when mounted in tracked vehicles. Instead of a conventional howitzer, the VDV selected the revolutionary new 2A60 120mm Nona howitzer/mortar. This weapon fired 120mm mortar bombs; unlike a conventional mortar, the ammunition was loaded from the breech end. The weapon could be fired at high elevation, like a mortar, or used in direct fire, like a gun or howitzer. Besides normal mortar ammunition, special projectiles were also developed, including a formidable shaped-charge antitank round that could penetrate twenty-four inches of steel armor, more than any contemporary main battle tank. The new 120mm weapon was mounted on a modified version of the lengthened BTR-D chassis, called the 2S9 Nona-S. The 2S9 resembled a tank, with a center-mounted turret instead of the usual rear-mounted turret common to self-propelled artillery. The gun system was fitted with a rammer to help load the heavy 120mm mortar ammunition. One of the clever innovations in the design was a small conveyor belt at the rear of the vehicle that allowed the crew to load ammunition from outside the vehicle when engaged in long fire-support missions.

The 2S9 Nona-S entered service in 1984. It is a remarkably powerful weapon for its small size and light weight. It replaced the 120mm towed mortars found previously in VDV regiments. But its direct fire capabilities made the ASU-85 unnecessary and considerably enhanced the fire support available to the paratroopers. The introduction of the 2S9 Nona-S was accompanied by the deployment of two other specialized artillery vehicles, the 1V118 and 1V119 Spektr fire control vehicles. The Spektr vehicles have a small fixed turret but lack any armament beyond self-defense machine guns. At the forward portion of the turret is an electro-optical sensor package that includes a laser range finder. The 1V118 Spektr serves as a forward artillery observation post and can also be used by air force forward air controllers when air support is needed by VDV units.

The 1V119 is similar in general appearance but has the necessary ballistic computers and communications equipment to serve as a fire direction center for the 2S9 Nona-S battery.

Experience with the BMD-1 in Afghanistan revealed serious problems with the design, especially its 73mm low-pressure gun armament. As a short-term solution, a new turret was developed for the BMD fitted with the more effective 30mm 2A42 autocannon found on the infantry's BMP-2 Yozh armored combat vehicle. This new version is called the BMD-2 and entered service in modest numbers in the mid-1980s. In the long term, a new BMD was developed under the code name Object 950. The new BMD is substantially larger and heavier than the BMD-1/2, with better armor protection and a more durable suspension. It was finally ready for service in 1993 and is designated the BMD-3. The Russian Army plans to base a future generation of armored vehicles around this chassis, much as the BMD-1 served as the basis for the BTR-D, 2S9, and other vehicles.

BMD DEPLOYMENT

The advent of the BMD changed the organization of the VDV airborne divisions. Although the divisions continued to train as light infantry, after 1969 they began to train as mechanized infantry as well. The key fighting elements of the airborne division were three airborne regiments, each with three airborne battalions. The airborne battalions prior to the arrival of the BMD each numbered about 600 troops. Each battalion had a machine-gun company; a mortar company (six 82mm mortars); an antitank company; an air defense company; and three airborne rifle companies, each with 110 men. With the introduction of the BMD, the number of troops in an airborne battalion shrank in size from 600 to 316 men. This was due in part to the elimination of most of the fire support companies, since the BMDs could provide direct fire-support and antitank defense. The new battalion had three airborne companies with 75 men, each with ten BMDs. In addition, there was a grenade launcher platoon with AGS-17 grenade launchers on three turretless BTR-Ds, and an air defense platoon with three BTR-Ds armed with a total of nine man-portable Strela 2 air defense missiles.

The airborne regiment showed a similar reduction in manpower and increase in firepower. The pre-BMD airborne regiment numbered about 2,060 troops; the mechanized airborne regiment saw a decrease to 1,450 troops. At the heart of the new organizational structure were the three BMD airborne battalions, which made up the bulk of the regimental strength. Their firepower was enhanced by an artillery battery with six 2S9 Nona-S, an air defense battery with six BTR-ZD/ZU-23 combinations, and an antitank battery with nine 9P148 tank destroyers (Konkurs antitank missile launchers on a wheeled BRDM-3 armored vehicle). The regiment also contained other necessary support elements such as a reconnaissance company, signal company, engineer company, transport company, parachute supply company, chemical defense platoon, and a medical team.

Of course, the mechanization of the airborne also had significant consequences on the portability of the units. The mechanization of the airborne added 156 armored vehicles to each regiment, plus more support trucks. The armored vehicles alone required an additional 52 Ilyushin IL-76 transports or 78 Antonov An-12 transports to carry them to the drop zone. A nonmechanized airborne regiment of the 1968 type would require only about 40 Antonov An-12 sorties or 20 Ilyushin IL-76 sorties. A BMD mechanized airborne regiment requires about 115 Antonov An-12 sorties or 65 Ilyushin IL-76 sorties, a threefold increase in the airlift requirement. Likewise, the daily resupply requirements of the regiment once it has landed increased dramatically with the addition of the BMD armored vehicles.

The airlift capability of the VTA increased steadily through the 1970s in an effort to accommodate the increasingly heavy airborne force. In 1970, the VTA had the capability to airlift about six BMD airborne regiments simultaneously, or roughly two of the VDV's six airborne divisions. This capability increased to nine BMD regiments (three VDV divisions) by 1987. Needless to say, the VTA could have airlifted a significantly greater fraction of the VDV at any point if it was more lightly configured without the full complement of BMD airborne assault vehicles. Also, the VTA could have been reinforced by absorbing IL-76 and An-12 transports from Aeroflot and other Soviet Air Force branches. This would have added about sixty-five aircraft, and the capability to lift an additional BMD regiment. The shortfall between the VDV order of battle and the actual airlift capability of the VTA was not particularly worrisome to the Soviet General Staff. The capability to airdrop two to three VDV airborne divisions simultaneously would satisfy most deployment scenarios.

Soviet Airlift Trends 1970–1990
VTA Transport Fleet

Year	An-12BP Cub	IL-76 M Candid-B	An-22 Cock	An-124 Condor	Total Aircraft	Total Payload (metric tons)
1970	730	0	10	0	740	15,400
1971	730	0	10	0	740	15,400
1972	730	0	17	0	747	15,960
1973	730	0	20	0	750	16,200
1974	680	0	40	0	720	16,800
1975	670	10	45	0	725	17,400
1976	630	40	50	0	720	17,400
1977	610	60	50	0	720	18,600
1978	600	80	50	0	730	19,400
1979	575	100	50	0	725	19,500
1980	425	125	50	0	600	17,500
1981	400	150	55	0	605	18,400
1982	360	180	55	0	595	18,800
1983	330	220	55	0	605	19,800
1984	260	250	55	0	565	19,600
1985	260	250	55	3	568	20,050
1986	210	310	55	3	578	21,400
1987	160	355	55	5	575	22,550
1988	160	380	55	11	606	24,450
1989	160	395	50	15	620	25,250
1990	150	435	50	29	664	28,750

NEW CAPABILITIES, NEW MISSIONS

The modernization of the VDV Airborne Force and the related VTA air transport force in the 1970s was undertaken to provide the Soviet armed forces with important new force projection capabilities. In the 1960s, the Soviet armed forces had developed the capabilities to engage in modern, high-intensity combat against NATO or China, under nuclear or conventional conditions. In the 1970s, the Soviet armed forces attempted to develop the capabilities to conduct military operations outside of these traditional theaters, much as the U.S.

armed forces were able to do with their strategic projection forces such as the 82nd Airborne Division and Marine Corps. Due to geographic differences between the United States and the Soviet Union, the Soviet mixture was different, with more emphasis on the airborne intervention forces and less on the naval infantry forces.

The deployment pattern of the VDV divisions in the 1970s reflected the broader orientation of the missions of the Soviet armed forces. Of the six VDV divisions, four were oriented toward operations in the new TVD (theaters of military operations): one in the Northwestern TVD oriented toward Scandinavia, one in the Western TVD oriented toward the NATO Central Front, one in the Southwestern TVD oriented toward the Balkans and western Mediterranean, and one in the Southern TVD oriented toward Turkey and the Mideast. Of the other two divisions, one was located near Moscow as a strategic reserve and one served for training purposes. Due to the exceptional mobility of the VDV, any of these divisions could have been quickly reoriented toward new theaters, such as China, if the need arose.

Some insight into the expanded mission of the VDV can be garnered from developments in 1973 at the time of the October war in the Mideast between Israel, Egypt, and Syria. The Soviet Union had supported the military buildup of Egyptian and Syrian forces since the 1967 Mideast War. Although the Kremlin did not foment the 1973 war, its supply of advisers and equipment to Egypt and Syria made the war possible. During Yom Kippur in October 1973, Egypt attacked Israeli forces in the Sinai in an attempt to wrest control of territories captured in the 1967 war. Syria attacked simultaneously on the Golan Heights on Israel's northern frontier. After suffering heavy losses, the Israeli Defense Force managed to take the offensive, attacking into Syria and Egypt. The 1973 war was a watershed in modern warfare. The level of expenditure of weapons and ammunition was on a scale not previously seen, and the intensity of the combat surprised not only the participants but the major powers as well.

The Kremlin was dismayed by the Arab reversals on the battlefield. The VTA was mobilized to airlift badly needed weapons, ammunition, and replacement parts and spares to Syria and Egypt, much as the United States did to support Israel. At the same time, three VDV

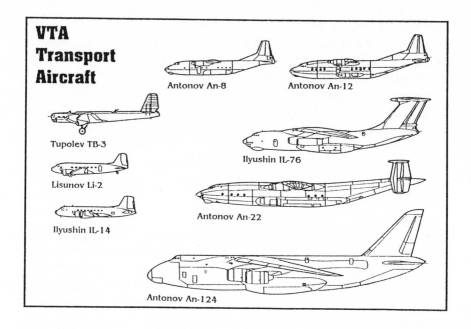

VTA Transport Aircraft

Antonov An-8

Antonov An-12

Tupolev TB-3

Ilyushin IL-76

Lisunov Li-2

Ilyushin IL-14

Antonov An-22

Antonov An-124

airborne divisions were mobilized as a possible intervention force in the region. It is not at all clear whether the Kremlin seriously considered introducing Soviet troops into the Mideast. The VDV mobilization was carried out in a particularly noisy and obvious fashion to ensure that U.S. intelligence observed it. The Kremlin apparently wanted to signal the United States that the Soviet Union would not tolerate further Israeli advances on Damascus or Cairo. This message was clearly understood, and the United States intervened with Israel to limit the scope of its counteroffensive.

The potential introduction of the VDV into the Mideast in 1973 was a remarkable change in the strategic capability of the Soviet armed forces. Until this point, the Soviet Union's ability to influence regional events much beyond its frontiers could not be easily stiffened by tangible military forces. The modernized VDV and VTA gave the Kremlin this capability for the first time.

The importance of the VDV in Soviet military doctrine was reflected in the annual summer and autumn war games. Since the 1967

Dnepr war games, the VDV had played a prominent role in nearly all subsequent exercises. During the March 1970 Dvina maneuvers, the 76th Guards Chernigov Airborne Division was parachuted or airlanded during a massive exercise in the Byelorussian Military District. The exercise pitted the Northern Force under the command of Colonel General Shavrov against the Southern Force of Colonel General Ivanovskiy. Shavrov's Northern Force managed to breech the Dvina River defense line of Ivanovskiy's force. Ivanovskiy responded by ordering a tank division forward from the area south of Orsha from the front reserves. The lead elements of Ivanovskiy's tank reinforcements were struck by a simulated tactical nuclear strike to slow their progress. Following the nuclear strike, the 8,000-man airborne division was dropped deep behind the Southern Front's lines to block the tank reinforcements. Two of the division's regiments parachuted into the drop zone northeast of the nuclear blast site in a massive twenty-two-minute drop; a third regiment airlanded later on a captured airfield outside Orsha. This exercise marked the first use of the new An-22 heavy transports, which airlanded heavy and bulky equipment such as Krug (SA-4 Ganef) air defense missiles and Luna (FROG-5) tactical nuclear delivery rocket systems.

In October 1970, an airborne regiment from the Group of Soviet Forces–Germany was employed for the first time in the "Brotherhood-in-Arms" exercise in East Germany alongside East German paratroopers. The tactical exercise employed the paratroopers to disrupt "enemy" defenses during the conduct of an amphibious landing along the Baltic coast. In June 1971, the 98th Svir Guards Airborne Division, based at Bolgrad near Odessa in Ukraine, was employed in the depths of "enemy" positions as part of an amphibious assault during war games in the Ukrainian Military District.

Besides the annual exercises, the airborne divisions continued to attract international attention during world crises. According to several newspapers in the United States and Europe, in July 1974 a threatened outbreak of fighting between Greek and Cypriot forces on Cyprus led to the mobilization of the VDV. The idea that Soviet paratroopers would intervene in an internecine conflict between ostensible NATO allies was completely preposterous. The Kremlin must have been delighted by such stories, as they enhanced the political value of their strategic projection forces.

THE CUBAN CONNECTION

The next international incident to involve the VDV and VTA occurred on the horn of Africa in 1977. The Soviet Union had been allied to both Ethiopia and Somalia since the early 1970s. In 1974, the Somali government sponsored the Western Somali Liberation Front (WSLF) in an attempt to annex portions of the Ogaden region of Ethiopia. In September 1977, the Soviet Union formally sided with Ethiopia in the conflict, beginning a massive airlift of arms and technical advisers. Under other circumstances, the Soviet advisory teams would have been much larger. But by this time, an alternative was available in the form of the extensive Cuban expeditionary force stationed in Angola.

The VTA began a secondary airlift of Cuban troops from Angola to Ethiopia. The introduction of Cuban troops on the Ethiopian side turned the tide of battle by early 1978. A further Cuban division with 6,000 troops was moved into Ethiopia in February 1978, bringing total Cuban strength to more than 11,000 troops. Soviet VDV advisers were brought in to plan an airborne envelopment of remaining Somali defenses in the contested territory. In early March 1978, Soviet VDV advisers oversaw a heliborne assault on the Somali stronghold at Jijiga, where an Mi-6 heavy-lift helicopter regiment was used to deliver seventy Cuban-manned BMD-1 airborne assault vehicles behind Somali positions. The shock of a large armored force suddenly appearing in their rear demoralized the remaining Somali troops, and a major retreat to the border began. On 9 May 1978, President Siad Barre of Somalia announced the complete withdrawal of his troops from Ethiopia in hopes of staving off an Ethiopian attack into Somalia itself. Soviet casualties in the fighting were modest—only fourteen dead—since the Cuban troops bore the brunt of the fighting. One of the rewards for "socialist solidarity" in Ethiopia was the transfer of surviving BMDs to the Cuban expeditionary force. The BMDs would later be used in fighting in Angola in the 1980s.

THE NEW ELITE

In the Khrushchev years, young and ambitious Soviet officers flocked to the ranks of the Strategic Missile Force. Nikita Khrushchev made no secret of the fact that the strategic nuclear force was his pet service and that its ranks would receive preference in recruiting and career advancement. Toward the end of the Brezhnev years, the fashion had changed. The VDV's sterling service in Czechoslovakia as the shock troops of the Brezhnev doctrine had won the Kremlin's favor. As the Soviet leadership became more enamored of foreign adventures, the VDV gradually usurped the Strategic Missile Force's status as the premier service. The best and the brightest sought the prized blue beret of the VDV. Much as American Special Forces and clandestine warfare forces flowered in the early Kennedy years, the Soviet power-projection forces flourished in the Brezhnev years. Margelov's dynamic leadership turned the VDV into a highly respected force, further reinforcing the VDV's mystique. The VDV reached its peak in the late 1970s, just in time to become trapped in the quagmire of Afghanistan.

Chapter 9
Battling Bumblebees

Parachute airdrops have inherent problems that have plagued airborne operations from the beginning. Parachute drops are subject to the vagaries of the wind: gusts scatter paratrooper units, disrupting the operation and diminishing the surprise effect. Paratroopers are exposed to fire from enemy forces on the ground as they descend. By the 1970s, the lumbering aircraft that transported paratroopers to the drop zone were becoming vulnerable to advanced antiaircraft guns and missiles. Parachutes are a one-way ticket. After an airdrop, the airborne unit must be relieved by attacking friendly forces or the paratroopers will be isolated and destroyed. The vulnerability of parachute operations is most evident from the fact that very few combat airdrops have been conducted since World War II. Since 1960, there have been only a handful of major parachute missions, and all in low-intensity conflicts such as Grenada and Panama. Besides its inherent problems, the parachute option has been undermined by the availability of another means of vertical envelopment: the helicopter.

Like many air forces, the Red Air Force of the 1930s experimented with various types of early rotary-wing craft, especially the autogyro. In 1941, the Red Air Force had seven A-7 autogyros in service for close reconnaissance and artillery spotting. An autogyro differs from a true helicopter in that its rotors are not powered; the aircraft derives its power from a normal forward-pointing propellor; the rotors, taking the place of conventional wings, merely add to the lift. Autogyros proved to be a technological dead end, and during the war, small-scale development work was undertaken on true helicopters. Ironically, it was a Russian, Sergei Sikorsky, who pioneered helicopters, but in the United States, not the Soviet Union. Both the United States and Germany fielded helicopters in small numbers during World War II, and they were used for liaison, observation, casualty evacuation, and other missions. The early helicopters did not have enough lift to carry a significant load, such as a squad of troops.

In the late 1940s, there were many Soviet attempts to develop helicopters, few of them successful. The most prominent aircraft design bureau, the Yakovlev OKB, attempted both a contrarotating design and a copy of the Sikorsky S-61 Dragonfly, neither of which was successful. The first truly successful Soviet helicopters were devised by an unknown young designer named Mikhail Mil. He would become synonymous with Soviet helicopters; more than 90 percent of the helicopters manufactured in the Soviet Union for the next fifty years were from his design bureau. Mil's first design was the Mi-1, a small two seater capable of carrying an additional two or three passengers in a small center compartment. The first Mi-1 was completed in 1948; production began in 1951 at State Aviation Plant Number 4 in Chkalov. The Soviet Air Force gained valuable experience in basic helicopter technology from the Mi-1, but the aircraft was not large enough to serve as a transport helicopter.

The first conflict to see the extensive use of helicopters was the Korean War of 1950–53. The U.S. armed forces used helicopters for a wide variety of roles, including air-sea rescue, medical evacuation, troop transport, and aerial observation. In October 1951, Joseph Stalin convened a meeting of the major Soviet aviation designers and rebuked them for neglecting the military potential of helicopters. Most of the design bureaus attempted to shield themselves from Stalin's wrath by pointing out that they were overwhelmed with work. This was certainly true, as at the time they were deeply involved in the jet revolution. With his Mi-1 helicopter already in production, Mikhail Mil was able to step forward and promise a new twelve-passenger helicopter. Stalin's favorite designer, Aleksandr Yakovlev, although unsuccessful to date in helicopter design, promised an even larger twenty-four-passenger transport helicopter. To give his edicts more bite, Stalin assigned the head of the Soviet special police, the sinister Lavrentiy Beria, to supervise the accelerated program.

Yakovlev's design, the Yak-24, was patterned after the American Piasecki H-21 "Flying Banana" helicopter, which used a twin-rotor configuration fore and aft. The Yak-24 was larger and heavier than the H-21, holding forty troops instead of twenty, and a rear ramp permitted small vehicles to be carried. Its long fuselage led to its popular nickname—Letayushchiy Vagon (Flying Boxcar). The first prototype flew in July 1952, but vibrations caused by torque and blade flutter in the twin-engine design plagued the type. Fortunately for Yakovlev's team, Stalin's death in 1953 prevented any police action against the bureau for the design flaws. The vibration problems were reduced but not eliminated, and the Yak-24 was accepted for production in April 1955. It was the world's largest production helicopter at the time. The production run was small; only about 100 were completed due to the lingering problems, and the Yak-24 soon disappeared from the scene.

Mil's Mi-4 design was patterned after the Sikorsky H-19 Chickasaw, with a nose-mounted radial engine, single rotor configuration, and double-decker fuselage design. As in the case of the Yak-24/H-21, the similarities were only skin deep. The Mi-4 was significantly larger than the H-19, and the larger size permitted the inclusion of a clamshell door at the rear of the fuselage so that light vehicles and other off-sized cargo could be carried. Mil's greater experience in helicopter design sped the program along, with the first flights taking place in April 1952, only six months after Stalin's ultimatum. The prototype helicopters were plagued with blade flutter problems, which were partly solved by the time the helicopter was rushed into production in the spring of 1953. Several early production machines were displayed at the August 1954 Tushino air display.

The early service use of the Mi-4 was plagued by reliability and maintenance problems. The blade life of the rotor system was only 100 hours, after which new blades had to be fitted or risk catastrophic failure. Improvements were gradually introduced that extended blade life to 300 hours by 1954, 600 by 1957, and 1,000 hours by 1960. Other reliability improvements resulted in the Mi-4A in 1957. In spite of the early problems, the Mi-4 (called Hound by NATO) was the most important Soviet helicopter in the formative years of the Soviet military helicopter force. A total of about 3,500 were built through the 1960s.

The intended role for the Mi-1 and Mi-4 helicopters was not well established in the mid-1950s. Clearly, the Mi-4 was intended for transport roles. The potential use of helicopters for delivering troops directly into battle had not escaped the Soviet Army. The most prominent example of such tactics took place with French army and marines in Algeria. Using American H-19 and H-21 helicopters, the French began to show the value of helicopters in a counterinsurgency campaign. The helicopters provided the French troops with both mobility and fire support in Algeria's rough, mountainous terrain.

The first demonstration of Soviet interest in air assault missions came during the 1956 Hungarian insurrection. The Soviet Army's Special Operations Corps decided to seize two Hungarian airfields in the outskirts of Budapest. On 28 October 1956, a squadron of Mi-4 helicopters with troops aboard were sent to one of the fields, expecting to encounter no resistance. Instead, Hungarian antiaircraft gunners opened fire and shot down three of the helicopters. It was an inauspicious start for the proponents of heliborne air assault.

In the late 1950s, Soviet air assault doctrine was constrained by the limitations of the technology. Mi-4 helicopters were entering service in significant numbers, but experienced crews and units were still quite few. Helicopter reliability was low, and maintenance demands were high, which led to the decision to keep the helicopters under air force rather than army control. This probably slowed development of air assault tactics. Armed forces where helicopters were integral to the army, such as in the United States and France, tended to more rapidly assimilate helicopters into their doctrine and begin experimentation in new roles such as fire support.

Soviet air assault doctrine germinated in the late 1950s as an offshoot of "the revolution in military affairs." Soviet theoreticians began to favor the use of helicopters over paratroopers for shallow tactical airborne operations—less than fifty kilometers from Soviet lines. Soviet planners considered the heliborne air assault tactics especially valuable for tasks such as seizing river crossings, bridges, or other tactical objectives that formerly would have been undertaken by paratrooper units. In the late 1950s and early 1960s, the main constraint was the simple lack of sufficient helicopters for large-scale operations. Soviet tactics at the time envisioned the use of a single helicopter regiment (about thirty Mi-4 helicopters) per army, although in reality each front* was lucky to have a single dedicated transport helicopter regiment.

At the time, the typical heliborne air assault mission was expected to involve between a company and a battalion of infantry. Troops were drawn from regular motor rifle divisions and did not receive much specialized training. The airborne operation was prepared at airfields about thirty-five kilometers behind the forward edge of the battle area. The assault force was equipped with typical infantry weapons, including mortars and recoilless rifles; conventional artillery normally was not possible. Like the airborne force, the air assault troops depended on surprise, timing, and good planning to strike the enemy where vulnerable. The tactics of this period expected that the heliborne force could hold its objective for about twelve hours—sufficient time to be reached by forward detachments of the advancing front. One of the most significant differences between heliborne missions and parachute missions was that the helicopters allowed the air assault force to be extracted if necessary. Early Soviet air assault doctrine did not envision the use of the helicopters themselves to provide fire support. This would be accomplished by traditional means such as strike fighters.

The use of helicopters in Soviet exercises became common after the 1950s. A popular scenario in Soviet war games was the use of combined airborne, heliborne, and amphibious forces to seize beachheads or river crossings. In some cases, the operation would be preceded by simulated tactical nuclear strikes. The heliborne assault force was usually the first group in, since its responsibilities were to land immediately behind the beach or over the river and take the actual landing site. The airborne force would then land a dozen or more kilometers deeper inside enemy territory to prevent any reinforcements

---

*A Soviet front consists of several armies; an army consists of several divisions.

from reaching the landing area. Finally, the main body would land and consolidate the beachhead.

A typical example of one of these special operations war games took place on 15 June 1961 in the Baltic Military District. The attack was launched across the Irbenskiy Strait from Latvia against the Estonian island of Saaremaa and was intended to simulate a wartime mission in the Danish straits. Three or four simulated nuclear devices were detonated along the coast, followed by the first wave of helicopter landing forces. A VDV airborne regiment dropped away from the beaches to disrupt any attempts to interfere with the landings. Finally, the main force of motor rifle troops was landed from assault ships.

The tactic of shallow heliborne penetration accompanied by deeper airborne penetrations became the standard distinction in air assault operations through the 1960s and 1970s. The heliborne assault force was always given a limited tactical role; operational and strategic missions were reserved for the airborne.

THE TURBINE REVOLUTION

As in the case of the airborne force, the development of heliborne air assault forces hinged to a large extent on the vehicles' airlift. In the first decade of helicopter forces, their size and capabilities were constrained by the limited lift, limited numbers, and limited durability of the Mi-4. Heavier helicopters were sought to enable the air assault to take along more capable weapons, including artillery and light vehicles. The Yakovlev Yak-24 had proven disappointing in this role. In the summer of 1954, Mil was authorized to begin development of a heavy-lift helicopter to replace the failed Yak-24. Designated the Mi-6 (NATO called it the Hook), the new helicopter was a revolutionary step forward in Soviet helicopter design. The reason was not so much its size, which admittedly was enormous, but its propulsion. Mil selected a gas turbine engine instead of the piston engines that had powered helicopters up to this time. The helicopter gas turbine, like the turbojet being fitted to Soviet transport aircraft at this time, was based around a jet engine for its power. This offered several attractive features. A gas turbine produced far more power for a given volume, a very important consideration in a heavy-lift helicopter.

Such engines also promised good fuel economy and easier maintenance than conventional piston engines. The prototype of the Mi-6
first flew in 1957 and was first publicly shown at the Tushino air
show in the summer of 1958.

The Mi-6 used a conventional pod-and-boom fuselage configuration, a hallmark of Mil designs since the first Mi-1. Fully loaded, the
Mi-6 could carry ten times the number of troops as the Mi-4—120
instead of 12. But the Mi-6 was mainly intended to carry heavy cargo
and in this role could lift twelve metric tons. This would enable it to
carry two ASU-57 assault guns, one ASU-85 assault gun, or various
assortments of towed artillery, trucks, or other weaponry. It was envisioned that each helicopter regiment of Mi-4s would be accompanied by up to a squadron of ten Mi-6s to deliver the needed heavy
equipment. Production of the Mi-6 began in 1957; by 1981 about
1,000 had been produced. More than half of these went to the Soviet
Air Force; the remainder went to Aeroflot or to foreign clients. In
Soviet service, the Mi-6 was nicknamed the *kishkaldak,* the "sausage
grinder," for its clanky, vibrating flying characteristics.

The success of the turbine-powered Mi-6 design prompted Mil to
propose a new assault helicopter to replace the cranky old Mi-4.
Originally called the V-8, the new helicopter resembled a shrunken
Mi-6. Like the Mi-6, it employed a pair of gas turbine engines. It
was designed to accommodate twenty-eight troops, more than double
the capacity of the Mi-4. Soon after its first flight in early 1961, it was
accepted for Soviet Air Force use as the Mi-8 (later called Hip by NATO).

The Mi-8 development paralleled similar efforts in the United
States and Europe. The trend toward the use of turbine-powered helicopters was nearly universal at this time due to the engine's higher
reliability, superior power output, and superior durability. However,
the U.S. approach to helicopter configuration was different from the
Soviet approach. Because the U.S. Army controlled the helicopter
force, the emphasis in basic troop-carrying helicopters was toward a
smaller, single-engine helicopter, which would be easier to maintain
in the field by the troops. This emerged as the famous UH-1 Huey.
The troop-carrying UH-1D could carry twelve troops; the Mi-8 could
carry double this. The Soviet Air Force preferred a smaller number
of larger helicopters as a more economical approach. The U.S. Army
did acquire larger helicopters as well, notably the CH-47 Chinook,

but this paralleled the Mi-6's mission. It is worth noting that the U.S. Marine Corps helicopter program followed the Soviet pattern, being based around the medium CH-46 Sea Knight, which is more similar in size and capability to the Soviet Mi-8 than the U.S. Army UH-1.

Series production of the Mi-8 began in 1966, more than a decade after the Mi-4. The Mi-8 has been the mainstay of the Soviet airborne assault force since then and is likely to remain so until the turn of the century, when its replacement, the Mi-40, is expected to appear. The Mi-8 in Russian service was popularly called the Shmel (bumblebee), a nickname that is now widely applied to Russian helicopters in general.

GUNSHIPS

Arming helicopters to provide fire support was first attempted during the Korean War on a small scale. The French army and marine forces in Algeria began the first systematic attempt to integrate armed helicopters into airlanding operations. The French were also the first to operationally fire guided antitank missiles from helicopters, using the Nord Aviation SS.11 wire-guided missile to attack guerrilla positions in caves in the Algerian mountains. The U.S. Army began an active program to study the role of armed helicopters in combat in the late 1950s.

Soviet experiments with armed helicopters also started in the late 1950s. Unlike U.S. Army helicopters, most of the original Mi-4 helicopters were armed from the outset, having a single 12.7mm heavy machine gun mounted in a bathtub under the fuselage. This was hardly adequate for any serious fire support but displayed an interest in this issue. The first serious attempt to develop a gunship took place in the late 1950s with the Mi-4AV (V for *vooruzheniy,* meaning armed). This was a standard Mi-4A fitted with reinforced mountings on either side for armament. The normal armament was four 57mm rocket pods, supplemented by four rails for Falanga wire-guided antitank missiles. This rocket capability was the most important single innovation in helicopter armament. A helicopter could carry several dozen rockets, each with the explosive power of a small howitzer round. It is not clear how many of these Mi-4AVs were built, or what tactics were intended for helicopter gunships in the Soviet

Air Force. The Mi-4AV appears to have been an effort to study the armed helicopter concept, rather than a response to established tactical doctrine.

The gunship idea was reinforced by the Vietnam War. Although Algeria was the first "helicopter war," the French experience with helicopters was little known except to specialists. In contrast, helicopters were far more evident in Vietnam, due to the scale of their use and the greater media attention. Helicopters revolutionized U.S. Army tactics, being used for troop transport on a daily basis as well as a host of other tasks, including scouting, medevac, and command and control. In 1965, the U.S. Army had 400 helicopters; in 1970 it had 4,000. Vietnam ended any doubts that might have existed about the importance of helicopters on the modern battlefield, especially in low-intensity conflicts. It also ended any further debate on the need for armed helicopters. The U.S. Army began by modifying existing UH-1B and UH-1D Huey helicopters with a wide variety of machine-gun mountings and rocket pods. The armed gunships provided a preliminary bombardment of the landing zone and overhead fire support once the helicopter landing force arrived. But it was acknowledged that the UH-1B gunships were simply an improvisation.

By the late 1960s, the U.S. Army had introduced the AH-1G Cobra gunship. This was developed on the basis of the UH-1 Huey but employed a streamlined forward fuselage, with two crewmen sitting in tandem, instead of the bulbous fuselage of the UH-1. The lighter structural weight of the Cobra gave it better aerodynamic performance, and the customized configuration made it more suitable for a variety of weapons and fire control systems.

The Soviet armed forces studied the Vietnam War with some interest, particularly in regard to technological innovations. Several captured American helicopters were shipped to the Mil design bureau in Moscow for detailed inspection. The Soviets also noted that in the late 1960s, the U.S. Army was developing a dedicated fire-support helicopter, the AH-56 Cheyenne. The Soviet approach was two pronged. As with the U.S. Army, armed versions of the standard troop-carrying helicopter were developed, in this case the Mi-8TB (TB for *transportno-boeviy,* meaning transport combat). As a long-term solution, a requirement was issued to the Mil design bureau to begin work on a dedicated attack helicopter in the summer of 1968.

The new attack helicopter was the Mi-24, better known by its NATO code name, the Hind. The Mil bureau took a significantly different approach to its gunship. The Mi-24 was an evolutionary outgrowth of the Mi-8, just as the U.S. Army AH-1 Cobra was an outgrowth of the UH-1. There the similarities ended. Because the Mi-8 was so much larger than the UH-1, the resulting Mi-24 was a monster. The larger size of the basic airframe allowed the designers to incorporate a small troop compartment in the center of the helicopter. It is not clear if this was driven by a doctrinal requirement, or whether the decision to build the helicopter around the Mi-8's dynamic elements left the designers with such a large fuselage that a troop compartment was inevitable. The idea of an attack helicopter with troop lift features was not new. The Sikorsky entry in the AH-56 Cheyenne competition, the S-67 Blackhawk, also had a troop compartment. The Mil bureau had long been influenced by Sikorsky designs, and it is possible that the Mi-24's configuration reflects some American influences. There have also been reports that the design was influenced by KGB Border Guards requirements, which sought an armed helicopter with troop-carrying capability to patrol the long Chinese frontier after the Ussuri River conflict with China in the late 1960s.

Whatever its origins, the first Mi-24 prototypes began flight tests in 1970, and limited production began in 1972. The original configuration of the Mi-24 proved unacceptable, and the definitive Mi-24D Hind D did not appear until 1975. It employed tandem seating for the two crewmen, much like the AH-1 Cobra. Due to the Mi-24's larger size, its firepower was formidable: four sixteen-round 57mm rocket pods, two multiple antitank missile launchers, and a chin-mounted 12.7mm heavy machine gun. On the other hand, its large size made it less agile than the smaller Cobra, and its use of stub wings hindered its hovering performance.

The role of the attack helicopter was not confined to fire support for heliborne operations. Indeed, the main motivation behind the later Mi-24 variants was similar to that of the U.S. Army's AH-1S Cobra attack helicopters: antitank fighting in support of the tank and mechanized forces. The Soviets intended their Mi-24s for a broader range of roles. For example, the Mi-24s often practiced dropping bombs, a practice never found in the U.S. Army. Whereas the U.S.

Army tended to concentrate on antitank missions, the Soviet attack helicopter regiments spent more time on general fire support.

AIRMOBILE ORGANIZATION

The availability of large numbers of the new Mi-8 transport helicopter, Mi-24 attack helicopters, and Mi-6 heavy-lift helicopters led to a gradual maturation of Soviet air assault tactics and helicopter organization. There are fundamental differences in the way Soviet helicopters have been deployed compared to the U.S. Army experience. The U.S. Army gradually integrated helicopters directly into armored and mechanized infantry divisions after the Vietnam War. In addition, the 101st Airborne Division was converted to a heliborne airmobile division at the time of Vietnam and has retained this special mission since then. The Soviet Army did not integrate helicopters into its tank or motor rifle divisions. Most divisions had a small complement of helicopters, usually less than a dozen, devoted to liaison and utility roles. Helicopters remained under the control of the Soviet Air Force, and were placed under Soviet Ground Forces control when the need arose. There were no dedicated heliborne units equivalent to the 101st Airborne Division. Heliborne operations employed normal motor rifle troops.

In the late 1960s and early 1970s, the standard Soviet helicopter formation was a multirole helicopter regiment, attached to each tactical air army. A tactical air army was assigned to each front, so the scale of helicopters available to conduct heliborne operations was very limited. Such a regiment tended to be composed of two battalions of transport helicopters (Mi-4 and Mi-8), a heavy-lift battalion with Mi-6s, and a fire-support battalion with Mi-24 helicopters. As more helicopters became available during the heavy military buildup of the 1970s, helicopter regiments were gradually provided to each army, as well as to the fronts. By 1980, most Soviet armies facing NATO countries had an organic helicopter regiment, and by 1990 they had two.

The first serious experiments with dedicated heliborne forces began in 1969 as a response to the Vietnam War. The Soviets had paid close attention to the extensive use of helicopters by the U.S. Army and U.S. Marine Corps in Vietnam, and began experimenting with their own formations. This led to a revival of the concept of "army aviation." Although the helicopters and crew were trained and equipped by the Soviet Air Force, they were subordinated to the Soviet Ground Forces during operations.

The closer integration of helicopters and infantry led to the first true airmobile helicopter units. The new airmobile brigades were an attempt to create a highly mobile force for operations in low-intensity conflicts. Three, and possibly four, of these formations were formed, located at Kutaisi (Transcaucasus Military District), Mogocha (Transbaikal Military District), and Magadachi (Far East Military District). A fourth may have been deployed in the Central Asian or Turkestan Military Districts. The airmobile brigades were based around three assault battalions and a heavy-weapons battalion, with a total of about 1,900 troops. These brigades were supported by the military district's special helicopter regiment equipped with thirty-two Mi-8 transport helicopters and twenty-four Mi-6 heavy-lift helicopters. The brigades had very little armor beyond a company of eight BRDM tank destroyers and a platoon of BRDM-2 armored scout vehicles. These airmobile brigades were intended as rapid-reaction forces for contingencies along the Soviet frontier, notably against China.

In parallel to the airmobile brigades, organization of another new type of force was taking place in the late 1970s in the NATO theaters: the air assault brigades (DShB, or Desantnaya Shturmvaya Brigada). These brigades were intended for use against NATO, so they were much more heavily armed than the airmobile brigades. They were equipped with BMD airborne assault vehicles and resembled a reinforced VDV regiment; these air assault units had nearly double the firepower per thousand troops as a normal motor rifle division. Their basic combat elements were two airborne assault battalions with BMDs, two airborne rifle battalions, and a composite artillery battalion with eighteen 122mm D-30 howitzers. DShB troops were recruited and trained like VDV troops, including parachute training. But their main means of airborne insertion was the helicopter.

These brigades were closely affiliated with a helicopter regiment, though the helicopters were not permanently attached, as was the case with the airmobile brigades. The air assault brigade was larger than the airmobile brigade, about 2,600 troops, and included 68

BMDs and other heavy equipment. Whereas lifting an entire airmobile brigade would take about 60 Mi-8s and 36 Mi-6s, lifting an air assault brigade with BMDs would take 40 Mi-8s and 125 Mi-6s. Lifting the brigade without BMDs and other armored equipment would take 75 Mi-8s and 36 Mi-6s. By the late 1980s, there was one of these brigades in each military district in the western USSR and with several of the Groups of Soviet Forces in the Warsaw Pact countries. This suggests an allotment of one air assault brigade per front in wartime.

The formation of these brigades reflected the continuing evolution of Soviet tactical doctrine in the 1970s and 1980s. The Soviet General Staff revived the concept of an operational maneuver group, a task-oriented mobile formation for special exploitation missions. An airmobile force was an excellent adjunct to such a formation, giving it the capability to rapidly insert a significant force behind enemy lines for a variety of critical tasks. The airmobile force was more convenient for such missions than the VDV, since it was simpler on short notice to coordinate the actions of the helicopter transport force than the VTA air transport force. Any VDV operations in a NATO environment would face the dilemma of confronting NATO air defenses. Helicopters, although not invulnerable, could be flown in at nap of the earth to avoid the most lethal radar-directed air defenses. Large air transports would require a significant suppression-of-enemy-air-defense (SEAD) operation to minimize air transport casualties, and this would cost time and the element of surprise.

The final type of heliborne force to appear in the 1970s was the separate air assault battalion. This unit contained about 500 troops and resembled a miniature air assault brigade. It was equipped with fourteen BMD airborne assault vehicles. Like the airborne assault brigade, it could be delivered by either helicopter or parachute, but clearly it was intended as a heliborne force. These battalions were meant to provide an air assault capability to armies for seizing key tactical objectives such as bridgeheads, important road junctions, headquarters, or vital geographic positions such as mountain passes.

The heavy-lift requirements imposed by the BMDs led to a reorganization of the airmobile forces in the 1980s, with the brigades and separate battalions losing their vehicles. At this point, they became indistinguishable from the airmobile brigades. There simply were not enough heavy-lift helicopters to make such formations practical. By 1990, there were only 200 Mi-6 and 55 Mi-26 heavy-lift helicopters in service with the Frontal Aviation helicopter regiments. It would have taken more than half of the available heavy-lift helicopters to carry a BMD-equipped brigade, and such a heavy concentration of helicopters was unlikely. Without BMDs, these brigades were readily transportable in the more common Mi-8 helicopter.

The emergence of these Ground Forces airmobile formations provided a tactical vertical envelopment force for army commanders. The VDV Airborne Force was a strategic force subordinate to the General Staff for operational and strategic objectives. The greater flexibility of heliborne delivery allowed the Soviet Army to allot these new formations in the 1970s and 1980s for tactical missions of the army and front-level commanders. These missions could be conducted without the complications or delays of coordinating the mission with the VDV Airborne Force.

Soviet Separate Airmobile Brigades 1985
Order of Battle

Unit	Location
11th Sep. Airmobile Brigade	Mogocha, Transbaikal Military District
13th Sep. Airmobile Brigade	Magadachi, Far East Military District
21st Sep. Airmobile Brigade	Kutaisi, Georgia
23rd Sep. Airmobile Brigade	Kremenchug, Ukraine
35th Sep. Air Assault Brigade	Cottbus, East Germany
36th Sep. Airmobile Brigade	Garbolovo, Russia
37th Sep. Airmobile Brigade	Chernyakovsk, Kaliningrad
38th Sep. Airmobile Brigade	Brest, Byelorussia
40th Sep. Airmobile Brigade	Nikolayev, Ukraine

By the 1980s, the usual configuration of the army helicopter force had been well established. Each military district (front in wartime) was allotted a composite helicopter regiment, typically equipped with thirty Mi-8 transport helicopters and twenty-four to thirty Mi-6 or Mi-26 heavy-lift helicopters. This regiment would be assigned the task of delivering the front's airmobile brigade in wartime. The fronts would also have a composite aviation squadron, but this was a utility and liaison unit, not generally employed by the airmobile forces. Most tank and combined-arms armies oriented toward NATO were assigned three helicopter units: a transport helicopter regiment (thirty Mi-8 transport helicopters and forty Mi-24 attack helicopters), a combat helicopter regiment (ten Mi-8 and forty Mi-24 helicopters), and a helicopter squadron (usually equipped with twelve to sixteen helicopters, including one or two Mi-6 heavy-lift helicopters and several Mi-2 light utility helicopters). The transport helicopter regiment could be used to deliver a separate airmobile battalion.

The main distinction between Soviet and U.S. Army practice in the 1980s was the allotment of helicopters at divisional level. American heavy divisions had an aviation brigade organic to their structure with more than forty attack helicopters; Soviet divisions were limited to a handful of utility helicopters.

There has been no Soviet Army organization to serve as an advocate for airmobile requirements as has been the case in the U.S. Army. As a result, Soviet transport helicopter technology stagnated in the 1970s after the introduction of the Mi-8. In the wake of the Vietnam experience, airmobile advocates in the U.S. Army pushed for an advanced transport helicopter with better resistance to battle damage. This emerged in the 1980s as the Sikorsky UH-60 Blackhawk, without question the best military transport helicopter in the world today. The Soviets continued to churn out the adequate but outdated Mi-8M. Its successor, the planned Mi-40, is unlikely to appear until the turn of the century, nearly two decades after the Blackhawk. The Mi-40 is heavily patterned after the UH-60 Blackhawk, but its progress has been delayed since the Soviet Air Force favored the development of new assault helicopters over transport helicopters. Two new attack helicopters entered trials in the late 1980s, the Mil Mi-28 Havoc and the Kamov Ka-50 Hokum: it was a wasteful competitive effort that could have resulted in an advanced transport design as well as an advanced attack helicopter design. These development abnormalities reflect the air force preoccupation with its traditional fire-support mission and the absence of an army counterweight to press for the less glamorous but equally essential transport designs.

The revolutionary impact of the Vietnam War on U.S. Army heli-copter forces was paralleled by the Soviet experience in Afghanistan, which was a helicopter war for many of the same reasons as Alge-ria and Vietnam. The terrain favored the local insurgents, and air-mobility was one of the few technological and tactical advantages enjoyed by the Soviet forces. As will become apparent in later chap-ters, Afghanistan had a profound effect on Soviet attitudes toward airmobile forces.

The air assault brigades were absorbed by the VDV after Afghani-stan and redesignated as airborne brigades. The VDV was used mainly as a heliborne force in Afghanistan, and its superior perfor-mance there led to a consolidation of all airmobile units under a single command. It is possible that the VDV regarded this growing airmobile force as a threat to its future and decided it was better to absorb the heliborne mission than compete with it.

The first experiments at integrating helicopters within normal mechanized infantry formations took place in Afghanistan in the mid-1980s. Special motor rifle brigades were organized, which had their own organic air assault battalion with its own helicopters. This type of unit proved highly successful in Afghanistan and is likely to form the basis for new combined-arms battalions in the late 1990s.

In the early 1990s, the author visited several aerospace design bureaus in Russia to discuss future aircraft developments. In nearly all cases, it was the same depressing story: heavy budget cuts, dras-tically reduced production, departure of the best engineers for more lucrative jobs elsewhere in the economy. The sole exception was the Mil helicopter design bureau in Moscow. The general designer, Mark Vineberg, had a broad smile on his face when asked about his company's future. Russia is placing great emphasis on airmobile forces, he said, and the helicopter business in Russia promises to be very good. The battling bumblebee has become an essential tool of modern warfare.

Chapter 10
The Other Elites

The VDV Airborne Force was the largest of the Soviet special operations forces, but not the only one. Four other forces deployed elite special operations units, though with different missions from the paratroopers. These included the navy's "Black Beret" Naval Infantry and naval Spetsnaz, the GRU military intelligence service's Spetsnaz, the KGB special operations units, and the MVD Dzerzhinskiy Division. Many of these forces interacted with the VDV for training, and in wartime they were intended to provide complementary capabilities.

SPETSNAZ

Of these elite forces, no doubt the most famous in the West are the Spetsnaz. Spetsnaz comes from the Russian words *spetsialnoye naznacheniye*, which roughly translated means "special purpose." The term "Spetsnaz" is used indiscriminately today to refer to nearly any Soviet special forces unit, whether under army, navy, KGB, or MVD control. In this book, it is used in the narrower sense to refer to the special operations forces of the Soviet GRU. The GRU Spetsnaz is also sometimes called the "gray wolves" due to the insignia the organization adopted in the early 1990s. The Soviet Union, like the United States, had two intelligence agencies: the GRU (the General Staff intelligence directorate, corresponding to the U.S.

Defense Intelligence Agency, or DIA) and the KGB (corresponding to the CIA and FBI all wrapped up in one). The GRU was a part of the military establishment, whereas the KGB was separate from both the Communist Party and the army, although deeply involved with both. The Spetsnaz forces were intended to bridge the gap between strategic intelligence-gathering personnel such as KGB and GRU spies, and tactical reconnaissance units attached to tank and motor rifle divisions.

The exploits of Spetsnaz have been trumpeted by Vladimir B. Rezun, alias Viktor Suvorov, a former Soviet GRU major who defected to the West in the late 1970s. Until Suvorov began writing his books on the subject, little attention was paid (publicly at least) to Soviet special forces aside from obvious elite units such as the Soviet airborne divisions. Certainly, there has always been some appreciation for Soviet partisan warfare and unconventional tactics, but not for the extensive type of special operations portrayed by Suvorov. He luridly depicts Spetsnaz as a bunch of highly trained multilingual sportsmen-killers, with a bent for assassination and other mayhem. He suggests they will be used in missions to eliminate NATO VIPs in the event of war, as well as carrying out more conventional commando-style operations against key NATO facilities. He has elevated Spetsnaz to mythical proportions, aided and abetted by a large number of credulous Western writers who echo his exaggerated portrayal.

This type of romantic mythmaking ignores the primary role of such forces, which is deep reconnaissance. Commando-type sabotage missions are a secondary mission of the Spetsnaz, and such activities would have distracted them from their main tasks. The Spetsnaz are inheritors of the long Russian and Soviet tradition of the *razvedchik,* or scout. The *razvedchik* is legendary in Russian military lore as the bravest of the brave, the intrepid adventurer carrying out missions deep behind enemy lines at great risk. This is hardly an unusual view of scouts and is found in most modern armies. The popular Willi Heinrich novels center around such scout teams in the German Wehrmacht in World War II and have been immortalized on the screen in Sam Peckinpah's film classic *Cross of Iron.* In the Red Army of World War II, each rifle division selected its best troops to serve as regimental or divisional scouts. In some cases, they were organized into traditional reconnaissance companies; in other cases the organization was less formal.

The *razvedchiki* were used for scouting and for especially demanding missions. For example, if a forward detachment was needed to seize an objective in advance of the main formation, it was usually assigned to the *razvedchiki*. If a division planned a sneak raid against enemy positions, the *razvedchiki* were the basis of the raiding force.

The development of deep reconnaissance teams for operational reconnaissance in the Red Army in World War II is a complicated subject due to its interaction with the partisan movement, which itself had intelligence collection as one of its major functions. But, in addition, the Red Army also dispatched deep reconnaissance teams into German-occupied territories in conjunction with partisan operations. Several organizations served in these functions. The OMSBON (*otdelnaya motostrelkovaya brigada osobogo naznacheniye,* or separate special operations motor rifle brigade) was used to prepare partisan units for special operations missions, both in the areas of intelligence and diversionary raiding. Red Army officers were often dispatched with these partisan units to provide professional assistance in conducting the missions. Many enlisted radiomen also formed a key element of these teams, operating radio networks for the partisan intelligence operations. Indeed, the distinction between partisan and regular army forces was often unclear, with the regular troops wearing local civilian dress for camouflage.

For particularly important demolition operations behind German lines, personnel were dispatched from an OGBM (*otdelniy gvardyskiy batalon minerov,* or separate guards sapper battalion). One of these OGBM was attached to each front for carrying out specialized combat engineer missions, and they often formed the cadre for rear-area raiding parties in conjunction with the partisan movement.

Aside from the deep reconnaissance teams connected with partisan operations, the Second Directorate of the General Staff coordinated special purpose detachments that were placed at the disposal of nearly all front commanders. These troops were more often called *razvedchik* than Spetsnaz, though other nicknames were used such as *osbon (osoboya naznacheniya),* or special operations. The Second Directorate was the element responsible for intelligence and became the GRU (Main Intelligence Directorate) in the postwar years. These detachments, usually of irregular size, from a few men to a few platoons, were used to carry out reconnaissance missions prior to offensive operations, or for other special tasks of utmost urgency. The detachments were the closest counterpart of the modern Spetsnaz, though the partisan connection cannot be forgotten. The detachments were used in situations where the local partisan movement was weak, for example in Ukraine, or for missions where coordination with the partisans was too time consuming or otherwise undesirable.

At the strategic level, the Red Army cooperated with the NKVD special police in deploying espionage and spy networks. Some of these were of a military nature, with teams parachuted deep behind German lines in military uniform. For example, the Red Army and NKVD began dropping intelligence teams into Poland, deep behind German lines, as early as the autumn of 1941. These strategic reconnaissance teams were on the fuzzy edge between military intelligence operations and conventional espionage operations, and it is often difficult to distinguish the two. Assassination missions deep behind enemy lines were more often the work of the NKVD than the military.

The Spetsnaz Reborn

In the immediate postwar years, the front-level deep reconnaissance detachments disappeared. They were finally re-formed in 1949 under the new designation *otdelnaya razvedyvatelnaya rota spetsialnoye naznacheniye* (separate special operations intelligence company). These were relatively small in number and were attached to a few of the tank and combined-arms armies, mainly in the Group of Soviet Forces–Germany. They were intended to conduct scouting missions between 95 and 125 miles behind the NATO front line. The units were quite secret, but specialized training was not much more extensive than that of the VDV airborne troops.

The "revolution in military affairs" that occurred in the wake of Stalin's death dramatically affected the Spetsnaz. The Soviet Army began to pay more serious attention to the nature of modern warfare, particularly the consequences of tactical nuclear weapons on the battlefield. A new mission was added to the Spetsnaz assignment—the elimination of U.S. Army tactical nuclear delivery systems such as the Honest John and Matador missiles. The Spetsnaz companies were expanded in size and formed into five new battalions. As during the war, these battalions were allocated to fronts rather than armies. The primary mission of the Spetsnaz battalions remained intelligence, but their operational area was deepened. They were trained to conduct missions 250 miles behind NATO lines. For such missions, airborne delivery became a vital tactic, and the Spetsnaz began to rotate through the VDV schools to learn the appropriate skills. The requirement to become airborne-qualified began a strong linkage between the Spetsnaz and the VDV, which has continued to the present day.

The changing depth of the modern battlefield led to foment in the Spetsnaz organization. The Spetsnaz were enlarged one last time in 1962, with the five battalions and several remaining separate companies being re-formed into six Spetsnaz brigades. The enlargement was accompanied by another extension of the Spetsnaz mission, from the 250-mile penetration capability to a 450-mile capability. This was in part to enable the Spetsnaz to deal with new NATO tactical nuclear systems such as the Lance and Pershing missiles.

The more demanding missions of the Spetsnaz required a greater level of professional training. Until the late 1960s, there were no specialist schools for enlisted men beyond VDV jump schools. In 1968, a training regiment was set up at Pechora in northeastern Russia for European assignments, and in 1970 another was formed in Chirchik in Uzbekistan for assignments in Asia and the Mideast.

In the 1970s, the new Spetsnaz brigades were deployed under the control of military district headquarters in peacetime. Their normal formation was three or four *otriadi* of 250 to 350 troops, which roughly corresponded to battalions. During wartime, one of these battalions was earmarked for deployment with a front for very deep reconnaissance and raiding missions. Two or three other battalions would be attached to the front's key tank and combined-arms armies. The Spetsnaz brigade also contained a combat engineer company, a descendant of the wartime OGBM, which prepared specialists in demolition. One of the special roles for these companies was the use of tactical nuclear munitions, sometimes called nuclear mines, or "suitcase nukes." The brigade also contained a communications detachment, which would furnish specialized communications personnel to the other Spetsnaz battalions.

The depth of the new mission also changed the training requirements of the brigades. For the first time, foreign language training was entered into the list of skills needed by the Spetsnaz. In fact, language training among the enlisted men was never adequate for anything more than the understanding of basic signs and words. Foreign language training was more serious for officers, but Spetsnaz were not fluent enough in German or English to be mistaken for locals, contrary to popular myth.

Some of the more sensationalized accounts of the Spetsnaz have suggested that this foreign language program was aimed at creating special assassination squads that could have operated behind NATO lines, disguised as NATO soldiers or as civilians. The idea is not entirely far-fetched. The German Wehrmacht in World War II operated the legendary Brandenburg units to disrupt enemy operations. A better-known example was Otto Skorzeny's improvised Operation Griffon during the Battle of the Bulge in the Ardennes in December 1944: German troops of Panzer Brigade 150 dressed in American uniforms in hopes of sowing confusion and disrupting the U.S. Army's response to the German offensive.

The Brandenburg and Skorzeny operations highlight the difficulty of such maneuvers, as well as their potential. It does not take a great many soldiers in disguise to seriously hinder an opponent's operations. However, it is difficult to organize large diversionary units of this type due to language barriers. Few soldiers have the language skills or the experience to convincingly pass themselves off as soldiers of another army, particularly in the Soviet Union where the youth had little opportunity for foreign travel prior to their conscription. The language training afforded the young Spetsnaz draftees was hardly adequate to give them a good reading knowledge of a new language, never mind any spoken fluency. The main reason behind the language program was to assist the units in carrying out missions behind NATO lines by helping the scouts read signs, question prisoners, and read captured documents.

The Spetsnaz were something of an oddity in the GRU. Headquartered at the legendary Steklyashka, the "glass house," at Khodynka Field in northern Moscow, the GRU always emphasized brains over brawn. The GRU leadership saw the Spetsnaz as a menacing bunch of Neanderthals stomping around in swamps and eating frogs for breakfast. It was a necessary job but one better left to the perpetually puerile. As technical and electronic means of intelligence collection began to dominate the GRU in the 1970s, the Spetsnaz's intelligence collection role became less important. What had been secondary missions, such as raiding NATO's nuclear sites, grew in importance to fill the vacuum. These commando missions overlapped with VDV missions and had little to do with traditional intelligence functions; Spetsnaz became estranged from its GRU headquarters.

Selection to become a recruit in the Spetsnaz was a great honor for a conscript soldier, but it amounted to only a two-year tour of duty. For an officer, selection for the Spetsnaz meant a tough duty assignment with little hope of future advancement. Spetsnaz was not a stepping-stone within the GRU, since most GRU assignments favored candidates with strong analytical and administrative skills, or with extensive experience in espionage functions during foreign assignments. Spetsnaz officers could hope to become majors or colonels and command one of the Spetsnaz brigades, but there were few prospects beyond that point. The Spetsnaz did attract many fine officers who preferred an adventurous lifestyle over the increasingly bureaucratic life of the average Soviet officer. But other services were a stronger magnet, particularly after Margelov revived the VDV in the 1960s. The VDV offered significant career opportunities since the force was more than ten times the size of the Spetsnaz. Under Margelov, the VDV began to be regarded as a prestigious assignment, whereas the Spetsnaz brigades remained obscure and highly classified until the very end of the Soviet Union.

The nature of reconnaissance changed rapidly after 1960. With the advent of reconnaissance satellites in the early 1960s, the need for deep reconnaissance teams began to diminish. The GRU expanded to take advantage of new means of collecting intelligence, and the smash-and-grab tactics of the Spetsnaz rapidly grew out of fashion. Automated means of reconnaissance collection continued to grow, not only satellites but reconnaissance drones and sophisticated electronic systems. By the 1970s, tactical reconnaissance in the tank armies and combined armies was undertaken by three formations: an attached Spetsnaz battalion; a separate reconnaissance and electronic warfare battalion (OBRiREB), which conducted electronic signal intelligence; and a separate target acquisition battalion (OBZR). These two new electronic intelligence battalions took over many of the functions that would have been performed by the *razvedchiki* in World War II. Of the three reconnaissance battalions, the Spetsnaz intelligence collection techniques were the most traditional and, perhaps, the most outdated for use on the modern battlefield.

The GRU was not ready to abandon the Spetsnaz, however, since they were well aware that electronic means of intelligence collection might be blinded in war by superior NATO electronic countermeasures technology. Spetsnaz provided a solid, traditional backup, and their secondary missions might prove useful as well. The Spetsnaz was not an expensive extravagance. The brigades seldom numbered more than 1,000 troops each in peacetime; in fact, they were closer to battalions than brigades in strength. Supplementing these brigades were Spetsnaz companies attached to each combined-arms or tank army, and numbering about 110 men each. Like the VDV, these Spetsnaz formations could always be employed in their secondary missions if their primary intelligence missions were no longer valuable. But there is little evidence that the Soviet General Staff placed much importance on their role in wartime, certainly not the grossly exaggerated importance given them by Western writers in recent years.

Suvorov has suggested that, by drawing upon reservists, the Soviet Army would have had up to 30,000 Spetsnaz troops available for operations in the event of war with NATO. This included Spetsnaz brigades at front level, Spetsnaz companies at army level, and various types of naval Spetsnaz forces. However, a GRU defector in 1990 put the number at about half that. In judging the quality of special forces, there is always a conflict between size and elite training. The larger the force, the more likely that its recruitment and training are less demanding. Although no one would deny the quality of the U.S. Marines as a fighting force, they do not compare in training and specialized skills to a unit such as the navy's SEALs. Likewise, British Paras are among the world's finest light infantry, but they are not equivalent to the SAS, nor are they intended to be. The type of force described by Suvorov was an elite force, but its sheer size suggests that it was more like the U.S. Army's LRRPs (long-range recon patrols) or Rangers rather than Delta Force, and probably not even that well trained.

It must be remembered that Spetsnaz, like most of the Soviet armed forces, was a conscript force. In a Spetsnaz detachment, eighteen of the twenty men were conscripts, and only two were professional soldiers; 90 percent of Spetsnaz tactical units were made up of eighteen- to twenty-year-old conscript soldiers with only a few months of specialized training. This does not imply the sort of James Bond characters that many people in the West associate with the word "Spetsnaz."

SOVIET NAVAL SPECIAL FORCES

The Soviet Navy had its own special forces, the Naval Infantry and the Naval Spetsnaz. The Naval Infantry was not an elite force in any real sense, since it did not traditionally enjoy special preference in recruiting, and its training program was not exceptional. It has been labeled an elite force more for its similarity to Western forces such as the U.S. Marine Corps or the Royal Marines than on its own merits.

The Naval Infantry, Morskaya Pyekhota in Russian, traced their lineage back to naval landing parties of the Imperial Fleet of Peter the Great. Peter formed the first naval infantry regiment, which first saw combat in 1714 during the wars with Sweden for the control of the Baltic Sea. Russian naval infantry forces, like most traditional marine forces, were quite small up to World War I. The story of the Soviet Naval Infantry often becomes mixed up with the use of other naval troops in ground combat. During the Russian Civil War in 1917–21, and again during the Great Patriotic War of 1941–45, the Red Fleet was bottled up in its ports and saw little action at sea. As a result, large numbers of sailors were idle, and they were often formed into improvised infantry formations.

During the Russian Civil War, sailors were a critical element of the Bolsheviks' new Red Army. The Russian Navy had a long-standing reputation for being a hotbed of revolutionary foment, and sailors took an active part in the 1905 revolution, including several mutinies. The Russian Navy did not suffer the appalling level of casualties endured by the army in World War I, but the proximity of the Baltic Fleet to Saint Petersburg ensured that many of the sailors were exposed to the revolutionary sentiment spreading through the Tsarist capital. When the revolution finally came in 1917, sailors played a prominent role in the ranks of insurgents. At the time of the storming of the Winter Palace in October 1917, sailors were about 35 percent of the strength of the Red Guard forces, far out of proportion to their strength in the Russian armed forces as a whole. The Baltic Fleet sailors were among the most radical, and flocked in large numbers to the Bolshevik cause. The sailors became the vanguard of Lenin's new armed forces, fighting not only in the Saint Petersburg area, but across most of Russia in the following years. Naval detachments formed the core of many special assault forces, including the vital armored train units.

The reputation of the naval detachments as the vanguard of the Red forces suffered badly in 1921 when the Baltic Fleet's key Kronshtadt garrison revolted against the growing authoritarianism of Lenin's rule. The revolt was crushed in a bloody fashion by the army, and the navy returned to its traditional mission. A small naval infantry force was formed in the 1930s for amphibious assault and traditional missions such as defense of key harbors. The Baltic Fleet had a separate special purpose brigade for these functions. This unit sent a special operations detachment to fight in the Russo-Finnish War of 1939–40. In 1940, this unit was re-formed as the 1st Baltic Naval Infantry Brigade. This was the only significant Soviet naval infantry formation at the beginning of the Great Patriotic War on 22 June 1941, when the Germans invaded.

The invasion included a small but successful naval campaign, which managed to bottle up the Baltic Fleet in Leningrad after the first few months of fighting. The Soviet ships kept skeleton crews aboard to man the guns as the Germans laid siege to Leningrad. The desperate need for manpower forced the Red Navy to form large numbers of naval infantry units to help defend the city. By the end of the year, the Baltic Fleet had formed ten naval infantry brigades, four regiments, and forty battalions and separate companies. Most of these units were turned over to Red Army command and fought through the 900-day siege on the front lines alongside regular Red Army formations.

In the Black Sea Fleet, two regiments and six smaller units of naval infantry were formed to assist in the defense of Odessa. At Sevastopol in the Crimea, the navy formed an additional three naval infantry brigades, two regiments, and four battalions. Other elements of the Black Sea Fleet formed eight more naval infantry brigades and about thirty battalions. The Northern Fleet formed a single brigade, three regiments, and two independent battalions of naval infantry. In total, about 100,000 sailors were assigned to these new naval infantry formations in the first few months of the war. These units were in no way elite. They were simply improvised units assembled in haste to make up for the disastrous losses of the regular army in the summer of 1941. The men received no special training for infantry combat. In later years, a number of regular army officers were assigned to command these units in the hope of improving their combat performance. One of these was Vasiliy Margelov, who would later lead the VDV Airborne Force after the war.

The Soviet Navy conducted about a hundred amphibious landings during World War II, mainly in the Black Sea. These ranged in size from small raids to full-scale assaults involving several divisions. Naval troops were used in many of the smaller raids, though not necessarily from the naval infantry formations. The larger assaults were conducted mainly with army troops with no special assault training. There were only four amphibious landings involving several thousand troops, three of these occurring on the Kerch and Taman peninsulas where the Azov Sea meets the Black Sea in southern Russia.

The first large operation took place on the Kerch peninsula from 25 December 1941 through 2 January 1942 and involved 42,000 troops. It was a horrific operation, occurring in the cold of winter under force eight gale conditions, but the Soviet Army did manage to seize the Kerch peninsula for a time in a vain attempt to regain the Crimea. Two years later, the Red Army was more successful in regaining this area. On 9 September 1943, the Northern Caucasus Front in conjunction with the Red Navy conducted an amphibious assault on the city of Novorossisk on the Taman peninsula, securing the city by 16 September. The rest of the Taman peninsula was seized in early October, permitting the Red Army to make another amphibious leap over the Taman straits to seize Kerch. The first amphibious landings took place near Kerch on 31 October 1943 as part of the effort to wrest the Crimea from German control. The landings stretched through December 1943 and eventually totaled some 85,000 troops, primarily from regular army formations but including the 83rd and 255th Naval Infantry Brigades and several naval infantry regiments. The only major amphibious landing not to occur in the Black Sea area was the landing on Moon Island in the Baltic.

The Soviet experience with amphibious landings was very different from the U.S. experience in the Pacific, where the Marine Corps was an integral part of the operations. The majority of the major Soviet landings were planned and executed by the Red Army, with little or no special role for the Naval Infantry. Although the Soviet naval infantry brigades were well regarded when provided with decent, experienced infantry leaders, their performance in World War II was not exceptional, and certainly did not create the type of mystique earned by the U.S. Marine Corps for its performance at Tarawa and Iwo Jima. A total of 122 naval infantry soldiers and officers received the Hero of the Soviet Union award, compared to 196 for the airborne troops.

In the immediate postwar years, nearly all of the naval infantry brigades and other formations were disbanded, and the sailors returned to their more traditional roles. There was a certain distaste in the postwar Soviet Navy for the whole subject of naval infantry: it was a painful reminder of the inadequacies of the Red Navy during World War II. Small naval infantry formations did remain with the major fleets through the early 1950s within the Coastal Defense Force, but their role was limited to base defense. The amphibious assault mission was taken out of the navy's hands and left to the army.

Khrushchev's rise to power after Stalin's death in 1953 led to a thorough reassessment of Soviet military doctrine. Khrushchev was firmly opposed to Stalin's plan for a traditional blue-water fleet, but the new navy commander, Admiral Gorshkov, managed to initiate a small-scale effort to build the first true Soviet amphibious assault ships. Gorshkov had commanded the Red Navy's Azov flotilla during the amphibious operations at Novorossisk and Kerch in 1943, and so was well aware of the need for improvement in this neglected area.

The latest effort included new ship designs such as the Project 188 class (MP-8) amphibious ships, as well as the conversion of freighters and coastal transports. Although Khrushchev argued that amphibious assault operations could be conducted by regular army units, as they had been during the war, he permitted Admiral Gorshkov to revive the Naval Infantry force on a small scale in 1961–62. The role of the new Naval Infantry would be to seize the beachhead, but regular army forces would be needed for any large amphibious operation. A Naval Infantry officer school was opened in Vyborg at this time to provide specialized training for the new formations.

The fortunes of the Naval Infantry improved dramatically after Khrushchev's overthrow in 1964. Under Leonid Brezhnev's government, Soviet foreign policy began to show more interest in involvement in the developing world. The Soviet Navy, and Admiral Gorshkov in particular, had been advocating a naval power-projection capability patterned after the U.S. Navy. This inevitably meant an enhanced amphibious warfare capability and a revival of the Naval Infantry. The new Project 1171 Nosorog (rhinoceros) class of heavy amphibious assault ships and the Project 770 class of tank landing ships began to enter navy service in significant numbers by the late 1960s.

Under the 1961–64 reorganization, the Naval Infantry added a regiment to the Northern, Baltic, and Black Sea Fleets, and a brigade to the Pacific Fleet. These regiments each numbered about two thousand troops based around three naval infantry battalions and a tank battalion with thirty-one PT-76 amphibious tanks and ten T-55 medium tanks. The first major field exercise of the new force took place in 1968 when the Baltic Fleet's naval infantry regiment conducted joint landings on the East German coast alongside the Polish 7th Naval Assault Division during the Sever war games. Most subsequent Warsaw Pact war games in the Baltic region involved naval landing exercises, often in conjunction with Polish or East German naval infantry formations. The Naval Infantry was gradually strengthened through the 1970s, including the expansion of its tank unit to a regiment, a new self-propelled artillery battalion, and air defense missile units; their expanded size led to their reclassification as brigades, and the Pacific brigade was expanded to form the first naval infantry division.

Even after the expansion, the Naval Infantry was still only a pale shadow of its American counterpart, the Marine Corps. Until the 1980s, the entire Soviet Naval Infantry force was only about the size of one U.S. Marine Corps division. In terms of size and importance, it was closer to Britain's Royal Marines. Whereas the U.S. Marines had about a third the number of divisions of the U.S. Army, the Soviet Naval Infantry was only about one-hundredth the size of the Soviet Ground Forces. This was largely due to the landlocked nature of the USSR, and the minor importance of the Naval Infantry in a war against NATO.

Had the Cold War turned hot, the Soviet Naval Infantry's missions would have been in peripheral operations against NATO. The 36th (later 336th) Naval Infantry Brigade of the Baltic Fleet would have been used in operations against Denmark in conjunction with similar Polish and East German naval assault units. The 63rd Guards Kirkenneskaya Naval Infantry Brigade (later re-formed into the 61st and 175th Naval Infantry Brigades) of the Northern Fleet would have been used in operations against northern Norway. The Black Sea Fleet's 810th Naval Infantry Brigade would have been used in any operations in the Mediterranean, but its main theater would have been Turkey.

The overseas power-projection role for the Naval Infantry was practiced on several occasions during the Brezhnev years. In July 1981, the Soviet Navy conducted its first overseas exercise outside the usual Warsaw Pact theater when Soviet naval infantry forces, including tanks, were landed on the Syrian coast as part of joint Soviet-Syrian exercises. Later exercises took place elsewhere in the developing world, including an exercise in the South China Sea with Vietnam in 1984. There were small-scale uses of naval infantry forces during several regional conflicts, including Angola in 1976, Ethiopia in 1979, and the Seychelles in the early 1980s. During the Afghanistan war, a detachment of mechanized Naval Infantry was used in ground combat, probably to provide the force with combat experience.

Naval Infantry Roles and Tactics
A key doctrinal difference between the Soviet Naval Infantry and the U.S. Marine Corps was the issue of the army's role in amphibious operations. The Soviet Naval Infantry was envisioned as a force for conducting coastal raids or spearheading an amphibious assault. None of the Soviet naval infantry units were large enough to conduct a major amphibious assault with their own resources, even after their expansion to brigade size in the 1980s. Throughout the Cold War years, the Soviets conducted naval landing exercises with the Naval Infantry securing the beach, followed by regular army formations in amphibious assault ships. In contrast, the U.S. Marines largely took over the amphibious assault role in the postwar years in spite of heavy army involvement in amphibious operations during the Pacific campaigns in World War II.

Soviet naval infantry tactics were different from U.S. Marine tactics in some key respects. In view of the U.S. experience in World War II assaulting contested beaches such as Tarawa and Iwo Jima, the Marine Corps was much more concerned about the capability to carry out forcible insertions. This meant that specialized assault vehicles were needed, such as the armored LVT amtracs. The Soviet Naval Infantry was issued standard army vehicles such as the PT-76 light tank and BTR-60PB armored transporter, which provided limited amphibious capabilities in calm seas, but it did not develop a dedicated amphibious assault vehicle such as the Marine amtracs, capable of operating in rough seas. Instead, the Soviets concentrated on another means of insertion—high-speed air-cushion vehicles. Since the NATO objectives were unlikely to be heavily contested beaches with conventional World War II–style shore defenses, the Soviet Navy felt that air-cushion vehicles were a more practical solution to the ship-to-shore problem.

Three different air-cushion landing craft were introduced in the 1970s in light, medium, and heavy configurations. The first were the light Project 1205 Skat (Skate, NATO: Gus class), which could bring in twenty-seven tons of troops or supplies at speeds of up to sixty knots. Thirty of these were built for the Naval Infantry in 1970–74. It was accompanied by a craft designed to carry tanks and heavy equipment, the Project 1232.2 Dzheyran (NATO: Aist). This massive craft was fitted with bow and stern ramps and could carry 220 troops and heavy loads such as four PT-76 amphibious tanks, or two T-55 tanks. Twenty were built in 1971–86. The medium Project 1206 Kalmar (Squid, NATO: Lebed) craft appeared in 1976. These could carry two PT-76 tanks or 120 troops. The most remarkable of the air-cushion landing craft to appear was the Project 1232.1 Zubr (Bison, NATO: Pomornik), which was designed to replace the Dzheyran class in the late 1980s. This was the largest and most powerful military air-cushion vehicle ever built; it could carry three medium tanks and 100 troops at speeds up to sixty-three knots. Four were built for the Baltic Fleet and three for the Black Sea Fleet in the late 1980s before the collapse of the USSR. The U.S. Navy finally introduced air-cushion landing craft (LCAC) in the late 1980s, but these did not approach the Zubr class in capabilities.

Another critical difference in tactics was in the area of airborne insertion. Heliborne insertion had become a major U.S. Marine approach by the 1960s, and the U.S. Navy eventually acquired specialized LPH and LHD helicopter assault carriers. By the 1980s, it was rare to see a Marine exercise without CH-46 and CH-53 troop helicopters involved. The Soviet Naval Infantry was very slow in adopting helicopters, instead seizing initial bridgeheads by using the more traditional means of airborne insertion—the paratroop drop. This tactic was demonstrated in several naval infantry war games, most notably the Zapad-81 exercise, in which seaborne landings by 5,000 naval infantry troops were preceded by an airdrop. In some cases, these preliminary air assaults were conducted by the VDV, but gradually the Naval Infantry began to qualify a larger fraction of its force for airdrop operations. The Naval Infantry finally began to acquire its own troop/assault helicopters in the form of the Kamov Ka-29TB in the late 1980s, but the Soviet Navy never acquired dedicated helicopter carriers for this mission, and the naval infantry helicopter force is still tiny.

Most assessments of the Soviet Naval Infantry place it well below the army's VDV or Spetsnaz in terms of combat quality. Due to its restricted role, the Naval Infantry has never had the prestige or conscription priority afforded the VDV, and the career of a naval infantry officer does not attract the most ambitious individuals. Although the Naval Infantry has attempted to create the mystique of an elite unit by traditional means such as its distinctive black uniform and black beret, it has not enjoyed the talented leadership of charismatic commanders such as Vasiliy Margelov. It is worth recalling that Margelov commanded the premier Soviet Marine unit, the 1st Baltic Naval Infantry Brigade, for a time in World War II, but he made his career in the regular army and the VDV.

Current Russian efforts to develop a rapid-reaction force for post–Cold War contingencies has not placed much emphasis on the Naval Infantry. This is not altogether surprising, as the post-1991 Russian military has been heavily dominated by senior VDV officers such as Defense Minister Pavel Grachev, and their allies in the air force. In 1993, the Russian Navy began to call for a major reorganization of the Naval Infantry to make it more suitable for modern combat conditions. It is one of the forces being earmarked for a larger percentage of professional (versus conscript) troops, but it is yet to be seen whether the navy will be able to extract the funds needed to bring the Naval Infantry up to true elite force status.

Naval Spetsnaz

Besides the Naval Infantry, the Soviet Navy also deployed a Spetsnaz diversionary brigade with most of the fleets. These correspond to the U.S. Navy's SEALs or the British SBS. These units have been far more secretive than the GRU's Spetsnaz formations, and they are still wrapped in mystery.

The Red Navy in World War II did not have an extensive underwater sabotage and special operations effort comparable to the U.S. Navy's UDT (underwater demolition teams), the forerunner of today's SEALs. The EPRON (*ekspeditsiya podvodnykh rabot osobogo naznacheniya,* or special purpose underwater rescue team) had deep-sea diving equipment for salvage and rescue work, but the navy lacked any advanced scuba technology and was only beginning to experiment with a primitive Aqua-Lung. The only specialized equipment available was a buoyant waterproof explosive device that the swimmer could tow behind him. Stalin ordered the development of a special "undersea torpedo boat" for use by naval commandos. The project was undertaken by a special NKVD design bureau. The boat was in fact a minisubmarine that would lie in wait at harbor entrances for an enemy ship and then fire a single torpedo. With the torpedo launched, the boat would surface and run away at high speed. The special hull design proved impossible, but work continued on the project through the Khrushchev years. The lack of suitable equipment, as well as the lack of opportunity to employ such forces with the fleet bottled up in harbor for much of the war, restricted the chances for the development of Soviet UDT forces.

Instead, the Red Navy's intelligence force concentrated on more traditional forms of reconnaissance and raiding. Each of the Soviet fleets had an intelligence department that was responsible for special operations. This department was generally organized into an agent detachment, a tactical reconnaissance detachment, an operational reconnaissance detachment, a signals intelligence detachment, and an analysis unit. The agent detachment controlled agents who operated behind German lines in cooperation with the NKVD special police. The tactical reconnaissance detachment controlled coastal reconnaissance missions and was the naval equivalent of the army's *razvedchiki*. The missions of the fleet reconnaissance detachments varied by theater. The Northern Fleet's reconnaissance detachment operated joint Russian–Norwegian teams of coast watchers who were instrumental in tracking German naval forces in the Barents Sea area. The Black Sea Fleet detachment was used extensively for raiding missions behind German lines and played a prominent role in the major amphibious operations. The river flotillas had their own small detachments, and the Baltic Fleet intelligence operated a Special Operations River and Lake Sabotage Detachment, which operated on Lake Ladoga and nearby waterways to harass German and Finnish forces near Leningrad. A separate fleet department controlled operational reconnaissance, the Soviet term for long-range reconnaissance missions, usually conducted by special parachute units or infiltration teams. It does not appear that the naval reconnaissance units had dedicated equipment, but high-speed craft and submarines were diverted to their use on a regular basis.

The first naval Spetsnaz brigades were formed in the 1950s by the Third Department of the Fleet Intelligence Directorate, the naval equivalent of the GRU. The role of these brigades was to formalize and coordinate the activity of the wartime intelligence departments. Although called brigades, these formations were in fact quite small in manpower, probably well under a thousand men per brigade. These units had a variety of roles but focused on reconnaissance, as did their land-based counterparts. In 1967, the Black Sea Fleet organized the first underwater sabotage detachments after learning of the deployment of such units by the Turkish navy in the Black Sea. Called antifrogman and minisub defense detachments (PDSS), these were the first Soviet units comparable to the U.S. Navy's UDT or SEALs. Gradually, these were extended to each of the four fleets and eventually became part of the Spetsnaz brigades. These units were structured not only for harbor defense but could be employed on sabotage missions, including those using portable nuclear devices. Some of the fleets operated minisubs and swimmer delivery vehicles both for the conduct of reconnaissance and the delivery of underwater sabotage teams.

Little is known about combat operations by the PDSS detachments. Russian accounts indicate that the Black Sea Fleet PDSS detachment was flown from Sevastopol to Angola in 1986 to protect Soviet merchant shipping. In June 1986, South African commando teams had damaged two Soviet merchant ships and sunk the *Havana* with limpet mines; they also landed teams ashore to destroy power lines and fuel depots. Russian accounts claim that the PDSS teams encountered U.S. SEALs during the Angolan operations, but in fact they were involved mainly with South African units. At least one South African was captured and later exchanged for several Soviet Army officers captured in the Angolan fighting. The PDSS has been used overseas for special assignments, for example at the Malta summit conference in 1989 when Mikhail Gorbachev met former U.S. president George Bush at sea.

Very little is known about the development of the Soviet swimmer delivery vehicles used by the naval Spetsnaz brigades. Recent Russian accounts suggest that four classes of minisubs were built, called Projects 865, 1806, 1832, and 1837. The two most recent types are the Piranya (Pirahna) and Triton, which were developed by the Malakhit design bureau in Leningrad. The Piranya minisubs displaced 219 tons submerged and had a crew of three. They could carry a Spetsnaz sabotage group of probably less than a dozen men. Their top underwater speed was six and a half knots and they had a combat range of one thousand miles. The Triton was much smaller, having a surface displacement of only 1.6 tons. It could carry two divers and had a combat range of thirty miles. It was intended as a replacement for the older Sirena-UM, which was a modified torpedo-type delivery vehicle much like the Italian Chariots of World War II fame. A specialized reconnaissance ship, the Project 1288.4 Bambuk class, was developed in the late 1980s; one of the two ships of this class, the SSV-189 *Pridnestrovie,* was assigned as a mother ship for the minisubs attached to the Black Sea Fleet. This ship was taken over by the Ukrainian Navy in 1993 and renamed the *Slavutich.*

Besides the minisubs, in 1992 the Russians revealed a whole family of secret weapons developed specifically for use by the naval Spetsnaz. This included both pistols and automatic rifles that fired underwater, the only weapons of their kind in the world, and a variety of unique antifrogman weapons to defend Soviet harbors, including special grenade launchers that fired mini–depth charges.

The naval Spetsnaz brigade of the Baltic Fleet probably has had the most active "peacetime" career of any Spetsnaz unit due to its participation in a controversial series of special reconnaissance operations in conjunction with Baltic Fleet submarines in Swedish coastal waters. Although the Soviet government, and the current Russian government, have strenuously denied Swedish allegations, it appears that in fact a series of reconnaissance operations was conducted by Soviet minisubs in the fjords leading into major Swedish naval facilities through much of the early 1980s.

PARAMILITARY ELITE FORMATIONS

Besides the Soviet armed forces, the Soviet state had several other organizations with elite, commando-type units. Most of these paramilitary elite formations were controlled by the KGB special police or the MVD Ministry of the Interior. These forces were considerably expanded in the 1980s, in part to deal with political unrest in Russia and in part to deal with the growing problem of terrorism and organized crime.

The KGB had several paramilitary formations that resembled elite military units. Until recently, the KGB controlled the Border Guards, roughly the equivalent of the U.S. Coast Guard and the U.S. Customs Service rolled into one. The Border Guards were recruited through conscription in the same manner as the regular army, wore the same uniform as the army, and received much the same training as light infantry. However, their peacetime role was more akin to that of a border police force, patrolling the frontier and manning customs posts. In the 1980s, the Border Guards numbered about 175,000 troops.

The Soviet Union does not enjoy as peaceful a border as the United States, and the military role of the Border Guards has often been very real. They were at the center of the fighting between the Soviet Union and China in the 1960s over the Ussuri River border disputes and played an important role in Soviet plans for any conflict with China. As a result, at least one Border Guards division was kept airborne-qualified through much of the 1970s and 1980s in the event of war. The Border Guards were intended for use as rapid-reaction forces in border areas where army units were few and far between. The Border Guards also have a sizable force of normal military

Mi-8 helicopters, which give them additional mobility in the event of hostilities.

The Soviet Ministry of the Interior (MVD) ran the state police force. The Soviet police system (and the Russian system today) is similar to European police systems. All police units belong to the national *militsiya* force, which is the equivalent of both local and state police in the United States. Besides the *militsiya,* the MVD also controlled the Interior Forces *(vnutrennie voiska).* This was a direct counterpart to the KGB Border Guards but aimed at combatting antistate activity by the Soviet citizenry. In its heydey in the 1980s, the Interior Forces numbered about 260,000 troops. These were not elite troops in any sense. Interior Forces soldiers were usually conscripted from poor, rural areas and served in areas far from home, away from their own ethnic group. Central Asian troops would be posted to Russia and vice versa. Since these troops were intended for use as riot control, it was desirable that they have no sympathy for the population they might be called upon to fight. Interior Forces units were used to suppress popular protests in Georgia in 1957 and in Novocherkassk in 1962.

Of the Interior Forces units, only one merits the description of an elite force, the 19th Dzerzhinskiy Special Operations Motor Rifle Division (19 OMSDON im. Dzerzhinskogo), which was stationed at Balashikha in the suburbs of Moscow near the Paveletskiy station. The division has an awkward history, closely connected to the political intrigue of Communist Party politics. The division was first formed in the wake of World War II; Stalin intended it to serve as a counterweight to the military. Should any military leader attempt a coup against the Communist Party in Moscow, the Dzerzhinskiy division would protect the political leadership. Its other mission was to quell any public disturbances.

At the time of Stalin's death in 1953, the party leadership was split over who would succeed the brutal dictator. During the face-off between the faction headed by Lavrentiy Beria and the faction headed by Nikita Khrushchev, the Dzerzhinskiy division sided with Beria. However, the two army divisions in the Moscow area sided with Khrushchev. When push came to shove, the Dzerzhinskiy division returned to its barracks without a fight, but several of its commanders were later sent to prison or shot for their mistaken allegiance to the losing side. In the 1964 coup against Khrushchev, the division sided with winners and backed Leonid Brezhnev. Soviet leaders have always tried to keep a trusted ally as head of the Dzerzhinskiy division and other special operations troops, and that remained the case right up to the troubles in 1991–93.

Smaller units patterned on the Dzerzhinskiy division were formed in other cities, and these became known as the Special Operations Troops of the Internal Forces. In recent years, these units were designated as OPNAZ troops (*operativnaya naznacheniya,* or operational missions troops). These OPNAZ motor rifle regiments were deployed primarily in Central Asia to provide a rapid-reaction force in the event of rioting. These units included armored vehicles, mainly BTR-60 or BTR-70 armored transporters. Since they were equipped like army units and wore the same uniform, OPNAZ units frequently have been mistaken for army troops in the Western media accounts of ethnic disturbances. The OPNAZ troops also had a long-standing role in controlling ethnic fighting in the army. For example, when rioting broke out among 700 Uzbeki and Georgian enlisted men in a motor rifle regiment in the Urals in December 1989, OPNAZ troops of the Internal Forces were brought in to end the fighting. They also were used in the Afghanistan war, and they have been active in recent years, particularly during the civil war in Tajikstan in the early 1990s.

Until 1989, the Internal Forces of the MVD were subordinated to army command for use in dealing with public disturbances. The leadership of the Soviet Army preferred to stay out of this role, however, realizing that army involvement in violent suppression of civil disturbances contributes to a rapid decline in public support for the armed forces. Army pressure was one element in the 1989 decision to remove the Internal Forces from armed forces' jurisdiction. In 1990, Defense Minister Dmitri Yazov expressed his hope that converting the OPNAZ troops of the Internal Forces to professional status would remove the need for future army involvement in civil disturbances. This did not prove possible prior to the Soviet collapse.

In the 1980s, the Dzerzhinskiy division began a modernization program to enhance its military capabilities. The troops began to undergo training very similar to that of the VDV. The mission of quelling popular discontent was not favored among the troops, and the training helped instill unit pride and distract attention from the real role of the unit.

The modernization of the OPNAZ troops had three main facets. To begin with, the 25,000 troops in this branch were inadequate in number given the sheer scale of the problem. MVD officials began to expand the force by another 25,000 to 35,000 troops to better handle the rapidly escalating number of civil disturbances. The experiences in 1988–89 also revealed that the military training and equipment of the Special Operations Troops left them ill prepared to handle civil disturbances. The troops were forced to use their rifles prematurely, since they did not have riot gear such as shields, protective clothing, and nonlethal weapons. This problem was partly remedied by a crash program to develop riot equipment based on Western European patterns. In addition, a new set of regulations was issued to OPNAZ troop leaders more clearly stipulating when lethal force might be used. One of the main complaints by military leaders has been that the Internal Forces were poorly trained and led.

The OPNAZ troops were supplemented by Special Police Regiments located in each major city. They probably numbered 40,000 men. These police units were organized on military lines but were not as heavily armed as the Special Operations Troops. The third and largest element of the Internal Forces was called Guards and Escorts; it numbered about 140,000 troops. They were used to guard key state installations, with the exception of select party headquarters, nuclear weapons sites, and other high-priority sites (which were patrolled instead by special KGB units). They were also used to guard prison camps, to escort certain types of rail shipments, and to guard large state supply dumps to prevent pilfering.

The standard Soviet approach to handling public unrest was incremental. Local MVD authorities used local resources, the Special Police Regiments, at the first sign of trouble. If these forces proved insufficient, local MVD authorities requested the intervention of OPNAZ troops of the Internal Forces. This took place, for example, in 1962 in Novocherkassk when food riots got out of hand. Such an action was considered a very serious matter and had to be approved by the Ministry of Internal Affairs in Moscow in consultation with the Council of Ministers. During the ethnic unrest of the late 1980s, this procedure proved to be needlessly time consuming, and local conditions often went out of control before the OPNAZ troops could intervene. As a result, a new temporary law was passed in March 1990 to streamline the process. One of the more controversial aspects of the new law was that it allowed the president, Mikhail Gorbachev, to deploy such troops without consulting the traditional bureaucracies.

The new law did not entirely remedy the problems afflicting the Internal Forces. During the rioting in Central Asia in 1988–89, the Internal Forces frequently proved unable to curb fighting among the various ethnic groups, and units would often break and run when confronted by unruly mobs. In the case of the Armenian-Azeri fighting in Nagorno-Karabakh, the army was forced to dispatch elite paratroop regiments of the VDV to supplement the Internal Forces units.

Antiterrorist Units

During the late 1970s, there was an increase in terrorist actions in the Soviet Union, mainly aircraft highjackings and kidnappings. By 1991, there had been 103 aircraft highjacking attempts leading to 120 deaths and 200 serious injuries. A significant increase in organized crime had also occurred. The government responded by organizing several dedicated antiterrorist units.

In December 1977, the MVD formed a special antiterrorist company in Moscow prior to the Olympics to take care of any problems that might arise. This unit was designated OMON (special operations state militia). The first company was commanded by Capt. I. Maltsev and became operational on 1 January 1978. In 1988, the OMON was considerably expanded, with units set up in every major city. The ostensible reason was to combat rising crime, but there was also concern about growing political discontent. The OMON units are often called "spetsnaz" in the Russian press, although there is no connection with the GRU's Spetsnaz brigades. The MVD formed another, more secretive, unit within the ranks of the Dzerzhinskiy division. This formation of about 360 to 400 men was used to develop new tactics and technology to deal with airliner highjackings, terrorist assaults, and other threats.

Several of the OMON battalions later took names to distinguish themselves from the many other special purpose units formed in the late 1980s. One of the Russian OMON battalions was named Vityaz (knight); it took part in many hostage and kidnapping rescues in the Caucasus in the late 1980s and early 1990s. The OMON units in five cities in Ukraine later formed the core of a special antiterrorist unit named Berkut (golden eagle).

The KGB antiterrorist effort was prompted by an incident in 1973 when a highjacker detonated a grenade aboard a Tu-104 airliner, causing it to crash. The KGB already had small, informal hit teams for special operations overseas. Until 1971, the First (Foreign Intelligence) Directorate of the KGB operated the secret V-Group for the conduct of assassinations overseas. This effort was reorganized under Department 7 in 1974. The KGB formed two new units—Alfa Group, specializing in antiterrorism, and Beta Group, to conduct overseas assassination ("wet") missions. These units are also sometimes called KGB OSNAZ (*osoboyogo naznacheniye,* or special purpose). The new Alfa/Beta Groups had considerable influence within the KGB, as they were commanded by a major general. Training for the KGB OSNAZ units was conducted at a special school at Balashikha, in the suburbs of Moscow near the Paveletskiy train station, and near the base of the 19th Dzerzhinskiy Special Operations Motor Rifle Division. The Beta Group has largely escaped public attention, but some of its activities have come to light. In 1985, for example, Lebanese extremists kidnapped four members of the Soviet embassy in Bierut and killed one of them. Rather than pay the ransom demand, a KGB antiterrorist team working in conjunction with Syrian intelligence agents grabbed twelve people, mainly relatives and political colleagues of the kidnappers. The Soviet team killed one of their hostages and shipped the mutilated body back to the kidnappers with the warning that the rest would soon follow. The Soviet embassy personnel were released soon afterward. Alfa Group was used repeatedly in the late 1980s during various disturbances in the Caucasus, including aircraft highjackings and kidnappings. There have been press accounts of another KGB special operations unit, called the Vympel Group, which is apparently a third element of the Alfa/Beta special operations force.* In 1994, the Vympel unit was turned over to the MVD, which suggests that its mission deals with internal security.

The KGB special operations units were among the most secretive in the entire Soviet system. There are probably other groups in addition

---

*Vympel (banner) starts with the third letter of the Russian Cyrillic alphabet (A, B, V, G, D, et cetera).

to those mentioned here, but most of these would be more clearly politically or intelligence oriented. The first large-scale combat use of KGB Special Operations Troops took place in December 1979 in Afghanistan, as we shall see in the next chapter.

The KGB has been in turmoil since the August 1991 coup against Gorbachev. It was officially disbanded in 1991, though, in effect, the component parts were simply renamed. The former First (Intelligence) Directorate, based in Yesenevo, was first renamed the Central Intelligence Service (TsSR) and then later renamed the Russian Foreign Intelligence Service (SVRR). The Second Directorate, based out of the notorious Lubyanka headquarters in central Moscow, was renamed the Russian Federation Security Ministry (MBRF). This agency retained the KGB's internal security, counterintelligence, and counternarcotics functions. Presumably, the former KGB special operations units for counterterrorism would be subordinated to this group. After the 1993 fighting between President Boris Yeltsin and the Russian Parliament, Yeltsin denounced the MBRF as "unreformable . . . obsolete, ineffective, a burden on the state budget and a restraining factor on the implementation of political and economic reform." As a result, a major change took place in early 1994, reorganizing the ministry as the Federal Counterintelligence Service (FSK). It would not be surprising to see additional changes occur.

Chapter 11
Storm over Kabul

I n the late 1970s, Afghanistan was a pesthole of intrigue and conspiracy. For the Soviet Union, the continual political turmoil in Kabul was a threat to the stability of its own republics in Central Asia. Something had to be done.

The "Red Prince," Mohammed Daoud, had seized power from the monarchy in 1973, declaring Afghanistan to be a republic. The move was not overly alarming to Moscow; at first, Daoud kept the country closely aligned with the Soviet Union. Afghan army officers continued to train in the USSR, and the Communist People's Democratic Party of Afghanistan (PDPA) remained a vital political movement among army officers and the intelligentsia. Gradually, Daoud grew mistrustful of his PDPA allies, however, and moved to consolidate his relations with neighboring regimes in Iran and Pakistan. By 1978, Daoud's rule was causing resentment among the urban Afghan intelligentsia, and the murder of a leading PDPA leader in April 1978 set off protests and riots. Daoud arrested the leading members of the PDPA in an attempt to quell the unrest. The plan backfired, as it prompted members of the armed forces sympathetic to the PDPA to stage a military coup. There are reports that the coup was backed by the Soviet Union. On 27 April 1978, the 4th and 15th Armored Brigades, supported by MiG-21s of the 322nd Air Regiment, attacked key facilities in Kabul. Daoud and his advisers were killed in a bloody firefight at the presidential palace, and the army officers installed Nur Mohammed Taraki, leader of the Khalq faction of the

PDPA, as the leader of the new Democratic Republic of Afghanistan (DRA). Taraki not only purged Daoud's followers from the government, but he also removed members of the rival Parcham faction of the PDPA.

Taraki's Khalq faction was the more radical of the PDPA wings, favoring a Stalinist reorganization of Afghan life in line with their crude Marxist world view. The Khalq wing embarked on a series of harebrained schemes to collectivize agriculture and to suppress the role of Islam in Afghan life. Not surprisingly, by the summer of 1978, open revolt was beginning in the ardently Islamic villages outside of Kabul. Taraki called on the Soviet Union for military aid. He signed a friendship treaty with Moscow in December 1978 and began to receive a steady stream of advisers and new military hardware. The connection between the anti-Islamic Taraki and Moscow led many Muslims in the growing Afghan resistance movement to call for a holy war, a jihad, against the Russian infidels they saw lurking behind the Kabul regime. In March 1979 when the mujahideen rebels seized the city of Herat, dozens of Soviet citizens were brutally tortured and murdered, including a Soviet Army advisory team. The escalating cycle of violence worried the Brezhnev regime, and it instinctively reacted by providing more military support to Kabul.

By the spring of 1979, Soviet helicopter pilots in mufti were flying Mil Mi-24 attack helicopters in support of the DRA Army against the mujahideen. In July, a battalion from the 345th Guards Airborne Regiment was installed at Bagram air base north of Kabul to ensure that the Soviet An-12 transport regiment there would be protected. The Soviet military aid did little good, however, and major DRA Army units were defeated by the rebels in the Panjsher valley and Paktia province in the summer of 1979. Taraki's regime grew increasingly intolerant of any political opposition, killing more than 17,000 Afghans in repressive purges in the cities.

The turmoil of civil war worsened as Hafizullah Amin, one of Taraki's rivals in the Khalq faction, began plotting to seize control of the PDPA and the government. One diplomatic communiqué from the U.S. embassy tellingly described the PDPA as "a bottle full of angry scorpions all intent on stinging each other." On 14 September 1979, Taraki invited Amin to a meeting, sponsored by the Soviet ambassador, at his residence in the Arque Palace to iron out differences.

Amin was ushered into Taraki's residence and met with Lt. Col. Said Daoud Tarun, ostensibly Taraki's bodyguard, but in fact a secret ally of Amin. Taraki had discovered Tarun's treachery and sent a squad of troops to kill Tarun and Amin. But Amin managed to escape. Amin had important allies in the DRA Army and, by the afternoon, army units loyal to him had seized most of the city. Several of Taraki's closest allies fled to the Soviet embassy and were secretly flown to Moscow for safety. Taraki himself was captured by Amin supporters within his own security force.

The Soviet ambassador met with Amin the next day; the Soviets were not pleased by the self-destructive behavior of the Afghan Communists, but they had few other immediate options. On 8 October, Amin ordered Taraki killed: he was smothered with a pillow by officers of the security police. Amin idolized Soviet dictator Joseph Stalin, and his explanation for the PDPA excesses was always the same: "Comrade Stalin has taught us how to install socialism in a backward country; at first there is pain and suffering, but later all will be splendid!" Ironically, Amin placed the blame for the disintegration of the Kabul regime on their Soviet advisers, arguing that their weak-kneed and cowardly recommendations were to blame for the escalating civil war.

Soviet embassy staff members were appalled by Amin's cruelty and stupidity. Informants within the Amin entourage disclosed that their new leader had lied to the Soviet ambassador about the circumstances of Taraki's death. Soviet specialists concluded that the situation in Afghanistan would continue to deteriorate in the hands of such a fool. In early December 1979, an attempt was made on Amin's life by surviving Taraki loyalists. The turmoil in Kabul was becoming intolerable to Moscow. There was a growing conviction in the Politburo in Moscow that a leader from the more moderate Parcham faction of the PDPA would offer a better chance of calming down the civil war. But the Parcham faction had been brutally suppressed by Taraki and Amin and could not hope to carry out a coup on its own against such ruthless opponents. Mikhail Suslov, the chief idealogue of the Soviet Communist Party, convinced Leonid Brezhnev that a small contingent of Soviet forces should be sent into Afghanistan to install Babrak Karmal of the Parcham faction and restore order.

In early December, the Soviet defense minister, Dmitri Ustinov, had conducted a series of meetings with high-ranking Soviet military leaders to discuss military options in Afghanistan. The General Staff had already prepared a variety of plans for intervention, but the military leadership was ambivalent about sending Soviet forces into the Afghan quagmire. The senile leadership of the Soviet Communist Party had no understanding of the difficulties of conducting a counter-insurgency campaign in the wilds of Afghanistan and no comprehension of the ferocity of the opposition.

On 10 December, in spite of military doubts, the first orders were issued to begin moving Soviet forces into position for the intervention. Neither Nikolai Ogarkov, the hard-line chief of the General Staff, nor I. G. Pavlovskiy, the commanding general of the Ground Forces, voted for intervention. Among the political leaders, Foreign Minister Andrei Gromyko was openly opposed. Regardless of these views, on 12 December 1979, Leonid Brezhnev convened a special commission of the Central Committee of the USSR, which decided "to provide military assistance to the DRA by means of sending a limited contingent of Soviet forces to its territory."

SPECIAL OPERATIONS IN KABUL

Earlier in 1979, when Taraki visited Moscow to confer with Brezhnev, the Soviet leader had promised to form a special Soviet unit to "protect the April Revolution movement." The Soviet General Staff was ordered to prepare a special bodyguard group of its best Dari- or Farsi-speaking Central Asian troops to serve in the new unit. Not surprisingly, the group quickly became known as the "Muslim Battalion." The task was assigned to Col. Vassily V. Kolesnik, on the Spetsnaz staff in the Glass House in Moscow, who had formerly commanded the Spetsnaz brigade in Uzbekistan near the Afghan frontier. The requirements were very specific. The unit was to be formed from troops serving in elite Spetsnaz or VDV units. One company would be organized around BMP-1 armored infantry vehicles, two companies in BTR-60PB armored transporters, and a fourth would be a heavy-weapons company with four ZSU-23-4 Shilka air defense gun vehicles, RPG-17 antitank rockets, and heavy-caliber machine guns. All told, the battalion would number 550 troops, all of Tadzhik, Turkmen, or Uzbek nationality who could easily blend in when stationed in Afghanistan.

Kolesnik selected Maj. Khabibdzhan Kholbayev to lead the battalion; Kholbayev had been his adjutant when he had commanded the Chirchik Spetsnaz brigade in Uzbekistan. The battalion was given carte blanche in terms of equipment and training facilities, and the new recruits were put through a grueling period of desert and mountain training. The main recruitment problem came with officers, since there were so few Uzbek and Tadzhik officers in the elite units. Also, there were concerns in some circles that a unit consisting entirely of Central Asians would not be entirely loyal. As a result, a small number of Slavic officers were assigned to the battalion "to dilute the command group." The Muslim Battalion would pose as an Afghan unit. The Spetsnaz troops would be dressed in Afghan uniforms, and the vehicles would be painted in Afghan markings. New Afghan uniforms were flown in from Kabul and subjected to several weeks of washing to get the proper worn and faded look.

The Muslim Battalion was scheduled to leave for Kabul on 14 September 1979, the very day of the shoot-out between Amin and Taraki. The men were ordered off their aircraft and told to return to training until the situation in Kabul clarified itself. In the middle of October, the battalion was airlifted to the Spetsnaz garrison at Chirchik in Uzbekistan to put it nearer the Afghan border. On 18 November, orders came from Moscow to depart for the Bagram air base near Kabul. Neither Amin nor his chief military adviser, General Yakub, was told of the original role of the Spetsnaz unit—to protect Taraki—and they presumed that it was simply a normal Soviet unit. The Muslim Battalion was eventually allowed to set up its tents in the southwest Darul-Aman district of Kabul near the old Taj-Bek Palace. In early December, following the attempt on his life, Amin decided to move his residence from the Arque Palace to the Taj-Bek Palace on the assumption that the Soviet unit there would be more reliable than an entirely Afghan detachment. It would prove to be a fatal mistake.

While the Spetsnaz Muslim Battalion was being formed, the KGB was putting together its own team for possible operations in Afghanistan, drawn from the Alfa, Beta, and Vympel special operations groups. An assault group, code-named Kaskad (cascade), was put under the command of Col. G. I. Boyarinov. Most members of the Kaskad assault group were recent graduates of the KGB's Balashikha special operations school, and Boyarinov was a former commander of the school. The group was divided into two, the Grom (hurricane) team and the Zenit (zenith) team, each of about thirty men. The Grom unit was infiltrated into Afghanistan in December under the guise of a sports team. The objective of the Kaskad group was to kill or capture Amin and his immediate entourage.

The Spetsnaz Muslim Battalion was not informed of any precise details of the assignment until the day before the assault; in fact, until the last moment, they thought the team was supposed to be protecting Amin. The KGB took great pains to hide the fact that Russians would kill Amin. The aim was to make the operation look like another Afghan blood feud.

The KGB also formed several "mobile groups," which were given other assignments in Kabul, including "working over" critical government centers such as the Central Committee building, Ministry of Defense, Ministry of Internal Affairs, the central telegraph exchange, the main post office, and the political prison at Puli-Charki. In cases where resistance was expected, these KGB units would be supported by additional Spetsnaz teams brought in from the USSR.

INTERVENTION PLANS

Mobilization of the Soviet Army for operations in Afghanistan had been under study since early 1979. In the autumn of 1979, two VDV divisions, the 103rd in Vitebsk and 104th in Kirovabad, and the independent 345th Guards Airborne Regiment from the disbanded 105th Airborne Division in Fergana, were ordered to move to a higher level of readiness. A special VDV working group was formed under Maj. Gen. Moussa Yevanov to plan the VDV operations in Afghanistan. In October, Gen. Ivan Ryabchenko, commander of the 103rd Guards Airborne Division, and his regimental commanders were flown to Kabul in civilian clothes to survey conditions around the Bagram air base and in the city itself. The first VDV unit scheduled to move into Kabul was the 345th Guards Airborne Regiment commanded by Lt. Col. A. Lomakin. One of his battalions had already been deployed at Bagram on 7 July, and the remainder followed on 1 December 1979.

At the same time, selected motor rifle divisions in the Turkmenistan and Central Asian Military Districts were brought up to war readiness, and reservists were called in to fill out these units. This mobilization program was designed to minimize the visibility of preparations. The VDV units were not a problem, since they frequently went to higher readiness and were isolated from other military units. The selection of motor rifle divisions at remote Central Asian bases was intended to minimize knowledge of the plans within the armed forces as a whole. Most of these motor rifle divisions were second-rate units with a largely Central Asian composition and Russian officers. The call-up of reservists in Central Asia would not be noticed by foreign intelligence as quickly as in European Russia.

Brezhnev's decision called for Soviet forces to occupy Kabul on 27 December 1979. This meant that Soviet forces would have to start moving south about two weeks earlier. The 103rd Guards Airborne Division was moved to its departure airfields near Vitebsk on 10 December, and on 14 December it was flown to forward air bases in the Turkestan Military District. The VTA began flying portions of the division into Bagram air base in Afghanistan on 24 December. The division suffered its first losses on the evening of 25 December, when an Ilyushin IL-76 transport carrying thirty-three paratroopers and two fuel trucks collided with a mountain peak, killing all aboard. By the afternoon of 27 December, forty-seven hours after the airlift had begun, the entire division was delivered to Bagram. The airlift required sixty-six An-22, seventy-six Ilyushin IL-76, and two hundred An-12 sorties.

On 25 December, two Soviet Army pontoon bridge regiments set up a sixty-ton bridge next to Friendship Bridge over the Amu Darya River outside Termez on the Soviet-Afghan frontier. Once this was erected, a *razvedchik* scout detachment from the 108th Motor Rifle Division was sent to the Afghan side. There was no activity near Termez, so the remainder of the division soon followed and began moving via the Salang highway toward Kabul, planning to arrive on 27 December.

By 26 December, a total of about 6,000 troops and KGB mobile group agents were in Kabul, including the Muslim Battalion, the 345th Guards Airborne Regiment, and a number of Spetsnaz teams. The official intervention would begin on 27 December with the final airlandings of the airborne force at Bagram air base, and the arrival of two motor rifle divisions into Afghanistan from Soviet bases north of the Afghan border. Unbeknown to Amin, in mid-December the Soviets had moved his chosen replacement, Babrak Karmal, and an entourage of his Parcham faction of the PDPA into the Chikhil-Sutun residence of the DRA Council of Ministers. Amin would be told in advance of the Soviet intervention, but only a day before the KGB hit team arrived to assassinate him.

OPERATION SHTORM-33

The attack on the Taj-Bek Palace in Darul-Aman was given the code name Shtorm-33 (storm 33). The role of the Spetsnaz Muslim Battalion would be to open up a path into the palace for the two KGB teams from the Kaskad group. The Muslim Battalion moved from Bagram air base to the area around the Taj-Bek Palace on 18 December and switched into their Afghan uniforms. They formed the second ring of a triple layer of defenses at the palace. The Taj-Bek Palace was built on a small hill and was protected by a personal bodyguard company of about 150 Afghan officers, supported by three guard groups that manned several sentry posts around the palace. The Muslim Battalion was positioned about 500 yards from the palace; the unit was housed about 800 meters to the west in a building that was being built for a new tank battalion of the Afghan Guards brigade. The outer defenses were garrisoned by the 1,200-man Guards brigade and included three motorized infantry battalions, a T-55 tank battalion, an air defense regiment with 100mm guns, and supporting units.

Colonel Vassily Kolesnik, who commanded the Spetsnaz mission in Kabul, was brought to the Soviet embassy on 26 December and told that he was to attack the palace instead of defending it. He was asked to prepare a plan of action on the spot, and it was immediately sent to Moscow by satellite. Kolesnik asked to expand his force to assist in the assault, and he was allotted a company of VDV airborne troops from Bagram and an antitank missile platoon to blow open the heavy doors at the palace. H hour for the operation was originally set for 21:00.

In order to catch Amin off guard, the KGB staged a deception. A PDPA Central Committee member from the Panjsher valley region returned from Moscow on 26 December with news of the Soviet military intervention. He described the Soviet invasion as an effort to bolster Amin's control of the country—a lie that Amin was all too willing to accept. He reassured Amin that Brezhnev had accepted the story about Taraki's fate, and informed him that the Soviet leader had extended an open invitation for him to visit Moscow to prepare for closer and stronger ties between the USSR and Afghanistan. Such good news from Moscow prompted Amin to stage a large formal dinner on 27 December, the evening of the invasion, inviting the entire Afghan Politburo, the government ministers, and their families.

Shortly after the dinner began, Amin and several of the guests fell ill. It is still not clear who was behind the poisoning, whether the KGB or one of Amin's many enemies. In any event, the commander of the Presidential Guard, M. Ekbal, called the Soviet embassy to ask for medical assistance. The chief Soviet military adviser in Afghanistan, Maj. Gen. I. Tutushkin, and several Soviet military doctors arrived shortly afterward. Unaware of the planned KGB assassination attempt, they set about trying to revive Amin by pumping his stomach and giving him transfusions. Amin was just beginning to regain consciousness when two red flares were seen arcing over the palace at around 19:25. These were the signals to begin Operation Shtorm.

The attack time had been moved up due to changing activities by Amin's Presidential Guard staff. After the poisoning attempt, Ekbal ordered additional Afghan troops to be brought closer to the palace since he suspected that something was going to happen. The commander of the Afghan reinforcements was captured by the Spetsnaz in a brief scuffle, and one of the replacement guards was killed using a silent pneumatic pistol. But the commotion alerted another Afghan guard, who opened fire on the Spetsnaz. He and the remainder of the guard platoon were killed with knives. This forced the operation to begin earlier than planned.

The Spetsnaz company assigned to neutralize the Afghan tank battalion noticed that crews were running out of their barracks and lining up on alert. The Spetsnaz team drove over to the group in their GAZ-66 truck and took the battalion commander and his company commanders prisoner, ordering them into the back of the truck. At first, the Afghan tankers stood by in stunned silence, but as the truck began pulling away, they ran after it. After driving some distance, the

Spetsnaz officer in command ordered three soldiers armed with PKM squad machine guns in the rear of the truck to set up a blocking position, and they began firing on the approaching Afghan soldiers at a range of about 150 yards. The Afghans ran away. The rest of the Spetsnaz company set about disabling the T-55 tanks.

The Spetsnaz assault party was led by BMP-1 armored infantry vehicles painted in Afghan markings. As the Spetsnaz column drove up to the palace, the sentries, alerted by noise from the earlier skirmish, opened fire on them with 12.7mm DShK heavy machine guns. This began an intense firefight as the Spetsnaz tried to secure several entryways into the palace. On seeing the determination of the Afghan defense, one of the Spetsnaz officers called up two ZSU-23-4 Shilka air defense vehicles from the rear of the column. The Shilka is armed with four 23mm automatic cannon and can unleash a spectacular burst of fire and tracers. Each one-second burst contains sixty projectiles totaling twenty-five pounds of steel and high explosive. The Shilkas resembled fire-breathing dragons as they spewed their deadly charges against the Afghan defenders. At the same time, two other Shilkas opened fire on the outer defensive positions of the Afghan Guards brigade. The Afghan position nearest the Spetsnaz compound was pummeled for several minutes by AGS-17 automatic grenade launchers.

As the firefight escalated, the KGB Kaskad team was huddled inside the troop compartments of the BMP armored infantry vehicles of Lt. R. Sharipov's company as they drove up a winding road leading to the palace. Sharipov ordered the BMPs to charge across the last 900 yards of open ground in front of the palace, assuming that the Afghans would have a harder time hitting fast-moving vehicles in the dark. The BMPs took the KGB teams directly inside the palace, where Colonel Boyarinov's Kaskad group took over. Sharipov's BMP company moved to the rear of the palace to create a possible escape route.

The fighting on the ground floor was intense, and the KGB teams suffered heavy casualties almost immediately. Colonel Boyarinov went back to the front gate to signal for reinforcements from the Spetsnaz, but he was accidentally hit by a blast from one of the Shilkas. By the time the first floor of the palace was cleared, the electrical power had been knocked out. The fighting took place in the dark, illuminated by flashes from automatic weapons and small fires set by grenade blasts. The KGB Kaskad group moved methodically through the second floor, grenading each room. Amin was helped from his stretcher by the Soviet doctors and attempted to hide behind a thick wood bar, his five-year-old son clinging to him. Hearing the shouts of the Russian KGB squad, the Soviet doctors decided it would be prudent to leave. Moments later, Amin was severely wounded by grenades and rifle fire. A coup de grace was administered some time afterward when he was found by a gang of Taraki supporters brought in by the KGB. His body was riddled with bullets.

The confusion and darkness in the palace led to many friendly fire casualties. The Spetsnaz Muslim Battalion lost 12 dead and 28 wounded. Casualties among the KGB group are in dispute: some accounts state that only 4 men were killed; others state that there were 14 survivors out of the original 60. Of the estimated 300 Afghan troops in the palace, about 150 were taken prisoner. About 500 other Afghan soldiers from the Guards brigade were killed in fighting with the Spetsnaz along the outer palace perimeter. Colonel Boyarinov and Colonel Kolesnik were secretly awarded the Hero of the Soviet Union gold star. Ironically, Col. V. P. Kuznechnekov, one of the doctors who had revived Amin before being killed by friendly fire, was also awarded the Order of the Red Banner.

While the firefight was taking place at the Taj-Bek Palace, other KGB and Spetsnaz teams assaulted key government buildings inside Kabul. Paratroopers from the 103rd Guards Airborne Division moved into Kabul to secure key road junctions. The two Afghan tank brigades near the city had been immobilized by their Soviet advisers a few days before when the tanks' batteries were removed for "periodic servicing." The only Afghan unit to offer sporadic resistance was the 26th Parachute Regiment, many of whose officers had trained with the VDV at the Ryazan airborne school.

The bulk of the Limited Contingent of Soviet Forces–Afghanistan, known by its Soviet acronym OKSVA, was in motion through most of 27 December 1979. The 357th Motor Rifle Division advanced along the Kushka-Herat-Shindand route; the 360th Nevel-Polotovsk Motor Rifle Division moved along the Termez-Kabul-Kandahar route. In addition, the 56th Air Assault Brigade was flown into Afghanistan.

On the day after the official start of the Soviet intervention, the 345th Guards Airborne Regiment escorted Babrak Karmal into Kabul. He gave a television and radio broadcast, beginning with a traditional Islamic benediction, a halfhearted attempt to regain the confidence of a people exasperated by Communist stupidity and brutality. In a belated attempt to give legitimacy to the Soviet invasion, he invited the Soviet Army to enter Afghanistan and announced that he was assuming the role of president and prime minister. The invitation was a farce, and the prayer was an insult to the faithful. The country was gripped by war fever, a jihad against the Soviet infidels and their puppets.

Chapter 12
Airborne in Afghanistan

Leonid Brezhnev hoped that the 27 December 1979 invasion of Afghanistan would be a repeat of his 1968 Czechoslovak success—a brief military action followed by a peaceful occupation. This was not to be the case. The Soviet forces sent into Afghanistan in 1979 were far smaller than those committed to Czechoslovakia, and the country was already embroiled in a violent and pervasive civil war.

The short-term objectives of the Limited Contingent were to establish road security along the Khairaton-Kabul, Kushka-Herat-Kandahar, Kabul-Jalalabad, and Puli-Kumri-Kunduz-Faizabad roads. In addition, Soviet garrisons were set up in all major cities, and at the air bases at Kabul, Bagram, Shindand, Kandahar, Kunduz, Jalalabad, Gardeyz, Herat, and Faizabad. The timing of the invasion was selected because it was presumed that the mujahideen rebels would be far less active in the harsh winter months, and that government control would be restored before the fighting weather returned. This opinion was widely shared by Western intelligence agencies, which expected that the Afghan resistance would be quickly crushed. The Soviet Army was, after all, the largest army in the world and had showed its ruthless behavior in Hungary and Czechoslovakia.

The Soviet Army's ostensible ally in the campaign was the Democratic Republic of Afghanistan (DRA) Army. The Afghan army was grossly understrength, however, as recruitment drives were met with resistance and desertion. Even when trained and organized, Afghan units had the alarming tendency to mutiny and go over to the side of the mujahideen. Following the Soviet invasion, DRA Army strength plummeted from 80,000 to 20,000 men. The Soviet political and military leadership (and that of the West as well) had sorely underestimated the tenacity of the mujahideen and were too blind to understand that any Afghan government aligned with the infidel Moscow Communists would be rejected by the Afghan resistance. The weakness of the DRA Army was soon evident. In January 1980, the DRA 4th Artillery Regiment in Nakrin mutinied and attempted to ransom its Soviet advisers. A task force from the 186th Motor Rifle Regiment was sent to crush the mutiny, which it did with minimal Soviet casualties. But this left Nakrin unguarded from the mujahideen; loyal Afghan troops were in short supply.

The Soviet operational plan was to first secure the major cities and road nets, then begin a systematic campaign of sweeps through rebel-controlled areas. By mid-February 1980, the first part of the plan was complete. The mujahideen, dormant because of the frigid winter weather, did not vigorously contest the Soviet presence. The first major counterinsurgency action began in late February when two regiments of the 103rd Guards Airborne Division and two regiments of the 108th Motor Rifle Division conducted a sweep of the Kunar valley. The Kunar valley controlled the Kabul-Jalalabad road leading eastward to the Pakistan frontier. It was one of the main strongholds of the mujahideen in the immediate Kabul area, so it was selected for the first blow. The airborne units quickly appreciated that they would have to adapt to local conditions. It was evident that parachutes were of no use in Afghanistan, so most specialized parachute equipment was put into storage at the Bagram and Kabul air bases or shipped back to the Soviet Union. Airmobility in Afghanistan would come exclusively from helicopters. The plan for the Kunar valley sweep was to deliver one paratrooper battalion high in the mountains to block the exit of the mujahideen, while the remainder of the force tightened the noose.

The operation was a fiasco. The heliborne battalion was quickly surrounded and had a hard time defending itself against attack. The mujahideen dynamited the roads leading from Jalalabad, and the road-bound Soviet armored columns soon were subjected to ambush. The trapped battalion lost thirty-eight dead but was finally extracted by helicopter. Two of the paratroopers killed during the fighting had become isolated from their units and were trapped by the mujahideen. One killed himself with a grenade as the Afghans approached, and the other set off a MON-100 mine, killing about thirty guerrillas as well as himself. These two VDV paratroopers were the first Soviet soldiers nominated for the Hero of the Soviet Union distinction during the Afghan war; ultimately only Sgt. A. G. Mironenko was awarded the distinction. The Soviets quickly learned to respect and fear their opponents. The original term for the mujahideen, *dushmani* (bandits), slowly evolved into *dukhi* (ghosts) for their ability to come and go as they pleased.

For the airborne forces, 1980 was a period of consolidation and reorganization. Helicopters were clearly going to become a critical ingredient in VDV operations in Afghanistan, and airborne commanders pressed Moscow for more Mil Mi-8T Shmel (bumblebee) transport helicopters and Mil Mi-24 Gorbach (hunchback) attack helicopters. By January 1980, there were still only three helicopter regiments in Afghanistan, and less than a hundred Mi-8T troop transports for the entire Soviet 40th Army.

The BMD-1 airborne assault vehicle proved a disappointment in combat from its first use in the Kunar fighting in 1980. Its suspension had been designed for light weight and as a result was very fragile. It soon became chewed up in Afghanistan's rocky terrain. It was too cramped for sustained operations, and its 73mm Grom low-pressure gun could not elevate enough to reach the mujahideen high in the mountains. Its small size made it very vulnerable to mine damage, and the paratroopers soon learned the Vietnam lesson that it was safer to ride outside of a vehicle than inside when mines were present. The VDV was stuck with the BMD for the first few years of the war. By 1982, the VDV began shifting to regular army vehicles, first the BTR-60PB wheeled armored transporter, and later to the much prized BMP-2 Yozh (hedgehog). The BMP-2 had a 30mm gun in a high-elevation mounting, which proved ideal for mountain fighting.

The Spetsnaz also underwent reorganization at this time. The Muslim Battalion was returned to Chirchik in 1980, where it was gradually amalgamated back into the 15th Spetsnaz Brigade. Two Spetsnaz detachments were transferred to Afghanistan in October 1980. One guarded the oil pipeline near Puli-Kumri, and the other was stationed at the southern opening of the Panjsher valley where so much fighting during the Afghan war was to take place.

Whereas the VDV and Spetsnaz forces proved to be adaptable to the local conditions, the same could not be said for most of the regular army units of the Soviet 40th Army. The airborne troops had been trained in light infantry tactics and were not particularly surprised by the conditions they encountered in Afghanistan. The motor rifle divisions had been trained in mechanized tactics developed for a war in Central Europe. They were accustomed to fighting from the safety of their armored vehicles, and both officers and enlisted men had a hard time adjusting to guerrilla warfare. In March 1980, a motor rifle company taking part in an operation in Paktia province became isolated from the main force. Rather than dismount and fight their way out, the troops stayed inside their armored infantry vehicles, firing off their remaining ammunition. When darkness fell, the mujahideen moved in and wiped out the unit. In the summer, a motor rifle battalion operating near Asmar tried to rescue an Afghan battalion trapped in a ravine. The road through the ravine was mined, and the battalion suffered heavy losses after it became bogged down in a series of bloody ambushes. The first year of fighting was an education for the Soviet Army, and one that came at a high price: 1,484 dead.

The Soviet Army was frustrated by the unwillingness of the mujahideen to stand and fight with conventional European tactics. The *dukhi* used traditional guerrilla tactics, waiting in ambush for isolated Soviet columns. Soviet casualties came from mines, snipers, and ambushes, amplified by atrocious field conditions and poor medical treatment. Large-scale engagements with the mujahideen were rare, and small-scale actions were the rule. The Soviet policy of sweeps was a failure as the mujahideen refused to become trapped and wiped out. In the mountainous terrain, the road-bound Soviet forces were far less mobile than the hardy Afghan mountain people.

The other problem faced by the 40th Army in the first year of the war was the composition of the invading Soviet units. Because the three motor rifle divisions had been raised in the Central Asian and Turkmenistan Military Districts, a large proportion of the Soviet soldiers were either Muslim, or from ethnic groups such as Tajiks and Uzbeks, kindred to the native groups of Afghanistan. The Soviet Army suffered an alarming level of desertions to the rebel side, which was completely unexpected. Furthermore, the enthusiasm of many of the troops was minimal, not only because of the ethnic issue, but because many were reservists who had already served their two years of army duty and had no interest in serving any longer. Morale was not helped by the level of secrecy on Soviet actions in Afghanistan, which limited communication with families back home. It took some time before the army realized the pervasiveness of the problems and took steps to remedy them. Eventually, the composition of the army units in Afghanistan shifted to a higher proportion of Slavic troops, who were more reliable.

The VDV played an important role in subsequent Soviet operations in Afghanistan because of its advantages over regular army units. The VDV divisions had enjoyed privileged recruitment for their units, so they did not suffer the ethnic problems troubling regular army units. The VDV units were the reservoir of the only really good light infantry in the Limited Contingent of Soviet Forces, even after the regular motor rifle troops were replaced by better troops. The quality of the airborne leadership and training was superior, and the airborne was officially out of the sclerotic 40th Army chain of command, giving the units more tactical flexibility. The VDV served as the key mobile assault force of the Limited Contingent in Afghanistan, taking part in nearly all major combat operations at the discretion of the General Staff.

At any one given time, about a third of the Soviet troops in Afghanistan were assigned to guard duty along the main routes into the Kabul area and other vital communications lines. This was the case with the airborne as well. The 317th Airborne Regiment of the 103rd Airborne Division was assigned to guard Babrak Karmal's residence and other key government buildings, but the remaining four regiments of the VDV force in Afghanistan were reserved for combat duty.

PANJSHER VALLEY

If any one area of operation symbolized the frustration of Soviet operations in Afghanistan, it was the Panjsher valley, straddling the road that ran north from Kabul, through Bagram, to the Soviet border. The valley put the mujahideen in a good location to ambush Soviet columns coming south from the USSR, and the forces there

were led by one of the ablest of the guerrilla commanders, Ahmad
Shah Massoud. The first Soviet effort to clear the Panjsher valley
involved a sweep by the 345th Guards Airborne Regiment in September 1980. It had little impact, and the operations that followed in
November 1980 and January 1981 were no more successful.

The VDV Airborne Force soon learned that intelligence was a key
asset in counterinsurgency warfare. For all the hoopla about the
physical training of paratroopers back in the Soviet Union, the hardy
condition of the tough mountain people of the Afghan valleys was
hard to match. Nor was the Soviet advantage in firepower of much
use unless the precise location of the enemy was known. When
Albert Slyusar took over command of the 103rd Airborne Division in
1981, improvement of the *razvedchik* units was given top priority.

Slyusar also learned that unconventional approaches to the enemy offered special rewards. The mujahideen groups often fought each other as enthusiastically as they did the Soviet Army, and on more than one occasion a bribe or a truce could convince the rebels to provide vital information on a rival rebel band. On several occasions, the Soviets were able to arrange a truce with the rebel groups in the Panjsher. This provided a respite for both sides, but, inevitably, the mujahideen broke the truce when it suited their purposes.

The VDV leadership was concerned by the high rate of casualties among the new recruits being sent to Afghanistan. Normal peacetime training was simply not rigorous or realistic enough. As a result, a training regiment was formed at Fergana in Uzbekistan to help prepare airborne soldiers and officers for combat duty. Although the 103rd Airborne Division was the only VDV division permanently stationed in Afghanistan, officers from all the other divisions were gradually rotated through the combat zone. The usual tour of duty was two years, and many officers served two or more tours through the nine years of fighting.

The young paratroopers soon learned to adapt to local conditions. The standard Soviet Army boot was nearly useless in mountain climbing, so Soviet paratroopers soon began sporting Kimris, a type of locally manufactured sneaker. The Soviet field kit was hopelessly inadequate, since it was designed for motor rifle troops, not for units that would operate on foot for weeks at a time. Surplus British and Pakistani rucksacks, sleeping bags, and other gear were acquired at local bazaars until the Soviet Union began to manufacture adequate equipment late in the war.

For all the airborne troops' tactical successes, the war proved enormously frustrating for them. Individual villages could be captured, but once the Soviets left, the mujahideen returned. The situation reminded more than one Russian officer of Alexander the Great's saying: "You can pass through the Orient, but you can't conquer it."

The frustrations and failures of the ground campaign led to more emphasis on airpower. The ground campaigns began to seem pointless, causing insignificant mujahideen casualties and usually leaving the rebels in control. The mujahideen movement prospered because of the support of the local Afghan population. Mao Tse-tung said that guerrillas must move among the people as a fish swims the sea. The Soviets decided to dry up "the sea" with high explosives. A bloody campaign of aerial attrition began in earnest in 1983, directed against the towns and the civilian population that supported the mujahideen. Villages were systematically bombed by Soviet and Afghan aircraft, and trade routes from mujahideen sanctuaries in Pakistan and Iran were indiscriminately mined by helicopter. When the mujahideen seized the city of Herat in 1983, the Soviets responded by bringing in Tu-16 bombers in attacks reminiscent of the Vietnam B-52 Arc Light strikes. Afghan casualties in the decade of war eventually totaled about 1.5 million, a large portion due to the air campaign.

WAR OF THE BUMBLEBEES

The Soviet Army had largely ignored or misunderstood the tactical lessons learned by the U.S. Army in Vietnam, and the French army in Algeria and Indochina. The Soviets were oblivious to the nature of modern guerrilla war, and they were both technically and tactically unprepared for the war in Afghanistan. This was evident in their faltering use of helicopters in the early years of the conflict.

Helicopters had proved invaluable in both Algeria and Vietnam. For all his training and equipment, the average American or French soldier was not much better than his Algerian or Vietnamese opponent in a guerrilla conflict. Both the French and American armies enjoyed firepower advantages, but these proved difficult to translate into real combat power since the enemy proved so elusive. A great deal of explosive was expended on empty jungle in Vietnam, and equally ample devastation was visited on many deserted mountains and villages in Afghanistan. Helicopters were the one technological advantage that mattered. They were a combat multiplier, allowing the Americans and French to rapidly position their forces. The aircraft allowed units to quickly maneuver against the enemy no matter how abysmal the terrain or how exhausted the troops. And they provided a genuine source of firepower that was readily available and easier to control than artillery or air strikes.

At the beginning of the war, Soviet helicopter forces consisted of a partial regiment of Mi-24 attack helicopters that had arrived in Afghanistan in 1979 to support the Afghan DRA, plus the 40th Army's own helicopter regiment. This amounted to about fifty to sixty helicopters, and grew to about a hundred later in 1980 after a third regiment was added. The VDV were the first to use helicopters during their initial mission in February 1980. Early attempts to employ airmobile helicopter tactics were stymied by the lack of helicopters and the lack of tactical experience with helicopters by the 40th Army command staff.

It took the Soviet Army about two years to fully integrate helicopters into their tactics. Although Soviet doctrine had long recognized the theoretical importance of helicopters, their high operating costs meant that few Soviet units actually trained with helicopters. Unit commanders were unfamiliar with helicopter operations, and helicopter units were inexperienced in the tactics of airborne assault. The VDV units were no different from most other units in this respect. Their preoccupation with parachute delivery had blinded them to the irrelevance of this technology in most circumstances.

The first lesson that had to be learned was that helicopters were not simply a means of troop delivery. In the U.S. armed forces, transport helicopters were part of the army; in the Soviet armed forces they were part of the air force. When a helicopter delivery took place in Afghanistan, the helicopters returned to the security of their remote air bases and awaited further instructions; they were seldom left under the jurisdiction of local army or VDV commanders to carry out missions. This practice changed, but it took time before the control of helicopters was coordinated between the ground and air contingents to make maximum use of the aircraft's capability. One of the most important innovations outside the VDV was the decision around 1984 to form a new integrated combined-arms brigade, the first of its kind in the Soviet Army to have an organized heliborne air assault element. The first of these in Afghanistan was the 70th Separate Motor Rifle Brigade, commanded by Lt. Col. A. G. Ivanov, operating in the Khandahar area. The brigade's organic air assault battalion was frequently supported by a flight of air force Mi-24 Gorbach attack helicopters, forming a potent mobile strike force. This mixed unit, containing its own armor, infantry, artillery, and airlift, continues to serve as the inspiration for new units in the Russian Army into the late 1990s.

By the summer of 1981, the Soviet helicopter force in Afghanistan had expanded to five times the size it was at the beginning of the war, with at least four regiments and several independent squadrons present. It stayed at this level for much of the war, though additional units were brought in from nearby bases in the Soviet Union for special operations. Of the 300 helicopters in Afghanistan in 1981, the backbone of the force was the Mi-8, which made up about 60 percent of the force. These performed the majority of air transport missions, though some were used for fire support and specialized roles. The Mi-24 Hind, known to its crews as the "hunchback" and to the mujahideen as the "devil's chariot," was the primary means of fire support during the air assault missions. It was not tied to airmobile missions, however, and was often used on independent assignments, including convoy security and fire support for mechanized columns. The remainder of the helicopter force was made up of specialized helicopters, including the Mi-6 Hook heavy-lift helicopter and the Mi-2 light utility helicopter.

The versatility of the helicopters in Afghanistan also meant that there was great demand for their services. The following figures were given in a 1993 Russian account of the use of helicopters in Afghanistan. They give a good idea of the varied activities of the bumblebees.

Helicopter Activities in Afghanistan by Type

	Mi-8	Mi-24	Mi-6
Air support of Ground Forces	9–1%	5–47%	—
Air assault	48–5%	7–9%	—
Convoy security	3–5%	25–27%	—
Supply missions	14–1%	2–4%	74%
Aerial reconnaissance	2–4%	10–12%	—
Air medical missions	3–5%	—	—
Aerial mining	1–3%	—	—

KISHLAKS AND CARAVANS

By 1984, the Soviet Army had concluded that the wide area sweeps of previous years were not an effective tactic. The attrition campaign against the Afghan *kishlaks* (villages) had flooded the massive refugee camps in Pakistan but had done little to curb the resistance. The emphasis began to shift to attempts to interdict the supply caravans coming into Afghanistan from mujahideen strongholds in Pakistan and Iran.

The interdiction mission was first given to the Spetsnaz in the autumn of 1983. The strength of the Spetsnaz in Afghanistan at this time was two brigades—the 1st Brigade (the former Chirchik 15th Brigade) based at Jalalabad and the 2nd Brigade based at Lashkar Gah in the southern Helmand province. However, this force was not sufficient to carry out the new Soviet policies. Although called brigades, these two elite units had a combined strength of less than 3,000 troops, roughly equivalent to a VDV regiment. The Spetsnaz forces in Afghanistan amounted to almost a third of the total Soviet Spetsnaz force, and the General Staff was reluctant to commit any more. For the expanded campaigns planned for the summer of 1984, more VDV troops were transported into Afghanistan, mainly from the 104th Guards Airborne Division stationed in Kirovabad in Azerbaijan. A dedicated interdiction campaign by the VDV began in 1984. The 1st Spetsnaz Brigade kept one of its detachments near Asadabad in the Kunar valley on the Kabul-Jalalabad road to Pakistan, where it continued its anticaravan campaign, sometimes with VDV support.

The Soviet Army launched its seventh attack into the Panjsher valley (Panjsher VII) in April 1984, intending once again to knock out Massoud's forces. Besides two veteran regiments of the 103rd Airborne Division and the 375th Airborne Regiment, a fresh regiment from the 104th Airborne Division was flown into Afghanistan. The operation was very sophisticated, synchronizing air strikes, heliborne assaults, and armored assaults. But the operation failed to engage or destroy Massoud's mujahideen forces. About 500 Soviet troops were killed, 900 Afghan DRA troops defected to the resistance, and the mujahideen claimed losses of only 200 dead. The losses in the airborne detachments were all the more bitter due to several instances of fratricide. During the operation, a Soviet bomber mission could not locate its targets and dropped their bombs on what they thought were empty areas. They landed in the midst of an airborne battalion, causing heavy casualties. Panjsher VII cost the Soviet Army nearly a quarter of the casualties it would suffer in Afghanistan that year. It was the bloodiest year of the war for the Soviet Union, with 2,343 dead.

NEW POLICY

Official Soviet accounts of the Afghanistan war break it down into
four phases. The first phase, from the December invasion to February 1980, consolidated the occupation. The period from March 1980
through April 1985, the second phase, represented a series of ever-
expanding efforts by the Soviet Army to crush the mujahideen. The
failure of the 1984 Panjsher campaign raised serious questions about
whether the war in Afghanistan could be won without making a
heavy commitment of additional Soviet forces. In March 1985, Konstantin Chernenko died and was replaced by the first Soviet leader of
the postwar generation, Mikhail Gorbachev. With a new leader in
power, the Afghan entanglement had to be reconsidered. The Soviet
Army had not been enthusiastic about the war, and now, with the
demise of the old hard-liners such as Chernenko and Suslov, new
thinking on the Afghan question was finally possible. The Kremlin
still could not stomach retreating from Afghanistan, but it did decide
to put limits on the depth of its involvement. By April 1985, Soviet
political and military leaders had concluded that Afghanistan was no
longer worth the bloodshed. The third phase of the war, from May
1985 to December 1986, was an attempt at "Afghanization," placing
a greater burden for the antiguerrilla campaigns on the backs of the
Afghan army, but still with support from Soviet airborne, tank, artillery, and air force units. During the fourth phase of the war, from
January 1987 to February 1989, the Soviet government attempted to
extricate itself from the Afghan morass, finally deciding on a complete troop withdrawal.

The performance of the Afghan DRA Army proved as frustrating
for the Soviets as the performance of the South Vietnamese ARVN
was to the Americans during the Vietnam War. The mujahideen were
as elusive and as tough as the Viet Cong. Although Afghanistan is
often called Moscow's Vietnam, there were as many differences as
similarities. The Soviet commitment to Afghanistan was far smaller
at its peak than the U.S. commitment in Indochina at its peak. Soviet
casualties were ultimately less than a third of those suffered by the
United States in Vietnam; annual Afghan war losses were actually
lower than training, hazing, medical, and other fatalities in the
peacetime army back in the USSR. There were seldom more than 6

Soviet divisions in Afghanistan out of the Soviet Army's 170, and these divisions were smaller than their American counterparts. The Soviets made extensive use of airpower in Afghanistan, but never on the scale of U.S. use in Vietnam. The essential similarity of the two conflicts lay in their ultimate futility.

The Kremlin decisions in the spring of 1985 envisioned a gradual shift of the combat effort from the Soviet 40th Army to the Afghan DRA. In the initial phase, Afghan infantry would take over from Soviet infantry but would retain support from Soviet tank and artillery units. The Soviet airborne force and Spetsnaz units would be the only Soviet infantry still committed to direct combat, but only for specific high-value operations. Soviet air support would continue or even increase. The tactical focus would be to interdict mujahideen arms supplies using air attack and Spetsnaz raids, and to conduct major ground operations near the Pakistan border to crush rebel strongholds.

The summer campaigns of 1985 saw the largest use of heliborne assault tactics of the entire war. In late May, the 40th Army began an assault in the Kunar valley to relieve the beseiged Afghan garrison at Barikot. The initial attacks were conventional ground operations, heavily supported by tanks and artillery. The second phase of the operation, code-named Operation Pustynya (desert), made heavy use of Spetsnaz from the 1st Brigade as well as VDV forces flown in by helicopter. In total, some 7,000 troops were carried aboard helicopters during this battle. At Barikot itself, a VDV battalion leapfrogged ahead of the tank columns, landing by helicopter directly in the perimeter of the fortified base once the Ground Forces were within striking range. The siege of Barikot was lifted. After the successful conclusion of the relief operation, the Soviet VDV pulled its troops back to the Kabul area for rest and rebuilding. The Afghan DRA set up a string of firebases and forts in the valley, hoping to keep control of the roads leading from Pakistan. Instead, the mujahideen methodically attacked the garrisons over the next few months, regaining control of the area. The war was stalemated. The Soviets could conduct and win operations anywhere they pleased using their new helicopter tactics, but the DRA was incapable of holding on to any gains in the major rebel areas of the northeast.

The next major offensive in 1985 used an even larger number of heliborne missions. Command of the 103rd Airborne Division was transferred to Gen. Pavel Grachev prior to the operation. Grachev was an Afghan veteran who had commanded the independent 345th Airborne Regiment in 1981; a decade later, after the 1991 coup attempt, he would be appointed to head the new Russian armed forces.

The attack into Paktia province began on 21 August 1985. Paktia was southeast of Kabul and controlled another key road leading eastward into Pakistan via Gardeyz and Khost. The operation was intended to crush large mujahideen forces in the province, to lift the sieges at Khost and Ali Khel, and to interdict the mujahideen supply routes running through the area. The pattern of the operation followed that set by the Kunar valley operation. The initial phase was a combined-arms assault preceded by heavy air strikes. Once the mechanized columns were well under way, the heliborne assaults by VDV and Spetsnaz units began. The helicopter operation was code-named Plotina (dam), a reminder that one of its major objectives was to staunch the growing flow of sophisticated arms to the rebels. In total, more than 12,000 troops were airlifted during the battle, the largest single airmobile operation of the war.

In one of the most dramatic actions of Plotina, three VDV battalions, along with three DRA Afghan battalions, were flown directly into the besieged garrison at Khost. The unexpected arrival of reinforcements caught the mujahideen off guard. By this time, the mujahideen were running out of ammunition and were forced to retreat. The reinforced Khost garrison went over to the offensive and began an attack on the mujahideen stronghold at Zhawar, up tight against the Pakistani frontier. Even with the heavy helicopter support, Zhawar proved unobtainable, and the Khost column was finally forced to return to the fortified city. Ultimately, Plotina had failed to meet its objectives: Zhawar would not be captured until 1986.

STINGER DIPLOMACY

The United States had condemned the Soviet invasion of Afghanistan in 1979 and had pulled out of the 1980 Moscow Olympics as a protest. In the early years of the war, American aid to the mujahideen became significant, most of it funneled through the Inter-Services Intelligence (ISI) branch of the Pakistani army. The vulnerability of the mujahideen to Soviet air strikes had been of particular concern to U.S. congressional supporters of the Islamic resistance, and they put pressure on the Reagan administration for several years to provide more effective weaponry. Both the CIA and the army objected to sending the most modern man-portable antiaircraft missile, the FIM-92 Stinger, to the mujahideen. The reluctance was in part due to the facade that the United States was not directly supporting the rebels; the appearance of such a state-of-the-art American weapon would undermine that transparent claim. The second reason was that missiles would inevitably fall into the hands of the Soviet Army. These could be used to help the Soviets develop their own counterparts, and would lead to the Soviet Air Force developing infrared countermeasures to undermine the effectiveness of the Stinger.

The mujahideen already had been receiving Strela-2 missiles from the CIA and Pakistan starting in 1982. The Soviet Strela-2 (NATO: SA-7 Grail) was an older man-portable missile and not particularly effective due to the use of outdated technology. It was almost completely ineffective against strike aircraft. A total of at least 118 Strela-2 missiles were fired against jet strike aircraft during the war, downing only three aircraft. The weapon was more effective against helicopters since they were slow, operated at low altitude, and gave off an alluring infrared signature. About 440 Strela-2 missiles were fired at Soviet and Afghan helicopters during the war, downing forty-two of them.

Strela-2 missiles were acquired from black market sources, including Soviet allies such as Romania, who manufactured the missiles. In addition, China built an unlicensed copy of the Strela-2 called the HN-5, and these were provided to the mujahideen as well. After losing many helicopters to the Strela-2s, the Soviet Air Force developed simple infrared countermeasures to bluff the missile's guidance system. Flares could be ejected, and the crude electronic logic of the Strela-2 would steer the missile at the bright flare instead of the helicopter. Also, large air mixers were placed over the engine exhausts to duct the hot gas into the rotor wash, reducing the infrared signature. The mujahideen grew increasingly frustrated at the declining results they were having with the already inadequate Strela-2.

As a compromise, in 1985 the CIA funded Shorts Brothers in Belfast, Northern Ireland, to acquire 300 of its Blowpipe man-portable missiles for the mujahideen. The British army was planning to adopt a new missile anyway, so technology transfer was not as great a concern. The Blowpipe worked in a fundamentally different fashion than the Strela-2 or Stinger. Instead of homing in on the infrared (heat) energy given off by the aircraft, the Blowpipe was command guided. The operator controlled the missile using a small thumb control unit in the launcher. This was fine and dandy on NATO proving grounds, but in the wilds of Afghanistan among illiterate and impatient mujahideen warriors, the complex firing routine of the Blowpipe proved too demanding.

The Blowpipe was first used during the fighting around Zhawar in April 1986. The Zhawar battle was another attempt to clear out this major mujahideen stronghold in the mountains on the Pakistani border. The only major Soviet unit committed to the fighting was a single regiment of the 103rd Guards Airborne Division, which was employed in its by-now traditional heliborne landing mode. An Afghan DRA commando force from the 37th Commando Brigade managed to land in broad daylight behind the main mujahideen positions. The mujahideen succeeded in downing three of the helicopters with the older Strela-2 missiles but cursed the fact that they didn't have better weapons. The Pakistanis consented to send forward some Blowpipes.

The Pakistani ISI opposed issuing this weapon from the outset, feeling that it was inferior and particularly unsuited to the mujahideen. Since there were not enough trained mujahideen Blowpipe gunners, several Pakistani army volunteers in mufti went forward, led by an air defense colonel. A total of thirteen missiles were fired, all missing their targets. The head of the Pakistani ISI later said, "The mujahideen, properly dug in at Zhawar with the Stinger, would have been unbeatable. Of that I have no doubt." Instead, Zhawar fell to the Afghan DRA forces in one of their rare victories.

The attack on Zhawar greatly disturbed Pakistan and the United States, as did the increasing number of Soviet Air Force incursions into Pakistan to attack mujahideen strongholds. It appeared that the war was now tilting in Kabul's favor, and that the Soviet policy of Afghanization of the war was succeeding. Some were convinced that the Stinger was the best way to help the mujahideen regain the advantage.

The Pakistani government had opposed supplying the mujahideen with the Stinger, partly on the grounds that its own army wasn't even allowed to acquire the missile. The fall of Zhawar changed the thinking of both the Pakistanis and the Americans. The previous October, the U.S. State Department's top intelligence officer, Morton Abramowitz, had visited Pakistan to discuss the progress of the war and come back advocating the Stinger as the best solution to shifting the war back in the mujahideen's favor. Abramowitz pressed hard to overcome CIA resistance and was soon bolstered by political support from Rep. Jim Courter and a Joint Chiefs of Staff recommendation in the spring of 1986. In April, President Ronald Reagan issued a directive to the CIA to supply limited numbers of Stingers to the mujahideen. Combat use of the Stinger had to wait, however, until sufficient Pakistani officers were trained on the weapon and, in turn, trained the first mujahideen crews at Rawalapindi.

Pakistani ISI officers directed the first Stingers to Gulbiddin Hekmatyar's fundamentalist Islamic Party when they arrived in the summer of 1986. They first went into action on 26 September 1986, shooting down a pair of Mi-24 attack helicopters outside Jalalabad air base. Only three missiles had been fired and two had hit, a remarkable performance compared to the earlier Strela-2 and Blowpipe. Additional successes soon followed. The Stingers had a more advanced infrared guidance seeker that made them less susceptible to infrared countermeasures such as flares and exhaust diffusion systems. Its warhead was larger and more lethal than that of the Strela-2, and it was easy to use after very basic training. Within a few weeks, the Soviet pilots quickly realized that they were dealing with a fundamentally different threat. And it was a threat directed at the main Soviet advantages in Afghanistan: airpower and airmobility.

The immediate success of the Stinger led to a larger number being shipped to the Afghan insurgents. They were issued to mujahideen groups operating near the main Soviet air bases at Kabul, Bagram, Jalalabad, Qandahar, and Shindand. They were then issued to units operating north of the Hindu Kush mountains along the Soviet border, which was the frequent site of attacks from nearby Soviet bases.

The impact of the Stinger was most clearly evident in the loss rate of Soviet combat aircraft. According to a recent Russian account, there were 60 missile launches in 1984 and only 10 aircraft lost; in 1985 there were 140 launches but only 15 losses, due to new countermeasures against the outdated Strela-2 missile. But when the Stinger was introduced in 1986, there were 600 launches and 100 losses. The official Soviet figures claim that only 65 aircraft were lost to all causes in 1986, but this does not include Afghan aircraft, which suffered quite heavily at the hands of the Stinger.

Soviet Aircraft Losses in Afghanistan
1980–89*

Year	Helicopters	Aircraft	Total
1980	42	4	46
1981	22	4	26
1983	26	8	34
1984	42	10	52
1985	56	8	64
1986	46	19	65
1987	48	17	65
1988–89	51	48	99
Total	**333**	**118**	**451**

*Figures do not include Afghan air force losses.

The impact of the Stinger on operations in Afghanistan was not simply in the number of aircraft shot down. Indeed, overall losses after 1986 were not significantly higher than in previous peak years. The Stinger's effectiveness lay in the fact that it gave the mujahideen protection against Soviet air attack for the first time, and thus deterred such attacks. Soviet and Afghan DRA attack missions were reduced in number due to the Stinger threat. New tactics were introduced to reduce the vulnerability of aircraft and helicopters, but this served to diminish the effectiveness of the Soviet aircraft during strike missions—aircraft would attack from higher altitudes, reducing the accuracy of their bombs and rockets.

Western journalists in the field with the mujahideen in 1987 immediately noticed the difference. Helicopter operations were sharply curtailed, often limited to missions made at night or far away from rebel positions. Bold helicopter raids were no longer conceivable. As early as March 1987, classified U.S. Army intelligence assessments noted the difference:

> Before the Stingers were employed in the area, Soviet helicopters flew wherever they wanted with impunity. They would hover anywhere they desired and fire into villages. Soviet crewmen would chase villagers and shoot them at will. But now when the helicopters approach villages at low altitude, they land quickly to discharge the troops. . . . The helicopters that used to fly up and down the valleys at low altitude now fly so high they can hardly be seen with the naked eye. The guerrillas have found it a little safer to live in their villages because the high-flying planes cannot bomb with the same accuracy as they once did. . . . The quantity of direct close air support of Soviet/ Afghan ground operations has been reduced significantly, and the application of all forms of close air support has been modified. More tactical and air support changes occurred in the last quarter of 1986 and the first quarter of 1987 than in the previous seven years of the conflict.

In the autumn of 1986, before the Stinger arrived, the war appeared to have reached a stalemate. Many Western analysts thought that a mujahideen victory was out of reach. After the Stinger arrived, the mujahideen regained the tactical initiative and turned around the course of the war. An Afghan resistance leader said: "For nine years the dragons have ruled the sky. Now the dragon is dead."

THE WAR WINDS DOWN

On 27 February 1986, the 27th Party Congress of the Soviet Communist Party began in Moscow. Gorbachev announced that the Soviet armed forces would be restructured and that Soviet military doctrine would become purely defensive. Instead of a continuing arms race with the United States, Moscow would aim for reasonable sufficiency in its military power. It was Gorbachev's first important step in bringing an end to the Cold War.

By this time, Gorbachev had already decided that the Soviet Union would withdraw from Afghanistan. The war was proving costly in human and material terms, and Gorbachev was completely unwilling to increase the Limited Contingent beyond its existing level. The Afghan invasion had poisoned relations with Arab client states in the Mideast and was an antagonizing stumbling block in U.S.-USSR relations. In April 1986, the Soviets forced out Babrak Karmal and replaced him with Maj. Gen. Mohammed Najeebollah, the former head of KhAD, the Afghan secret police. Karmal was regarded as a Brezhnev protégé, and his departure signaled the important changes Mikhail Gorbachev was about to announce. In July, Gorbachev declared a limited pullout of about 7,000 troops. The U.S. ridiculed the pullout as a hoax, saying that the units had been brought into Afghanistan specifically for the purpose of staging a publicized withdrawal. But Gorbachev had made up his mind. Najeebollah was informed of the decision during meetings with Gorbachev in December 1986. The aim of the Gorbachev plan was to completely withdraw the Soviet 40th Army within two years. Soviet combat operations in Afghanistan would be significantly reduced, and the DRA Army would have to take over the brunt of the fighting.

The new war policy did not affect the VDV paratroopers or the Spetsnaz as much as the other Soviet Army units. The Soviet General Staff was intent on helping the DRA crush several key mujahideen strongpoints before they pulled out, and the VDV would remain the last major Soviet force to engage in these battles, aside from air force helicopters and strike aviation. Two of the airborne division's regiments were tied down in the Kabul area, in part to conduct sweeps to keep the Stinger-equipped mujahideen away from the airport. This left only a single regiment, along with Lt. Col. V. A. Vostrotin's independent 345th Airborne Regiment, to support the DRA Army efforts.

Luckily for the Soviets, the Stinger was still not available in large numbers in mid-1987. Stingers were most widely used around Kabul and along the Pakistani border near Khost. In May 1987, Vostrotin's 345th Airborne Regiment took part in the first large-scale operation of the year, code-named Operation Parachinar, supporting an Afghan DRA sweep near Ali Khel in Paktia province aimed at destroying major mujahideen supply dumps. The 345th Airborne Regiment was assigned to seal off the routes into the area from the nearby Pakistani border. The Afghan DRA Army was responsible for the attacks on the rebel strongholds. The fighting was at times intense, and the Stingers succeeded in limiting Soviet air operations. About four aircraft were shot down, but in fact the restrictions placed on Soviet helicopter mobility were of far greater consequence than the actual losses. Two of the paratroopers involved in the operation were later awarded the Hero of the Soviet Union distinction for their efforts in this skirmish. The mujahideen claimed that the battle had "humiliated" the airborne troops, though Russian accounts suggest otherwise. Vostrotin was nominated a second time for the Hero of the Soviet Union distinction, but he did not finally win it until 1988.

The last major Soviet offensive campaign took place at the end of the year, near the perennially besieged city of Khost. The objectives of the mission, code-named Operation Magistral (highway), were as much political as military. Najeebollah's government desperately wanted a major victory over the mujahideen to give credibility to his regime before the Soviets pulled out. The operation included the largest concentration of Soviet airborne forces in any single mission since the beginning of the war, including not only Vostrotin's 345th Airborne Regiment, but a regiment from General Grachev's 103rd Airborne Division, the 56th Air Assault Brigade from Gardeyz, and a large contingent of Soviet combat engineers, to help breach the many minefields along the road from Gardeyz to Khost. On the Afghan side, it involved the elite 37th Commando Brigade, one of the few reliable DRA Army units.

The main attack by Afghan mechanized columns, supported by Soviet engineers, began along the highway on 19 November 1987. In a bold move, a regiment from the Afghan 37th Commando Brigade was flown by helicopter into the Shabek Khel valley in an effort to seize the key Sato Kandao mountain pass and cut off the mujahideen forces of Jalaladin Haqani. Soviet airborne forces were not committed to the opening phase of Magistral, except for reconnaissance units and a company serving as convoy escorts with the Soviet engineers.

With the mujahideen concentrating on wiping out the beleaguered 37th Commando Brigade forces, the 103rd Guards Airborne prepared to seize its intended objective, the Sato Kandao pass. A dummy parachute operation began the mission, with Soviet aircraft dropping cargo parachutes weighted down with sandbags. The dummy airborne drop was intended to pinpoint Afghan mujahideen forces near the pass. The mujahideen fired at the parachutes, and Soviet air strikes soon followed. The actual helicopter landing by a single VDV regiment took place on the night of 18–19 December, since a large daytime landing was judged too risky if Stingers were present. The airborne troops finally captured the pass on 23 December, and a critical roadblock on the way to Khost was cleared. During the subsequent operations near Khost, the two airborne regiments were mainly involved in clearing out mujahideen supply depots. The 345th Guards Airborne seized one of the main depots at Srana, although mujahideen resistance was fierce. One of the battalion commanders and several of his staff were severely wounded in the fighting. But the fighting was far from over.

Russian accounts claim that on 6 January 1988, reinforcements were flown into the area from neighboring Pakistan, totaling about 450 mujahideen and Pakistani troops in local garb. This force managed to cut off the 9th Company, 345th Airborne Regiment, which was holding defensive positions on a mountainside to block the approach to the Srana arms caches. The Pakistani/mujahideen force soon threatened to overrun the Soviet company. As the regiment's two battalions were already heavily committed in the fighting around the arms caches, Vostrotin was forced to cobble together a relief force from headquarters troops, including many of the regimental staff officers, bolstered by a couple of platoons of the best *razvedchik* scouts. The VDV column set off in several BTR-70 and BMP-2 armored vehicles but eventually had to dismount due to the rugged terrain.

The beleaguered company was isolated on the side of a mountain; unable to dig foxholes, they had erected rock barriers for defense. The relief column fought its way to the company shortly before they expended their last ammunition. The troops were down to two magazines each. The company had suffered many casualties, but to their great surprise as Mi-8MT helicopter suddenly appeared to evacuate the most seriously wounded. The mountainside was too steep to permit the helicopter to land, so the wounded had to be loaded awkwardly and painfully through the side door over the arms of other soldiers as the helicopter hovered. To the amazement of the paratroopers, the same helicopter pilot returned some time later with a substantial amount of ammunition. The reinforcement of men and equipment allowed the survivors of 9th Company to hold the rock defenses against several later attacks. Whether by coincidence or intent, Mikhail Gorbachev finally authorized the award of the Hero of the Soviet Union distinction to Vostrotin while the relief of the 9th Company was going on—an award based on his regiment's performance the year before.

The heaviest fighting during the Magistral operation ended by the second week of January with the Soviet units firmly in control of the arms dumps. The road between Gardeyz and Khost was kept open until the end of January, and the bloodied 345th Airborne Regiment was transported back to Bagram. As was so typical of the war, within a week the mujahideen took control of the road again from the DRA Army, and the destroyed arms dumps were replaced by new supplies from Pakistan. Russian officers disgustedly called Magistral "the most idiotic and unnecessary airborne operation of the war."

Vostrotin nominated the helicopter pilot who had so bravely flown in to rescue the 9th Company for the Hero of the Soviet Union distinction. But the helicopter regiment staff had already rebuked him for his reckless act and shipped him back to Russia. Three other airborne soldiers were decorated for Operation Magistral. The 103rd Airborne Division commander, Gen. Pavel Grachev, received the Hero's gold star, the second of the division's Afghan commanders to be so honored. Grachev had already served two tours in Afghanistan and was widely admired by his men for not wasting their blood in careless actions. Two young paratroopers, Sgt. V. A. Aleksandrov and Pvt. Andrey Melnikov, were decorated posthumously for their heroism during the defense of the 9th Company's mountain positions.

AFGHAN WITHDRAWAL

After Magistral, the Soviet VDV and Spetsnaz units began to limit their participation in major operations. There were many small-scale actions in 1988, but the 6 January 1988 announcement by Foreign Minister Eduard Shevardnadze made it clear that the Soviet pullout was only a matter of time. By spring, Soviet units began to leave the garrisons in the southwestern regions of Afghanistan, concentrating on Kabul. The main route would be along the Kabul-Bagram highway, through the Panjsher valley and the Salang pass back into the Soviet Union. There was considerable fighting along this route to ensure that it stayed open, and truces were arranged with several rebel commanders to minimize the clashes. The first major columns of Soviet troops began to withdraw along the Kabul-Salang route in May 1988; several airborne units, including Vostrotin's 345th Airborne Regiment, were assigned to keep portions of the highway open. There was intermittent fighting with mujahideen forces under Massoud through January as they harassed the withdrawing Soviet units along the narrow mountain roads. The last column drove across the Amu Darya bridge linking Afghanistan and the Soviet Union on 15 February 1989. The last unit out of the country was a VDV company, followed closely by Gen. Boris Gromov, the last commander of the Soviet 40th Army in Afghanistan.

Soviet Casualties in Afghanistan*

Year	Killed in Action	Officers	Enlisted Men
1979	79	9	70
1980	1,399	170	1,229
1981	1,188	155	1,033
1982	1,838	215	1,623
1983	1,236	179	1,057
1984	2,345	285	2,060
1985	1,792	240	1,552
1986	1,266	198	1,068
1987	1,193	189	1,004
1988	745	106	639
1989	55	9	46
Total	**13,136**	**1,755**	**11,381**

*Figures do not include 697 noncombat deaths, or 572 KGB Border Guards and Special Operations Troops or 28 MVD Interior Forces troops killed during the war.

Afghanistan left the VDV bloody and weary. The airborne forces had borne the brunt of the war more than any other branch of the Soviet armed forces. Some idea of the VDV's central combat role in the Afghan war can be seen from the decorations awarded the troops of the Soviet Army. A total of fifty Hero of the Soviet Union distinctions were awarded to the ground troops. The VDV paratroopers earned fifteen, compared to twenty-eight for the Ground Forces, even though the Ground Forces outnumbered the airborne troops by a factor of at least seven to one. No Ground Forces' divisional commander was awarded the Hero's gold star, but it was awarded twice to the commanders of the 103rd Guards Airborne Division—to A. E. Slyusar in November 1983 and to Pavel Grachev in June 1988. At least four Spetsnaz members were awarded the Hero's gold star, starting with Col. Vassily V. Kolesnik, who commanded the Muslim Battalion during the attack on Amin's Taj-Bek Palace in December 1979. The last Hero of the Soviet Union award went to an airborne officer, Maj. O. A. Yurasov, after he was killed during the skirmishes to keep open the Salang highway during the withdrawal in January 1989. After losing so many men in the mountains of Afghanistan, few paratroopers could bear to call the war a waste. One of the veterans, Lt. Col. B. Sergeyev, summed up the thoughts of many:

> I live! And yet I vainly endeavor
> To forget all that has wounded my soul.
> We will recall for the rest of our lives
> How joyless was this war.

Chapter 13
The Time of Troubles

T he 103rd Airborne Division returned to a very different Soviet Union from the one it had left in December 1979. The country was in the throes of Gorbachev's reform, perestroika. By removing the repressive control of the Soviet police state, Gorbachev had opened a Pandora's box of long-ignored social and political problems.

The exceptional performance of the Blue Berets, as the airborne had become popularly known in Moscow, brought them to the attention of Moscow's power brokers. The VDV had been the reliable backbone of the Afghan adventure and had proven their steadfast reliability where the regular army had occasionally stumbled. The top Soviet leadership began to look at the VDV as the most likely candidate for restoring order if the reforms led to turmoil. The KGB began intrigues to put the battle-hardened 103rd Airborne Division under its control for special internal missions.

The head of the VDV in 1990 was Vladislav Achalov, a very different sort of VDV commander from his predecessors. Vasiliy Margelov, the charismatic leader of the VDV at the height of the Cold War, had retired in 1979 and been replaced by his deputy, Dmitri Sukhorukhov. Another career paratrooper, Sukhorukhov was cut of the same cloth as Margelov. He was replaced in 1987 by Gen. Nikolai Kalinin, who was promoted to head the Moscow Military District in 1989.

Achalov had been trained as a tank officer but was put in command of an airborne regiment in the 1970s when the arrival of the

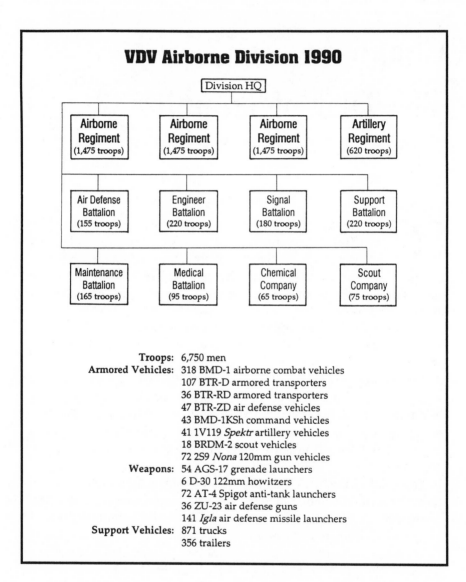

VDV Airborne Division 1990

Division HQ

| Airborne Regiment (1,475 troops) | Airborne Regiment (1,475 troops) | Airborne Regiment (1,475 troops) | Artillery Regiment (620 troops) |

| Air Defense Battalion (155 troops) | Engineer Battalion (220 troops) | Signal Battalion (180 troops) | Support Battalion (220 troops) |

| Maintenance Battalion (165 troops) | Medical Battalion (95 troops) | Chemical Company (65 troops) | Scout Company (75 troops) |

Troops: 6,750 men
Armored Vehicles: 318 BMD-1 airborne combat vehicles
107 BTR-D armored transporters
36 BTR-RD armored transporters
47 BTR-ZD air defense vehicles
43 BMD-1KSh command vehicles
41 1V119 *Spektr* artillery vehicles
18 BRDM-2 scout vehicles
72 2S9 *Nona* 120mm gun vehicles
Weapons: 54 AGS-17 grenade launchers
6 D-30 122mm howitzers
72 AT-4 Spigot anti-tank launchers
36 ZU-23 air defense guns
141 *Igla* air defense missile launchers
Support Vehicles: 871 trucks
356 trailers

new BMD armored airborne assault vehicle required officers with armored vehicle experience. His success as an airborne regimental commander led to his later appointment to command an airborne division. He returned to a more conventional career track afterward, serving in a number of key staff positions in the Ground Forces and finally as the commander of the prestigious Leningrad Military District in the early 1980s. His appointment to command the VDV was odd: Kalinin had gone from the VDV to district command; Achalov had done the reverse, from district command to command of the VDV. In fact, Achalov's selection was not so surprising given his personality. Gorbachev and the General Staff knew Achalov to be a no-nonsense, conservative, hard-line Soviet patriot. If the VDV was to serve as a stabilizing force in the turbulent years ahead, the Kremlin needed a ruthless and reliable commander such as Achalov.

VDV Airborne Force 1990

UNIT	LOCATION
7th Guards Airborne Division	**Kaunus, Lithuania**
97th Airborne Regiment	Alitus
108th Airborne Regiment	Kaunus
119th Airborne Regiment	Mariyampole
1141st Artillery Regiment	Kalvariya
744th Air Defense Battalion	Kaunus
143rd Combat Engineer Battalion	Kaunus
6th Maintenance Battalion	Kaunus
743rd Signal Battalion	Kaunus
185th Air Transport Squadron	Kaunus
76th Guards Airborne Division	**Pskov, Russia**
104th Airborne Regiment	Pskov
234th Airborne Regiment	Pskov
237th Airborne Regiment	Pskov
1140th Artillery Regiment	Pskov
29th Air Defense Battalion	Pskov
83rd Combat Engineer Battalion	Pskov
7th Maintenance Battalion	Pskov
728th Signal Battalion	Pskov

VDV Airborne Force 1990 (Cont.)

UNIT	LOCATION
242nd Air Transport Squadron	Pskov
98th Guards Airborne Division	**Bolgrad, Ukraine**
217th Airborne Regiment	Bolgrad
299th Airborne Regiment	Bolgrad
300th Airborne Regiment	Kishniev
1065th Artillery Regiment	Veseliy Kut
100th Air Defense Battalion	Bolgrad
112th Combat Engineer Battalion	Bolgrad
15th Maintenance Battalion	Bolgrad
674th Signal Battalion	Bolgrad
243rd Air Transport Squadron	Bolgrad
103rd Guards Airborne Division*	**Vitebsk, Byelarus**
393rd Airborne Regiment	Vitebsk
583rd Airborne Regiment	Vitebsk
688th Airborne Regiment	Vitebsk
271st Artillery Regiment	Vitebsk
Air Defense Battalion	Vitebsk
Combat Engineer Battalion	Vitebsk
Maintenance Battalion	Vitebsk
Signal Battalion	Vitebsk
Air Transport Squadron	Vitebsk
104th Guards Airborne Division	**Gyandzha, Azerbaijan**
328th Airborne Regiment	Gyandzha
337th Airborne Regiment	Gyandzha
345th Airborne Regiment	Gyandzha
1180th Artillery Regiment	Shamkhor
103rd Air Defense Battalion	Gyandzha
132nd Combat Engineer Battalion	Gyandzha
24th Maintenance Battalion	Gyandzha
729th Signal Battalion	Gyandzha
116th Air Transport Squadron	Gyandzha

*This division was under KGB rather than armed forces command at this time.

106th Guards Airborne Division	**Tula**
51st Airborne Regiment	Tula
137th Airborne Regiment	Ryazan
331st Airborne Regiment	Kostroma
1182nd Artillery Regiment	Tula
107th Air Defense Battalion	Donskoy
139th Combat Engineer Battalion	Tula
43rd Maintenance Battalion	Tula
731st Signal Battalion	Tula
110th Air Transport Squadron	Tula
242nd Airborne Training Center (Division)	**Gayzhyunay, Lithuania**
(Separate VDV Units)	
11th Separate Airborne Brigade	Ulan-Ude, Russia
13th Separate Airborne Brigade	Magadachi, Russia
21st Separate Airborne Brigade	Kutaisi, Georgia
23rd Separate Airborne Brigade	Kremenchug, Ukraine
35th Separate Air Assault Brigade	Cottbus, Germany
36th Separate Airborne Brigade	Garbolovo, Russia
37th Separate Airborne Brigade	Chernyakovsk, Russia
38th Separate Airborne Brigade	Brest, Byelarus
40th Separate Airborne Brigade	Nikolayev, Ukraine
56th Separate Airborne Brigade	Volgodonsk, Russia
83rd Separate Airborne Brigade	Ussurisk, Russia

ETHNIC BLOODSHED

One of the immediate consequences of Gorbachev's liberalization policy was an outburst of ethnic friction throughout the Soviet Union. The USSR was a vast empire, consisting of scores of different, and mutually antagonistic, ethnic groups. In the Communist police state, ethnic friction was firmly suppressed under the veneer of fraternal brotherhood. As soon as police control was relaxed, the age-old antagonisms quickly resurfaced. One of the first areas to suffer from the festering nationalistic tensions was the Caucasus. The territory of Nagorno-Karabakh was a mountainous Christian Armenian enclave located within the Muslim Azerbaijan republic. The

Azeris governed the enclave, much to the chagrin of the Armenians. In February 1988, fighting broke out in Armenia's captial, Yerevan. Armenian crowds hounded Azeris. A regiment from the 104th Airborne Division, stationed at Kirovabad in neighboring Azerbaijan, was dispatched to Yerevan to quiet the situation after the local MVD Interior Troops proved incapable of maintaining order. The situation calmed down quickly, as most Azeris had already fled the city. But the ethnic turmoil in Yerevan led to counterdemonstrations in the Azeri capital of Baku, a major oil-producing center with a large Armenian population. No sooner did the 104th Guards Airborne return to Kirovabad than they marched into Baku to put down an anti-Armenian pogrom.

The situation in the Caucasus continued to heat up through 1989. In April, the capital of Georgia, Tbilisi, erupted in demonstrations. Georgian nationalists led by Zviad Gamsakhurdia demanded independence from the USSR. It was one thing for the locals to engage in blood feuds; it was another thing to demand seccession from the

Soviet Union. Gorbachev personally ordered that the 106th Guards Airborne Division at Tula, remaining regiments from the 104th at Kirovabad, and MVD troops from the 19th Dzerzhinskiy Special Operations Division in Moscow be sent to Tbilisi to put down the disturbances. The MVD forces were intended to provide crowd control, with the VDV forces to serve as backup. The most violent clash occurred on 9 April 1989, when the MVD troops attempted to break up a rally by Georgian nationalists. The MVD police forces used *cheremukha,* a type of riot-control gas, and in the ensuing melee, dozens of civilians were killed and wounded. Videotapes of the savage and inept police action were soon on television channels around the world, embarrassing the Gorbachev government. The army was blamed for the brutal handling of the whole affair. The MVD Internal Troops wear essentially the same uniform as the army, so the international press condemned the Soviet Army. Gorbachev had no appreciation of the distinction, and he sacked the commander of the Transcaucasus Military District, even though it was MVD conduct that was suspect.

The VDV commanders were unenthusiastic about their new role as peacekeeper among the various ethnic factions in the Soviet hinterlands. The 106th Airborne commander, Aleksandr Lebyed, had been a young boy in June 1962 in Novocherkassk, site of the largest civil disturbances in Russia in the immediate Cold War years, and he had nearly been killed by indiscriminate MVD police violence against the protesters. This memory colored his view, and many other senior VDV officers felt the same way. In many cases, the VDV had little choice. In the summer of 1989, fighting flared up between Meskhetians and Uzbeks near the garrison of the independent 387th Airborne Regiment in Fergana, Uzbekistan. More than a hundred Meskhetians were killed during a riot by Uzbeks, and the MVD police failed to calm the situation. The surviving Meskhetians fled in fear to the VDV base, and to calm the situation the paratroopers had to threaten the pursuing Uzbeks with automatic weapons.

THE WALL COMES TUMBLING DOWN

Gorbachev's speech at the United Nations in December 1988 signaled a rejection of the Brezhnev doctrine about Soviet intervention in the internal affairs of the neighboring Warsaw Pact states. It was the first inkling that Moscow would tolerate real independence in Poland, Czechoslovakia, and the other countries on the Soviet Union's western frontier. But loosening the ties with the Warsaw Pact countries also led nationalists in the outlying republics of the Soviet Union to demand independence as well. In November 1989, the Berlin Wall came crashing down, the ultimate symbol of the end of the Cold War. Soviet military officers were shocked that Eastern Europe had been allowed to pull itself free from the Soviet Union without a fight, and they were equally dismayed to see chaos beginning to envelop the Soviet Union itself.

By January 1990, the situation in Azerbaijan was sliding into civil war. The Armenians were attempting to win control of the Nagorno-Karabakh region, and the ethnic tension had degenerated into rampage and slaughter on both sides. Azeri nationalists were insisting that the Soviet Army intervene in the dispute on their side and, when nothing was done, began attacking Soviet garrisons in Azerbaijan. The commander in chief of the Ground Forces, General of the Army Valentin Varennikov, flew to Baku to assess the situation. Gorbachev ordered Achalov and the MVD minister, Vadim Bakatin, to join him there. Varennikov's report to the Kremlin was so alarming that Gorbachev and the Politburo ordered that martial law be declared and that forces be moved into the republic to quell the unrest. The MVD *militsiya* in the area was completely unprepared to handle the well-armed insurgents, and many *militsiya* units had simply broken and run when confronted by the local mobs.

The only forces mobile enough to rapidly respond were the VDV divisions, which soon found themselves winging southward to the beleaguered republic. Three divisions were ordered into action: the entire 106th Airborne from Tula, the 76th Guards Airborne from Pskov, and one regiment from the 98th Guards Airborne from Bolgrad in Ukraine. On landing at Kala airfield outside Baku, the 106th Guards Airborne found the road into the city blocked by armed insurgents huddled behind barricades. The paratroopers mounted their BMD armored vehicles and began moving on the city. The insurgents quickly realized that they could not hope to win against armored airborne units and began abandoning their defensive positions. At one point, a large amount of gasoline was poured onto the main road by the Azeri militants, creating a fiery ribbon nearly a mile long. The

BMD armored vehicles simply drove off the road and continued to the city. The paratroopers were ordered to hold their fire, even though several were wounded by snipers.

The regiments from the three airborne divisions converged on Baku from different directions, and each was assigned a different section of the city. The anti-Armenian pogroms were forcibly stopped. Many Azeris were ashamed of the behavior of the extreme nationalists and supported the actions of the Soviet troops in restoring order. The 331st Guards Airborne Regiment of the 106th Airborne was ordered to seize the command post of the Azeri nationalists, located on a ship in Baku harbor. This was accomplished after a short skirmish. Azeri nationalists on another cutter tried to intervene, but four BMD armored vehicles responded with a salvo of 73mm high-explosive rounds, which set the cutter on fire. It eventually sank. Several days later, a task force from the 217th Guards Airborne (98th Airborne Division) was sent to the city of Dushanbe when anti-Armenian killings began there. The paratroopers arrived before the situation deteriorated to the point it had in Baku. With conditions temporarily stabilized, the VDV divisions were withdrawn, leaving behind the 104th Airborne at its base in Kirovabad.

PSEUDO-COUP

Achalov's capable handling of the Armenian disturbances brought him into frequent contact with Gorbachev. The situation in the hinterlands was very worrisome to conservative members of the army, who feared that the troubles might spread into Russia itself. In September 1990, Defense Minister Dmitri Yazov and KGB chief Vladimir Kryuchkov helped Gorbachev plan an unusual military exercise intended to intimidate his opposition in the Russian Republic. Gorbachev's main political opponent was Boris Yeltsin, who had won a stunning election victory over Gorbachev and the Communist Party in the March 1989 Congress of Peoples Deputies election. The aim of the exercise was intentionally ambiguous. It took place while Gorbachev was on a visit overseas, raising the specter of a coup attempt. To some, it appeared that by hinting of unknown forces contemplating a coup, Gorbachev was trying to evoke sympathy in the West in his fight against remaining hard-liners in the Russian government.

To the opposition headed by the Russian Republic's president, Boris Yeltsin, the use of military troops in Moscow was a signal that Gorbachev would use the military if necessary to counter any threat to his regime. The September exercise remains one of the most bizarre incidents in the string of coups and countercoups that rocked Russia in the early 1990s. It suggests that Gorbachev had come to regard the VDV as his own personal Praetorian Guard to protect himself should Yeltsin or others attempt to seize power.

At 11:00 on 9 September, elements of the 76th Guards Airborne Division in Pskov were placed on alert; the warning was limited to the key regimental commanders, who received the orders directly from Achalov, not through the usual divisional command structure. All BMD-1 airborne assault vehicles were ordered out of mothballs. The 103rd Guards Airborne Division in Vitebsk was also put on alert, and rumors circulated that control of the division had been shifted from the General Staff to KGB authority "for a special mission." On the evening of 10 September, the 137th Airborne Regiment, stationed near the VDV Academy at Ryazan, was alerted and put under a special operational group headed by Colonel Kolchenoveniy. Officers on leave were called back to the unit. Thirty IL-76 transport aircraft from VTA Military Transport Aviation regiments in the Leningrad area were dispatched to Ryazan to lift the regiment to an undisclosed location. The 331st Airborne Regiment at Kostroma was also airlifted. One of the regiments had only recently returned from Osh in Central Asia where it had been involved in quashing ethnic fighting.

The airborne troops received no prior warning of the exercise, which was not typical Soviet practice. Field exercises away from base were always placed into an annual schedule and were well known in advance to unit commanders. All troops were equipped in "southern style," Soviet slang for arming troops to the combat standards used in Afghanistan. The paratroopers were issued flak vests, steel helmets, and live ammunition. This was very unusual in VDV airborne units, as helmets were seldom worn, even in field exercises. Paratroopers usually wore the distinctive blue beret of this elite force; helmets were a special issue item seen only in wartime. Also, live ammunition was never issued in advance in field exercises; it was usually distributed at the last moment at the firing range. To the paratroopers involved in the exercise, the preparations were reminiscent of actual combat deployments such as the 1979 Afghanistan operation, or recent deployments of VDV troops to quell disturbances in Central Asia republics.

Neither enlisted men in the unit nor junior officers were told anything about their assignment. One battalion officer stated that "the informals," army slang for Yeltsin and the other reformist politicians and activists in Moscow, were planning to forcibly remove the Soviet government and that the paratroopers were being dispatched to prevent it. Two days later, the same officer told his junior officers that the unit had been flown into the Moscow area since "the informals" planned to prevent their usual rail journey to the capital in time for the 7 November Red Square parade.

Pilots flying the task force to Moscow informed the Moscow Air Defense District that the transports were loaded with food for children displaced by the Chernobyl disaster, or that they carried vitamin pills. This detail suggests the exceptionally high level of secrecy attached to the mission—which also suggests the simulation of a mission opposed by other units of the armed forces. One of the paratroop regiments landed at a small airstrip west of Moscow and the other at an airstrip to the southwest. At first, the paratroopers were ordered to stay aboard the aircraft, but subsequently they were ordered to take up defensive positions in woods around the airstrip. Thirty-four hours later, one unit was withdrawn and flown back to its home base near Pskov via Bryansk. Later, on 13 September, the elite reconnaissance companies of the two regiments, still in the Moscow area, donned civilian garb and were deployed to the Moscow suburb of Odintsovo to "guard" the dachas of top Soviet generals. The exercise ended prematurely on 18 September due to public outcry, and the remaining units returned to base by ground transport, arriving on 20–21 September. While the exercise was going on, Boris Yeltsin was involved in a suspicious car "accident" and suffered a concussion, widely believed to have been staged by the KGB.

The unusual alert at Ryazan immediately attracted the attention of local political leaders. Valeriy Ryumin, the chairman of the Ryazan City Council and a former paratrooper lieutenant colonel and instructor, called friends at the base to find out about all the unexpected commotion. The staff at the academy denied that any exercises were in effect. Ryumin dispatched several council deputies, who noted the extensive preparatory activity at the base, including the arming of troops and the loading of armored vehicles aboard the transports. The deputies were barred from talking to the troops, and no explanation was given about the alert. Inquiries to the head of the VDV Airborne Force, Col. Gen. Vladislav Achalov, elicited the unconvincing response that "many paratroopers are helping with the potato harvest." Statements by Defense Minister Dmitri Yazov were equally unbelievable, and KGB head Vladimir Kryuchkov stated that he knew nothing of the alert, even though nine KGB counterintelligence officers were assigned to the units in the exercise.

Under these circumstances, wild rumors about the intentions of the alert spread through the media. On 24 September, forty-two reformist deputies from the Russian Republic went so far as to issue a public appeal to the troops not to use their weapons against their own people. Various television broadcasts aired talk shows where guests debated whether the alert was meant to prevent a coup against Gorbachev by radical reformers, or to stage a coup by right-wing opponents of Gorbachev in the military and KGB. Establishment newspapers such as *Izvestiya* denounced press coverage of the alert, and further obscured the origins of the alert by revealing an alleged plot called Action Program-90 by a previously unknown "Russian Democratic Forum" that envisioned mass protest to overthrow the regime. The top military leadership offered only evasive answers to the press, but some of the more prominent young generals were less circumspect. Colonel General Boris Gromov, the last Soviet commander of the 40th Army in Afghanistan and a firebrand regarded by democratic forces as a potential Russian Napoleon, deemed the coup rumors to be "totally unfounded idiocy." Coup hysteria had reached the point when a column of derelict World War II–vintage tanks, being dragged into Moscow by volunteer vehicle enthusiasts for a new museum, were reported to authorities as a column of "rebel" tanks.

The coup craze in Moscow, lasting until November 1990, was symptomatic of the disintegration of authority in the Soviet Union and Gorbachev's feckless dealings with the military. It created grave doubts in the minds of many Russians about the future stability of their government. Gorbachev needed solid military support in order to carry out his reform activities, but his use of the military in such an irresponsible manner created an impression among the hard-liners that he would seriously entertain a real crackdown if reforms went too far. A year later, many of the participants in the pseudo-coup, including KGB chief Kryuchkov and Defense Minister Yazov, would attempt to stage a real coup patterned on the phony exercise, expecting that Gorbachev could be forced to take part. Their miscalculation led to the downfall of the Soviet Union.

THE AIRBORNE RESURGENT

Achalov's willingness to participate in the dubious September exercise, and his able leadership of the VDV in squashing the ethnic disputes in Central Asia, created a favorable impression on Mikhail Gorbachev. In December 1990, Gorbachev appointed Achalov as the deputy defense minister. Achalov later stated that his appointment was due to Gorbachev's recognition that army support, and especially VDV support, would be crucial in the upcoming year. The army, and the VDV in particular, was increasingly seen as a critical stabilizing force for the times of trouble ahead. Achalov was clearly viewed as a Gorbachev loyalist. His place at the head of the VDV was taken over by Pavel "Pasha" Grachev, the young 103rd Airborne Division war hero. Another young Afghanistan veteran, Aleksandr Lebyed, gave up his command of the 106th Airborne at Tula and was installed as the head of the Ryazan training school, which also controlled the airborne regiment used for any special missions in the Moscow area. By the early 1990s, the generation of young Afghan veterans was being thrust into critical positions of leadership in the Soviet Army. A disproportionate number were VDV officers.

One of Achalov's first tasks was to coordinate a plan to deal with further nationalist outbreaks in the republics, especially the Baltics. The plan had two parts, under the code names Operation Metel (blizzard) and Taifun (typhoon). Operation Metel was planned as a limited response to civil disturbances. As mentioned in earlier chapters, Yazov had sponsored efforts to professionalize the OPNAZ troops of the MVD Internal Forces to make them better suited to handle civic actions. Under the scenario envisioned by Operation Metel, the MVD's elite 19th Dzerzhinskiy Special Operations Motor Rifle Division, not VDV paratroopers, would be the primary force behind the operation. Operation Taifun would be enacted if conditions were far more serious. This plan would result in the declaration of martial law, and MVD troops would be quickly reinforced by army units, primarily the VDV airborne regiments.

The plan was enacted sooner than anyone anticipated and before the modernization of the MVD troops had any effect. Instead, Gorbachev ordered the KGB and the army to reassert Soviet domination in Lithuania in the face of growing separatist sentiment. In January 1991, regiments from the 76th Guards Airborne Division in Pskov were flown into Vilnius. They were ordered to take control of key government installations and protect them from any actions by the Lithuanian nationalists. They were supported by small detachments from the KGB's Alfa Group and other KGB special operations forces. The plan was carried out brutally, and at least fourteen civilians were killed, most notoriously during the action at the Vilnius television tower. The VDV attack was recorded on video and soon was broadcast worldwide as another example of Soviet barbarism. Gorbachev's actions were clumsy and ill advised. They accomplished nothing in Lithuania. Instead of satisfying the demands of military hard-liners for a crackdown on separatists, they led to questions about Gorbachev's willingness to firmly defend the Soviet Union against disintegration. The VDV was all too willing to fight for Soviet unity, but the airborne officers were dismayed by the tendency to use military force in political disputes.

The chaotic situation was especially worrisome for the VDV, since more than half their units were in the breakaway republics. The 98th Guards Airborne, under the command of Afghan war hero Valery Vostrotin, was located in Ukraine. The 7th Guards Airborne was based around Kaunus in Lithuania. The 104th Guards Airborne was stationed in the most precarious location, near Kirovabad in Azerbaijan, where the officers' families were often at risk of attack from disgruntled Azeri nationalists. The 103rd Airborne Division was based near Vitebsk, in Byelarus.

MOSCOW COUP

On Saturday, 17 August 1991, Achalov ordered all VDV airborne divisions on the alert. Although there had been rumors of an "action" for months, most officers assumed that the divisions were preparing for another deployment into the hot spots in the Caucasus. Major General Aleksandr Lebyed, an Afghanistan veteran and commander of the 106th Guards Airborne Division in Tula, was told to prepare an "operational group," the Soviet term for a combat-ready task force. Like many Russians, Lebyed was on an August vacation. Curiously enough, so was Mikhail Gorbachev—resting at his dacha at Foros in the Crimea.

On Sunday, 18 August, the KGB mobilized the Alfa and Beta Groups, calling many of the key detachment commanders back from vacation. The group officers originally were told to prepare two Alfa detachments, about 200 troops in total, which were to be sent to the Transcaucasus region to free a group of Soviet soldiers being held hostage by local separatists. The "mission" was a complete fabrication.

A group of hard-liners calling themselves the State Committee for Emergency Rule (GKChP), including Defense Minister Yazov and KGB head Vladimir Kryuchkov, had decided to launch a surprise coup. A later Russian Republic KGB investigation fingered Kryuchkov as the prime organizer of the plot, and Oleg Baklanov and Oleg Shenin as his "clients." Baklanov was the head of the Soviet military industries; Gorbachev's "defense sufficiency" doctrine had led to massive defense cuts, and orders to this industry had declined 50 percent. Shenin was a leader of the conservative wing of the Communist Party; he feared that the upcoming union treaty on 20 August 1991 would place more power in the hands of non-Communist republic presidents such as the charismatic Russian leader Boris Yeltsin. The KGB had bugged a conversation between Yeltsin and the head of the Kazakh republic, Nursultan Nazarbayev, in which Yeltsin described Defense Minister Yazov, KGB chief Kryuchkov, and military industry chief Lukyanov as "particularly dangerous," and had pledged to reorganize the army and the KGB once the union treaty came into effect. The front man for the coup was the little-known Soviet vice president, Gennadiy Yanayev, whom the KGB judged to be suitably pliable.

The coup leaders were frustrated by Gorbachev's lack of resistance to the demands of the republic leaders for decentralizing control from Moscow and giving the regions more power. As the 1989 ballot had so clearly shown, any free elections led to sharp upsets for the ruling Communist Party, and the party bureaucrats were unwilling to give up their privileges or power. Army leaders such as Yazov and Achalov were dismayed by Gorbachev's surrender of the Warsaw Pact countries and felt that he was selling out to the United States through one-sided treaty concessions and military cutbacks. Gorbachev had effectively alienated every major power center: the Communist Party, the military-industrial complex, the KGB, and the army. All wanted him removed and replaced by a conservative ruling group more sympathetic to their interests.

The coup plan called for the army to deploy its two Moscow units, the 2nd Taman Guards Motor Rifle Division and the 4th Guards Kantemirovets Tank Division, into the city, supported by Lebyed's operational group of paratroopers, to "restore order." In fact, Moscow was quiet, with many families away on vacation on the Black Sea or resting in their tiny garden dachas in the Moscow suburbs. The plotters sent a delegation to Gorbachev's dacha on Sunday, 18 August, and put him under house arrest. No major armed detachments accompanied the delegation in spite of Gorbachev's formidable assortment of bodyguards and the extensive military patrols around the Foros compound. The coup plotters expected Gorbachev to accede to their demands, and perhaps even join in their action. Although Gorbachev refused to join their operation, his reaction was odd. He made no effort to resist the coup or communicate with other Soviet leaders during his house arrest even though he had the means to do so. Many of the plotters assumed that he was waiting to see the reaction to the coup. If accepted by Moscow and by world leaders, he could always change his mind and join his former colleagues; if resisted by Moscow and by world leaders, he could wash his hands of the whole affair and proclaim his innocence.

At 04:00 on Monday, 19 August, VDV commander Pavel Grachev was awakened at home and told to report to VDV staff headquarters in Sokolniki. Aleksandr Lebyed was ordered to begin moving his operational group into Moscow via Tushino air base in the Moscow suburbs. At 06:00, Moscow radio announced that the hitherto unknown State Committee for Emergency Rule, headed by the obscure Yanayev, had declared martial law "in order to root out shameful manifestations which discredit our society and humiliate Soviet citizens."

The general reaction in the Soviet Army was ambiguous. Many senior officers were away on vacation. Most officers were profoundly upset by the changes befalling the Soviet Union, but military action against the legal government had long been considered anathema to the Soviet officer corps. Few officers liked Russian leader Boris Yeltsin, and most presumed that the martial law decree had something to do with a Gorbachev-Yeltsin confrontation. But many of the officers were contemptuous of the plotters, viewing them as a bunch of mediocrities.

Grachev was one of the officers who was comfortable with Yeltsin's brand of Russian nationalism, and he received a telephone call from Yeltsin shortly after the radio announcement. Grachev promised that his paratroopers would not be used against Russian citizens. Relieved to hear Grachev's sensible declaration, Yeltsin asked him to dispatch a company of paratroopers to the Supreme Soviet of Russia, better known as the White House. Ironically, Grachev had already done so on the instructions of Yazov and the coup plotters, based on an earlier plan he had developed with Yazov under the Operation Metel/Operation Taifun scheme.

Yeltsin and the other leading Russian reformers gathered at a special government dacha complex at Arkhangelskoye, about thirty miles from the Kremlin. Unknown to them, the area was surrounded by a detachment of the KGB's Alfa Group. The team had been assigned by KGB chairman Kryuchkov to arrest Yeltsin. However, two of the three detachment commanders had serious reservations about attacking the dacha complex. While they were arguing, Yeltsin's limousine slipped out of Arkhangelskoye, heading toward central Moscow. About fifteen minutes later, an armored unit surrounded Arkhangelskoye, but by now the prey had fled. It was a critical failure, and symptomatic of the plotters' lack of legitimacy among the military and paramilitary leaders.

Units from Tula's 51st Guards Airborne Regiment and Ryazan's 137th Guards Airborne Regiment reached the outer ring road around Moscow by 10:00. Grachev ordered the 137th Guards to deploy its 2nd Battalion at the White House and its 3rd Battalion at the nearby Moscow City Council building. Other units were converging on the city by road from Tula and Ryazan, using their BMD armored vehicles.

By the time the paratroopers arrived, Boris Yeltsin had already climbed on a T-72B tank from the 2nd Guards Taman Motor Rifle Division and denounced the coup plotters. Moreover, Yeltsin announced that the armed forces stationed on Russian soil were now under the command of the lawfully elected Russian Republic government, not the self-appointed coup plotters. Radio broadcasts of the speech prompted thousands of Muscovites to gather around the White House to show their support of the reformers. The army units exhibited no interest in harming any of the curious spectators.

The plotters had seriously miscalculated in choosing the two army divisions to back up their plans. The 4th Kantemirovets Tank Division and 2nd Guards Taman Motor Rifle Division were "show" divisions used in the annual October Revolution and May Day parades in Red Square. They were pampered units that frequently choreographed displays of military firepower for foreign dignitaries at their bases outside Moscow. For many years, prominent Muscovites had pulled strings to get their sons sent to these divisions, since the soldiers received better food and accommodations and the conscripts were not subjected to the hazing or ethnic violence that had plagued the Soviet Army in its last decades. As a result, many of the raw recruits manning the tanks were from the Moscow area and had friends and family in the crowds. They either stayed neutral in the events of the day or openly sided with Yeltsin and the reformers. Furthermore, the tanks did not carry ammunition for their main guns, and the machine-gun ammunition was still under lock and key. The tanks were meant to intimidate, not fight, and the friendly smiles of the boyish tankers did not inspire fear in Yeltsin or the crowds. On Monday evening, the commander of the tank battalion stationed at the White House announced his unit's allegiance to the Yeltsin government.

It was evident to everyone by late afternoon that the coup had gone seriously wrong. No one had counted on Yeltsin mounting the tank and stirring up the crowd, and the plotters had failed to control radio and TV broadcasts of Yeltsin's inspiring call to action. The plotters had no control over the military forces in the city, and it appeared that the military units were siding with Yeltsin and the Parliament against Yanayev's State Committee. By evening, General Lebyed still had not been able to move a paratrooper battalion into the White House due to the size of the crowd. The plotters in the Kremlin grew concerned when they learned that Lebyed had been speaking with Yeltsin since 18:00. There were press reports on the international news services such as CNN that Lebyed and the paratroopers had gone over to Yeltsin's side.

In fact, Lebyed was trying to negotiate with the pro-Yeltsin forces to allow his paratrooper battalion to move into the White House, as ordered by the coup plotters themselves. The crowd did not trust the paratroopers, however, and would not let them pass through peacefully. Finally, around 23:00 on 19 August, the two battalions were allowed into the White House and the City Council building, but they were not allowed to move their BMD vehicles. The reformers still suspected that the paratroopers were loyal to Defense Minister Yazov, whereas Yazov and the coup plotters were concerned that they had gone over to Yeltsin's side. Everyone's nerves were frayed from the chaotic nature of the coup, and it was clear that the army units were entirely confused about their mission. It was quite possible that some units would refuse to obey orders, or that civilians might provoke some soldiers and start an unwanted fight.

There were signs that the plotters planned to seize the White House on the night of 19–20 August using elements of Major General Gusha's KGB special operations units and the Dzerzhinskiy Division. However, the Dzerzhinskiy division troops had a difficult time reaching the White House due to roadblocks set up by Afghan veterans and students. The attack was probably called off because of uncertainty about the loyalty of Lebyed's paratroopers and fear that fighting between army units and the internal security units could precipitate civil war.

OPERATION GROM

On Tuesday, 20 August, more airborne units were arriving at the main staging area at Tushino air base in Moscow's northwest suburbs. Two regiments from Vostrotin's 96th Guards Airborne Division in Bolgrad, Ukraine, were scheduled to leave for Moscow in the afternoon to further reinforce the growing VDV presence in the capital. By early Tuesday morning, Grachev had grown worried that his troops at the White House might be provoked by the crowds, leading to unwanted bloodshed. Contrary to his orders from Yazov, he decided to pull back his two battalions from central Moscow. Ironically, the Yeltsin forces in the White House, who had resisted allowing the paratroopers into the building for much of the previous day, suddenly felt uncomfortable having the men leave. Yeltsin's military adviser, Yuri Rodionov, tried to telephone Grachev to ask him to keep the paratroopers in place to protect Yeltsin, but he was unable to reach him.

The questionable loyalty of army and KGB units already in Moscow led the plotters to take desperate measures. The KGB chairman, Kryuchkov, sent a special coded command to KGB special operations units, and to the 103rd Guards Airborne Division in Vitebsk, to move into Moscow. The 103rd Airborne had been specifically subordinated to the KGB in the early 1990s for contingencies such as these. Yazov ordered the 28th Guards Motor Rifle Division, which had been used in the 1990 Baku operation, to be flown to Moscow. Yazov and Kryuchkov did not know that air force commander Yevgeniy Shapashnikov had already taken steps to prevent the air force from undertaking any such airlifts.

At 14:00, Grachev and Lebyed were called to Defense Minister Yazov's office and asked to report on the situation. With a straight face, Grachev said that his units "were ready to fulfill their orders"— when in fact he had pulled out his troops hours before. Yazov, exhausted and distracted, assumed this meant that his battalions were still stationed at the White House.

On Tuesday afternoon around 14:30, a special meeting was held in the Ministry of Defense building on Arbat Street. It included Colonel General Achalov, chief of the General Staff Mikhail Moiseyev, and Gorbachev's personal military adviser, Marshal S. K. Akhromeyev. The group was visited periodically by Marshal Yazov. By evening, it was clear that the regular army units were unwilling to take any violent action against Yeltsin or other opposition leaders. Instead, the military decided to dust off a variation of Operation Metel, called Operation Grom (thunder). The 19th Dzerzhinskiy Special Operations Motor Rifle Division of the MVD would use water cannon, tear gas, or force to create a corridor through the crowds at the White House, and the paratroopers would provide any backup needed. This would enable the KGB Alfa Group personnel to get into the building, where they would arrest Yeltsin and Russian Parliament leaders. The Alfa Group would be backed up by Beta Group, part of which would be landed on the roof of the White House. Besides the 200-man Alfa Group unit, there were about 400 other KGB troops involved in Operation Grom.

The head of Alfa Group, Maj. Gen. Viktor Karpukhin, was given his orders: H hour would be 03:00 the following morning, Wednesday, 21 August. Karpukhin was a rare KGB officer, having seen extensive combat duty and having been awarded a secret Hero of the Soviet Union distinction for his role in KGB special operations in Afghanistan. Karpukhin was now faced with the same dilemma of many Russian commanders: he had no enthusiasm for the junta leaders, was wary of participating in the rapidly unraveling coup attempt, and had no interest in ordering his men to attack—and possibly kill—prominent Russian political leaders such as Yeltsin. Karpukhin also knew that if he refused to carry out his orders, the KGB leaders aligned with the plot would simply replace him with a more pliant KGB officer. He received a telephone call from the chairman of the Russian branch of the KGB, Maj. Gen. Viktor Ivanenko, warning him not to allow his unit to take part in any actions against Yeltsin. Other officers at the conference recalled that Karpukhin looked extremely depressed. The stress had a telling effect, and Karpukhin was obliged to take an extra dose of his heart medication. In the late afternoon, he visited the White House with the airborne commander Aleksandr Lebyed and surveyed the site for possible deployments.

At 17:30, Karpukhin returned to the Alfa Group base and called to his office the two officers commanding the mobilized Alfa Group detachments. Both were told that they were under government orders to carry out Operation Grom. The two officers, Lt. Col. Mikhail Golovatov and Lt. Col. Sergey Goncharov, looked at each other and rolled their eyes. They asked who had issued the order, and Karpukhin repeated that it was "a government order." After leaving the office, Goncharov and Golovatov decided that they would drag their feet. They gathered together their unit commanders and, in an action completely out of character with the KGB, they told their unit leaders to poll the men about the mission. Almost unanimously, the men answered that the order was illegal and against the constitution. When Karpukhin was so informed, he threatened to court-martial both officers, although he realized that without their cooperation, it was unlikely that Alfa Group would be a viable combat unit. Preparations were made in a halfhearted fashion, but there was a consensus that no action would be taken.

Karpukhin attempted to confer with Kryuchkov, head of the KGB and one of the main coup plotters. When Kryuchkov declined to meet, Karpukhin made it clear to Kryuchkov's deputy that his unit had refused to storm the White House. The KGB was not the only source of problems. Air force helicopter units would not become involved in the plan to land part of the KGB force on the roof of the White House. The accumulating refusals had a domino effect, and group after group rebuffed the plotters.

Following the afternoon Ministry of Defense meeting, Pavel Grachev returned to the VDV Airborne Force headquarters at Sokolniki and brought his staff together. He informed them that the commands to attack the White House were illegal and that the VDV was now under his personal command. He also told the officers that should he be arrested, they were to take orders from his fellow Afghanistan comrade Aleksandr Lebyed, who he knew was opposed to the coup. By late afternoon, it was clear that many military leaders had finally decided against supporting the coup. Grachev spoke with air force commander Yevgeniy Shapashnikov, who had been attempting to obstruct Yazov's orders through much of the day. Shapashnikov and Grachev agreed that their military units would avoid any actions that would lead to "irreversible consequences." Shapashnikov at one point had two strike aircraft loaded up with bombs to attack the plotters in the Kremlin if necessary. Grachev and Shapashnikov considered conducting a paratrooper attack on the Kremlin but ruled it out, fearing that the large KGB detachments would have the advantage since they knew the terrain inside the old fortress complex. The two leaders decided instead to continue their passive resistance.

At 01:00, two hours before the scheduled mission, Karpukhin had nearly broken under the strain and was drunk. He telephoned Pavel Grachev, head of the airborne forces. Obviously upset, Karpukhin told the younger commander that he had decided against the attack. Grachev had already made the same decision himself, and told Karpukhin so.

Colonel General Achalov went to the White House at 01:00 on the morning of 21 August 1991, expecting that Operation Grom would soon take place. Instead, he found a scene of utter confusion, with a hugh crowd of more than seventy thousand civilians milling about. Three KGB and MVD companies did get into the immediate area of the White House, but it must have been readily apparent that something had gone terribly wrong. The police were spotted by informal security units protecting the White House, but the KGB and MVD units made no attempts to execute their phase of Grom alone. When Achalov realized that the operation was not taking place, he returned to the Ministry of Defense building and reported to Yazov that any further action before dawn would be very difficult and might not succeed anyway. There was no one the plotters could trust to carry out their schemes. Exhausted and depressed, Yazov decided to withdraw military support from the coup attempt.

At an 08:00 meeting at the Ministry of Defense, Shapashnikov recommended to Yazov that he resign and that the military declare the coup illegal. The military leaders agreed to withdraw all forces from Moscow. By afternoon, the troops were pulling out of the city and the coup had completely crumbled. Within a few days, Marshal Yazov and the other coup leaders had been arrested; Colonel General Achalov was sent to a sanitorium "for health reasons"; and Gorbachev's personal military adviser, Marshal Akhromeyev, committed suicide for his role in the plot and his personal betrayal. Major General Karpukhin was replaced as head of Alfa Group by Colonel Golovatov.

Why did the Soviet elite formations refuse to obey orders and cause the coup to collapse? It is premature to make any definitive assessment, since the subject is still a political hot potato in Moscow. The few personal accounts by participants are self-serving, contradictory, and distorted by subsequent events. Some suppositions are possible. The inaction by most of the military during the coup was the result of a passivity deliberately cultivated over generations by Russia's leaders. Boris Yeltsin later wrote in his memoirs: "There exists a very peculiar attitude towards power in Russia. The government has always been perceived as the incarnation of some kind of all-pervasive force, so terrifying and invincible that even the thought of attempting an overthrow, a coup, a rebellion, seems quite absurd." But a handful of key officers were not guided by timorous passivity and took action in spite of the risks.

One link between most of the groups refusing to participate or passively resisting orders was the common experience of Afghanistan. There was a widespread sense of victimization among many of the officers of the VDV and KGB special forces who had served during this hard-fought war. The Kremlin had censored the war until the final dismal year, denying the officers the glory and honor they felt they deserved. Returning Afghan veterans were not greeted by the type of adulation and respect afforded their fathers' generation after World War II; instead they were ignored. Many senior officers felt that the Afghan war had been a mistake: not a valiant-but-failed effort, but a malign, stupid error by geriatric political hacks. Disillusioned by their war experiences, the VDV leadership was sympathetic to reform efforts. American readers might draw some parallels between the post-Afghanistan experience and America's post-Vietnam experience, but this would be stretching the point too far. The Soviet Army was far more politicized than the U.S. Army, and the Soviet Army had been a king maker several times in the past, most notably the 1953 power struggle. This tradition made some Russian officers far more willing to act on their own once the legitimacy of the orders came under question.

The commitment of the officer corps to the Kremlin also was being undermined by other forces let loose by Gorbachev's perestroika. The Soviet Army's influential *Military History Journal (Voenno-Istorichesskiy Zhurnal)* had begun running a series of articles detailing the previously suppressed story of the purges of the Red Army in 1937–39, the mistreatment of senior officers by Trotsky during the civil war, the humiliation of senior army and navy commanders in the 1950s by Khrushchev, and other abuses by the Communist Party and the KGB against the armed forces. At the same time, there was a revival of Russian nationalism in the army, which had the unintentional consequence of corroding allegiance to the Communist Party. Russian military traditions, particularly those associated with the glories of the Napoleonic Wars, were being recalled after decades of Communist suppression. The ethnic conflicts in the Caucasus led many VDV officers to question why Russia should continue to bear the economic and social burdens of the Soviet empire.

This brewing stew of discontent flavored the reaction of commanders such as Grachev and Shapashnikov when instructed to carry out the coup. Many officers feared that any military participation in the coup would eventually lead to significant bloodshed in the streets of Moscow, pitting Russian soldiers against Russian civilians, and perhaps even leading to civil war. The VDV officers, who had first-hand experience with the horror of civil war in Armenia, Azerbaijan, and Afghanistan, could not contemplate unleashing these hellish forces on their own people. Also, the coup plotters had little respect among the military leaders; most realized that it was the KGB and Communist Party bureaucrats behind the plot, and not the feckless Marshal Yazov. Against these negative influences, some officers saw positive alternatives. Yeltsin and the reformers were not widely liked by the military, but they were recognized as representing a legitimate Russian revival in the face of Communist decay. Some officers half-heartedly obeyed the plotters' commands but recognized that the rank-and-file conscripts might switch sides if violence was ordered. Most officers found the choice of supporting or not supporting the coup too difficult, and dragged their feet. Only a few officers actively disobeyed their orders; even then, they did so in a conspiratorial fashion to minimize the risk of being arrested by pro-coup forces. But this confusing blend of reactions, combined with the halfhearted, drunken conduct of the plotters themselves, was sufficient to doom the coup.

The plotters' startling ineptitude led to precisely the events they had hoped to prevent. They had unwittingly provided the Russian reformers with the pretext for a real coup to sweep away the rotting remnants of the Communist Party. There was lingering suspicion that Gorbachev was somehow linked to the plot and that his opponents used his muddled reaction to the August events to circumvent his authority. On 8 December 1991, Presidents Boris Yeltsin of the Russian Republic, Stanislav Shushkevich of the Republic of Byelarus, and Leonid Kravchuk of Ukraine signed a document attesting to the fact that "the USSR, as a subject of international law and a geopolitical reality, ceases to exist."

Chapter 14
Russian Airborne

The demise of the Soviet Union, and with it the Soviet Army, had an agonizing impact on the VDV Airborne Force. Of its six airborne divisions, four were located in republics outside of Russia. From 1992 to 1994, the central focus of the VDV was to return these units to Russia and rebuild them. The special attention paid to the VDV was based on the increased importance that such highly mobile units have in the post–Cold War world. Not surprisingly, several of the newly independent republics were also impressed with the VDV's record and took steps to include airborne units in their new armed forces, often based on VDV units. The VDV divisions have been involved in peacekeeping attempts in the former Soviet Union almost continually since 1988, and this situation is unlikely to change in the foreseeable future. The problems afflicting the airborne formations in these turbulent years were a reflection of the changes occurring throughout the former Soviet Army. In the long run, Russian military planners expect that the VDV will play a central role in the new Mobile Force that will form the core of the reconstituted Russian Army.

RETURN TO THE HOMELAND

Some Soviet Army units left outside of Russia were allowed to transfer their allegiance to the local republic's government, but the new Russian General Staff specifically identified the VDV units as strategic assets that would not fall under republic control. In any case, the VDV's troop strength was disproportionately Russian, Ukrainian, and Byelorussian, since the division had enjoyed preferred recruitment of conscripts through the last three decades of the Soviet Union. At first, the Russian Federation hoped to establish an alliance system called the Confederation of Independent States (CIS, or SNG in Russian). Each republic would control its own tactical army and air force units, whereas strategic units would come under joint CIS control. The most important of these strategic units were, of course, the strategic nuclear missile and strategic air defense systems. But Moscow placed a high premium on the VDV and included these among the strategic joint forces.

The head of the new CIS Unified Forces was Marshal Yevgeniy Shapashnikov. Shapashnikov, former head of the Soviet Air Force, won Boris Yeltsin's approval for his role in resisting the August 1991 coup. Shapashnikov's task was daunting. The former Soviet Army was in chaos, with units moving back to Russia from Germany, Poland, and Czechoslovakia. There was little or no housing at the new bases, and soldiers and their families were living in tents and warehouses at the height of the Russian winter. The Yeltsin government wanted to cut back on the size of the armed forces. Troops were demobilized without any system to ease them back into civilian life. At the same time, the Soviet Army was in the process of switching from a conscript-based army to a partly professional army in the enlisted ranks, which only added to the chaos.

Several of the newly independent republics, notably Ukraine, were not happy with the CIS concept, feeling that it was nothing more than a Russian attempt to reassert control over their armed forces. There was vigorous debate between Moscow and the newly independent republics over which units would be allowed to revert to local republican control and which would return to Russia. In the case of the Caucasus and Central Asia, the Russians wanted as few sophisticated weapons as possible to fall into local hands, rightly fearing that a sudden weapons glut would feed the flames of interethnic conflict and civil war.

The dilemma with Ukraine and Byelarus was somewhat different. There was little fear that either republic would pose a direct conventional threat to Russia. But the deployment pattern of Soviet forces during the Cold War had put a disproportionate share of the most modern conventional weaponry in the western sections of the USSR, namely Byelarus and Ukraine. The weapons stockpiles in Russia, ironically, were old and outdated, since they constituted the rear area in any Warsaw Pact/NATO confrontation. Moscow was reluctant to part with all this hardware and suggested that it be placed under CIS control. Byelarus was far more pliant in these cases than Ukraine, as nationalist sentiment there had never been as strong.

These arguments dragged on for nearly two years. But by the summer of 1993, the CIS Unified Forces concept was a dead issue. Ukraine had nationalized nearly all of the units on its soil, as had Byelarus. Strategic nuclear weapons and the Black Sea Fleet remained bones of contention, but the conventional forces issue resolved itself in favor of local control. One of the few exceptions was the VDV Airborne Force, which remained under Russian control through these turbulent years.

Complicating the chaos in the new Russian Army was the bloodshed occurring along Russia's frontiers. The former Soviet republics, now called the "near-abroad," were disintegrating in a wave of ethnic bloodshed and turmoil. The worst-hit areas were the Caucasus, but fighting also flared up in European areas such as Moldova, and in Central Asia. Russian units were sometimes being withdrawn under fire.

While Shapashnikov, as head of the CIS Unified Forces, argued with the republics, young Pavel Grachev was faced with the formidable problems confronting the Russian armed forces. Grachev's refusal to back the August 1991 coup had won the favorable attention of Boris Yeltsin, who appointed him Russian defense minister in May 1992, at the ripe old age of forty-four.

Grachev's strong ties with the VDV divisions in the separate republics were a major factor in Russia's retention of these units. Grachev saw the VDV as a reliable core for the new Russian Army, and an indispensable force for the turbulent years ahead. The VDV's unique capabilities were unavailable elsewhere in the Soviet Army. Grachev convinced Shapashnikov and the rest of Russia's military leaders to categorize the VDV as a strategic asset and not allow it to slip under the control of the republics. "Pasha" Grachev could count on the loyalty of the airborne officers, having served with nearly all of the divisional commanders at one time or another in Afghanistan.

Fate of the VDV Airborne Divisions

Unit	1990 Location	1994 Location
7th Guards Airborne Division	Kaunus, Lithuania	Novorossisk, Russia
76th Guards Airborne Division	Pskov, Russia	Pskov, Russia
98th Guards Airborne Division	Bolgrad, Ukraine	Ivanovo, Russia
103rd Guards Airborne Division	Vitebsk, Byelarus	Byelorussian army
104th Guards Airborne Division	Gyandzha, Azerbaijan	Ulyanovsk, Russia
105th Guards Airborne Division	Fergana, Uzbekistan	Disbanded
106th Guards Airborne Division	Tula, Russia	Tula, Russia

THE FIRST WAVE IN UKRAINE

In the summer of 1991, the 98th Guards Airborne Division at Bolgrad (Belgorod in Ukrainian), near Odessa, received instructions from the new Ukrainian government to swear allegiance to the Ukrainian armed forces. The division staff and most of the troops simply refused. The division had a large number of Ukrainians in it, but divisional loyalty and loyalty to the VDV Airborne Force took precedence over ethnic roots. The Odessa region around the airborne base is heavily Russian, and Ukrainian officials prudently avoided confrontations with the airborne forces over this issue. At the time, the new Kravchuk government had its hands full with arguments over the fate of the Black Sea Fleet and strategic nuclear weapons in Ukraine.

The situation on many Soviet bases in Ukraine deteriorated through 1991 and 1992. There were arguments over whether the Russian or Ukrainian government was responsible for pay and food, so frequently the units went without both. This led to demoralization and desertion. Some officers began to sell off army property, such as trucks or fuel, to pay for essentials. These improvised attempts at army finance sometimes degenerated into widespread theft and looting. The VDV units fared better, since their neighboring VTA transport units gave them a link to Russia for supplies. In February 1992, a confrontation occurred when Ukrainian authorities prevented the 98th Airborne Division from being mobilized when ordered by the Kremlin to move into Chechenia to calm down an ethnic dispute. Ukrainian forces were sent to block the runways at the base. Bloodshed was avoided only because the Ukrainian commander was an old friend of the airborne commander, and neither side wished to come to blows. The mission to Chechenia was canceled as a result of the dispute.

Ukrainian pressure was more successful outside the division. In February 1992, the independent airborne brigade stationed at Bolshaya Korenikha went over to the Ukrainian army against the wishes of its commander, Col. A. Loginov, and without Moscow's knowledge. The troops in the unit were allowed to decide for themselves whether to stay in Ukraine or not, and they had become fed up with the constant problems over food and pay. The example set by this brigade convinced the Russian General Staff to negotiate over the fate of the 98th Guards Airborne Division before similar events happened.

A year later, agreement was reached that the 98th Guards Airborne Division would be withdrawn from Belgorod, and its major equipment divided between Russia and Ukraine. The Ukrainian army wanted to keep much of the specialized airborne equipment to form its own 1st Mobile Air Assault Division. A significant number of Ukrainian paratroopers agreed to stay, about 40 percent of the division; others transferred from divisions still in Russia. The pullout began in January 1993, and by April most of the 98th Airborne Division had been moved to the Ivanovo district, northeast of Moscow in the Russian Federation. Both the 23rd Separate Airborne Brigade at Kremenchug and the 40th Separate Airborne Brigade at Nikolayev were left under Ukrainian control, but the airborne training regiment at Lvov was transferred to Saratov in Russia, where it was reconstituted as the 159th Separate Airborne Training Regiment.

The Spetsnaz suffered a particularly hard blow when the 10th Spetsnaz Brigade in Izyaslav was turned over to the command of Col. Pavel Davidyuk of the Ukrainian army in 1992. This brigade had served in the 1968 Czechoslovak invasion. Its 2nd Battalion had served in Afghanistan, where three of its soldiers were awarded the Hero of the Soviet Union distinction, making the unit the most highly decorated of its size in the Soviet Union. The Spetsnaz brigades were particularly vulnerable to amalgamation into local armies, since they tended to depend more heavily on reservists in the local area who were not interested in moving their families to Russia under such uneasy conditions.

The fate of the 810th Naval Infantry Brigade of the Black Sea Fleet in Sevastopol was somewhat more complicated. Because of disputes between Ukraine and Russia over the fate of the fleet, the Russian officers heading the fleet strongly urged the brigade's commander, Col. A. Kochenkov, to prevent heavily Ukrainian units from voluntarily taking the Ukrainian oath. In March 1992, however, after a series of disagreements, Maj. Vitaly Rozhman's battalion decided to take the Ukrainian oath, and the unit was attached to the Ukrainian armed forces. The rest of the brigade remained under Russian control. With Rozhman's battalion gone, the brigade soon earned a reputation for being one of the most nationalist Russian units in the fleet. In February 1993, it was involved in a mock attack on a nearby Ukrainian air defense missile regiment, which nearly resulted in the first major outbreak of fighting between Ukrainian and Russian forces.

THE MOLDOVAN MORASS

Trouble was also brewing in Moldova, on the Ukrainian border. The Moldovan Republic was a region that had been seized from Romania in 1940. The area of Moldova west of the Dnestr River was mainly Romanian-speaking, but the region east of the river was predominantly Ukrainian. Moldova had attempted to separate from the remains of the USSR in 1991, and laid claim to the east-bank area as well. The Ukrainians and Russians in this region were unwilling to join Moldova, since they worried that it would soon merge with Romania. They announced the formation of a separate state called the Dnestr-Moldovan Republic (PMR). As a result, there was continual fighting between the PMR and Moldova through 1992. Much of the military equipment for the PMR came from former Soviet Army arsenals, and their troops were a mixture of former Soviet Army volunteers, mercenaries, and newly formed "Cossack" units. The position of the former Soviet 14th Army was awkward: it was supposed to maintain neutrality, but most Russian and Ukrainian troops had no sympathy for the Moldovan separatist movement. Tensions were further heightened when in December 1991, the Moldovan government laid claim to all former Soviet Army units on its soil. The 300th Guards Airborne Regiment was in a particularly awkward position due to its location near Kishniev, the Moldovan capital. The regiment was commanded by Col. Aleksei Lebyed, the younger brother of Gen. Aleksandr Lebyed.

In June 1992, after a string of Moldovan provocations, General Lebyed was sent to the region by Yeltsin to determine what should be done. Lebyed judged the situation intolerable and mobilized a cadre unit, the 59th Guards Motor Rifle Division, which was the only major element in the 14th Army, aside from the paratroopers, that was still under Moscow's control. Lebyed's actions were the source of considerable controversy, since it was widely suspected that he had been given secret orders to crack down on the Moldovans. He was widely portrayed as a local warlord, carrying out his own agenda.

Lebyed's reservists were not entirely adequate for peacekeeping but managed to put a lid on the troubles until a more substantial force could be organized. Given his paratrooper background, Lebyed asked a friend, Defense Minister Pavel Grachev, to dispatch a VDV formation. By late summer, an operational group was formed by taking an airborne battalion from VDV units in Pskov, Ryazan, and Kostroma. This operational group was used to impose order in the border areas between the left and right banks of the Dnestr River. It was replaced by the 137th Airborne Regiment of the 106th Airborne Division in 1992. The 300th Airborne Regiment was withdrawn from Kishniev in the autumn of 1992 and transferred to a new base in Abakan, Siberia. A portion of their BMD armored vehicles was left behind for the Moldovan forces, who planned to form their own airborne unit.

BYELORUSSIAN SPECIAL OPERATIONS FORCES

The Russian General Staff was less reluctant than the units in Ukraine to see special operations units in Byelarus take the oath of allegiance to the new republic. The Byelarus government had far more amicable ties with Moscow than did the Ukrainian government, and had been one of the earliest supporters of the CIS Unified Forces concept. Although Byelarus did nationalize most of the conventional forces on its soil in 1992, it refrained from creating any incidents by allowing the 103rd Guards Airborne in Vitebsk to remain under CIS control. By 1993, the CIS had become a dead issue, and the 103rd

Airborne was transferred to Byelorussian command. The neighboring VTA regiment, however, flew many of its IL-76T transport aircraft back to Pskov in Russia to reinforce the 76th Guards Airborne Division.

The Spetsnaz lost another of its premier units in Byelorussia. The 5th Spetsnaz Brigade in Marina Gora was transferred to the Byelorussian army in 1992. This was the largest single Spetsnaz brigade, because it was usually kept on a wartime footing due to its proximity to NATO borders. It had served as a test bed for experimental tactics and technology, including recent experiments in the use of powered hang gliders for the insertion of Spetsnaz troops behind NATO lines.

Russian Spetsnaz Force 1993

Unit	Location	Military District
2nd Spetsnaz Brigade	Pskov	Leningrad
3rd Spetsnaz Brigade	Samara	Urals
12th Spetsnaz Brigade	Lagodekhi	Transcaucasus
14th Spetsnaz Brigade	Ussurisk	Far Eastern
16th Spetsnaz Brigade	Chuchkovo	Moscow
22nd Spetsnaz Brigade	Aksai	North Caucasus
24th Spetsnaz Brigade	Kyakhta	Baikal
67th Spetsnaz Brigade	Berdsk	Siberian
1071st Spetsnaz Training Regiment	Pechori	Leningrad

AIRBORNE IN THE BALTIC

Although the Russian General Staff was willing to transfer units to Byelarus, hard feelings still remained between the Russians and the Balts. The 7th Guards Airborne Division was stationed at Kaunus, Lithuania. Russian nationalist hard-liners were reluctant to allow the Baltic states to leave Russian control, since the area's excellent ports represented a significant strategic interest to Russia. The 7th Guards Airborne Division remained in Kaunus as part of Russian pressure on Lithuania and the other Baltic states in ongoing disputes over sovereignty and the future of Russian military installations in the Baltic. After a series of agreements with the Lithuanian government, the 7th Guards Airborne Division began its move in 1993. It was transferred to Novorossisk in southern Russia near the Caucasus as part of an effort to build up the new Group of Russian Forces–Transcaucasus (GRVZ) near this troubled region. The 242nd Airborne Training Regiment was moved from Jonova (Gaujunai) to Omsk in the Urals.

CENTRAL ASIAN AIRBORNE

A fifth, partial VDV division was left behind in Uzbekistan. The 105th Guards Airborne Division was disbanded in 1978–79 to provide troops for the expanding air assault brigades. Its 345th Guards Airborne Regiment had served as an independent unit in Afghanistan, and its 387th Airborne Regiment had formed the basis for the Afghan VDV combat training regiment. In 1991, amidst all the turmoil, it was decided to bring the division back up to strength using the 387th Airborne Regiment as its cadre. Only two of the division's three regiments were actually in Uzbekistan; one was located at Eolotan, Turkmenistan, and another at Kapchugai in neighboring Kazakhstan. Considering the incomplete status of the division, in 1992 it was agreed to leave it behind to help the Uzbek government form a reinforced airborne regiment. Many Russian officers remained behind due to the lack of airborne-qualified Uzbeks. The independent airborne brigade at Kapchugai, Kazakhstan, was left under Kazakh control to form the basis for a Kazakh VDV force.

Another veteran formation from the Afghanistan war also transferred to the Uzbek army. The 15th Spetsnaz Brigade in Chirchik, Uzbekistan, was transferred over to the Uzbek army in 1992. The 15th Spetsnaz Brigade had provided most of the troops of the famous Muslim Battalion that spearheaded the 1979 Afghanistan invasion, and the brigade had formed the basis for one of the two Spetsnaz brigades that served in Afghanistan later in the war.

Uzbekistan formed the staging area for one of the most difficult VDV missions in 1992. In August, nearly four years after the Soviet pullout from Afghanistan, the mujahideen finally overcame their bickering and assaulted Kabul. The Kremlin thought it prudent to evacuate Russian embassy personnel but realized that a military escort would be needed. The job, needless to say, fell on the airborne troops. A special task force was prepared of thirty-four troops headed by Lt. Col. Nikolai Ivonik, an Afghan veteran familiar with Kabul airport. The task force was raised from Maj. Gen. Aleksandr Kolmakov's 106th Guards Airborne Division in Tula.

The task force landed at Kabul airport in two IL-76 transport aircraft and came under immediate mortar and small-arms fire from nearby hills. The Soviet embassy personnel, along with most of the Chinese and Mongolian delegations, were already huddling in one of the airport buildings. The evacuation took place under continual fire from the mujahideen in neighboring hills. The first aircraft was loaded safely and departed with only minor damage, but the second transport was badly damaged. Much to their chagrin, the paratroopers and embassy personnel had to wait for another aircraft. The paratroopers established a defensive perimeter near one of the airfield buildings, and the group settled down for an uneasy night. The VDV commander located a functional Afghan transport at the base, and the Russian ambassador convinced the Afghan government authorities to provide fuel and allow the group to use it in place of the damaged transport. The embassy group was quickly loaded aboard the aircraft and took off with the dull thuds of small-arms fire heard ripping into the plane's fuselage and wings. It recalled the evacuation of the American embassy in Saigon two decades earlier. One of the paratroopers assigned to the mission, Sen. Sgt. Sergei Arefiev, was awarded one of the first "Hero of Russia" distinctions for valor for his bravery during the operation.

BLOODY CAUCASUS

Amidst all the turmoil of the early 1990s, the VDV remained the Kremlin's choice when it came to rapid-reaction forces for peace-keeping missions. Its most unhappy experiences took place in Azerbaijan in the Caucasus region. The Caucasus had been a hot spot for the Tsarist army for centuries, and it promises to remain so over the next decade. As described earlier, the airborne had been involved in peacekeeping missions there in the Soviet era in 1988–90. The area is extremely mountainous, and such terrain fosters isolated ethnic groupings and deeply rooted hatreds. The ethnic disputes in the Caucasus paralleled the wars in Yugoslavia and were equally as bloody; the fighting was less publicized in the West, however, as few sensible journalists would venture into this dangerous area.

The 104th Guards Airborne Division was based at Gyandzha, Azerbaijan (formerly Kirovabad). The paratroopers were widely hated by the local Azeris, who felt that the Russians invariably supported their enemies, the Armenians. This sentiment stemmed from the Soviet intervention in January 1990 when Russian units, including the 104th Airborne, were used to put down the bloody Azeri rampage against the Armenians in Baku. Nearly a thousand Azeris were killed or wounded in the fighting. Even after Azerbaijan declared its independence, Moscow was reluctant to pull out the division, since it might prove useful in peacekeeping operations in the tense Caucasus area. From 1989 to 1993, the 104th Airborne endured nearly four years of fighting, sometimes within the main garrison at Gyandzha. Local Azeri militias made repeated raids on divisional warehouses in attempts to steal arms. More worrisome to the officers were the attacks on base housing. The division finally had to set up patrols in the city to prevent injury to their families. On numerous occasions, unarmed officers and enlisted men would be kidnapped off the street. They were often humiliated or tortured before their release by the militants as a reminder of who was now in charge in Azerbaijan.

By 1991, a full-scale war had broken out between Azerbaijan and neighboring Armenia over the fate of the isolated Nagorno-Karabakh region. Although the Russian General Staff had planned to use the airborne forces for such peacekeeping missions, this was made difficult by the Azeri campaign of harassment and intimidation directed against the Gyandzha base. In May 1992, an agreement was finally reached between Moscow and Baku for the evacuation of all Russian forces from Azerbaijan over a two-year period. It was precipitated in part by a controversial operation in the disputed Nagorno-Karabakh area that involved the paratroopers. This was a rare case where two Russian units almost came to blows.

This odd and bitter encounter took place in May 1992. Nagorno-Karabakh is a mountainous valley region inside Azerbaijan but populated mainly by Armenians. It is separated from Armenia by a narrow strip called the Nachin corridor. After enduring years of harassment by the Azeris, the Armenians were determined to reunite Nagorno-Karabakh with the remainder of their newly independent country.

The 366th Motor Rifle Regiment, stationed in Stepanakert since 1986, was the only major Russian formation in the disputed area. It had earned the enmity of the local Armenian population in July 1990 when it took part in a crackdown after a decree by Mikhail Gorbachev banning the paramilitary militias in the province. Following the abortive coup of August 1991, the situation had rapidly deteriorated: both Armenia and Azerbaijan declared their independence from Moscow. The garrisons in the valleys were pummeled by Armenian artillery fire, and sniper fire from the hills was a constant threat. Russian sources claimed that the fedayeen guerrilla militias numbered 140,000 men, a figure that was widely regarded as an exaggeration. Although the region was clearly in the grip of war fever, Moscow instructed the regimental commander that under no circumstances were the Russian troops to return fire, since negotiations were under way to bring the fighting to an end.

The situation in the regiment was complicated by the number of Armenian officers and troops in the unit, along with some Russians who were sympathetic to the local fedayeen militias. In December 1991, several of the younger officers began to organize a scheme to mount up the regiment and their family members in the armored troop carriers and drive out of the mountains into Russia, using armed force if necessary. In all likelihood, the plotters were intending to head for the 104th Airborne garrison at Gyandzha, about seventy miles away. Word of the plotting reached Moscow, and a delegation was sent to make it clear to the young hotheads what their fate would be if they took matters into their own hands.

The near mutiny led Moscow to allow the regimental commander greater discretion in carrying out military actions to defend the unit. Tragedy resulted. During the last week of February 1992, units from the regiment took part in combat actions alongside Armenian forces near the Azeri town of Khodzaly. Some of the troops were apparently sympathetic to the Armenians, but others had been paid off by the local Armenian militias. There was a massacre in Khodzaly on 26 February, and the 366th Regiment was held to be complicitous in the atrocities. Azeri officials threatened to retaliate against Russian units, such as the 104th Airborne, elsewhere in Azerbaijan if action wasn't taken. The Russian Ministry of Defense decided to pull the unit out before further troubles erupted.

Rumors spread that the regiment was to be withdrawn to Gyandzha, in Azerbaijan. Armenian troops in the unit were infuriated that they were being transferred into the middle of "enemy" country. Russian soldiers felt they had been betrayed. The Azeris surely would view them as pro-Armenian after the Khodzaly massacre and would probably try to retaliate. Moscow received word that the regiment was on the verge of disintegrating, with pro-Armenian elements in the unit going over to the fedayeen side with their equipment, and the Russians trying a suicidal "breakout" attempt for Russia. Finally, the regiment was ordered to prepare to be airlifted out of the Stepanakert area.

The airlift was preceded by the dispatch of a VDV airborne group and a Spetsnaz detachment. Although the objective of this operational group was to prevent Armenian irregulars from interfering with the airlift, the group was ordered to take control of the 366th Motor Rifle Regiment, by force if necessary, to prevent desertions or other unauthorized actions. On 1 March 1992, the operational group landed near the regimental headquarters, took command of the unit, and arrested a number of troops. Several soldiers were found to have unusually large amounts of cash, which seemed to give evidence to Azeri charges that the unit had been bribed to provide support to the Armenians. One of the regimental officers, distraught over the charges of treason and mutiny, wrapped himself in the regimental flag and committed suicide. Over the next several days, the regiment was evacuated by helicopter to other Russian bases in the region while the airborne operational group kept watch. Even with the Spetsnaz and paratroopers present, a few units "surrendered" to the fedayeen while moving toward the departure area, providing the local Armenian forces with several ZSU-23-4 Shilka self-propelled air defense vehicles and most of the regiment's artillery equipment. The airborne troops destroyed any material that could not be airlifted out by helicopter. Following the withdrawal, about 180 troops were still unaccounted for; it was not clear if all the missing were deserters, or whether some might be hostages to local Armenian or Azeri militias. The VDV paratroopers were bitter about being sent in to "capture" a unit of their own army, but Grachev and the Russian

General Staff saw no other alternative, given the tense conditions in Nagorno-Karabakh.

After repeated attacks on the base housing, evacuation of families from the 104th Airborne Division finally began in April 1992. Some of the first to leave were families of the VTA transport regiment stationed near the airborne base, which was isolated and less well protected. The skirmishing between the paratroopers and Azeri militias intensified in the summer of 1992 as the Azeris sought arms and military equipment to bolster their forces in the disputed Karabakh region. In September 1992, the former Soviet 4th Army was disbanded, leaving the 104th Airborne Division as its last major unit in Azerbaijan. During the spring of 1993, the Azeri government pressed Moscow to pull out the airborne division due to evidence that Russian troops had supported the Armenian seizure of Kelbadzar in early April. By now, the Russian Defense Ministry was fed up with attempts to mediate the Armenian-Azeri dispute, and so the 104th Airborne Division was ordered to evacuate Gyandzha. The last elements of the division departed on 25 May 1993 for its new base at Ulyanovsk in the Urals area of central Russia. Not a single piece of equipment was left for the Azeris, and the paratroopers sabotaged many of the facilities that were left behind.

In spite of Azeri hatred for the paratroopers, the Armenian militias were impressed by their performance during the troubles. In March 1992, when the new Armenian army was created, the first unit formed was the 1st Airborne Assault Regiment. It was created in Yerevan on the basis of a heavily Armenian MVD Internal Forces battalion. The initial Armenian units were patterned after Soviet airborne formations in the hope that a core of elite, highly mobile professional units could make up for the mediocre capabilities of the disparate militias that composed the rest of the army. Armenia's ambition was to become "the Israel of the Caucasus" with a potent military force.

THE GEORGIAN MAELSTROM

Georgia was the scene of some of the most confused and bitter fighting in the "near-abroad" in the early 1990s. It was also an example of the byzantine Russian defense policy, which consisted of an odd mixture of peacekeeping efforts, informal help for favored militias, and surreptitious involvement of Russian forces for murky foreign policy goals. Although Yeltsin nominally supported independence movements in the republics, the army pursued a policy of intimidation to push states such as Georgia back into the Russian embrace. When Georgia showed no interest in joining the Moscow-dominated CIS Unified Forces, intrigue began to coerce them to reconsider.

Georgia, to the north of Armenia and bordering the eastern end of the Black Sea, declared its independence from the former Soviet Union after the August 1991 coup. For a short time, the newly independent republic was ruled by Georgian nationalists under the virulently anti-Communist Zviad Gamsakhurdia. But a civil war broke out on 22 December 1991 between Gamsakhurdia's militia forces and other political militias headed by Tengiz Kitovani. Russian nationalists in the army were very unhappy to see Georgia become independent under the intensely anti-Russian Georgian nationalists, and there have been many reports that Russian military units were partly responsible for the outbreak of fighting. On 28 December, when it appeared that Kitovani's militia was about to be defeated, Russian troops intervened on his side. It is difficult to determine whether the Russian actions were part of a plan initiated by Moscow, or if the involvement was due to bribery and corruption. Russian units in the country had a reputation for widespread corruption involving the sale of arms and supplies to militants on all sides, and the military district there was labeled the "Mercenary Military District," even by the Russians. Gamsakhurdia was eventually overthrown, but troops still loyal to him battled incessantly with the Georgian National Guard through 1994, and even managed to seize buildings in the capital of Tbilisi in the summer of 1992. Both sides made raids on Russian garrisons still in Georgia in hope of securing arms. A 13 June 1992 attack on the Gori garrison was fought off by the 901st Paratroop Battalion, one of the few VDV units permanently stationed in the region.

The civil war in Georgia led other ethnic groups in the mountainous enclaves of the republic to declare their own independence. The Abkhazians, located in northwestern Georgia, and the Ossetians, located in the mountains of north-central Georgia, both attempted to secede from Georgia. The Southern Ossetians wanted to unite with their kin across the Russian border in Northern Ossetia.

Several thousand people were killed in the fighting in Southern Ossetia in the summer of 1992 in battles between Georgian and

Ossetian militias. Finally, the warring parties agreed to Russian mediation. The 104th Airborne Regiment from the 76th Guards Airborne Division was sent to Ossetia on 15 June 1992 as the main Russian contribution to the peacekeeping force, led by deputy VDV commander Maj. Gen. Aleksandr Chindarov. The airborne force was often involved in firefights with extremists, including a series of engagements with Ingushetian irregular militias in the autumn of 1992.

The threat posed to the Abkhaz forces proved more serious to Georgia than did the Ossetian war. Abkhazia declared its independence from Georgia on 25 July 1992. The head of the Georgian "Mkhedrioni" National Guards, Tengiz Kitovani, led an assault on Abkhazia in August 1992 with about 3,000 troops. Moscow pressured both sides to a cease-fire, which was declared on 3 September. On 19 September, Georgia decided to use the lull to move six infantry battalions and tanks into Abkhazia to reinforce Kitovani's forces. The Abkhazians replied by capturing the town of Gagry from the ill-disciplined Georgian units. The war broke out again with full force, and allegations were made that Russia was supporting Abkhazia to lure the Georgians back into the bear's embrace.

After recapturing their own homeland by early 1993, the Abkhaz army decided to try its luck in storming down the Black Sea coast. On 15 March 1993, the Abkhaz army crossed the Gumista River and headed for the key Georgian port city of Sukhumi. There were many accusations that the sudden military competence of the Abkhaz army was due to an influx of troops and equipment from Russia. Some credence to the charges can be inferred from the ability of the Abkhaz forces to launch a successful amphibious assault against Sukhumi. The MiG-29 and Su-25 aircraft supporting the Abkhazians were clearly from Russian bases. Eduard Shevardnadze, Gorbachev's former foreign minister and head of the coalition Georgian government at the time, described the fighting as a virtual Russo-Georgian war. The Russian Ministry of Defense categorically denied involvement, but the Georgians claimed that 80 to 90 percent of the Abkhaz forces were Russians. This was probably an exaggeration. One of the main sources of arms was the semiautonomous Chechen republic, a mountain people sympathetic to the Abkhazians. The Georgian position was somewhat hypocritical in any case, since most Georgian combat aircraft were flown by mercenary Russian pilots. After a prolonged siege, the Abkhaz forces captured Sukhumi on 27 September 1993. Shevardnadze finally succumbed to Russian pressure. With Russian support, Sukhumi was back in Georgian hands by the end of 1993. With Georgia returning to the Russian fold, the Abkhaz forces were abandoned by Moscow.

An operational group based on the 345th Guards Airborne Regiment was deployed in Abkhazia during several of the short-lived truces to protect Russian military facilities located there; it was the only officially "Russian" unit in Abkhazia. The VDV forces were involved in the cease-fire that ended the war late in 1993. With Abkhazia secure, the Georgian army turned its attention to remnants of Gamsakhurdia's forces still active in western Georgia. Gamsakhurdia was widely regarded as a traitor for having continued his rebellion while Abkhazia threatened central Georgia. In January 1994, Gamsakhurdia committed suicide, and it appeared that the Georgian civil war might finally be over.

MOSCOW COUP, PART TWO

After a series of escalating conflicts between Boris Yeltsin and his erstwhile allies in the Russian Parliament, the crisis came to a head in October 1993. Yeltsin declared the parliament dissolved; the parliamentary leaders led by the speaker, Ruslan Khasboutlatov, and Vice President Aleksandr Rutskoy claimed that the Russian government rested with them. The parliament leaders informed the armed forces that they should take their orders from a new defense minister appointed by parliament, General Achalov. Ironically, this left two paratroopers "in charge" of the Russian armed forces, Achalov on the parliament side and Grachev on President Yeltsin's side.

Yeltsin had taken considerable pains to make certain that the armed forces and security apparatus would support him in the event of a crisis. Grachev was firmly in Yeltsin's camp; not only had Yeltsin elevated him to his position as head of the armed forces, but the dissolution of the CIS Unified Forces in the summer of 1993 had given Grachev further power. In September, Yeltsin made a series of visits to critical units in the Moscow area, including the 2nd Taman Guards Motor Rifle Division and the 4th Kantemirovets Tank Division. Yeltsin had made certain that the MDV OMON troops were under firm control, and had supported a modernization of the 19th Dzerzhinskiy Special Operations Motor Rifle Division after the 1991 coup. The division was one of the first MVD units to begin hiring professional soldiers, and under Lieutenant General Anatoliy Kulikov, steps were taken to convert the unit into a true elite formation with combat training and specialized skills at a higher level than those of normal police units. To bolster the image of the division, the red beret was adopted as a unit motif, clearly intended to suggest that the division had been elevated to the status of the Blue Beret VDV. The Russian press began to refer to the Dzerzhinskiy division as the MVD Spetsnaz, though there was little evidence that the division was any better trained than a normal army unit.

At the height of the crisis, on Sunday, 3 October 1993, supporters of the parliament went on a rampage in central Moscow after a provocative speech by Vice President Aleksandr Rutskoy. The level of violence came as a complete surprise to the Moscow police, and the local *militsiya* forces were unable to cope with the crowds. Small numbers of troops were moved into the city later in the day, taking part in a brief but bloody fight for the Ostakino television center. Early on Monday, 4 October, Yeltsin met with Grachev and the deputy defense minister, Konstantin Kobets, and planned military actions to prevent another riot. The 2nd Taman Guards Motor Rifle Division dispatched several battalions of infantry in BTR-80 armored transports, which arrived in the city early in the morning. In addition, several platoons of T-80U tanks from the 4th Kantemirovets Tank Division began occupying positions in the center of the city. The 27th Separate Motor Rifle Brigade was also moved to Moscow. After the experience of 1991, the Russian Army had reorganized the 27th Brigade in Tepliy Stan for counterinsurgency work. This unit was trained in light infantry and urban combat tactics and would be useful should heavy fighting break out.

Grachev mobilized both the 76th Guards Airborne in Pskov and the 106th Airborne in Tula, but there was never a need to move them into the city. The only VDV unit to take part in operations in Moscow during the October dispute was the 119th Airborne Regiment, based at Naro-Fominsk near Moscow. The 218th Spetsnaz Battalion of the 2nd Spetsnaz Brigade was moved into the city from Chuchkovo.

Unlike the August 1991 coup, in 1993 there was no question about military loyalty. Although the army was not happy to be fighting against Russian civilians, the rampage by parliament supporters on Sunday had outraged many army officers and troops. The attack on the White House began around 07:30; it involved the whole panoply of special forces units, leading many observers to conclude that each of the units had been selected to demonstrate their loyalty to the Yeltsin government.

The 119th Airborne Regiment was assigned the capture of the Moscow City Council building. Parliamentary militias resisted, and a company commander, Lt. Sergei Smirnov, was killed; the deputy regimental commander, Lt. Col. Mikhail Korkin, was severely wounded. The outcome of the fighting was never in doubt, and by early afternoon the White House had been captured. The second Moscow coup led to further calls from military leaders to improve the MVD units so that the army could stay out of political squabbles. It remains to be seen whether this will ever be possible.

MOBILE FORCE

The end of the Cold War forced the Russian Army to come to grips with the changing security threats it faces. For several years, the army simply attempted to reconstruct the same sort of tank-heavy force it had become accustomed to deploying in the NATO versus Warsaw Pact confrontation. Grachev was isolated from this debate, in part due to his involvement in the day-to-day chaos of the withdrawing Soviet Army, and in part due to his VDV background. The VDV had always been independent from the Ground Forces, and the General Staff was dominated by Ground Forces officers. Not only was Grachev a representative of an upstart branch of the armed forces, but his young age and lack of Moscow experience alienated him from the mainstream Russian military leaders.

Grachev's independence had its positive side. He was able to take a fresh look at Russia's defense dilemma and come up with a plan very different from the stale ideas of the former military leadership. In May 1990, the General Staff Academy had first raised the idea of creating a rapid-deployment force as the core of a reorganized Russian Army. This idea was roundly criticized at the time by tradition-bound tank and motorized infantry officers. On 18 December 1992,

Grachev threw his backing behind the idea of a Russian Mobile Force (*mobilnie sily rossii,* or MSR). The mobile force concept was similar in many respects to the American Rapid Deployment Force of the 1980s. Under the plan, certain units would be earmarked for participation in any contingencies, and these units would be kept at a higher state of preparedness than the rest of the army. This concept can also be traced back to roots deep in Russian national tradition. The Russian border is so extended that it is impossible to deploy enough forces to defend it; instead, the idea was to create central reserve forces that could be rapidly deployed forward when and where they were needed. The Russian Mobile Force would be located in the Volga and Urals Military Districts and organizationally would probably have its own interbranch command structure similar to that of a military district.

The proposed Mobile Force is to consist of two main elements, the Immediate Reaction Force *(sily nemedlennogo reagirovaniya)* and the Rapid Deployment Force *(sily bystrogo razvyortyvaniya)*. The Immediate Reaction Force is to be configured from light, easily transported units, with the VDV as its core. It would constitute the first wave in any contingency action. The Rapid Deployment Force is to be the heavy portion of the force, based around three army corps with traditional tank, motorized rifle, and heavy artillery units. It would differ from the rest of the Russian Army in being maintained at a high state of readiness with a full complement of troops and a high percentage of professional, rather than conscript, enlisted men.

The Immediate Reaction Force would be based around five VDV airborne divisions, essentially the entire reconstituted VDV force. One division would be sacrificed to build up a larger number of independent airborne brigades and other specialized units for smaller contingencies and peacekeeping missions. The plan envisions fielding eight independent brigades; the experimental air assault units of the 1980s would be disbanded except for two independent air assault battalions. For missions where greater ground mobility is required, six light motorized rifle brigades would be formed. These would have a lighter tank component than traditional motorized rifle units to make them more transportable, and would have an organic heliborne air assault battalion such as the experimental 70th Rifle Brigade in Afghanistan. The force would also be supported by at least one Spetsnaz brigade. The Russian Navy's Naval Infantry branch would be subordinated to the Immediate Reaction Force, and the plan calls for the retention of six naval infantry battalions.

One of the key elements of the plan is the creation of supporting airlift forces. The Immediate Reaction Force would have four of the air force aviation transport divisions assigned to it for possible airlift or airdrop missions. In addition, to give the force greater tactical mobility, at least twelve helicopter regiments would be assigned to the force. Air support would be provided by seven fighter regiments, five bomber regiments, and two strike regiments.

The plan gives greater priority to Mobile Force divisions, including personnel selection and equipment modernization. Since 1991, the Russian defense procurement budget has fallen ninefold, and procurement is at about 10 to 15 percent of Soviet levels. Under such circumstances, not all army divisions will be modernized at the rates seen during the Cold War, and the Mobile Force plan specifies a rationale for allotting these reduced resources.

This plan would require a substantial reconfiguration of the Russian Army, which is unlikely to be accomplished until the end of the century. Advocates of the plan have suggested a short-term grouping to serve as the core of the full Mobile Force, which would consist of two airborne divisions and three airborne brigades already in Russia, plus several helicopter regiments. The core groups would constitute the Immediate Reaction Force until the airborne divisions being withdrawn from the republics are fully rebuilt. The Rapid Deployment Force would be based around a special division of peacekeeping forces formed in the Volga Military District in the early 1990s, plus five or six reinforced motor rifle battalions. In 1993, Russia had only one peacekeeping battalion, drawn mostly from VDV units, stationed outside the former Soviet Union in Bosnia.

WHITHER THE AIRBORNE?

The Russian VDV has not conducted a parachute assault in combat since the Dnepr operation more than fifty years ago. Is there still a place for paratroopers in modern armies? The Russians believe that there is, for several reasons. Parachutes provide a degree of strategic mobility that still cannot be provided by any other means. Although helicopters are a much more practical means of delivery at ranges of 100 miles, parachute operations can occur at ranges of 500 miles. Second, the Russians argue that parachute training is an essential ingredient in creating and training an elite force. Parachute jumping requires a level of personal courage and determination that helps separate the paratroopers from the rest of the army. It attracts the bold and the brave, traits that are much prized in special operations units. Parachuting helps to build self-confidence in a soldier, which is essential in the chaotic conditions of special missions.

The symbolic importance of the parachute to the VDV has hampered modernization of Russia's helicopter assault force. The heliborne units developed in the 1980s were mostly abandoned in the early 1990s to provide troops to the VDV. Although the VDV has come to depend on helicopters for tactical mobility, the organizational separation between the helicopter force and the VDV has not encouraged the VDV's advocacy of helicopter development. The U.S. Army has retained a paratrooper unit, the 82nd Airborne Division, but it converted its other paratrooper division, the 101st Airborne, to a heliborne air assault unit after the Vietnam War. The VDV did not follow this natural evolutionary course after Afghanistan. As a result, the Russian helicopter force is relatively backward in equipment and tactics. In the mid-1990s, the Mi-24 attack helicopter is badly dated, and its replacement, the Mi-28, only began to enter production in 1994, almost fifteen years after its American counterpart, the AH-64 Apache. More importantly, the principal troop carrier, the Mi-8, will not be replaced by the proposed Mi-40 until the turn of the century; in contrast, the U.S. Army began receiving its UH-60 Blackhawk in the early 1980s. Heliborne forces lack a strong voice, but it is possible that the new light motorized rifle brigades will serve this function as they grow and mature.

In spite of its checkered history, the Blue Berets of the VDV remain Russia's main elite combat force. They have proven to be well suited to the type of low-intensity battlefield so typical of warfare in the late twentieth century. Their exceptional performance as the storm troopers of the old Soviet empire, and their reliable service as the Praetorian Guard of the Kremlin, will make them one of the most critical elements in the future Russian Army.

Bibliography

There has been a general lack of significant publications on the Soviet VDV airborne, with two important exceptions. Colonel David Glantz's study, *The Soviet Airborne Experience,* was the first serious study in English on the Soviet airborne in World War II. It was published in a very limited run primarily for internal use by the U.S. Army and is not easy to find except at a few major libraries and defense research centers. It is worth hunting down for anyone interested in the World War II period. Carey Schofield's remarkable *The Russian Elite* is a journalistic account based on years of interviews with Russian airborne officers. It is particularly strong on Afghanistan and the 1991 coup but also contains excellent material on the Spetsnaz. There are several Russian accounts of the VDV such as Lisov's and Sukhorukhov's, but for the English reader the Glantz study is a superior, professional synthesis.

In the area of government studies, there is a wide range of U.S. Army and DIA publications dealing with the Soviet VDV. In some cases, these are specialized monographs; in other cases there are chapters contained in standard handbooks such as the FM-100-2 series of field manuals. These are excellent sources for anyone interested in detailed information on tactics and tables of organization and equipment (TO&E). They are generally better in the 1980s than in the previous decades. Although the studies listed here are either unclassified or have been declassified, few of these publications are publicly available; they can usually be obtained by a determined researcher through Freedom of Information Act requests. I have listed only the major handbooks since there are so many.

In the area of declassified intelligence documents, a wealth of material is available for the prewar years of 1930–41 from the Military Intelligence Division G-2 records of the U.S. War Department in the National Archives (Record Group 165). (Some of these are available in microfiche collections such as the *U.S. Military*

Intelligence Reports: Soviet Union 1919–1941, from University Publications of America.) Consisting mainly of military attaché reports from Moscow or the surrounding countries, these documents are best on subjects such as the airborne participation in the annual war games; they are suspect when dealing with order of battle. I have not listed all of the documents here as they are too numerous and of too narrow an interest. I have not found U.S. Army wartime intelligence documents on the VDV airborne to be very helpful. In the postwar years, documents have generally been declassified into the early 1960s. The usual order-of-battle documents have not been useful, as the United States didn't manage to locate and identify the VDV divisions in documents that have been released to date. Several of the longer intelligence reports on the airborne contain useful technical details and assessments, and I have listed some of the more significant ones here. I located copies at the U.S. Army Military History Institute at Carlisle Barracks, Pennsylvania.

On the VDV in World War II, several documents are worth special mention. The *Soviet Documents on the Use of War Experience,* Vol. 3, contains a handy Soviet assessment of the 1942 Vyazma operation; there is also a useful overview of Belov's cavalry operations. Glantz's article on the VDV mission against the Demyansk pocket is the only source available on this forgotten episode and is up to his usual high quality. The 1943 Dnepr drop is not well covered in Russian sources, but the U.S. Army collected the assessments of a number of German officers in *Russian Airborne Operations P-116,* cited below. This is a fascinating account; I located a copy (as usual) at the U.S. Army Military History Institute at Carlisle Barracks, Pennsylvania. There is no adequate study of Soviet airlift in World War II. The account here was pieced together from many sources. There are several good accounts on both glider development and glider operations in Russian, but they are generally hard to find outside of Russia.

The development of the VDV in the immediate postwar years is poorly covered in any language. Western intelligence on Soviet subjects was still weak in the 1950s, and it shows in the documents cited below. The Hungarian uprising has been the subject of a series of articles in the Russian military history journal *Voenno-Istorichesskiy Zhurnal,* and these are cited below. By the 1960s, a clearer picture of the Soviet Army was emerging, and U.S. and British military publications begin to become essential at this stage. Over the past decade, I have collected an enormous file of U.S. government reports, magazine articles, and government translations on the VDV. This file stands several feet thick; for example, I have collected a file nearly an inch thick simply on the BMD airborne assault vehicle. I have avoided trying the readers' patience by listing only the better overviews. I have also avoided listing all of the general surveys of the postwar Soviet Army, many of which contain short sections on the VDV. The invasion of Czechoslovakia has been the subject of a host of books and articles, including Kyrov's recent *Krasnaya Zvezda* article, which provided unique insight into the actual VDV objectives.

Afghanistan has been the subject of several Russian journalistic accounts that have been translated into English; Borovik's is still the best. There are several very good English accounts, of which David Isby's and Mark Urban's are the best; both visited Afghanistan during the war. David Isby's articles on special operations in Afghanistan are the best source available, along with the personal accounts in the Schofield book. The Russian General Staff has completed two studies of the Afghanistan war; the first of these will be serialized in the *Journal of Slavic Military Studies* in 1994–95.

Carey Schofield's book is the best account of the VDV for the post-Afghanistan operations and is especially interesting on the 1991 coup. The best overview of the 1991 coup so far is the Dunlop study. My main sources on the many border wars involving the VDV have been translations of the Russian press undertaken by the Foreign Broadcast Information Service (FBIS) and Joint Publications Research Service (JPRS), such as the FBIS *Central Eurasia Daily Reports* and the *Central Eurasia Military Affairs* periodic digest, and the daily Russian army paper, *Krasnaya Zvezda*. The *Daily Reports* can be found at federal document depositories; I used the collection at the Lehman Library at the Columbia University School of International Affairs. I have listed only a small number of these translations, as most provided only tidbits of information. Recent Russian order-of-battle information in this book comes mainly from the documents released in conjunction with the Conventional Forces–Europe Treaty.

UNPUBLISHED DOCUMENTS

Chief of the General Staff, Royal Army. *Tactics of the Soviet Army: Notes for Regimental Officers,* 1959.

Chief of the Imperial Staff, Royal Army. *Notes on the Soviet Army,* 1956.

————. *The Soviet Army: Tactics and Organization,* 1949.

U.S. Defense Intelligence Agency. *Soviet Military Transport Aviation: Prospects for the 1970s,* DIE SOV 8-72, 18 September 1982.

————. *The Soviet Airborne Forces,* DDB-1110-2-82, April 1982.

————. *The Soviet Naval Infantry,* 1979.

U.S. Department of the Army. *Handbook on Aggressor Military Forces,* FM 30-102, February 1959.

————. *Handbook on Aggressor Military Forces,* FM 30-102, June 1960, 1973.

————. *Opposing Forces: Europe,* FM 30-102, 1977.

————. *Russian Airborne Operations,* Foreign Military Studies Manuscript No. P-116, U.S. Army Historical Division, 1953.

————. *The Soviet Army: Specialized Warfare and Rear Area Support,* FM 100-2-2, 1984.

————. *The Soviet Army: Troops, Organization, and Equipment,* FM 100-2-3, 1984, 1989, 1991.

Military Intelligence Division: U.S. War Department. "Airborne Equipment & Airborne Defenses of the Major Powers," IRP-8420, 14 February 1953.

————. "Airborne Equipment & Airborne Defenses of the Soviet Union," IRP-8908, 17 July 1955.

————. "Distribution of (Soviet) Parachute Units," IG No. 9115, 30 December 1940.

————. "Parachute Troops in the Finno-Soviet War & Finnish Countermeasures," G-2 Report No. 0132, 2090-391-14, 21 May 1940.

————. "Preliminary Report on the Soviet Air Force," 26 June 1945.

————. "Soviet Airborne & Aerial Supply Operations," IRP-9805, 1 October 1956.

————. "Soviet Airborne Capabilities," IRP-6849, 10 December 1951.

————. "Soviet Airborne Capabilities," IRP-7311, 4 August 1952.

————. "Soviet Long Range Force," IRP-3119, 3 April 1946.

————. "Tactical Capabilities of the USSR," IRP-4691, 21 April 1949.

Office of the Secretary of Defense, Director of Net Technical Assessment. *A Comparison of U.S. and Soviet Military Airlift Aircraft,* March 1976.

USSR Ministry of Defense. *Information on the Command Structure of the Ground Forces, Air Force, and Air Defense Forces Aviation of the Armed Forces of the USSR,* 18 November 1990.

BOOKS AND PUBLICATIONS

Alexiev, Alexander. *Inside the Soviet Army in Afghanistan.* Santa Monica, Calif.: Rand Corporation, 1988.

Armstrong, John, ed. *Soviet Partisans in World War II.* Madison: University of Wisconsin Press, 1964.

Baumann, Robert. *Russian-Soviet Unconventional Wars in the Caucasus, Central Asia, and Afghanistan.* Leavenworth Papers No. 20. Fort Leavenworth, Kans.: U.S. Army Command and General Staff College, 1993.

Beitler, Stephen. "Spetsnaz: The Soviet Union's Special Operations Forces." Master's thesis, Defense Intelligence College, June 1985.

Borovik, Artyom. *The Hidden War: A Russian Journalist's Account of the Soviet War in Afghanistan.* New York: Atlantic Monthly Press, 1990.

Burgess, William, ed. *Inside Spetsnaz: Soviet Special Operations, A Critical Analysis.* Novato, Calif.: Presidio Press, 1990.

Butowski, Piotr. *Smiglowiec szturmowy Mi-24.* Warsaw: WMON, 1990.

Carell, Paul. *Hitler Moves East 1941–1943.* New York: Ballantine Books, 1971.

Cooper, Matthew. *The Nazi War against Soviet Partisans 1941–1945.* New York: Stein and Day, 1979.

Dubcek, Alexander. *Hope Dies Last: The Autobiography of Alexander Dubcek.* New York: Kodansha International, 1993.

Dunlop, John. *The Rise of Russia and the Fall of the Soviet Empire.* Princeton: Princeton University, 1993.

Everett-Heath, John. *Soviet Helicopters: Design, Development and Tactics.* London: Jane's Information Group, 1988.

Foye, Stephen, ed. *Post-Soviet Armies.* RFE/RL Research Report, Vol. 2, No. 25. New York: 1993.

Fuller, William. *The Internal Troops of the MVD SSSR.* College Station Papers No. 6. College Station, Tex.: Texas A & M, 1983.

Furtatov, V. M. *Ognennye desanty: o muzhestve parashyutistov VVS Chernomorskogo Flota.* Moscow: Voenizdat, 1989.

Galvin, John. *Air Assault: The Development of Airmobile Warfare.* New York: Hawthorn Books, 1969.

Glantz, David. *The Soviet Airborne Experience.* Fort Leavenworth, Kans.: U.S. Army Command and General Staff College, 1984.

Goncharenko, V. T. *O. K. Antonov: Desyat raz snachala, rasskazy.* Kiev: Veselka, 1981.

Green, William. *Gorbachev and His Generals: The Reform of Soviet Military Doctrine.* Westport, Conn.: Westview Press, 1990.

Gribovskiy, K. V. *Razvitie transportnogo planerizma.* Moscow: Mashinostroenie, 1993.

Gromov, I. I., and V. N. Pigunov. *Chetvertiy vozdushno-desantniy: voenno-istorichesskiy ocherk o boevom puti 4-go vozdushno-desantnogo korpusa.* Moscow: Voenizdat, 1990.

Grzegorzewski, Jerzy. *Smiglowiec Mi-1.* Warsaw: WMON, 1975.

———. *Smiglowiec Mi-4.* Warsaw: WMON, 1982.

———. *Smiglowiec Mi-6.* Warsaw: WMON, 1988.

———. *Smiglowiec Mi-8.* Warsaw: WMON, 1984.

Guskov, A. S. *Podgotovka parashutista.* Moscow: Izd. DOSAAF, 1976.

Irving, David. *Uprising: One Nation's Nightmare, Hungary 1956.* London: Hodder and Stoughton, 1981.

Isby, David C. *Russia's War in Afghanistan.* London: Osprey, 1986.

———. *War in a Distant Country: Afghanistan, Invasion and Resistance.* London: Arms and Armour Press, 1989.

Ivonin, V. I. *Krylataya gvardiya: Sbornik.* Moscow: Izd. DOSAAF, 1978.

Kaitanov, K. F. *Pod kupolom parashyuta.* Moscow: Izd. DOSAAF, 1984.

Kamalov, Kh. Kh. *Morskaya pekhota v boyakh za Rodinu.* Moscow: Voenizdat, 1983.

Kazakov, V. B. *Boevie aerospetsepki.* Moscow: Izd. DOSAAF, 1988.

————. *Nebo Pomnit.* Moscow: Molodaya Gvardiya, 1988.

Kempski, Benedykt. *Samolot tranportowy IL-14.* Warsaw: WMON, 1982.

Konieczny, Jerzy. *Samolot Transportowy An-12.* Warsaw: WMON, 1973.

Knight, Amy W. *The KGB: Police and Politics in the Soviet Union.* Boston: Unwin Hyman, 1988.

Krivosheyev, G. F. *Grif sekretnosti snyat: poteri vooruzhennikh sil SSSR v voinakh, boevikh deistviyakh i voennikh konfliktakh.* Moscow: Voenizdat, 1993.

Krolikiewicz, Tadeusz. *Szybowce Transportowe.* Warsaw: WMON, 1985.

Lasky, Melvin J., ed. *The Hungarian Revolution.* New York: F. Praeger, 1957.

Leonov, Viktor. *Blood on the Shores: Soviet Naval Commandos in World War II.* Annapolis, Md.: U.S. Naval Institute, 1994.

Lewis, Edward. *A Comprehensive Examination of the Soviet Naval Infantry.* Garmisch, Germany: U.S. Army Russian Institute, 1977.

Lisov, I. I. *Desantniki: Vozdushniye desanty.* Moscow: Voenizdat, 1968.

Luttichau, Charles von. *Guerrilla and Counterguerrilla Warfare in Russia during World War II.* Washington, D.C.: Office of the Chief of Military History, U.S. Army, 1963.

Lyakhovskiy, A. A. *Tainy afganskoy voiny.* Moscow: Planeta, 1991.

Malinowski, Tadeusz. *Spadochrony.* Warsaw: Wyd. Komunikacji i Lacznosci, 1974.

Mrazek, James. *The Glider War.* New York: St. Martin's Press, 1975.

Musialkowski, Lechoslaw. *Samolot transportowy C-47.* Warsaw: WMON, 1988.

Nazarewicz, Ryszard. *Polacy-spadochroniarze-wywiadowcy na zapleczu frontu wschodiego.* Warsaw: WMON, 1974.

Orenstein, Harold. *Soviet Documents on the Use of War Experience: Military Operations in 1941–42.* Vol. 3. London: Frank Cass, 1993.

Pavlov, A. S. *Voenno-morskoi flot Rossii i SNG 1992g.: Spravochnik.* Yakutsk: Baltika, 1992.

Pikov, N. I. *Voina v Afghanistane.* Moscow: Voenizdat, 1991.

Poirier, Robert, and Albert Conner. *The Red Army Order of Battle in the Great Patriotic War.* Novato, Calif.: Presidio Press, 1985.

Pryce-Jones, David. *The Hungarian Revolution.* New York: Horizon Press, 1970.

Reinhardt, Hellmuth, et al. *Airborne Operations: A German Appraisal.* Washington, D.C.: Government Printing Office, 1988.

St. Croix, Philip de. *Airborne Operations.* London: Salamander, 1978.

Sarin, Oleg, and Lev Dvoretsky. *The Afghan Syndrome: The Soviet Union's Vietnam.* Novato, Calif.: Presidio Press, 1993.

Schofield, Carey. *The Russian Elite: Inside Spetsnaz and the Airborne Forces.* Mechanicsburg, Pa.: Stackpole Books, 1993.

Smirnov, S. M. *Tak prikhodit muzhestvo.* Moscow: Voenizdat, 1985.

Sukhorukhov, D. S., ed. *Sovetskie Vozdushno-Desantny.* Moscow: Voenizdat, 1986.

———. *Vertikalniy okhvat.* Moscow: Molodaya Gvardiya, 1981.

Suvorov, Viktor [pseud.]. *Spetsnaz: The Story of the Soviet SAS.* London: Hamish Hamilton, 1987.

Szuman, Boleslaw. *Samolot transportowy Li-2.* Warsaw: WMON, 1976.

Thompson, Leroy. *Unfulfilled Promise: The Soviet Airborne Forces 1928–1945.* Bennington, Vt.: International Graphics, 1983.

Udalov, K. G. *Samolety Aeroflota: Samolet IL-14.* Moscow: Izd. Transport, 1991.

Urban, Mark. *War in Afghanistan.* New York: St. Martin's Press, 1990.

Vali, Ferenc A. *Rift and Revolt in Hungary*. Cambridge, Mass.: Harvard University Press, 1961.

Voinov, A. A. *Chelovek i parashyut*. Moscow: Izd. DOSAAF, 1977.

Volodko, A. M. *Vertolet v Afganistane*. Moscow: Voenizdat, 1993.

Wood, Alan. *History of the World's Glider Forces*. Wellingborough, UK: Patrick Stephens Ltd., 1990.

Yousaf, Mohammad. *The Bear Trap: Afghanistan's Untold Story*. London: Leo Cooper, 1992.

Zaitsev, V. P. et al. *Voennie svyazisti v boyakh za Rodinu*. Moscow: Voenizdat, 1984.

Zaloga, Steven. *Anti-Tank Helicopters*. London: Osprey, 1986.

Zaloga, Steven, and James Loop. *Soviet Bloc Elite Forces*. London: Osprey, 1985.

ARTICLES

Badurkin, Viktor. "The Grey Wolves." Trud (31 July 1993): 1; translated by JPRS-UMA-93-032, 54.

Belovetskiy, Dmitriy. "They Refused to Storm the White House." Literaturnaya Gazeta (28 August 1991): 5; translated by JPRS-UMA-91-023, 69.

Bobrakov, A. "Quick Reaction Forces: The Naval Component." *Voenniy Vestnik* 2 (1993): 24–26.

Brusstar, James. "Soviet Airborne Training." *Review of Soviet Ground Forces* (July 1982): 9–12.

"Budapesht-osen 1956." Krasnaya Zvezda (5 November 1991): 3.

Burton, Chris. "The Myth and Reality of the Soviet Paratrooper." *Military Review* 65/1 (January 1985): 26–41.

Cruchter, Michael. "The Soviet Airborne Division." *Review of the Soviet Ground Forces* (March 1980): 1–4.

"Die Luftlande und Luftsturmtruppen der Sowjetunion." Osterr. Milit. Zeitschrift (February 1985): 152–56.

"Einsatz sowjetischer luftlandetruppen." Allgemeine Schweizerische Zeitschrift (November 1961).

Glantz, David. "The Ghosts of Demiansk: In Memory of the Soldiers of the Soviet 1st Airborne Corps." The Journal of Military History 56 (October 1992): 617–50.

Goncz, Arpad. "Budapest 1956." *New Times* 35 (1991): 28–31.

Gubarev, V. "Props of Power." Moscow News 30 (1991): 20.

Hansen, James. "Soviet Vanguard Forces–Spetsnaz." *National Defense* (March 1986).

Hauterive, Robert. "Les Troupes Aeroportes Sovietiques." *Raids* 65 (October 1991): 22–31.

Holcomb, James. "Soviet Airborne Forces and the Central Region." *Military Review* 67 (November 1987): 36–47.

———. Holcomb, James. "Recent Developments in Soviet Helicopter Tactics." *Soviet Studies Research Centre Papers* B34 (March 1988).

"The Ilyushin Candid Family." Air International (April 1990): 173–210.

Isby, David C. "Soviet Tactics in Afghanistan." *Jane's Defence Review* 7 (1983): 681–93.

———. "Panjsher VII: Soviets Smash Afghan Resistance in Vital Valley." *Soldier of Fortune* (February 1985): 34–39.

———. "The Vertical Threat: Air Assault and Airmobile Brigades of the Soviet Army." *Amphibious Warfare Review* (August 1985).

———. "The Spetsnaz in Afghanistan: Soviet special operation forces in action." *Military Technology* 10 (October 1985).

———. "Soviet Special Operations Forces in Afghanistan: The Interdiction Mission." *Free Afghanistan* 7 (1987): 18–20.

"Afghanistan: Low-Intensity Conflict with Major Power Intervention" in *Low-Intensity Conflict: Old Threats in a New World.* Boulder, Colo.: Westview Press, 1992.

Isherwood, Julian. "Warsaw Pact Planned to Nuke its way Across Europe." *Armed Forces Journal International* (June 1993): 15.

Ivanov, Nikolai. "How the Afghan War Started." *Soviet Soldier* 7 (1991): 14–25; 8 (1991): 22–33; 10 (1991): 16–28; 11 (1991): 14–30; 12 (1991): 12–23.

Keller, Bill. "General recalls Soviet rift on war." *New York Times,* 19 March 1989.

Kohler, David R. "Spetsnaz." *U.S. Naval Institute Proceedings* (August 1987).

Kostenko, I. K. "Osnovnie etapy razvitiya konstruktsii planera" in *Issledovaniya po istorii i teorii razvitiya aviatsionnoy i raketno-kosmicheskoy nauki i tekhniki* 5 (1986): 133–87.

Kyrov, A. M. "The Danube Burst Its Banks in August: washing away the Prague Spring." *Krasnaya Zvezda* (21 August 1993): 5.

———. "Zabudet li otechestvo pogibshikh desantnikov?" *Voenno-Istorichesskiy Zhurnal* 6–7 (1992): 60–64.

Lashchenko, P. N. "Vengriya, god 1956–y." *Voenno-Istorichesskiy Zhurnal* 9 (1989): 86–89.

Liebl, Vern. "The War in Nagorno-Karabakh: Background and Developments." *Command Magazine* (September–October 1993): 47–51.

Likhanov, Dmitriy. "Spetsnaz." *Ogonyok* 38 (September 1989): 30–32.

MacKenzie, Robert. "SOF Jumps in Mother Russia." *Soldier of Fortune* (January 1990): 62–90.

Malashenko, Ye. I. "Osobiy korpus v ogne Budapeshta." *Voenno-Istorichesskiy Zhurnal* 11 (1993): 44–51; 12 (1993): 33–37.

Maryukha, Vladimir. "Sea Devils Attack." *Soldier* 1 (1993): 43–45.

Musatov, Valery. "Operation Whirlwind." *New Times* 49 (1991): 28–31.

Oden, Richard. "The Soviet Airborne Troops." *Review of the Soviet Ground Forces* (March 1980): 5–12.

Perezhogin, V. A. "Joint Operations of Partisans with Troops in the Rzhev-Vyazma Operation." *Voenno-Istorichesskiy Zhurnal* 2 (1987): 26–32.

Petrichenko, Aleksey. "Smiglowce w Afghanistanie." *Nowa Wojskowa Technika* 1 (1993): 14–16.

Podkolzin, Ye. N. "Vyazemskaya vozdushno-desantnaya operatsiya-yanvar-iyun 1942 goda." *Voennaya Mysl* 3 (1993): 44–51.

———. "The Airborne Troops, as Always, Are on Guard." Argumenty i *Fakty* 12 (March 1993): 1–6; translated by JPRS-UMA-93-011, 1.

Prados, John. "Parachutes across the Dnepr: Kanev 1943." *Strategy & Tactics* 115 (December 1987): 16–48.

Shortt, Jim. "A visit to the Soviet Ryazan Higher Airborne Forces Command School." *International Defense Review* 6 (1989): 730–33.

Stapanov, A. "Berety v vooruzhennikh silakh SSSR." *Tseykhgauz* 1 (1993): 42–46.

Sukhorukhov, D. S. "Airborne Assault Forces in Front Offensive

Operations of the Great Patriotic War." *Voenno-Istorichesskiy Zhurnal* 12 (1985): 14–21.

Suvorov, Viktor [pseud.]. "Spetsnaz: The Soviet Union's special forces." *International Defense Review* (September 1983).

————. "Soviet Airborne Forces." Military Review (April 1973): 60–70.

Turbiville, Graham. "Soviet Airborne Forces: Increasingly Powerful Factor in the Equation." Army (April 1976): 18–27.

"Paradrop at the Bukrin Bridgehead: An Account of the Dniepr Airborne Operation." *Military Review* (December 1976): 26–40.

Urban, Mark. "The 76th Guards Red Banner Chernigov Airborne Division." *Armed Forces* (December 1982): 413–17.

"Vengriya, god 1956–y." *Voenno-Istorichesskiy Zhurnal* 8 (1993): 86–87.

Vladykin, Oleg. "Mobilnie sily Rossii." *Krasnaya Zvezda* (18 December 1992): 2.

————. "Protektsiya po-Margelovski." *Krasnaya Zvezda* (31 July 1993): 2.

"Grave is the Fate of the Elite: Spetsnaz Units have their own problems." *Krasnaya Zvezda* (29 October 1993): 1; translated by JPRS-UMA-93-042.

Zhdankin, Andrey. "The 'A' Team: Portrait against a Background of Stagnation, the Putsch and October." *Rossiya* (7 December 1993): 8; translated by JPRS-UMA-94-003 (19 January 1994): 1–4.

Zhitarenko, Vladimir. "Komandir 'Letuchey Myshi.'" *Krasnaya Zvezda* (26 November 1993): 2.

Glossary

ABON: Special Purpose Airborne Brigade. The original 1933 Soviet airborne unit.

A-7: A World War II Antonov assault glider.

Abkhazia: A region in the former Soviet republic of Georgia.

ADD: Long-range aviation, The Soviet World War II strategic bomber force.

AGS-17: A Soviet 30mm grenade launcher first commonly used in the Afghanistan war.

Alfa Group: Code name for a KGB special operations unit.

An-8: Antonov transport aircraft of the 1950s, code named Camp by NATO.

An-12: Antonov transport aircraft of the 1960s roughly equivalent to the U.S. Lockheed C-130 Hercules; NATO code named it Cub.

Army: Besides its usual meaning as a branch of the armed forces, "army" can also refer to a field formation consisting of several divisions. For example, the Soviet forces in Afghanistan constituted the 40th Army.

ASU-57: 57mm airborne assault gun. A lightweight tank destroyer with a 57mm gun used by the Soviet airborne since the early 1950s, retired in the 1980s.

ASU-85: 85mm airborne assault gun. A medium tank destroyer with an 85mm gun used by the Soviet airborne since the early 1960s, retired in the late 1980s.

AT-4 Spigot: NATO name for the Soviet 9M111 Fagot antitank missile, roughly equivalent to the European Milan antitank missile system.

AT-5 Spandrel: NATO name for the Soviet 9M113 Konkurs antitank missile, roughly equivalent to the European HOT or American TOW antitank missiles.

Bf-110: A twin-engined German Messerschmitt fighter from World War II.

Black Beret: Russian nickname for the Naval Infantry.

Blue Beret: Russian nickname for the paratroopers of the VDV Airborne Force.

BMD: Airborne combat vehicle. A Soviet air-transportable armored vehicle used as a troop transporter and combat vehicle.

Border Guards: A paramilitary branch of the Soviet KGB used to patrol the USSR frontiers and conduct border customs duties. This force was sometimes used in combat, for example, in Afghanistan.

BRDM: Armored reconnaissance vehicle. A Soviet four-wheeled armored car used for reconnaissance.

BTR-D: Armored airborne transporter. A derivative of the BMD, without the normal gun turret, used as an armored transporter and command vehicle in VDV airborne units.

Byelarus: A former republic of the USSR, also called Byelorussia or White Russia, located between Russia and Poland with its capital in Minsk.

C-47: World War II American transport aircraft, also used by Soviets after being supplied under Lend-Lease program. USSR manufactured a copy under the name Li-2.

Central Committee: The Central Committee of the Communist Party was the highest body of the former Soviet Communist Party and played a key role in all major national decisions.

Chechenia: An autonomous region of the Russian Caucasus.

CIS: Confederation of Indepedent States. The name given to a short-lived union of the former republics of the USSR. Its armed forces sometimes were called the Unified Forces.

Cossack: Under the tsars, the Cossacks were an independent military caste living mainly in southern Ukraine. They were persecuted under Stalin for allying with the White forces in the 1918–20 civil war. The Cossack concept has been revived in recent years.

Council of Ministers: The highest governmental administrative body in the former USSR. The Council of Ministers consisted of representatives of key state organizations and were particularly important in authorizing major Soviet weapons programs.

Crimea: A peninsula in the Black Sea originally part of the Russian republic. Since 1954, a disputed part of Ukraine.

CSLA: Czechoslovak Peoples Army.

D-30: A type of Soviet 122mm howitzer in service since the 1960s.

DB-3: A type of Ilyushin twin-engined bomber used by the Red Air Force since the late 1930s.

DFS.230: A type of German World War II assault glider.

desantnaya: Russian word for special purpose troops; no direct English equivalent. In the designation VDV, it can be translated as airborne or airborne assault.

DP: A type of Russian light machine gun.

DRA: Democratic Republic of Afghanistan.

DShB: Airborne Assault Brigade. A type of Soviet heli-borne unit.

DShK: A type of Soviet 12.7mm heavy machine gun first introduced in 1938 but widely used in the Afghanistan war.

dukhi: Russian word meaning ghosts or spooks, used to refer to Afghan guerrillas.

dushmani: Russian word for bandits, especially those in Central Asia.

falanga: Soviet term for a type of antitank missile called AT-2 Swarter by NATO.

Federal Counterintelligence Service: One of a number of names given the former Second Directorate of the KGB after the collapse of the USSR. Responsible for internal security and similar in role to the FBI.

Foreign Intelligence Service: One of a number of names given the former First Directorate of the KGB after the collapse of the USSR. Responsible for overseas espionage and similar in role to the CIA.

FROG: Free-rocket-over-ground. A NATO term for the Soviet Luna-series of tactical ballistic rockets.

front: Soviet term for a battlefield formation consisting of several armies.

gas turbine engine: Another word for a jet engine; the preferred technical term since many such engines transmit their power mechanically via a shaft (in a helicopter for example) rather than by the reactive force of their exhaust.

GAZ-67B: A type of World War II–era Soviet jeep.

Georgia: A former Soviet republic located in the Caucasus at the eastern end of the Black Sea.

Gorbach: Russian nickname for the Mil Mi-24 attack helicopter, meaning "hunchback."

Ground Forces: Soviet term for a branch of the Soviet armed services comparable to the U.S. Army. The term "Soviet Army" refers to the Ground Forces, PVO Air Defense Forces, RVSN Strategic Missile Forces, and VVS Air Force, that is, all branches of the armed forces except the navy.

Group of Soviet Forces: Soviet term for Soviet military units in the former Warsaw Pact countries. For example, Group of Soviet Forces Germany or Northern Group of Forces (in Poland).

GRU: Main Intelligence Directorate. The intelligence gathering arm of the Soviet armed forces, comparable to the U.S. Defense Intelligence Agency (DIA).

Guards: An honorific given to Soviet military units for distinction in battle.

GVDB: Guards Airborne Brigade.

GVDD: Guards Airborne Division.

Hero of the Soviet Union: The Soviet armed forces' highest military distinction, roughly comparable to the U.S. Medal of Honor.

IL-12: A type of Ilyushin transport aircraft, followed by the improved IL-14.

Jihad: Islamic holy war.

Junkers Ju-52: German World War II troop transport aircraft.

Kazakhstan: Former Soviet republic in Central Asia.

KGB: Committee of State Security. One of the names of the successor organizations to the World War II NKVD. The Soviet special police that combines the functions of the American CIA, FBI, and Coast Guard.

KhAD: The Afghan secret police, patterned after the Soviet KGB.

kishlak: Afghan village.

LCAC: Landing craft air cushion. A type of amphibious assault craft that rides on an air cushion instead of a conventional boat hull.

Limited Contingent of Forces-Afghanistan: Soviet term for Soviet armed forces in Afghanistan at the time of the Afghanistan war.

Lisunov Li-2: Soviet licensed copy of the Douglas DC-3 transport aircraft, originally called PS-84.

MAON: Moscow Special Purpose Aviation Group. A special transport unit created by absorbing the pre–World War II Soviet civil air fleet into the military in 1941.

Mi-8: A type of Mil transport helicopter, called Hip by NATO.

Mi-24: A type of Mil attack helicopter, called Hind by NATO.

militsiya: Russian term for the state police.

Moldova: Region of the former USSR between Ukraine and Romania seized by the Soviet Union in 1940.

MVD: Ministry of Internal Affairs. The Soviet government branch responsible for the state police force.

Naval Infantry: The Soviet term for their Marine force.

NKVD: Peoples Committee for Internal Affairs. The Soviet special police in the 1930s and 1940s. Successor to the OGPU of the 1920s, precursor of the KGB.

OKSVA: Limited Contingent of Soviet Forces-Afghanistan.

OMON: Special Purpose Militia. The antiterrorist special police units of the Soviet MVD.

OMSDON: Special Purpose Division. Russian acronym for the MVD's Dzerzhinskiy division in the Moscow area.

Osoaviakhim: Soviet state organization to encourage sports and other public activities to benefit military preparedness, followed after World War II by the DOSAAF.

otriadi: Russian for units.

panzer: German for armor, also used as slang for a German tank.

panzerfaust: A small antitank rocket grenade launcher.

panzergrenadiers: The German term for mechanized infantry.
panzerjaeger: The German term for tank destroyer units (literally, "tank-hunters").

panzershreck: A type of World War II German antitank rocket launcher, similar to the U.S. Army bazooka.

PDMM: Airborne equipment container. Special containers for parachute dropping supplies.

Pe-8: A type of World War II Soviet Petalyakov heavy bomber, roughly comparable to the American Boeing B-17 Flying Fortress.

PKM: A type of Soviet squad light machine gun used since the 1960s.

PMR: Transdniester Republic. A breakaway region of Moldova in the early 1990s.

PPSh: A type of Soviet automatic pistol commonly used in World War II, roughly similar to the U.S. Army's M3 "Grease Gun," British Sten gun, or German MP.40 Schmeisser.

PRSM: A type of parachute pallet system with a retro-rocket to slow down the final descent.

PT-76: A type of Soviet amphibious light tank in service since the early 1950s, armed with a 76mm gun.

Pz.Kpfw.IV: The standard German medium tank of World War II.

razvedchik: Russian for a scout.

Red Army: Soviet term for the armed forces (minus the navy) from 1918 to 1947. The full name was "Workers and Peasants Red Army." In 1947, it was renamed Soviet Army. Same applied to Red Air Force and Red Navy.

SACLOS: Semi-automatic-command-to-line-of-Sight. A type of guidance, frequently used with antitank missiles.

SAM: Surface-to-air missile.

SAS: Special Air Service, a British special forces unit.

Sd.Kfz. 251: A type of German World War II armored half-track infantry carrier, sometimes nicknamed a Hanomog after the firm that manufactured it.

SEAD: Suppression of enemy air defenses. The initial stage of a modern air campaign when an air force attempts to eliminate enemy radars, command centers, anitaircraft missiles, and other air defenses in preparation for an air attack.

shilka: Russian word for awl. A type of armored, tracked antiaircraft vehicle armed with four 23mm cannon and used for air defense, also known as ZSU-23-4.

shturmovik: Soviet attack aircraft, especially the World War II Ilyushin IL-2.

SNG: Russian acronym for the Confederation of Independent States.

spetsnaz: Russian slang for special purpose; usually refers to the special operations troops of the GRU.

STAVKA: Soviet wartime high command.

Strategic Missile Force: Independent branch of the Soviet Armed Forces responsible for the strategic ballistic missile force. Russian acronym is RVSN.

Strela-2: Soviet manportable antiaircraft missile also known in NATO as SA-7 Grail.

TB-3: Soviet heavy bomber of the 1930s, also used as an improvised transport aircraft for paratroopers.

TO&E: Table of organization and equipment. A prescribed pattern for a military unit.

U-2: A type of Soviet two-seat biplane, later called Polikarpov Po-2.

UPA: Ukrainian Insurgent Army. Nationalist Ukrainian guerrilla force active against the Germans and Soviets in 1943–47.

Uzbekistan: Former Soviet republic in Central Asia.

VDV: Russian acronym for Airborne Forces.

VTA: Russian acronym for Military Transport Aviation.

ZiS-3: A type of Soviet 76mm divisional gun used since World War II.

ZSU-23-4: A Soviet air defense armored vehicle armed with four 23mm guns, also known as Shilka.

ZU-23: A type of Soviet towed, twin-barreled 23mm antiaircraft gun.

Index

About the Author

Steven J. Zaloga holds B.A. and M.A. degrees in history from Union College and Columbia University and did graduate research at the Uniwersitet Jagiellonski in Krakow, Poland. A recognized authority on the Russian and Soviet armed forces, he is the author of more than thirty books and hundreds of articles. He is a special correspondent for *Jane's Intelligence Review,* writes a monthly column on Russian military affairs for Armed Forces Journal International, and is on the executive board of the *Journal of Slavic Military Studies.* He wrote and produced the Firepower television series which appeared on The Discovery Channel and a multi-part documentary on Operation Desert Storm for the Arts & Entertainment Network. He currently works as a senior analyst with the Teal Group, specializing in missile technology and arms export issues, and has served as a consultant to agencies of the U.S. Department of Defense.